From Political Economy to Economics

In a new major work of critical recollection, Dimitris Milonakis and Ben Fine show how economics was once rich, diverse, multidimensional and pluralistic. The book details how political economy became economics through the desocialisation and dehistoricisation of the dismal science, accompanied by the separation of economics from other social sciences, especially economic history and sociology. It ranges over the shifting role of the historical and the social in economic theory, the shifting boundaries between the economic and the non-economic, all within a methodological context.

Schools of thought and individuals, that have been neglected or marginalised, are treated in full, including classical political economy and Marx, the German and British Historical Schools, American institutionalism, Weber and Schumpeter and their programme of *Sozialökonomik*, and the Austrian School. Developments within the mainstream tradition from marginalism through Marshall and Keynes to general equilibrium theory are also scrutinised, and the clashes between the various camps from the famous *Methodenstreit* of the 1880s to the fierce debates of the 1930s and beyond brought to the fore.

The prime rationale underpinning this account is to put the case for political economy back on the agenda. This is done by treating economics as a social science once again. It involves transcending the boundaries of the social sciences through the reintroduction and full incorporation of the social and the historical into the main corpus of political economy, by drawing on the rich traditions of the past.

Economists, advanced students and researchers engaged in interdisciplinary approaches to the study of economic phenomena, scholars interested in the history of economic thought, economic historians and other social scientists will find this book of compelling interest.

Dimitris Milonakis is Associate Professor and Head of the Department of Economics at the University of Crete.

Ben Fine is Professor of Economics at the School of Oriental and African Studies, University of London.

Economics as Social Theory

Series edited by Tony Lawson
University of Cambridge

Social Theory is experiencing something of a revival within economics. Critical analyses of the particular nature of the subject matter of social studies and of the types of method, categories and modes of explanation that can legitimately be endorsed for the scientific study of social objects, are re-emerging. Economists are again addressing such issues as the relationship between agency and structure, between economy and the rest of society, and between the enquirer and the object of enquiry. There is a renewed interest in elaborating basic categories such as causation, competition, culture, discrimination, evolution, money, need, order, organisation, power probability, process, rationality, technology, time, truth, uncertainty, value etc.

The objective for this series is to facilitate this revival further. In contemporary economics the label 'theory' has been appropriated by a group that confines itself to largely asocial, ahistorical, mathematical 'modelling'. Economics as Social Theory thus reclaims the 'Theory' label, offering a platform for alternative rigorous, but broader and more critical conceptions of theorising.

Other titles in this series include:

From Political Economy to Economics

Method, the social and the historical in the evolution of economic theory

Dimitris Milonakis and Ben Fine

Routledge
Taylor & Francis Group

LONDON AND NEW YORK

First published 2009
by Routledge
2 Park Square, Milton Park, Abingdon, Oxon, OX14 4RN

Simultaneously published in the USA and Canada
by Routledge
270 Madison Avenue, New York, NY 10016

Routledge is an imprint of the Taylor & Francis Group, an informa business

Typeset in Times New Roman by
Taylor & Francis Books
Printed and bound in Great Britain by
CPI Antony Rowe, Chippenham, Wiltshire

British Library Cataloguing in Publication Data
A catalogue record for this book is available from the British Library

Library of Congress Cataloging in Publication Data
Milonakis, Dimitris.
    From political economy to economics : method, the social and the
    historical in the evolution of economic theory / Dimitris Milonakis and
    Ben Fine.
        p. cm.
    Includes bibliographical references and index.
    1. Neoclassical school of economics–History. 2. Economics–History. I.
    Fine, Ben. II. Title.
    HB98.2.M55 2008
330.15′7–dc22   2008022095

ISBN 978-0-415-42322-9 (hbk)
ISBN 978-0-415-42321-2 (pbk)
ISBN 978-0-203-88711-0 (ebk)

Walls

Without consideration, without pity, without shame
they have built great and high walls around me.
And now I sit here and despair.
I think of nothing else: this fate gnaws at my mind;
for I had many things to do outside.
Ah why did I not pay attention when they were building the walls.
But I never heard any noise or sound from builders.
Imperceptibly they shut me from the outside world.

Constantine P. Cavafy (1897)

Τείχη

Χωρίς περίσκεψιν, χωρίς λύπην, χωρίς αἰδώ
μεγάλα κ' ὑψηλά τριγύρω μου ἔκτισαν τείχη.
Καί κάθομαι καί ἀπελπίζομαι τώρα εδῶ.
Ἄλλο δέν σκέπτομαι: τόν νοῦν μου τρώγει αὐτή ἡ τύχη·
διότι πράγματα πολλά ἔξω νά κάμω εἶχον.
Ἀ ὅταν ἔκτιζαν τά τείχη πῶς νά μήν προσέξω.
Ἀλλά δέν ἄκουσα ποτέ κρότον κτιστῶν ἤ ἦχον.
Ἀνεπαισθήτως μ' ἔκλεισαν ἀπό τόν κόσμον ἔξω.

Κωνσταντίνος Π. Καβάφης (1897)

Contents

Preface

This book started with the relatively modest aim of bringing together two separate but connected areas of our previous research. One is the study of the shifting relations between economics and the other social sciences. The other is the case study provided by economic history, especially in light of the rise of cliometrics. In the event, these goals have not so much been set aside as surpassed in depth and breadth almost beyond recognition of the initial starting point. The case study, for example, has become a broader study of the shifting relations between economic theory and economic history, stretching back into the nineteenth century, long before economic history became a separate academic discipline. The study has now warranted a separate book in its own right, Milonakis and Fine (forthcoming).

Stripped of its intended case study, the original volume has become reoriented towards examining the role of the historical in economic theory, especially in light of current attempts by neoclassical economics to address history and the social through the process of 'economics imperialism'. As with the study of economic history itself, the depth and breadth of what has ultimately been covered has expanded enormously beyond original intentions and expectations. Attention to the historical content of economic theory has been complemented by its social and methodological content. What was originally intended to be two chapters on 'economics imperialism', or the colonisation of the other social sciences by economics, has thereby become the subject of a separate book, Fine and Milonakis (2009). It not only brings our account of the shifting relation between the economic and the non-economic in the evolution of economic theory up to date, but also reflects upon the limited extent to which economics imperialism has drawn upon earlier, richer understandings of the social and the historical within economic theory and the aspirations for a deeper integration of economics with the other social sciences.

Similar divisions and extensions have applied to the chapters covering the passage from classical political economy through the marginalist revolution to general equilibrium theory within this volume. And, entirely unanticipated at the outset, separate chapters have been drafted on American institutionalism, the Austrians and social economics. All this proved essential if we were to provide a relatively full picture of the newly identified subject matter. This book then uncovers the way in which the social and the historical, but also the methodological, have shifted in presence and content within economic theory during the passage from classical political economy to general equilibrium theory. Inevitably, it involves an account of their reduction in scope and substance within economics, greatly contributing to, and reflecting, the process of separation of economics from the other social sciences. The resistances and responses to these processes are as much a part of our account as the outcomes themselves.

In retrospect, we were delighted by what can only be described as the magnificent and insightful contributions that have informed our study. These belong both to the past and to the present, and are a remarkable testimony to the diverse nature of economics, its history as a discipline, its relationship to other social sciences, and the debates that these have inspired. Equally telling, though, is the extent to which these positive elements are unknown to the profession of economists today, beyond a few dedicated and often specialised scholars. Whilst we have not intended a history of economic thought, we hope to have brought its importance to the fore and to have offered some broader insights into how it might be approached in light of the topics, characters and more general themes that we have covered. In addition, whilst the subject matter addressed is far from arbitrary, its depth and breadth is uneven, reflecting both our relative expertise on different topics and areas covered, and what we have discovered and found both interesting and important as the volume itself evolved.

The book is intended for advanced undergraduate and postgraduate students of economics and other social sciences, researchers in political economy, scholars interested in interdisciplinarity and the history of economic thought, and other social scientists.

Many people have helped us in a number of ways in achieving what we have in hand. We owe special thanks to Michel Zouboulakis and Nikos Theocharakis, who read an earlier draft of the entire manuscript and made extensive and constructive comments. Also our thanks go to Thanassis Giouras amd Giorgos Stassinopoulos for comments on various chapters of the book at various stages. Last, our gratitude is extended to all those, too numerous to mention, who have given us encouragement and who have offered both advice and criticism.

1   Introduction

'A person is not likely to be a good economist who is nothing else. Social phenomena acting and reacting on one another, they cannot rightly be understood apart'.

J. S. Mill quoted by Marshall (1959, p. 637)[1]

'The papers by Arrow, Davis, Solow and Temin all reach the same conclusion, that knowledge of and appreciation for history is important for economics and ought to be an integral part of the discipline'.

Gavin Wright (1986, p. 77)[2]

1 General outline

If we were to describe the essence of this book in two words, they would certainly be *political economy*. If we were to use four words, they would be *economics as social science*. In short, the book is about the shifting boundaries between the economic and the non-economic, all set within a methodological context. It deals with the process by which political economy became economics, through the desocialisation and dehistoricisation of the dismal science, and how this heralded the separation of economics from the other social sciences at the beginning of the twentieth century.

In part, this development is explained through the identification of two great schisms in economic thought which played a decisive role in the process. The first is the schism between the abstract/deductive and the inductive/ historical methods, which is diachronic in content. Although this begins in classical political economy with the first skirmishes between Ricardo and Malthus, it cuts across the whole time horizon up to the Second World War, reaching a climax in the 1880s with the famous *Methodenstreit*, between the marginalist, Carl Menger, and the leader of the German Historical School, Gustav Schmoller. The second rupture exists primarily in the movement from classical political economy to neoclassical economics, via the marginalist revolution, and is both methodological and substantive in content.

All classical writers wrote at a time when political economy was the only identifiable social science, with the fragmentation of the latter lying far ahead in the future. As such, most of them were able to range freely across the economic and the non-economic, to incorporate the social and the psychological into their analyses, and to move from historical narrative to theoretical discourse without apology. Indeed, for most classical writers, especially Smith, Mill and Marx, political economy was seen as a unified social science, rather than simply as the science of the economy.

This state of affairs changed drastically during and after the marginalist revolution and the subsequent move from (classical) political economy to (neoclassical) economics, although marginalism did not signal the end of attempts to keep the relationship between the economic and the non-economic alive. Such attempts, however, increasingly had to find refuge either in alternative schools of thought – such as the German and the British Historical Schools, American institutionalism or the Austrian School, whose members' work was non-marginalist in principle and interdisciplinary in character – or in the efforts of individual writers like Weber and Schumpeter, each of whom emphasised multi-disciplinarity, albeit with different emphases. The end result of these processes was the establishment of neoclassical orthodoxy as the dominant school of thought within economics, and the concomitant separation of economics from other social sciences, especially economic history and sociology. Within economics, this process was rounded off through two parallel developments: the Keynesian revolution of the 1930s, and the further mathematisation and formalisation of mainstream economics following developments in microeconomics and general equilibrium theory. In short, our aim is to trace the route from political economy to economics and the corresponding, and to some extent subsequent, separation of economics from other social sciences.

2 Main themes

The focus of this book, then, is the relationship between economic theory and the social and historical – what might loosely be termed the non-economic – all attached to a methodological context. Considerable ambiguity is necessarily involved here unless 'the economic' is understood in extremely narrow and specific terms. If it is simply the study of supply and demand in the framework of proximate factors defined by economic orthodoxy (such as given preferences, technology and endowments), then there would appear to be no lack of precision. 'The non-economic' then, would simply be everything else, and would be taken as exogenous or, more likely, irrelevant. In this case, our volume would be short (and far from sweet) and confined to the study, like much of contemporary economics, of the relationship between select exogenous and endogenous variables. Shift preferences or technology, for example, and there is a corresponding shift in demand and supply, respectively.

Matters are not so simple, however, for a number of reasons. First and foremost, economic theory as currently constituted is the exception rather than the rule as far as the history of economic thought is concerned. The way in which it handles the relationship between the economic and the non-economic is both recent and, in a longer perspective, peculiar. In the past, the relationship and the boundaries between the two have been very different. This is because the social and the historical content of economic theory, most notably symbolised in the terminology of 'political economy', has been substantial and, often, explicit. But we should clarify what we mean by this, as it is something that is more often claimed in criticism of the orthodoxy than it is explained.

By the social content, we mean the extent to which the nature of the particular society or societies under consideration, consciously or unconsciously influences the economic concepts deployed. Necessarily, such social content of economic theory delimits its scope of application to particular societies, those for which the theory's concepts are appropriate (historical specificity). Thus, for example, how we construct and use the notion of capital will have a bearing on its relevance for capitalist economies as such – or not, if it is entirely inappropriate.

The historical content of (economic) theory is closely related to the social, and the two might be used interchangeably. But 'the historical' includes the question of how the specificity of the past affects the analysis. What is different, for example, about German capitalism as opposed to another system? To answer this, we need to know what is socially different about capitalism (itself a more general, or grander, historical question) from other forms of economic organisation, in order to highlight differences between one capitalism and another by setting aside what they have in common.

These definitional conundrums need not detain us further, and probably offer little of novel substance to the non-economist. For economics as a discipline, however, it has become commonplace to accept concepts of analysis uncritically, and not to interrogate their historical and social content. Little attention has been paid to the issue of why there should be swings in analytical content, from monetarism to Keynesianism and back again, for example. Indeed, as a discipline, economics tends to pride itself (inevitably erroneously) on being value-free and independent of external influence.

It is therefore salient to remind economists that this has not always been true of their discipline, and that the social and historical content of what they do (or do not do) now is worthy of critical attention through the prism of the past. This is especially so for two reasons. On the one hand, in its methods and technical apparatus, economics has become asocial and ahistorical, in the sense of deploying universal categories without reference to time, place or context – such is the nature of categories of analysis like production and utility functions. Further, the intellectual passage to these universal categories is one of qualified acceptance, if not total resistance. The resulting reservations over what economics was becoming – even or especially by those pushing it forward – have only too readily been forgotten, and are worthy of restoration to our attention.

This involves discussion of issues that have been neglected, if not increasingly set aside, by today's mainstream economics. It is now commonplace to observe that discussion of economic methodology belongs to a field of study separate from economics itself, more attuned to the philosophy of science. As a result, mainstream economists not only deploy a method or methods that have long been discredited, not least by the natural sciences that they seek to emulate, they also prove themselves incapable of understanding the terms under which such methodological issues are discussed.

Critical recollection is the intention of this volume. Its subject matter will range over how the relationship between economic(s) and the non-economic has changed over time both in extent and content, why it should have changed, and it will also offer judgements over the merits of how economics has treated the historical, the social and the methodological.

These are surely ambitious tasks, but – however well and fully we have grappled with them – do they warrant close attention? Although the book is primarily about economics, the topics treated here are anything but fashionable within the profession. In this respect, our book fills a huge gap in the relevant literature, with Hodgson's *How Economics Forgot History* (2001) being the only major exception. This is not because the central issue of the relationship between economics and the social and the historical has been explicitly and fully settled as far as the orthodoxy is concerned. On the contrary, as Solow (1986, p. 21) puts it, 'economic theory learns nothing from economic history'. It is arguable that the vast majority of today's academic economists, especially the younger generations, are unaware that there might be an issue over the appropriate contribution to be made to their endeavours by the historical or the social. For the vast majority, even to try to explain the problem would prove futile. There is a sense in which, whilst economics profoundly reflects historical and social processes both materially and ideologically, it is blissfully ignorant of them and wishes to remain so. If this book helps in redressing this balance, even by a little, it will have achieved its aim.

This points to some remarkable features of economics as a discipline that set it apart as not only separate from but also alien to the other social sciences. First and foremost – for otherwise the disregard for the historical and the social could hardly be sustained – economics has become totally intolerant of approaches other than its own mainstream. It has become dominated by the neoclassical approach, taught almost exclusively as standard, and often without reference either to irrefutable criticism or to alternative approaches that at most cling for survival upon its margins. Variously referred to as autistic, as monoeconomics, or as subject to Americanisation, homogeneity of thought and approach within the discipline has since the Second World War been strong, but it has also intensified over the past decade or so. Paradoxically, within the UK, heterodoxy within economics is increasingly to be located in burgeoning schools of management, business studies, marketing and (tellingly) accountancy. These previous bastions of orthodox economics as supply and demand, of the firm and the consumer, have been far more open to root economic considerations in a more rounded approach than economics itself. This is both in method and by incorporating the insights of other social sciences and the historical. Even accountancy has begun to recognise that economic calculation is socially constructed in response to material and ideological practices!

A second fundamental feature of economics that allows it to disregard (the issue of) the historical and the social is its method. It has strengthened its commitment to falsifiability (or to close consistency with empirical evidence through statistical methods), to axiomatic deduction from abstract assumptions, to methodological individualism of a special type (utility maximisation), and to equilibrium (and efficiency) as an organising concept. It is a moot point whether these principles are more observed selectively for convenience in the practice of mainstream economics, and whether they are mutually compatible with one another in any case. Be this as it may, the conventional wisdom about its own principles and practices tend to prevail without question despite debates over methodology over the past few decades (let alone those of longer standing) that have long since departed from and shown such nostrums to be invalid. As a result, economics has been marked by an almost exclusive reliance, at least in principle, upon abstract mathematical formalism married to statistical testing or estimation against given evidence, i.e. data. Anything within the discipline that does not conform to these dictates is dismissed as lacking science and rigour (with the same attitude that has been imperiously adopted towards other social sciences).

As already indicated, though, the early chapters of this book establish that economics has not always been like this. Classical political economy, from before Adam Smith, had a profound sense of the historical and the social, and consciously incorporated this both in its concepts and its theory, as we will see in Chapters 2, 3 and 4. Not only was Adam Smith a great virtuoso in combining the economic with the philosophical, the psychological, the social and the historical, but in his *Wealth of Nations* can be found the sperm of most subsequent developments in economic theory related to these issues. Deduction and historical narrative were combined with individualistic and collective modes of reasoning, sometimes in a dynamic way, at other times in a comparative static analysis of the capitalist economy.

On the other hand, despite their presumed common adherence to the labour theory of value, Ricardo and Marx lie at opposite extremes in the historical content of their economics. Ricardo pioneered the deductive method within economics by seeking to explain the categories of capitalism by appeal to the labour theory of value. By contrast, Marx understands the labour theory of value in terms of concepts that consciously correspond to the material conditions and organisation of the capitalist economy itself.

These differences between Ricardo and Marx in part reflected, but were not reducible to, a difference in emphasis on the deductive as opposed to the inductive method, respectively. Nonetheless, Marxism apart, Ricardo's deductivism offered a focus for the emergence of alternative schools of thought in support of, or reacting against, this method not least as Ricardianism lost its intellectual stranglehold in the later part of the nineteenth century. The most prominent early reaction against Ricardianism, pre-dating but surviving beyond the marginalist revolution, was provided by the German Historical School with its emphasis upon historical study, as we will see in Chapter 5. Its presumed antipathy to theory in general and marginalism in particular provoked the *Methodenstreit* or 'Battle over Method', which is covered in Chapter 6. The relative merits of induction and deduction were heavily debated on a broader front across the positions adopted in the *Methodenstreit*, highlighting a long-running controversy that is itself inevitably and explicitly concerned with the historical content of economics. In particular, in the context first of Ricardo's deductivism and, subsequently, the axiomatics of marginalism, attention focused on the extent to which universal, abstract theory could prevail independently of the cultures, nations and traditions of the economies under consideration.

In a wonderful illustration of the history of the subject being written by the victors – and, it should be added, subsequently forgotten – it is commonly claimed that the marginalists and deductivism won the debate, with the fatal flaw in the Historical School being its lack of theory (rather than their opponents' lack of history). This is only true in the sense that the marginalists prevailed. Indeed, at least from the 1870s until the 1950s, marginalist economics continued to be marked by its failure to vanquish those committed to the historical and social as a part of, but increasingly frequently as an adjunct of, economics. For the marginalist revolution was attached to a huge intellectual compromise. On the one hand, its analytical principles are universal, not historically or conceptually rooted by time, place, activity, stage of development, etc. Such is the nature of abstract appeal to utility, production function and other categories that survive, primarily unmodified, to the present day. On the other hand, economics detached itself from the other social sciences and confined its subject matter to the science of the market. Thus economic history itself – an offspring of the historical economics of the German and the British Historical Schools – emerged as a separate discipline, as a reaction against the inadequacy of the historical content of marginalism, as charted in Chapter 8 and to be covered in detail in a subsequent book.

Thus, paradoxically, one of the outcomes of the marginalist revolution, and its confrontation with classical political economy and the *Methodenstreit*, was to limit the scope of application of its universally applicable concepts. Instead, social science was fragmented into separate disciplines. This process, however, involved a number of different aspects beyond those for which the *Methodenstreit* is usually remembered (if it is remembered at all). These include not only the relative merits of induction and deduction, but also the relationship between the separate disciplines, the nature and significance of economic rationality, individualism versus holism, and the nature and origins of (modern) capitalism as an economic and social system. The discussion in later chapters is guided by two elements that are characteristic of the results of the marginalist revolution, but which can also be shown to precede it. These are: a shift in emphasis from more synthetic methodological approaches to purer and more deductive methods, and the narrowing of the scope of economic enquiry. As already suggested, with the shift from (classical) political economy to (neoclassical) economics, not only has there been a shift of method but there has also been a gradual loss of discussion of methodology itself.

Looking forward from this time, it is easy to recognise how such concerns have been set aside or reduced to simplistic nostrums around mainstream neoclassical economics. Looking back, however, not least through the economic and social theorists of the time, such issues had to be addressed as part of their intellectual heritage; not surprisingly, there was by no means universal agreement upon, or response to, the various conundrums involved. This is illustrated through Chapters 7 to 13 by reference to a range of contributors, across the various strands of the Historical School and beyond, from Marshall through Veblen and the old institutionalists, to Weber and Schumpeter, finally leading to Robbins' squaring off of the marginalist revolution and Hutchison's positivist response, let alone the (neo-)Austrians. In this process, the separation of economics from sociology and the latter's birth and further consolidation through the work of Weber, Pareto and Parsons is brought to the fore.

What they all shared in common, whatever the stance towards what was at their own time a less extreme (or old Marshallian) marginalism, is that it is sorely inadequate as a means to address economic, let alone broader, issues sufficiently fully on its own. In short, these writers can be read as reflections of the intellectual tensions running through the creation and evolution of the system of social sciences as we know them today. As such, in each case, it is occasionally a moot point how and whether they stood in the path of the 'progress' of economics as it was to become, or propelled it on its way. As the interdisciplinarity of American institutionalism, Chapters 9 and 10, the social economics of Weber and Schumpeter, Chapter 11, the neo-Austrian economics of Hayek and Mises, Chapter 13, and the sociological writings of Pareto and Parsons, Chapter 12, fell by the wayside as far as mainstream economics is concerned, so the latter gathered the technical and disciplinary content and confidence to broaden its scope of application and reclaim the historical and social that had been expunged as a condition for its creation in the first place.

Thus, as already remarked in the case of the *Methodenstreit*, marginalism progressed by setting aside rather than overcoming the arguments of its opponents. Much the same is true, then, of the period of consolidation following the marginalist revolution that gave rise to the prodigious development of microeconomics as the technical core of mainstream economics – and (Keynesian) macroeconomics as its counterpart, at least in the beginning, in deference to economic realities, especially in relation to functioning of the economy as a whole, Chapter 14. The formal apparatus attached to the theory of supply and demand took on a life of its own, most notably in the development of microeconomics and its ultimate triumph in the ever-esoteric concerns of general equilibrium theory. By accepting the limitations of its scope of application, economics consolidated its method and theory into a formidable apparatus and core of analytical principles from which even minimal dissent – endogeneity of preferences, for example – is unacceptable except by way of curiosum. This is despite the transparent lack of realism on which this apparatus is constructed.

As will already be apparent, the breadth of subject matter within this volume is extensive, ranging over the history of economic thought and methodology in seeking to pinpoint the shifting relationship between economics and the social and historical. Of necessity, the coverage is uneven in depth and style. At times, at one extreme and more often, the text explicitly delves into detailed scholarship at the levels of both primary and secondary sources. At other times, and less often, the discourse is more informal, and concentrates on the arguments and their relevance to our themes rather than extensive textual evidence. Each of the chapters is intended to be more or less self-contained, although, despite cross-reference between them, there is some trade-off in avoiding undue repetition to this end. There are also incursions into the elaboration of economic theory and political economy, but these are kept to a minimum (with reference to fuller accounts) and motivated more by illustrating our arguments concerning the historical and social content of theory than providing exposition. Care has been taken to clarify all or most of the concepts used, taking into account the vast deficit existing in the training of modern economists on issues of methodology, history of economic thought, other social sciences, etc. We hope this will make the task of reading the book easier for the uninitiated, without putting unnecessary strains on the more knowledgeable reader.

Taking all this into account, it is extremely difficult in such a project to satisfy all readers to the full. Despite our best efforts, some (uninitiated) may find the arguments in this book somewhat difficult to follow to begin with, while others (especially the experts on specific areas) may find our attempt at approaching their subject wanting. Significantly, some readers of initial drafts have complained of insufficient attention to their own specialisms, which indicates the overwhelming relevance of our arguments for a wide swathe of social science and the topics addressed. No doubt, then, the specialised scholar will occasionally be disappointed with our treatment of many of the topics, schools or individuals that warrant books to address them in their own right. Hopefully, the range of what we have covered and the broader narratives and themes to which each topic is attached will still prove of value to the expert. To do more is to go far beyond our capacity and ambition, and our book has already been lengthened inordinately. On the whole, however, we hope to have struck the right balance between introducing the subject of each chapter, albeit at an advanced level, and offering something of value, on the broader canvas, to the more accomplished.

3 Main objectives

Writing this book has led to a very interesting, refreshing and fascinating journey, but also, in some important respects, a depressing journey. This is because we realised, even more than before we began, how reduced our science has become, compared to how it has been. For one thing, mainstream economists, trapped between perfecting their increasingly esoteric and formalistic models and techniques, no longer show any interest in anything that lies outside their mode of thinking and their field of competence, including the history of their own subject and the methods employed. Increasingly, as already emphasised, whatever is not comprehensible through their state-of-the-art tools (model building, econometrics, game theory, etc) is considered as lying outside the scope of the economists' research interests, and is cast aside as either non-economic or non-scientific – and usually both.

Another sad aspect of an otherwise challenging and rewarding exercise that is also deserving of emphasis, is how much the history of our subject is one, when not neglected, that has been written by the victors and through the prism of what has become the current orthodoxy. Even worse, this history has often not been written but has simply been presumed to be an unproblematic passage from the imperfect discoveries in the past to their refinement and improvement in the present. In this respect, ours is an alternative story that is written from the perspective of political economy, i.e. from the confines of what nowadays would be called heterodox economics; we find many invaluable commentaries from the mainstream neoclassical economists of the past, however, not least because they were involved in both promoting, qualifying and defending the changes they were making, rather than simply accepting them as a conventional wisdom.

Nonetheless, since our focus is on the role of the social and the historical, and given the totally asocial and ahistorical nature of most modern economics, it was inevitable that our story would include all those schools and individuals for whom these factors form an integral, usually major, part of their academic endeavours. Hence our inclusion of chapters on classical political economy and Karl Marx, the German Historical School, the British Historical School, Max Weber and Joseph Schumpeter and their programme of *Sozialökonomik*, the Austrian School, and American or old institutionalism, most of which (with the exception of classical political economy and Karl Marx) hardly even warrant a mention in most history of economics textbooks.

On the other hand, this journey was also very refreshing and rewarding because we discovered to a much fuller extent how rich, diverse, multidimensional and pluralistic this science once was; if this was once the case, then nothing can preclude the possibility that it could be so again. It is with this hope in mind that we embarked upon writing this book. Is this an easy task? Not at all. We would even argue that, given the present state of the dismal science, it is a very difficult task. If our book adds a small stepping stone in this direction, then our task will have been accomplished.

As a small indication of the difficulties ahead of us is the fact that, although this is a book it is an exercise in economic thought written by two economists, or more accurately by two political economists, we anticipate that this book will appeal more to heterodox economists, to historians of economic thought, economic historians and other social scientists, than to (orthodox) economists. Explaining why this is the case, and how we reached this state of affairs, is one major objective of this book. The other, and perhaps the prime, objective, is to argue the case of putting political economy back on the agenda. This is done by treating economics as a social science once again, rather than as a positive science, as has been much the case since the time of Jevons and Walras. More than that, it is a plea for transcending the boundaries of social sciences, but in a particular way that is exactly in the opposite direction to the economics imperialism we are now witnessing – i.e. through the reintroduction and full incorporation of the social and the historical into the main corpus of economic theorising. It is interesting that the participants at a symposium held at the meeting of the American Economic Association in 1984, among economists and economic historians at the forefront of their disciplines on the relationship between economic history and economic theory reached a similar conclusion as far as the role of history in economic theory is concerned, see opening quote by Wright (1986, p. 77). If our account of how economics has related to the historical and social inspires further critical attention, we will consider our efforts to have been worthwhile, especially the more it contributes to a reconstruction of political economy and its incorporation within social theory.

2 Smith, Ricardo and the first rupture in economic thought

'The integration of history with analysis and theory so superbly, and uniquely, achieved in Adam Smith's work was shattered, hardly ever after to be fully recovered in a major treatise (except, perhaps, in its own historicist way. Karl Marx's *Capital*)'.

Hutchison (1978, p. 54)

'With Ricardo economics took a major step toward abstract models, rigid and artificial definitions, syllogistic reasoning – and the direct application of the results to policy. The historical, the institutional, and the empirical faded into the background, and explicit social philosophy shrank into a few passing remarks'.

Sowell (1994, p. 113)

1 Introduction

The role of historical and social investigation in economic theorising is chiefly a function of what one considers the *scope* and *method* of economic inquiry to be, J.N. Keynes (1999 [1890]). On the basis of these two elements, as already indicated in the introduction, two great divides can be discerned in the history of economic thought. The first is diachronic in content, reflecting differences between the inductive/ historical and the deductive/abstract methods. It cuts across the chronological divisions by persistence of differences across the various schools of economic thought. The second exists primarily in historical time, in the movement from classical political economy to neoclassical economics, across the marginalist revolution which narrowed the scope of scientific inquiry. This had its most significant moment in the 1870s.

The purpose of this and the next two chapters is to demonstrate that it is and has been possible to incorporate a social and historical element in economic theory. This is done by reference to the political economy of the eighteenth and nineteenth centuries prior to the marginalist revolution of the 1870s (which is not to suggest that the social and historical disappeared altogether with marginalism). Later chapters will demonstrate that, in different ways, it retained its presence albeit to differing degrees and in differing ways, at times limited to a token nod of acceptance, before more or less total excision (before reappearing in reversed form with economics imperialism).

Whilst Chapter 4 focuses on the social and historical in the value theory of Smith, Ricardo and Marx, this and the following chapter are more concerned with the methodological content of these and other authors' contributions, and the praise or criticism that these correspondingly attracted. For method is intimately related with whether and how the social and historical are incorporated.

In what follows in this chapter, and to a varying extent in others, reference to differences with today's orthodoxy is desirable, if not unavoidable, in providing exposition of the economic theory of the past, and its methodological, social and historical content. In addition, this allows for a more nuanced understanding of the rise of marginalism and its passage to the current mainstream. For the marginalist revolution of the 1870s, in broad brush, is usually seen as a watershed in the history of economic thought, which marked the separation between classical political economy of the nineteenth century and neoclassical economics of the twentieth. But that increasingly rare creature, the historian of economic thought (and of economic methodology), has recognised that it is misleading to interpret the marginalist revolution as a short and sharp event that reshaped economic theory once and for all. Was *everything* different before when compared with after, simply because so much was different?[1] And were differences correspondingly realised in an acute transition that saw classical political economy swept aside extremely rapidly and replaced by marginalism (and, ultimately, mainstream economics) with little or no overlap between them? Putting this more constructively, in terms of continuities rather than change or rupture, what aspect(s) of classical political economy prepared the way for the marginalist revolution, what influence, if any, did it continue to exert over marginalism, and for how long?

In Section 2, we examine some general methodological themes relating to the whole classical edifice. In Section 3, we examine the work of Smith and Ricardo, and the debates and interpretations that have been inspired by them, by drawing attention to the many dualisms that penetrate Smith's analysis and the abstractness of Ricardo's system. It will be shown that Ricardo was heavily responsible for pioneering the deductive method, long before marginalism so fully embraced it. In doing so, the mixture and balance of deduction and induction to be found in Smith is, to a large extent, set aside in the period leading up to the marginalist revolution; but it was not entirely lost in a moment and once and for all. The first skirmishes around the method of political economy between Ricardo, and Malthus and Jones, which initiated the first methodological rupture in economic thought, are the subject of Section 4, with concluding remarks in Section 5. Yet, whilst the relative merits of deduction and induction may have symbolised both divisions within economic methodology and the prospect of the triumph of deduction in the wake of the marginalist revolution, it is important not to reduce methodological issues to these alone, as is apparent from later chapters.

2 Classical political economy: general themes

The question of what constitutes classical political economy has been highly controversial in the history of economic thought. The three most famous statements on this are those of Marx, Keynes and Schumpeter, and they are widely divergent. For Marx, classical political economy starts in England with the work of the mercantilist William Petty and ends with its greatest representative David Ricardo.[2] Keynes included in his definition all the writers who did not reject Say's Law, from Ricardo to his contemporary Pigou.[3] And for Schumpeter (1994 [1954], pp. 379–80), the 'classic period of economics' spanned the period from 1798 to 1871, and included those as diverse as Malthus and Jevons, see also Perlman and McCann (1998, p. 229). Classical political economy will be defined here to include the writers from Adam Smith to John Stuart Mill, including Bentham, Ricardo, Senior, Malthus, Mill and Cairnes. Classical political economy, through its main representatives Smith, Ricardo, Malthus, and Mill, showed great concern for the nature and causes of the wealth of nations and its distribution to different fractions of society (classes). According to Mill (1974 [1859], pp. 124–5):

> the definition most generally received among instructed persons, and laid down in the commencement of most of the professed treatises on the subject, is to the following effect: That Political Economy informs us of the laws which regulate the production, distribution, and consumption of wealth.

A similar concern ('to reveal the economic law of motion of modern society') is also the 'ultimate aim' of the work of Karl Marx (1976 [1867], p. 92), who wrote in a manner close to the classical tradition but also broke with it in many, and fundamental, respects. All these writers were interested in questions of long-term economic development, and focused their attention on the evolution of the economic system as a whole, at the level of economic aggregates. Such methodological holism or methodological collectivism gives primacy to the social whole or totality, as opposed to individuals, without necessarily precluding analysis pitched at the level of the individual. What it implies, however, is that the social whole and collectivities – such as institutions, classes, national economy and society at large – rather than being explained by individual action as in the case of methodological individualism (see below) have an autonomous existence and, as such, mould and influence the behaviour of individuals. Primacy is given here to the social and collective whole, rather than the individual actor, and the former is presented as something more than the mere aggregation of its individual parts, Rutherford (1994, pp. 27–37). Not all classicals, though, were pure methodological holists.

Although Ricardo and Marx mostly used, or proceeded from, aggregate modes of reasoning, Smith and Mill adopted both aggregate and individualistic arguments, while Bentham was a pure methodological individualist. Methodological individualism refers to the method of explanation whereby the whole is explained in terms of the properties of its individual parts (members). As Watkins (1968, pp. 270–1) puts it in a classic statement:

> The ultimate constituents of the social world are individual people who act more or less appropriately in the light of their dispositions and understanding of their situation. Every complex social situation, institution or event is the result of a particular configuration of individuals, their dispositions, situations, beliefs and physical resources and environment ... We shall not have arrived at rock-bottom explanations of large-scale phenomena until we have deduced an account of them from statements about the dispositions, beliefs, recourses and interrelations of individuals.

With this methodological principle, only individuals have goals and interests, and the whole becomes a mere aggregation of its individual parts with no existence outside them. Jon Elster (1982, p. 48) defines methodological individualism as 'the doctrine that all social phenomena (their structure and their change) are in principle explicable only in terms of individuals – their properties, goals and beliefs', see also Mises (1996 [1949], p. 42).

For Ricardo and Marx, the economic system as a whole is the object of investigation, while classes form the basic units of analysis. Such a macrodynamic view of the economy both requires and provides ample space for the social and historical processes to become valuable and integral parts of economic analysis. As will be argued, one of the key elements in this context is the role played by value theory, and the extent to which it either stands alone to a greater or lesser extent, or embodies an understanding of the economy as a whole, its relationship to society more broadly, and the dynamics of historical change. Overgeneralising and unduly homogenising in view of their differences, the main representatives of classical political economy subscribe to an objective theory of value, based on material cost of production, with the special case of the quantity of labour needed for production particularly prominent.

Further, the classicals have a view of society as a self-existent entity with an autonomous presence, independent of its individual members, and of the economy as part and parcel of this wider entity. Indeed, economic relations are inseparable from social relations and the analysis focuses on collective economic agents such as social classes. As Swedberg (1990, p. 9) rightly observes, 'what distinguished Smith, Marx and Mill from many later sociologists and economists was their ambition to define economics in a broad manner and to be interested in the insights of other social sciences'. Thus, it is no accident that most classical economists had some training in philosophy or were themselves philosophers: Smith was a moral philosopher;

Malthus studied mathematics and natural philosophy; Mill was trained in both political economy and philosophy, and published books in economics, philosophy, politics and social theory; and Marx studied law and wrote his doctoral thesis on the philosophy of Epicurus! Only Ricardo differs from the others in this respect, more a practical man of business than scholar as such, although he is the exception that proves the rule.

This tradition of 'economics plus' came to an abrupt, if not complete, end after the marginalist revolution with a major and, as will be seen in Chapter 7, significant exception. Alfred Marshall, the founder of orthodox neoclassical economics in its partial equilibrium form, studied moral sciences (and mathematics) before turning to economics.[4] Today, economists are more liable to be recruited at higher levels from science (and mathematics) than from the social science disciplines, in deference to technical capacity for mathematics and statistics as opposed to more general knowledge of the economy and the method and techniques of the social sciences.

Hence, although for the classicals political economy is a science defined by its subject matter, i.e. the science of the economy, the latter is treated as part of the wider social context. In particular, the class structure – the three main classes being landlords, workers and capitalists – is of prime importance. The explicit recognition of context in this manner renders classical political economy a historically specific social science: it is the science of the *capitalist* economy and its corresponding classes, rather than of the economy or the economic in the abstract. Indeed, most, if not all, the classicals are concerned to unravel what is distinctive about capitalism as opposed to previous epochs, and for this to be reflected in their theory, see Chapter 4.

These common traits notwithstanding, classical political economy also witnessed the *first great divide in economic thought*, the schism between the inductive and the deductive methods, which reflects what Tabb (1999, p. 5) calls 'a pervasive and deep cultural divide' in economics.[5] This schism has played a major role in the separation of economic science from history, and in the emergence of economic history as a separate discipline, for more on which see Chapter 8. Having said this, it should be stressed at the outset that such sharp divisions, although useful for heuristic purposes, should always be used with care in order to avoid overgeneralisations and over-homogenisation, and the danger of over-reading contributions through the prism of such schisms alone.

Deduction is defined as the method of developing a theory by starting with given assumptions and premises, and, through syllogism and the use of the rules of logic, moving to what are effectively conclusions predetermined by the starting points. It is an abstract scientific method based on a priori reasoning and, as such, can purport to be devoid of history (other than that determined by the terms and conditions set by the practitioner's own context that are far from negligible, i.e. through introspection). *Induction*, on the other hand, refers to the method of moving from the specific to the general, from observed facts to theoretical generalisations, by identifying characteristics of a specific phenomenon or situation and transposing it to the totality of similar phenomena or situations. In this approach, historical investigation of the subject matter occupies centre-stage. As Pheby (1988, p. 3) puts it,[6] 'inductivism is a general approach that emphasises observation and systematic empirical work as the major means of attaining knowledge', see also Blaug (1980, pp. 2–4, 11–12, 14–17).

This divide in economic thought is the reflection of a more general divide in western thought, between what Dow (1996, pp. 10–13) has called Cartesian/Euclidean and Babylonian modes of thought. The first works methodologically by 'establishing basic axioms, which are either true by definition or "self-evident", and using deductive logic to derive theorems, which are not self-evident', p. 11.[7] The second 'starts from the view that it is impossible in general to establish watertight axioms' and considers knowledge to be 'generated by practical applications of theories as examples, using a variety of methods', p. 12. In other words, the Euclidean/Cartesian mode of thought is a 'closed system of axiomatic logic', a prime example of which is mathematics, whereas the Babylonian tradition is more open-ended and can employ 'several strands of argument', generally encompassing the more applied sciences, pp. 12–13. Granted this division, within each mode of thought, it is possible to combine deduction with induction in order to counterbalance their mutual shortcomings, p. 25.

3 Smith's dualisms, Ricardo's abstractions

Although the classical approach allows ample space for the combination of these two methods (deduction and induction), it does not make it mandatory. Thus, as will be seen, Smith is recognised to have made extensive use of both methods, whereas Ricardo's system lies at the opposite extreme by deliberately and totally abstracting from empirical reality. Moreover, the roots of this methodological divide within economics can be traced back to Adam Smith (1723–90). 'Adam Smith's methodology was eclectic. The empirical, the theoretical, the institutional, the philosophical, the static, and the dynamic were all intermingled', Sowell (1994, pp. 112–13). In Smith can be found several dualisms; one is between his macro-dynamic theory of economic development and his micro-theory of market exchange (the invisible hand), Screpanti and Zamagni (1993, pp. 62–5). The former is expounded in the first three chapters of Book I of the *Wealth of Nations*, where Smith identifies the growing division of labour as the basic cause of the growth of the wealth of nations through the improvement in the productive power of labour it brings about. For Smith (1981 [1776], p. 13):

> The greatest improvement in the productive powers of labour, and the greatest part of the skill, dexterity, and judgement with which it is anywhere directed, or applied, seem to have been the effects of the division of labour.

The division of labour, in turn, is the result of 'a certain propensity in human nature ... to truck, barter, and exchange one thing for another', itself an expression of the individual's pursuit of self-interest. For, as endlessly quoted, pp. 26–7:

> It is not from the benevolence of the butcher, the brewer, or the baker, that we expect our dinner, but from their regard to their own interest. We address ourselves, not to their humanity but to their self-love, and never talk to them of our own necessities but of their advantages.

Pursuit of self-interest is a basic attribute of human nature, but not the only one. Smith's *homo economicus* is not the single-minded and selfish utility maximiser of modern neoclassical economics. On the contrary, economic agents are conceived as part of the wider social context, Perlman and McCann (1998, p. 239). As Smith argues in his *Theory of Moral Sentiments*, human motivation is varied, encompassing self-interest but also benevolence and sympathy, the last of which meaning the ability to put oneself in another's place. Yet, on the other hand, the *Wealth of Nations* does tend to lean heavily on the motive of self-interest. Its realisation, however, is through the propensity to 'truck, barter, and exchange' and the division of labour this brings about is limited by the extent of the market. Smith (1981, p. 31) suggests, 'as it is the power of exchanging that gives occasion to the division of labour, so the extent of this division must always be limited by the extent of that power, or, in other words, by the extent of the market'.

Such is a brief overview of part of Smith's overall vision of the capitalist economic system.[8] It is, however, complemented by a micro-theoretic element that takes the form of the additive or components theory of price as expounded in Chapters 6 and 7 of Book I, after Smith has rejected the labour theory of value, certainly once capital stock has been accumulated in the hands of individuals, if not before with settlement of land and emergence of rent. This gives rise to the second dualism in Smith's method. It concerns the use of both individualistic and holistic/collectivist modes of reasoning. Thus, although Smith's theory of economic development in the first chapters of Book I of the *Wealth of Nations* is built on the individualistic premises of self-interest and natural human propensities, his theory of distribution presented in the final chapters of Book I is conducted in structuralist, collectivist and hence aggregate terms. Individuals have become members of classes, the individual self-interest has given way to class interests, and individuals have been substituted by collective agents, Urquhart (1993, pp. 190–1). Thus, the distribution of income is treated in terms of the remuneration of different *classes* (landlords, capitalists and workers) with different types of income (rents, profits and wages, respectively), before the task of explaining the sources of these incomes and tracing the dynamics of their distribution both deductively and historically is engaged.

This last remark brings us to a final (methodological) dualism in Smith, that of his utilisation of both deductive and inductive types of reasoning. Cliffe Leslie (1879 [1870], p. 151), the Irish historical economist, in his essay on 'The Political Economy of Adam Smith', was one of the first to highlight this dualism in Smith. He identified it as the source of the division of political economy into two schools that use opposing methods. One of these is represented by Ricardo as the founder of the deductive method; the other, of which Malthus and Mill are the chief representatives, combines the a priori and inductive methods. Blaug (1980, p. 57), on the other hand, following Skinner (1974, pp. 180–1), has argued that Smith applied the 'Newtonian method first to ethics and then to economics' in both *The Theory of Moral Sentiments* and in *The Wealth of Nations*.[9] Yet, as Pheby (1988, p. 16) observes, Smith:

> certainly employed deductive reasoning, but not of an axiomatic nature. He was a keen observer, of history and different societies and frequently used facts to illustrate his arguments. In short, his deductions were usually empirically founded. Therefore we cannot say that Smith rejected or did not employ inductive arguments.

This view is shared by Alfred Marshall, who also emphasised Adam Smith's methodological balance in 'having shown how inseparable induction and deduction are ... He was always inductive, but never merely inductive' (quoted in Hutchison 1998, p. 45).[10] Accordingly, Redman (1997, pp. 212–13), in her careful study, summarises Smith's method in the following steps:

1 abstract and isolate social (including economic) motivations and processes;
2 examine the interdependencies between the component parts;
3 generalise the relationships discovered to all similar situations (establish principles via induction, the process of deducting an inference from the facts);
4 draw inferences from the general or universal principles (deduction) to form a system, illustrate the theory, and show and explain the effects of the workings of the principles on social institutions.

In his exposition of the theory of economic growth, Smith makes use of the abstract/deductive method, which takes the form of deductive assumptions concerning human nature. But he also makes extensive use of empirical and historical material of the 'orthodox' type for illustrative purposes.

This is not the only type of historical argument used by Smith, however. Being one of the most prominent members of the Scottish Historical School, he also deployed what has been termed a 'theoretical' or 'philosophical' type of history. According to Blaug (1980, pp. 56–7), 'Books III, IV and V of *The Wealth of Nations* and most of the *Theory of Moral Sentiments*, exemplify the methods of the so-called Scottish Historical School'. Contrary to the 'orthodox', descriptive type of history, the latter refers to the Newtonian type of history, which is based on certain basic principles or assumptions, by analogy with the study of the effects of gravity, Skinner (1975, pp. 154, 169, 170).[11]

Thus, in Books III and V of the *Wealth of Nations*, Smith presents his view of development as proceeding through four normally consecutive stages, each based on a particular 'mode of subsistence' – hunting, pasturage, agriculture, and commerce, Meek (1971, pp. 9–10). In Book III, 'Of the Natural Progress of Opulence', in particular, Smith tackles the question of the origins of the 'present establishments' in Europe through 'the natural course of things', in the form of the four stages schema of the process of historical evolution. This historical part of Smith's work relies on the proposition that social change depends on economic development. One last premise on which Smith's argument is built refers to his more deductive assumption, according to which, 'man is self-regarding in all spheres of activity', Skinner (1975, p. 155), through 'the uniform, constant and uninterrupted effort of every man to better his condition', Smith quoted in Coleman (1987, pp. 10–11) and Hutchison (1978, p. 10). In sum, history plays a dual role in Smith; its 'philosophical' type forms an integral part of his analysis, while historical and empirical material of the 'orthodox' type is used throughout his writings for illustrative purposes.

Indeed, there is scarcely a page of *The Wealth of Nations* where history and theory are sundered apart. Overall, then, Smith's theoretical edifice is highly selective but also rich and multifaceted, encompassing philosophical, psychological, social, historical and economic elements. His is the first comprehensive attempt at approaching political economy as a unified social science, or as a part of the Moral Sciences greater whole, with no attachment to ethical or practical neutrality.

In opposition to Smith's pluralistic approach, the utilitarian philosopher Jeremy Bentham (1748–1832) was the only major classical writer who was purely and consistently individualistic. His importance, from our point of view, lies not only in the influence he exerted on other political economists as far as his utilitarian philosophy is concerned (these include John Stuart Mill and at least two of the marginalists, Jevons and Menger), but also because his philosophy provided one of the pillars on which the whole marginalist edifice was erected, see later chapters. This is none other than 'the principle of utility', otherwise known as 'the calculus of pleasure and pain'. According to Bentham (1970 [1789], p. 11):

> Nature has placed mankind under the governance of two sovereign masters, *pain* and *pleasure*. It is for them alone to point out what we ought to do, as well as determine what we shall do. On the one hand the standard of right and wrong, on the other the chain of causes and effects, are fastened to their throne. They govern us in all we do, in all we say, in all we think: every effort we can make to throw off our subjection, will serve but to demonstrate and confirm it.

Here all human action is reduced to rational responses to the relative weight of pleasure and pain. So what is the exact meaning of the term 'utility'? Bentham, p. 12:

> By utility is meant that property in any object, whereby it tends to produce benefit, advantage, pleasure, good, or happiness, (all this in the present case comes to the same thing) or (what comes again to the same thing) to prevent the happening of mischief, pain, evil, or unhappiness to the party whose interest is considered: if that party be the community in general, then the happiness of the community: if a particular individual, then the happiness of that individual.

Individuals strive to maximise their happiness, or their utility, by maximising their pleasure and minimising their pain. And since society is simply the sum of its individual members, the interest of society is also 'the sum of the interests of the several members who compose it' (Bentham quoted in Perlman and McCann 1998, p. 244). Hence by promoting the greatest happiness for the greatest number of people, society's welfare is also maximised, Perlman and McCann (1998, pp. 243–51).

If Jeremy Bentham is the only purely individualist classical writer, David Ricardo (1772–1823) is considered the first (unwitting) champion of the abstract/deductive method in economics, whose writings set its methodological division with induction in economics into motion. At the same time, and in opposition to Bentham's individualism, Ricardo employed a more collectivist type of reasoning. Although he did not write explicitly on method, his analysis in *On the Principles of Political Economy and Taxation* (1973 [1817]), is the archetype of abstract/deductive reasoning, thus helping to push political economy in this direction. It is no accident that Ricardo is the only classical economist with no training in philosophy (or any other moral science). He was a broker by profession and never attended university. Redman (1997, pp. 288–9) partly attributes Ricardo's narrow perspective (his 'one-track mind') to his professional shortsightedness:

> His working on the London stock exchange required the ability to make quick decisions and assess the situation by reducing the problem to simple analytical relations ... For a political economist, however, this method can only lead to what might be termed ... 'brokers' myopia'.

Specifically, in his own words, 'My object', he writes to Malthus, '[is] to elucidate principles, and to do this I imagined strong cases that I might shew the operation of these principles', Ricardo (1952b, p. 184).[12] Ilyenkov (1982, p. 182) appropriately sees Ricardo as:

> the first to distinguish, consciously and consistently, between the task of properly theoretical consideration of empirical data (the task of expressing

these data in concepts) and the task of simple description and cataloguing of phenomena in the form in which they are immediately given in contemplation and notion.

Using the power of abstraction, Ricardo was able to focus upon the quantity of labour as the essence of value and hence the basis for explaining all phenomena of the capitalist economy, and so to 'determine the laws which regulate this distribution ... among three classes of the community, namely, the proprietor of the land, the owner of the stock or capital ... and the labourers', Ricardo (1973, p. 3) and Zeleny (1980, p. 11).

Thus, whilst substantively he continues in Smith's footsteps in many respects, Ricardo's analysis is completely devoid of Smith's dualisms. First, he focuses exclusively on the macro rather than the micro level. His is mostly a macrodynamic analysis. Second, being primarily concerned with long-term trends in the distribution of the product between different classes, Ricardo is committed to an aggregate and holistic rather than an individualistic mode of analysis. Third, Ricardo did not adopt Smith's rich, if eclectic, methodological stance. His main work is mostly devoid of any historical or empirical references.[13] Although Ricardo tried to erect a dynamic theory of the distribution of the product based on his labour theory of value, he did so through the exclusive use of the abstract/deductive method, as in the speculative invention that Portugal should have absolute advantage over England in production of both cloth and wine. For Coleman (1987, p. 23), Ricardo 'hardly ever appealed to history to make a point, to support an analytical proposition, even to illustrate an argument', and for Schumpeter (1994, p. 472), he had no historical sense. Redman (1997, pp. 284, 285), though, is more tempered on this, arguing that 'the belief that Ricardo was not a man of facts' is a myth:

> Although facts play a different, more restricted role in his theorizing than in Malthus', Ricardo believes they shape his conclusions. In formulating bold hypotheses, he relied on general observation and his knowledge of the commercial world.

But this is very different from the historical being directly and explicitly incorporated. Although Ricardo was acutely attuned to the economic policy context of his own time, he deliberately and successfully sought to abstract from this in building his theory (although he was probably mindful of the policy conclusions, especially Repeal of the Corn Laws, that he sought to reach). Hutchison (1978, p. 54) elevates the importance of this methodological rupture in excising the historical to the extreme, by claiming that 'the contrast in method with *The Wealth of Nations* seems sufficiently profound, extreme and consequential, as to justify the adjective "revolutionary"'. As indicated in our opening quotation, Hutchison finds that Smith's blend of economic theory and history is set aside except in Marxist political economy, see below and Chapters 3 and 4.

Whether in his search for an 'invariable standard' to measure the value of commodities (ch. 1, p. 17) his theory of rent based on the diminishing fertility of land (ch. 2), his theory of wages (ch. 5), his attempt to establish theoretically 'the natural tendency of profits ... to fall' (ch. 6, p. 71) or his theory of foreign trade (ch. 7), Ricardo's main concern is to establish the 'laws' that govern the behaviour of these economic categories or the 'principles' on which they are based. He does so mostly by using the rules of logic to make the necessary abstractions and simplifying assumptions, to the almost total exclusion of any other mode of reasoning, be it historical, empirical or otherwise. He attempts to give economic science a status equivalent to that enjoyed by natural sciences. However, 'it was not simply that Ricardo and the Ricardians constructed abstract models, but that they applied the conclusions from the highly restrictive models directly to the complexities of the real world', Sowell (1994, p.122). In Schumpeter's (1994, p. 472) words, 'his interest was in the clear-cut result of direct, practical significance'. This 'habit of applying results of this character to the solution of practical problems', Schumpeter, in his erstwhile famous phrase, dubbed 'the Ricardian Vice', p. 473.

Substantively, the social element is still an important part of Ricardo's analysis, as evidenced by his use of social categories such as social class. But, methodologically, 'the use of the Ricardian technique permitted economic theory to develop independently of other social sciences', Deane (1978, p. 84). The process initiated by Ricardo came to final fruition as a result of the marginalist revolution. Being the first classical economist to employ the abstract, a priori method with such consistency and vigour, Ricardo became one of the principal poles of the first great divide in economics between the deductive and the inductive methods. As is widely acknowledged, Ricardo's greatest influence in economic science was in terms of his method. In Hutchison's (1978, p. 26) words, 'if the changes brought about by Ricardo's work, and the influence which it exercised, may validly be regarded as "revolutionary", this must surely be primarily, or largely, because of the novelty, and subsequent importance for the subject, of its *methodological* contribution'.[14] In other words, 'the *methodological* claim that problems in political economy are problems of "*determining laws*" ... (and) the *method* of extreme abstraction'.

4 The first methodological rupture

Ricardo's abstract mode of reasoning gave rise to a major debate on method in the history of economic thought. This debate concerned the relative merits of induction and deduction and, at a deeper level, how apposite it is to counterpose the two methods (rather than simply accepting the necessity and desirability of elements of both). Especially prominent were the exchanges between Ricardo himself and Malthus (1776–1834). According to the latter, the basic vice of authors like Ricardo, who rely exclusively on the deductive method, is their 'precipitate attempt to simplify and generalise', as well as their 'unwillingness to bring their theories to the test of experience', Malthus

(1986 [1820], pp. 4, 8). This desire to simplify is the result of the 'unwilling-ness to acknowledge the operation of more causes than one in the production of particular effects'. Since, however, very few phenomena have mono-causal explanations, reversion to the facts is inevitable. 'Before the shrine of truth, as discovered by facts and experience, the fairest theories and the most beautiful classifications must fall', p. 6. In contradistinction to Ricardo's abstract, deductive type of political economy, for Malthus, 'the science of political economy is essentially practical, and applicable to the common business of life', p. 9. As such, the initial premises of any theory must be based on empirical observation. On this basis, certain propositions can be derived which can again be empirically checked and confirmed 'by the state of society as it actually exists in every country', p. 8. In essence, Malthus is adhering to a mixture of the abstract and the inductive methods, with emphasis on the latter. According to Schumpeter (1967 [1912], pp. 81–2, n. 1), although 'Malthus appears to us more "inductive" than Ricardo ... the essence of his thought process and the manner of his argumentation is just as "theoretical", though not as bold and precise as is the case with Ricardo'. Further, for Malthus (1986, p. 1), 'the science of political economy bears a nearer resemblance to the science of morals and politics than to that of mathe-matics', not least because the effects of 'the laws which regulate the move-ments of human society', as opposed to the effects of physical laws, 'are continually modified by human interference', p. 10.

Paradoxically, albeit for different reasons, both Mill and Marx sided with Ricardo in this methodological battle, whilst Keynes was later to embrace Malthus' approach. As Schumpeter (1994, p. 480) puts it, 'Marx poured on [Malthus] vitriolic wrath [while] Keynes glorified him'. Indeed, in view of his focus on demand for consumption, Keynes regarded Malthus as one of the most important precursors of his own work (cited in Redman 1997, pp. 261–2; see also Blaug [1958, pp. 238–40]):

> the almost total obliteration of Malthus' line of approach and the complete domination of Ricardo's for a period of a hundred years has been a disaster to the progress of economics ... If only Malthus, instead of Ricardo, had been the parent stem from which nineteenth-century economics proceeded, what a much wiser and richer place the world would be today.

Malthus is mostly remembered, and notorious, for his descriptive work on population although, in fact, 'he collected his material in order to verify views which he had already developed', Schumpeter (1967, p. 82, n. 1). Ricardo, on the other hand, is heavily associated pejoratively with his attachment to the labour theory of value with its potentially normative, if not necessarily socialist, connotations concerning the source of value (not least following its adoption and adaptation by Marx).

Another early attack on Ricardo's abstract axiomatic approach in the 1820s and 1830s comes from Richard Jones (1790–1855), who is considered a precursor of the British Historical School to be discussed in Chapter 8. Jones was unhappy with the abstract and non-empirical nature of Ricardo's economics, and called for a more empirically-based and historical approach to political economy, Pheby (1988, p. 10) and Hodgson (2001, p. 65). For Jones, quoted in Miller (1971, p. 199):

> We must get comprehensive views of facts, that we may arrive at principles which are truly comprehensive. If we take a different method, if we snatch at general principles, and content ourselves with confined observations, two things will happen to us. First, what we call general principles will often be found wanting; ... and, secondly, we shall miss a great mass of useful knowledge, which those who advance to principles by a comprehensive examination of facts, necessarily meet with on their road.

However, despite Jones' strong emphasis on inductivism and on getting a comprehensive view of the facts, he did not simply, 'let facts tell their own story, but tried to impose theories on the facts and even made an effort to use deduction to develop the theories', Miller (1971, p. 204). And William Whewell (1794–1870), a close friend of Jones, shared his views on methodology: 'The science of Political Economy', says Whewell (1999 [1862], p. 8), 'does not rest upon Definitions. It rests upon facts. But facts are to be described in a general manner – that is, by means of general terms. And these terms should be well chosen, so as to enable us to assert true propositions'. At the same time, however, Whewell, also wrote three articles in which he tried to put the Ricardian system into mathematical form, Gordon (1991, p. 203).

Jones is one of the first political economists to stress the (historical) relativity of economic laws, and 'to urge economists to pay greater attention to the historical differences between economic institutions', Roll (1992 [1937], p. 283). As Roll (1992, pp. 285, 289) observes in concise summary of Jones' work:

> [He] was anxious to lay bare the distinction between that which was common to all social structures and the different forms in which it appeared as a result of differences in the social structure ... His explanation of the historical evolution of different economic structures, and his extraordinarily penetrating distinction between the universal categories of economic activity and their varying social expressions put him in the select group of those who were able to combine rigorous deductive analysis with an understanding of the broad sweep of history.

Jones applied these principles consistently. His penetrating and detailed analysis of the problem of rent and his insistence on the problem of historical relativity of economic laws attracted Marx's attention and praise in the *Theories of Surplus Value*, Marx (1991, pp. 320–71). It can be argued that

Jones' distinction between different forms of social production in the course of history anticipates Marx's periodisation through different modes of production, Marx (1991, p. 320), Roll (1992, p. 285), and see also next chapter, Section 3.

Although Ricardo was certainly the first economist to use the abstract method so fully, Nassau Senior (1790–1864) wrote one of the first explicit essays on method in 1826, Hutchison (1998, p. 46). Between them they set off what Hausman (1992, p. 1) has called 'traditional methodological wisdom', or what Hutchison (1998, p. 44) has characteristically termed 'empirically minimalist ultra-deductivism'. Senior's advocacy of the axiomatic method is made explicit in his *An Outline of the Science of Political Economy* (1965) [1836], from which he can be interpreted to hold that, 'introspection and casual observation were sufficient to provide such an axiomatic basis', Pheby (1988, p. 17). Senior (1965, p. 1) defines political economy as 'the Science which treats of the Nature, the Production, and the Distribution of Wealth', and he goes on to add that the premises of the political economist, pp. 2–3:

> consist of a very few general propositions, the result of observation, or consciousness, and scarcely requiring proof, or even formal statement, which almost every man, as soon as he hears them, admits as familiar to his thoughts, or at least as included in his previous knowledge; and his inferences are nearly as general, and, if he has reasoned correctly, as certain, as his premises.

So these 'few general propositions' are mostly the result of introspection, and they consist of the following: first, in typical Benthamite fashion, 'that every person is desirous to obtain, with as little sacrifice as possible, as much as possible of the articles of wealth', Senior, quoted in Hutchison (1998, p. 46); second is the Malthusian population principle; third is that the productivity of labour and capital can be increased by using their products for the production of other products; and fourth is that agriculture faces diminishing returns, Hutchison (1998, p. 47) and Pheby (1988, p. 17).

For Senior (1965, p. 3), although the general principles governing the production of wealth are universally valid, 'those which relate to the distribution of Wealth are liable to be affected by the peculiar institutions of particular Countries', and are hence historically specific. Senior was also one of the first writers to make explicit the distinction between economics as a science and economics as an art, p. 3:

> The business of a Political Economist is neither to recommend nor to dissuade, but to state general principles, which it is fatal to neglect, but neither advisable, nor perhaps practicable, to use as the sole, or even the principal, guides in the actual conduct of affairs ... To decide in each case how far those conclusions are to be acted upon, belongs to the art

of government, an art to which Political economy is only one of many subservient Sciences.

This distinction was further consolidated during the marginalist revolution, before becoming one of the cornerstones of modern neoclassical economics following its seizure, especially through Robbins, of the distinction between positive and normative economics as developed in 1890 by John Neville Keynes, see Chapter 7.[15]

5 Concluding remarks

If Smith was the pioneer and the great synthetic mind of classical political economy, with Ricardo the latter reached its analytical apogee. Although certainly Ricardo's work should be seen in many respects as contributing to and continuing in Smith's footsteps, his writings also represented an analytical and deductivist turn compared to Smith's multifaceted and methodologically mixed political economy. Between them, they provided the seeds of most subsequent developments in political economy. Thus Marx should be seen as drawing on the more holistic and abstract aspects of their methods in conjunction with their theories of value, radically reconstructed, as his main analytic tool. Marginalism, on the other hand, is an offspring of the individualistic aspects of Smith's method in conjunction with Ricardian deductivism and Benthamite utilitarianism. Another major difference is that although Marx saw his political economy as a continuation of, as well as a break with, classical political economy, all marginalist writers considered their work as a conscious departure from most aspects of classical political economy, especially in substantive terms, the main exception being Ricardo's 'marginalist' rent theory. Karl Marx and John Stuart Mill are the subject of the next chapter, whereas marginalism will be treated in Chapter 6.

3 Mill's conciliation, Marx's transgression

'The extraordinary durability of [Mill's *Principles of Political Economy*] was due in large part to its blending of classical and anticlassical elements. It represented the final synthesis of Ricardian doctrine with many of the qualifications and refinements introduced by Ricardo's critics hinting just enough at the "real cost" of capital and the role of demand in determining prices to reconcile Ricardian notions with the new utility theory of value'.

Blaug (1997, p. 172)

'Political economy cannot be the same for all countries and for all historical periods ... Political economy is therefore a *historical* science'.

Engels (1972 [1878], pp. 211–12)

1 Introduction

Despite its many critics, Ricardian economics dominated the scene from the 1820s to the 1870s, and even beyond. John Stuart Mill's (1806–73) text, *Principles of Political Economy* (1976) [1848], which was written in the Ricardian tradition, became the bible of political economy, and was not displaced until the publication of Marshall's *Principles of Economics* in 1890.

In the previous chapter, we discussed two early critics of Ricardo's political economy, both coming from an empiricist and inductivist perspective, Richard Jones and Robert Malthus. Other early attacks came from writers such as Bailey, Scrope, Lloyd, Longfield and Senior, who were the first to replace Ricardo's labour theory of value with utility theory, even though, at the time, it did not gain any currency. Ricardo, however, was also fortunate enough to win extremely loyal disciples, among them James Mill, McCulloch, Torrens and John Stuart Mill, who were largely responsible for the dominance of Ricardian economics, if in a modified form, for the next half century after Ricardo's death in 1823, Blaug (1958, pp. 1–4, 221–7). It is in light of these early critiques that Mill's peculiar defence of the Ricardian system should be seen. As discussed in Section 2, Mill's own interpretation, and adaptation, of the Ricardian system occupied a middle-ground between Ricardo's political economy and its critics, while remaining largely Ricardian in character.

Karl Marx, on the other hand, although an offspring of classical political economy, also departed from it in important ways, and built an alternative theoretical system of his own. It is no accident that Marx himself called his work in *Capital* 'a critique of political economy'. In addition to the labour theory of value inherited from the classicals, Marx's other influences included German philosophy (mainly Hegel and Feuerbach), and what he himself labelled 'Utopian' socialists, including Saint-Simon, who also exerted an influence on Mill, Fourier, Owen and Proudhon. On this basis, Marx manages to erect an extraordinarily rich theoretical construction, combining in a dialectical way abstract, social and historical elements. Section 3 offers an account and assessment of Marx's method and the dialectics of history in light of his reconstruction of political economy, in a way that cuts across rigid methodological divisions such as the one between induction and deduction.

By contrast, the concluding remarks point briefly, if sharply, to the loss of methodological wealth and debate within economics – to the point of its being unaware that these losses have taken place – apart from in increasingly marginalised heterodoxies. This conclusion is unavoidable in broad contrast between then and now. How it came about occupies much of the rest of this book, a tale of piecemeal if often rapid change in thought, propelled by the reluctant acceptance of what was being lost in principle, but its being set aside in practice without regard.

2 John Stuart Mill: consolidation and crisis

Although his *Principles of Political Economy* were written in the Ricardian tradition, Mill tried to introduce subjectivist utilitarian elements in the form of 'the laws of human nature' in his otherwise Ricardian system. For Mill, moral science can be divided into the science of human nature and the science of society, the former logically preceding the latter. Social phenomena are the effects of individual action, so the science of the individual (the science of human nature) must precede the science of society (social science), Redman (1997, pp. 332–4). His utilitarianism, however, is different from Bentham's. As Riley (1994, p. xvi) puts it:

> [Mill's] aim in the *Political Economy* was to rework Smith's practical approach by applying Ricardo's advanced scientific principles in the light of a suitably 'enlarged' utilitarian philosophy that would go beyond narrow Benthamism to make room for a more complex psychology (admitting the possibility of higher kinds of pleasures and characters) and for improved ideas of social co-operation and equal justice.

Thus, in his work *Utilitarianism* he stressed his preference for 'ethical utilitarianism' as opposed to Bentham's 'hedonistic utilitarianism'.

Ethical utilitarianism depicts the individual as a social animal whose utilitarian calculus, in addition to hedonistic factors, includes other ethical and moral factors that are not innate but culturally derived, such as 'the hope of favour and the fear of displeasure, from our fellow-creatures or from the ruler of the Universe', Mill (1962 [1863], p. 280), but also the 'pure idea of duty', sympathy, love, fear, religious motives, self-esteem, desire of the esteem of others etc., p. 281, see also Perlman and McCann (1998, pp. 273–6). This infusion of social factors in individual conduct has led commentators to describe both Mill's and Smith's partly individualistic method as 'institutional individualism', as opposed to the 'psychological individualism' of the marginalists and neoclassical theory, see Zouboulakis (2002) and later chapters. Mill's specific combination of Ricardianism with his brand of utilitarianism is depicted in his 'correct and accurate' definition of political economy as 'the science which treats of the production and distribution of wealth, *so far as they depend upon the laws of human nature*', Mill (1836, p. 133), emphasis added.

This mixture of Ricardianism with anti-Ricardian elements is what, according to Blaug (1997, p. 172), lies behind its immense success, see opening quote. What Mill did not realise, however, was, as de Vroey (1975, pp. 431–2) observes:

> the long-term consequences which would result from the infiltration of subjective elements into the Ricardian system. More precisely, he did not realize that the labor and subjective theories of value, which he tried to synthesize, belong to opposed methodological approaches. Indeed, the labor component of his theory of value was linked to a definition of economic processes as relations between classes. On the contrary, the subjective component depended upon a vision in which the object of analysis was the relation between the individual and his desires.

Paradoxically, then, the push by Mill to complement an objective theory of value with subjective elements, in order to account for the historically and socially situated individual, in part had the perverse effect of paving the way for ahistorical and asocial subjectivity (marginal utility) to prevail.

The eclectic nature of Mill's *Principles* is not accidental. It was the product of an epoch (between the 1830s and 1870s) that has been described as 'a long period of hybrid equilibrium', de Vroey (1975, p. 431), during which the attacks on the Ricardian system (which started as early as 1825 by Bailey) co-existed with the long-drawn-out gestation process of the marginalist revolution. These early attacks on Ricardianism led Schumpeter (1994, p. 478) to declare, somewhat prematurely, that by the 1830s, 'it is clear that Ricardianism was ... no longer a living force'. However, it is now well-established that, despite these early attacks on the Ricardian system, it did not show serious signs of expiring until at least the 1870s, and Mill played no small part in this. Part of the explanation lies in the fact that, according to Blaug (1958, p. 229):

> Nothing better was found to take its place. In an era of rapid industrial expansion, dominated by the conflict between the landed gentry and the manufacturing interests, a theory which dealt with the major issues of

capital accumulation and functional distribution in terms of a few aggregate variables had all the advantages of popular appeal and practical significance. On this level of analysis Ricardo had no competitors.

Untangling Mill's methodological views is not an easy task. Part of the reason for this is that Mill went through 'several changes of mind, some of which produced almost mutually contradictory views; ambiguities that may never be resolved; and a plethora of special terminology that can be semantically demanding', Redman (1997, p. 321). Mill was influenced by the French positivist philosopher Auguste Comte.[1] In his more philosophical work, such as *A System of Logic*, Mill (1884) [1843] espouses a radical empiricist approach to science, according to which, 'the only source of knowledge was sense experience; knowledge was obtained inductively; and scientific laws were simply empirical event regularities', Wade Hands (2001, p. 16), see also Randall (1965, p. 60) and Giddens (1977). In his political economy, however, he adhered to the more deductive approach of the Ricardian system. In this light, Mill's 'greatest challenge was the reconciliation of *empiricist epistemology* and (Ricardian) *economic theory*', Wade Hands (2001, p. 16). For him, the important distinction is not between induction and deduction – for Mill only inductive inference is possible – but 'between sciences that *can be made deductive* and those that *must remain experimental*', p. 18. He gives Newtonian mechanics as an example of the former; chemistry of the latter. Coming to political economy, granted that the experimental (a posteriori) method is not available, it has to recourse to the Newtonian, deductive (a priori) method, p. 21.

Significantly, Mill (1836, p. 143), in an earlier work, provides, together with Senior, one of the first explicit essays on the method of political economy. He emphasises that the dichotomy between deduction and induction is false, since 'those who disavow theory cannot make one step without theorizing', while 'both classes of inquirers do nothing but theorize, and both of them consult no other guide than experience', p. 142. In other words, 'both the "theorists" and the empirical or "practical" men used systematic reasoning, starting from given assumptions, and both derived those assumptions from something in the real world', Sowell (1994, p. 123). The difference between the two, according to Mill (1836, p. 143), is that:

> those who are called practical men require *specific* experience, and argue wholly *upwards* from particular facts to a general conclusion; while those who are called theorists aim at embracing a wider field of experience, and, having argued upwards from particular facts to a general principle including a much wider range than that of the question under discussion, then argue *downwards* from that general principle to a variety of specific conclusions.

Theorisation is inescapable because of the sheer complexity of the real world, which renders the deduction of general laws through the inductive process impossible, pp. 148–9:

it is vain to hope that truth can be arrived at ... while we look at the facts in the concrete, clothed in all the complexity with which nature has surrounded them, and endeavour to elicit a general law by a process of induction from a comparison of details.

Following the rejection of pure inductivism as the method of political economy, Mill defines political economy in typical Ricardian fashion, as 'essentially an *abstract* science, and its method as the method a priori', the latter meaning 'reasoning from an assumed hypothesis', p. 143. Further, p. 144:

Political Economy ... reasons from *assumed* premises – from premises which might be totally without foundation in fact, and which are not pretended to be in accordance with it. The conclusions of Political Economy ... like those of geometry, are only true ... *in the abstract.*

One such assumed abstract hypothesis is what came to be known as that of 'economic man' or 'homo economicus'. Mill defines *homo economicus* as 'a being who desires to possess wealth', while abstracting from 'every other human passion or motive', p. 137. Having thus begun, though, Mill goes on to qualify his argument by noting that, p. 150:

when the principles of Political Economy are to be applied to a particular case, then it is necessary to take into account all the individual circumstances of that case ... These circumstances have been called *disturbing causes* ... When the disturbing causes are known, the allowance necessary to be made for them detracts in no way from scientific precision, nor constitutes any deviation from the a priori method.

Thus, although Mill considers political economy as dealing with the economic man who is driven by his 'desire for wealth', he also modifies this view by treating political economy as a partial and approximate science, whose premises and deductions need to be modified by non-economic factors and the results of other social sciences. It involves 'a mixed method of induction and ratiocination' and 'reasoning from assumed premises', Mill quoted in Redman (1997, p. 339). At the same time, empirical evidence is relevant to moral sciences in general, and political economy in particular, for the purposes of verifying theories, because 'it is seldom in our power to make experiments in them', Mill (1836, pp. 146–7), and see Deane (1978, p. 89).[2] All these remarks by Mill regarding the method of political economy have to be seen in the context of his overall empiricist epistemological framework, Wade Hands (2001, p. 23). Even Hutchison (1998, pp. 44, 48), who includes Mill in his list of ultra-deductivists, qualifies the latter's deductivism as being 'less extreme', because Mill 'was in several respects more empirical than the others'.

Following in Senior's footsteps, Mill also makes the distinction between the science and the art of economics, quoted in Deane (1978, p. 88):

Science is a collection of *truths*; art, a body of *rules*, or directions for conduct ... Science takes cognizance of a *phenomenon*, and endeavours to discover its *law*; art proposes to itself an *end* and looks out for *means* to effect it. If, therefore, Political Economy be a science, it cannot be a collection of practical rules; though, unless it be altogether a useless science, practical rules must be capable of being founded on it.

So Mill was in favour of a purely scientific political economy, but one which is also practically relevant. In this direction, Mill did try to connect his theoretical principles with practical problems – a connection that 'requires consideration of a broader range of social and ethical matters than most economists are accustomed to examine. So we find in Mill far more material of a historical and descriptive or institutional nature than in Ricardo's, Gordon (1991, p. 205). 'Thus', suggests Hutchison (1998, pp. 50–1), 'Mill did admit ... the *potential* importance of a historical dimension to political economy, or the longer-term factor of evolutionary change, as emerged in his distinction between the laws of production and the laws of distribution'. At the same time, Mill was also sensitive to the specific historical context.[3] His inductive and historical side is more evident in his writings on applied and policy issues such as the Irish land question: 'no one is at all capable of determining what is the right political economy for any country until he knows its circumstances', he declared in Parliament, opposing Lowe's attack upon the Irish land legislation, Mill quoted in Koot (1975, 321). Mill was also a great social reformer and liberal, as laid out, for example, in his *On Liberty*, Mill (1974) [1859]. Influenced by other socialist writers such as the French Saint-Simon, he thought of himself as a socialist, albeit of his own peculiar type. In his *Chapters on Socialism*, he envisaged a sort of decentralised cooperative socialism, based on small-scale and cooperative forms of property, see Mill (1994 [1848], pp. 369–436).

John Elliot Cairnes (1823–75), a close disciple of Mill, is regarded as the last and one of the more strident supporters of the Ricardian system, his *The Character and Logical Method of Political Economy* having been published in 1857. He denied that 'economic theories can ever be refuted by a simple comparison with the facts', pp. 77–8. Economic laws, according to Cairnes, 'can be refuted only by showing either that the principles and conditions assumed do not exist, or that the tendency which the law affirms does not follow as a necessary consequence from this assumption', p. 110. In other words, a theory is refuted only if the assumptions on which it is based are proven to be invalid, or if it is proven to be logically inconsistent, Blaug (1980, p. 80). This led Hutchison (1998, p. 51) to declare that 'Cairnes was the most emphatic exponent of one of the main doctrines of ultra-deductivism'.

Despite the more or less qualified defences of the Ricardian system and its underlying abstract/deductive method by Senior, Mill and Cairnes, Ricardian economics came under increasing attack during the 1860s and 1870s from many quarters and from different – even opposing – viewpoints. These attacks were taking place against the background of the repeated failure of the Ricardian theory to yield accurate predictions, as was made evident in the 1840s by the increasing availability of statistical data, Blaug (1958, p. 227). 'It is evident', writes Jevons (1957, p. xvi), one of the leading marginalists, in 1879, 'that a spirit of very active criticism is spreading, which can hardly fail to overcome in the end the prestige of the false old doctrines'. And he goes on: 'But what is to be put in place of them?'. Three main critiques of the classical school had emerged during this period, giving rise to three different answers to Jevons' question, but also to three competing schools of thought: the Marxist School, the Historical School and marginalism. While Marx saw himself as providing a critical reconstruction of Ricardian economics, the anti-Ricardian reaction – first of the Historical School and later of the marginalists – was prompted, among other reasons, by the appropriation of Ricardian economics by socialists. This underpins the total abandonment by both schools of Ricardo's principal theoretical tool, the labour theory of value, which became Marx's cornerstone in his critique of political economy. By the 1870s, the classical paradigm in its Ricardian form was in crisis.

We now turn our attention to the three major reactions against Ricardianism, although not in chronological order: in the next section, we deal with Marx's critique of (classical) political economy, followed in Chapter 4 by the German Historical School. Marginalism, which brought about the second great rupture in economic thought, will be dealt with in Chapter 5.

3 Karl Marx, dialectics and history

'The philosophers have only *interpreted* the world, in various ways; the point, however, is to *change* it', posited Marx (1968 [1888], p. 30) in his *Theses on Feuerbach*. The explicitly stated aim of Karl Marx's (1818–83) lifetime work was to change the world, although this should itself be interpreted as a way of understanding the world and not just exhortation to action. Thus, the way in which he set about reaching his goal in his major work, *Capital*, is by examining the way the modern capitalist system works, through unravelling its basic law of motion, Marx (1976, p. 92). Marx's theoretical corpus was erected on three pillars: classical political economy, German philosophy and French utopian socialism. From classical political economy, he inherited the labour theory of value, his collectivist mode of reasoning, and class as a unit of analysis; from German philosophy, Hegel's dialectics and Feuerbach's materialism; and from the French socialists, their critique and rejection of the optimism of classical liberalism, their emphasis on social justice, and their support for alternative forms of collective/social ownership.

Through Marx, classical political economy reaches a climax in all its multi-dimensional complexity, including its abstract, social, holistic, historical and dynamic elements. Marx praises both Smith and Ricardo for furnishing the premises for a 'scientific' political economy, but he also criticises them for what he considers to be inadequacies of method. In particular, he criticises Smith for his methodological eclecticism, and for failing to apply the abstract method consistently. As he puts it in *Theories of Surplus Value*, Marx (1969b, p. 165):

> with Smith both methods of approach not only merrily run alongside one another, but also intermingle and constantly contradict one another. With him this is justifiable ... since his task was indeed twofold. On the one hand he attempted to penetrate the inner physiology of bourgeois society but on the other, he partly tried to describe the externally apparent forms of reality for the first time ... [T]his results in completely contradictory ways of presentation: the one expresses the intrinsic connections more or less correctly, the other ... expresses the *apparent* connections without any internal relation.

For Marx, in other words, as Ilyenkov (1982, p. 181) observes, Smith 'unfolded a theory in which properly theoretical consideration of facts was continually interwoven with extremely untheoretical descriptions of empirical data', what Marx (1969b, p. 166) himself called 'the esoteric and exoteric part of his work'. An instance of 'esoteric' analysis in Smith is his determination of value by 'the quantity of labour', whereas an instance of 'exoteric' analysis is his additive theory of value in terms of wages, profits and rents, Smith (1981, book I, chs. V and VI) and Marx (1969a, p. 97), see also Chapter 4.

Smith's labour theory of value as a theory of price (which he rejects beyond the rude society, see Chapter 4), is esoteric because it deploys an abstract causal category that has no immediate connection to what is to be explained. There is the need to show how the inner workings of the economic system translate such value to its more obvious outcome as price. By contrast, the additive theory of price is exoteric since it seeks simple connections between immediately observable elements. Price is made up of its constituent parts (of wages, profits and rents), which means little more than identifying its parts and adding them together just as two plus two equals four. As such, it is deductive in the most immediate sense.

Ricardo's work, on the other hand, represents a 'determined break with the contradiction that pervades Adam Smith's work' by consistently following and expanding the 'esoteric' part of Smith's analysis, through, in other words, the consistent application of the abstract theoretical method, Marx (1969b, p. 169). 'At last', Marx says, p. 166:

> Ricardo steps in and calls to science: Halt! The basis, the starting-point for the physiology of the bourgeois system – for the understanding of its internal organic coherence and life process – is the determination of *value by labour-time*. Ricardo starts with this and forces science to get out of the rut, to render an account of the extent to which the other

categories – the relations of production and commerce – evolved and described by it, correspond to or contradict this basis, this starting point ... and in general, to examine how matters stand with the contradiction between the apparent and the actual movement of the system. This then is Ricardo's great historical significance for science.

Note, however, that the praise for Ricardo is not so much because of his deductive method as the wish to apply the labour theory of value as an underlying concept in explaining capitalism. For Marx, by accident or design, Ricardo has stumbled upon the appropriate socially and historically derived category for analysing capitalism, however well he may have understood this category of value itself or the reasons for its suitability for this purpose.

Despite, however, the merits and the consistent application of the abstract/ deductive method, Ricardo's work suffers 'scientific deficiencies'. One is that, out of the 32 chapters of his *Principles*, only the first six ('On Value', 'On Rent', 'On the Rent of Mines', 'On Natural and Market-Price', 'On Wages' and 'On Profits') are devoted to the elaboration of the Ricardian theory and, of these, the first two contain 'the entire Ricardian contribution'. The rest merely deal in applications of the theoretical principles, pp. 166–7.

Even the theoretical part of his work, however, exhibits what Marx calls 'faulty architectonics'. This is not accidental, 'rather it is the result of Ricardo's method of investigation itself and of the definite task which he set himself in his work. It expresses the deficiencies of this method of investigation itself'. Thus, although Ricardo tried to apply his deductive method consistently, his use of the power of abstraction is deficient and one-dimensional for this reason. This is evident, for example, in 'On Value', where the problem of value is examined. This is done by assuming, 'not only commodities exist – and when considering value nothing else is required – but also wages, capital, profit, the general rate of profit and even the various forms of capital ... and also the difference between "natural and market price"', pp. 167–8. Ricardo fails to ask what are the social and historical conditions that underpin the presence of commodities, let alone the prices and distributional forms of revenue to which they are attached. It is as if these, alongside classes, are natural.

Thus, Marx concludes, p. 191:

> Though Ricardo is accused of being too abstract, one would be justified in accusing him of the opposite: lack of the power of abstraction, inability, when dealing with the values of commodities, to forget profits, a factor which confronts him as a result of competition.

This scientific inadequacy 'not only shows itself in the mode of presentation ... but leads to erroneous results because it omits some essential links and *directly* seeks to prove the congruity of the economic categories with one another', pp. 164–5. Elsewhere, Marx characterises Ricardo's abstraction as 'incomplete', 'formal' or simply 'wrong', p. 106, see also Sayer (1979, pp. 119–41). As Himmelweit and Mohun (1978, p. 81–2) put it:

> Ricardo's theory is ... a model built upon assumptions rather than the theorization of a real world process by means of abstraction. Assumptions are thought-constructs which have no real existence but are invented in order to simplify and to structure the complexity of the analysis ... Assumptions are of course designed in order to be able to say something about the real world, but to the extent that they do this ... they do so purely by virtue of being imposed upon empirical 'facts' in order to render appearances coherent and plausible. Hence they are expressions of surface phenomena which see in such *immediate* forms the whole nature of the phenomena in question. But descriptions of surface phenomena exclude the possibility of necessary contradictions as the determinants of the motion of these immediate forms ... [It] follows that nothing can be deduced from assumptions which is not already entailed by those assumptions; hence theory becomes tautology, the deduction of conclusions from assumptions.

In short, and more specifically, Ricardo seeks to deduce price, or whatever, quantitatively from a labour theory of value, without examining how value and price are connected to one another qualitatively, i.e. in terms of the historically evolved societies from which they are drawn and to which they apply.

It is already apparent from these critiques that Marx was firmly in favour of abstract theorising and opposed to both 'vulgar empiricism' and 'vulgar eclecticism'. The task of science, according to Marx (in Volume III, ch. 48, section 3), is to go behind the appearances of things and reveal their true essence. Indeed, 'all science would be superfluous if the outward appearance and essence of things directly coincided'. To achieve this, Marx makes use of the method of dialectics, which he derives from Hegel. In the Hegelian system, says Engels (1968 [1883], p. 408):

> for the first time the whole world, natural, historical, intellectual, is represented as a process, i.e. in constant motion, change, transformation, development; and the attempt is made to trace out the internal connection that makes a continuous whole of all this movement and development.

Dialectics as a mode of reasoning captures the movement of any social entity and depicts contradiction as the motor behind it, Stedman Jones (1987, pp. 125–6). In Hegel's idealist dialectics, however, 'the process of thinking ... is the creator of the real world'. To the contrary, in Marx's materialist dialectics, 'the ideal is nothing but the material world reflected in the mind of man, and translated into forms of thought'. In other words, with Hegel, the dialectic 'is standing on its head. It must be inverted, in order to understand the rational kernel inside the mystical shell', Marx (1976, pp. 102–3).

Marx (1973 [1953], pp. 100–1) identifies two methods for analysing the concrete world. In the 'method of inquiry', through which one starts from ('a chaotic conception' of) the concrete world itself and moves analytically to ever simpler concepts. In the 'method of presentation', on the other hand, these simple concepts form the starting point from which the concrete whole is (re)constructed, this time not as a 'chaotic conception' but as a 'rich totality of many determinations and relations'. It is the latter that Marx considers 'the scientifically correct method'. In order for the human mind to arrive at these simple concepts, however, the power of abstraction is needed. As he puts it, 'in the analysis of economic forms neither microscopes nor chemical reagents are of assistance. The power of abstraction must replace both', Marx (1976, p. 90). As opposed to Smith's and Ricardo's 'incomplete' and 'formal' abstractions, however, Marx's abstractions are 'real', 'concrete', 'rational' abstractions, in accordance with material reality, Fine and Harris (1979, pp. 6–8), Fine and Saad-Filho (2004), and Chapter 4 below.

This is an essential element of Marx's method of dialectical logic (or materialist dialectics) according to which the concrete whole (e.g. the capitalist mode of production) is regarded as an integral whole whose individual parts are mutually constitutive. Thus, contrary to metaphysical forms of abstraction which take the form of pure mental generalisations based on 'arbitrary selection of certain relations or common properties' of the concrete whole such as 'labour', 'utility' or what have you, dialectical logic 'selects the most important feature of the concrete, and reconstructs the other features systematically on the basis of this essence', Saad-Filho (2002, pp. 8–15). Based as it is on the method of dialectical logic, Marx's analysis takes a holistic form. The social whole takes precedence over its individual elements, and is analysed in terms of the inner connections and relations of its constituent parts. Studying the capitalist mode of production as an integral totality through its inner connections and relations, Marx is able to reveal its 'economic law of motion', which is his explicitly stated aim.

In the deductive/inductive dichotomy, Marx is a case apart because of his deployment of the method of materialist dialectics. In this approach, the traditional distinction between deduction and induction is transcended. Ilyenkov (1982, p. 162) puts the point eloquently, if obliquely:

> The old opposition of deduction and induction is rationally sublated in materialist dialectics. Deduction ceases to be a means of formal derivation of definitions contained a priori in the concept, becoming a means of actual development of knowledge of facts in their movement, in their internal interaction. This deduction organically includes an empirical element: it proceeds through rigorous analysis of empirical facts, that is, through induction. In this case, however, the names 'induction' and 'deduction' express only the external, formal resemblance between the

method of materialist dialectics and the corresponding methods of ratiocinative, intellect-oriented logic. In actual fact, that is neither induction
nor deduction but rather a third method including the other two as
sublated moments.

As already indicated on a number of occasions, the point is neither to reduce
method to induction versus deduction, nor to strike a balance between them.
To a large extent, the preoccupation with this dualism has been inspired by,
even if it does not originate with, the rise to predominance of neoclassical
orthodoxy, its obsession with the deductive, and ignorance and neglect of
methodology in wake of attaining its own intellectual hegemony.

An insightful but esoteric debate has recently taken place around the notion
of 'new dialectic' that was put forward by Marxist philosopher Chris Arthur
(2002 and 2005).[4] Arthur makes a sharp distinction between systematic and
historical dialectics. Following Hegel's *Logic* closely, he picks up the former
as his guiding methodological principle in analysing capitalism, at the total
expense of the latter. In this way, he reformulates Marx's theory in *Capital*
through the prism of systematic dialectics by totally dispensing with the historical dimension in Marx's analysis. Dialectics and historical analysis, however,
as seen from Marx's own materialist-dialectical perspective, go hand-in-hand.
As such, they should not be treated as mutually exclusive modes of reasoning
in analysing any concrete social entity such as capitalism, as in Arthur's 'new
dialectic' approach, but as indispensible complements. Indeed, as seen below,
the distinction between the two is transcended in Marx's materialist-dialectical
method, which includes both systematic dialectics and historical analysis as
constituent elements. Although the former is the guiding principle, the latter
is also indispensible in any materialist analysis firmly anchored in reality.

Marx, following in the footsteps of Smith and Mill, conceives the object of
political economy in the broadest possible terms to include both social and
historical elements. In this way, he forges a link between economics and
other social sciences. Indeed, it could be argued that his political economy
represents a sort of *unified social science*. Economy and society become
inseparable (i.e. an integrated unity), and the social character of economic
relations assumes central importance. The basic object of his holist analysis
is the mode of production, while the basic units of analysis are not individuals but social classes. Indeed, 'individuals are dealt with here only in so far
as they are personifications of economic categories, the bearers of particular
class relations and interests', Marx (1976, p. 92). At the same time, his analysis is *historically specific*. What Marx (1976, pp. 90, 92) analyses in *Capital*
is 'the capitalist mode of production and the forms of intercourse that correspond to it' in order to 'reveal the economic law of motion of modern
society'. Such a law, as are all economic and social laws, is specific to the
historical conditions under consideration. In society there are no eternal or
universal laws irrespective of the specific social conditions. 'Political economy',
says Engels (1972, pp. 211–12):[5]

cannot be the same for all countries and for all historical periods ... Political economy is therefore a *historical* science. It deals with material which is historical, that is, constantly changing; it must first investigate the special laws of each individual stage in the evolution of production and exchange, and only when it has completed this investigation will it be able to establish the few quite general laws which hold good for production and exchange in general. Marx was the last of the foremost nineteenth century theoretical economists to have made extensive use of history in his economic theory.

Indeed, history forms an *integral* part of Marx's method. In his writings, one finds at least four different usages of historical argument – in addition, that is, to the historically specific character of his analysis. One such use is in the course of what Marx calls the method of *scientific inquiry or investigation*. Marx's materialist-dialectical method makes such a use imperative, since actual historical development is closely intertwined with the notion of dialectics. According to this principle, historical processes are being created by the dialectical nature of social relationships. So by studying the course of historical development one can gain many insights into the dialectical nature of these relationships. Similar considerations apply to the role of history in Marx's *mode of presentation or exposition*. What is being constructed through this method is the developed whole itself: its inner structure, its beginning, development, maturation and decline, Zeleny (1980, p. 38). So the method of presentation has to capture this movement; it must accurately depict the development of the object of inquiry through its own internal contradictions, from its beginning to its decline and replacement by another more advanced object. For the object being studied is not static but in continuous movement. This is one of the most basic principles of dialectics, a notion of things in the state of becoming. It implies a continuous developmental process, one played out materially, ideologically, through time and, thereby, inevitably incorporating elements of history. So history must be an indispensable part of Marx's analysis. A necessary corollary of this historical dimension in Marx's approach is its dynamic nature and, equally, the rejection of equilibrium as a category for organising analysis.

Marx makes clear on many occasions that what dictates the sequence in which the categories appear in his analysis is their inner arrangement inside the developed whole (e.g. the capitalist mode of production) so that the (dialectical) logical mode of presentation is called to play the leading role, see Marx (1973, p. 107) for example. But this serves to reinforce rather than to negate the historical and social component of his approach, as is evident, for example, in his choice of the starting point for the analysis in *Capital*. It is dictated by the inner structure of the object under investigation. In the case of the capitalist system, the *commodity* is chosen exactly because it is 'the economic cell-form' of this system, from which all other more developed aspects and concepts of this system, such as capital, can be theoretically (i.e.

dialectically-logically) derived. The commodity, however, is also a *historical* starting point of capitalism. This is no accident since 'the historically necessary conditions of the emergence of the object are preserved in its structure throughout its development', thus becoming decisive moments of this structure, Ilyenkov (1982, p. 210).

The historical dimension of Marx's mode of reasoning also becomes apparent when theoretical analysis and the historical process itself move in parallel directions. In the opening chapters of *Capital*, where Marx starts his analysis with the commodity and then goes on to analyse money and capital, we find an example of the use of the logico-historical mode of presentation. This is exactly the sequence in which these categories appeared historically, i.e. how capital emerged in history. As Marx (1973, p. 310) puts it, 'we are present at the process of its becoming. This dialectical process of its becoming is only the ideal expression of the real movement through which capital comes into being'. Similar considerations apply to his discussion of the origins and essence of money through a logico-historical analysis of the development of different forms of value: from the simple or accidental, to the total or expanded, to the general, which heralded the emergence of the money form of value, pp. 138–63. This is complemented by the presentation of the historical evolution of the exchange process and of the money-form in Chapter 2 of Volume I of *Capital*, which rounds up the dialectical-materialist analysis of money. 'The continuous oscillation between abstract dialectical development and concrete historical reality pervades the whole of Marx's *Capital*', Zeleny (1980, p. 36), see also p. 58.

One last example is the so-called historical transformation problem, the relationship between value and price formation through historical time. This refers to the question of whether Marx's famous transformation of values into prices of production was not simply a theoretical transformation but also an historical one. In other words, whether this transformation took place not only in logic, but also as an actual historical movement. Says Marx (1981 [1894], p. 277):

> Apart from the way in which the law of value governs prices and their movement, it is also quite apposite to view the values of commodities not only theoretically prior to prices of production, but also historically prior to them.

Engels (1981 [1895]), and following him Meek (1973b and 1976), have interpreted this as saying that exchange at value ruled pre-capitalist exchange, whereas exchange at prices of production rule in the capitalist market, so that the movement from values to prices of production was also a historical process. Meek (1973b) went even further, by saying that Marx applied his logico-historical method to the transformation problem. Although this is an exaggerated claim, it is beyond doubt that, for Marx, this transformation also had an important historical dimension, Milonakis (1990 and

1995).[6] It has to be emphasised, however, that it is *not* necessarily or generally the case that the logical sequence of concepts in Marx's analysis follows their historical evolution. In *Capital*, for example, we also find instances where theoretical presentation and historical development move in opposite directions. Merchant capital and ground rent represent two such cases, since they are theoretically analysed after industrial capital, although in reality they have had a historically prior existence. Once again, the sequence in which the concepts appear in his mode of presentation is dictated by the inner structure of capitalism. Marx also uses historical and empirical material extensively throughout his writings for illustrative purposes. As Engels (1970 [1859], p. 227) puts it, 'the logical exposition ... requires historical illustration and continuous contact with reality'. His discussion of the length of the working day in Chapter 10 of Volume I of *Capital*, and the crudest forms of exploitation of the workforce, is full of such historical illustrations.

There is, however, at least one occasion in Marx's writings where historical analysis is used as a substitute for theoretical analysis. This is in his discussion of the origins of capitalism. In *Capital*, as seen already, Marx analyses the capitalist mode of production as a developed whole. But how does capitalist production come into being? For Marx (1976, p. 873):

> The accumulation of capital presupposes surplus-value; surplus-value presupposes capitalist production; capitalist production presupposes the availability of considerable masses of capital and labour-power in the hands of commodity producers. The whole movement, therefore, seems to turn around in a never-ending circle, which we can only get out of by assuming a primitive accumulation ... which precedes capitalist accumulation; an accumulation which is not the result of the capitalist mode of production but its point of departure.

Marx nowhere gives a theoretical account of the emergence of capitalism. What he offers instead is a descriptive, historical account of the process of primitive accumulation. 'So-called primitive accumulation', he says, 'is nothing else than the historical process of divorcing the producer from the means of production', pp. 874–5. And he goes on to describe how this divorce, which gave rise to the wage-labourer, was effected historically by the forcible expropriation of the direct producers from their land through the enclosure movement and 'the transformation of arable land into sheep-walks', 'the usurpation of common lands', 'the dissolution of monasteries', 'the theft of state lands', etc., ch. 27. This process was complemented by the genesis of the capitalist-farmer, on the one hand, who was borne out of the richer peasant-farmers themselves, through the process of the differentiation of the peasantry, and the industrial capitalist, on the other, who had accumulated wealth mostly through usury and commerce, chs 29, 31. Although Marx's analysis of the capitalist mode of production is mostly theoretical in nature, his exegesis of its emergence is mostly historical in character. Indeed, of all Marx's writings, his discussion of the process of primitive accumulation comes closest to what would nowadays be called orthodox, narrative-type economic history, although it is profoundly dependent upon his theoretical understanding of what is the capitalist mode of production (to which transition is being made).

Last, history itself becomes the object of investigation in Marx's *materialist conception of history* (or historical materialism), where an attempt is made to unravel the causes of long-run societal change in the process of historical evolution through the deployment of the concept of mode of production. Contrary to his discussion of primitive accumulation, however, where he deploys a traditional, descriptive type of economic history, his materialist conception of history represents one of the best examples of a 'philosophical' or 'theoretical' type of history, or what Schumpeter called 'reasoned history', see Chapter 5. This is presented in summary form in Marx's (1970 [1859], pp. 20–1) well-known passage in the preface to his *A Contribution to the Critique of Political Economy*, where he writes that:

> In the social production of their existence, men inevitably enter into definite relations, which are independent of their will, namely relations of production appropriate to a given stage in the development of their material forces of production. The totality of these relations of production constitutes the economic structure, the real foundation, on which arises a legal and political superstructure and to which correspond definite forms of social consciousness. The mode of production of material life conditions the general process of social, political and intellectual life … At a certain stage of development, the material productive forces of society come into conflict with the existing relations of production or – this merely expresses the same thing in legal terms – with the property relations within the framework of which they operated hitherto. From forms of development of the productive forces those relations turn into their fetters. Then begins an era of social revolution. The change in the economic foundation leads sooner or later to the transformation of the whole immense superstructure.

This passage is as controversial as it is widely quoted.[7] The dialectical, social, historicist and dynamic nature of Marx's theoretical approach to history is immediately apparent. Represented is the application of Marx's dialectical mode of reasoning to the whole historical trajectory, rather than to any mode of production in particular. It enables Marx to identify and isolate what he thinks are the basic explanatory variables in the course of historical evolution. This is done in a holist and materialist fashion through the identification of the 'economic structure' or 'mode of production of material life' as the basic unit of analysis. 'The materialist conception of history', says Engels (1968, p. 411), 'starts from the proposition that the production of the means to support human life and, next to production, the exchange of things produced, is the basis of all social structure'. It represents conclusions drawn abstractly from historical study which then serve as the basis for continuing investigation of both theoretical and empirical issues (and, as such, is a mode of analysis that is not reducible to a trade-off between, or mixture of, induction and deduction). It is 'the general result at which I arrived and which, once reached, became the guiding principle of my studies', Marx (1970, p. 20).

A mode of production is defined as a social entity structured by the contradictory unity of the technical aspects of the production process – what Marx calls productive forces – and its social aspects as expressed in the prevalent relations of production. Productive forces include a physical aspect – the means of production (objects and instruments of labour) – and a human aspect – labour-power – in their complex interaction with one another in the labour-process. Relations of production, on the other hand, refer to the social relations that individuals enter into in the production process. The mode of production, according to Marx, represents the economic base, the 'real foundation on which arises a legal and political superstructure', which together form what later came to be known in the literature as 'the socio-economic formation'. The technological determinist reading of Marx's passage regards the development of productive forces as the sole source of social change, Cohen (1978). The view taken here, however, is that what fuels social change, according to Marx, is the contradictory unity between productive forces and relations of production. The latter unity represents the answer to Marx's quest for the motor of social and economic development and change. The catalyst of this change is the force of class conflict. As the opening remark of the *Manifesto of the Communist Party* puts it, 'the history of all hitherto existing society is the history of class struggles'. When the dynamics of this contradictory unity bring about a revolutionary change in the mode of production through the force of class action, then the whole superstructural edifice is transformed. On the basis of this schema, Marx (1964, p. 21) identified four different epochs or stages in the history of mankind:[8]

> In broad outlines Asiatic, ancient, feudal, and modern bourgeois modes of production can be designated as progressive epochs in the economic formation of society. The bourgeois relations of production are the last antagonistic form of the social process of production ... This social formation brings, therefore, the prehistory of human society to a close.

Different theoretical categories correspond to each of these modes of production, although production, class, etc., provide the conceptual threads on which historical specificity is woven.

In short, Marx made extensive use of history both as an integral part of his theoretical exposition and in the form of historical narrative or the 'orthodox' type of history, both for illustrative purposes and in order to explain the emergence of capitalism. He also deployed history in its more philosophical or theoretical form to explain the long-term process of social change. Schumpeter (1987 [1943], p. 44) eloquently sums up Marx's use of history:

> Economists always have either themselves done work in economic history or else used the historical work of others. But the facts of economic history were left to a separate compartment. They entered theory, if at all, merely in the role of illustrations, or possibly of verification of results. They mixed with it only mechanically. Now Marx's mixture is a chemical one; that is to say, he introduced them into the very argument that produces the results. He was the first economist of top rank to see and to teach systematically how economic theory may be turned into historical analysis and how the historical narrative may be turned into *histoire raisonnée.*

It is this type of philosophical history, or what he terms 'historicism', that Popper (1986 [1957]) attacked in his famous *The Poverty of Historicism*. In this book, Popper identifies historical prediction as the defining feature or principal aim of 'historicism' or of theoretical history of the Marxian type. A historical prediction that can be attained 'by discovering the "rhythms" or the "patterns", the "laws" or the "trends" that underlie the evolution of history', p. 3. His refutation of theoretical history lies in the fact that, 'we cannot ... predict the future course of human history' which is based on the 'future growth of knowledge' which is also non-predictable, pp. vi–vii.

Marx's method has already explicitly been seen to incorporate methods of abstraction, investigation and presentation, none of which necessarily parallels any of the others exactly. The commodity, for example, is the starting point in *Capital* from which Marx deduces the categories of capital and exploitation, and their relationship to classes (capital and labour and, ultimately, in Volume III of *Capital*, landlords). But it would be foolish to suggest that Marx's order of presentation had not already been fully informed by investigation through conscious abstraction. Further, the causal relationship between his concepts equally cuts across how they are abstracted, investigated and presented.

4 Concluding remarks

Marx's was just one of the three main reactions to what was an eroding faith in Ricardianism. The second response, that of the German Historical School, whose origins chronologically predate the other two, retained its commitment to the inductive historical method with a corresponding abhorrence of a purely deductive method. This will be examined in Chapter 5, before coming in Chapter 6 to the triumphant marginalism which, unlike German historismus, was built prodigiously upon the deductive strand pioneered by Ricardo – the two schools resolving their differences in the methodological battle between the marginalist Carl Menger and the German historicist, Gustav Schmoller. Before this, however, in the next chapter, we return to the value theories of Smith, Ricardo and Marx, in order to examine in more detail how the historical and the social are explicitly incorporated into economic theory in different ways and to different extents that are not reducible to the induction/deduction prism.

As will be seen, with the passage from classical political economy to neoclassical orthodoxy, a number of great divides in the history of economic ideas are at least partially traversed, from holism to methodological individualism, from a plurality and multiple use of different methodological principles to pure and simple deduction, from dynamics to statics, etc. Although, as a result, there is a sense in which the intellectual journey has been historically accomplished, the same is not true logically. The purveyors of today's economic theory rest upon the accomplishments (if such they are) of their predecessors, but they do not show any awareness of the debates and conflicts they engendered nor the nature of, and reasons for, alternatives. For this reason, it proves appropriate both to re-introduce the issue of the loss of the historical, the social, the methodological and so much more, from the orbit of economic theory, and to demonstrate their presence within the practice of the lost world of nineteenth century political economy, see also Hodgson (2001).

4 Political economy as history

Smith, Ricardo, Marx

'Since it is a changing world that we are studying, a theory which illuminates the right things now may illumine the wrong things another time. This may happen because of changes in the world (the things neglected may have grown relatively to the things considered) or because of changes in our sources of information (the sorts of facts that are readily accessible to us may have changed) or because of changes in ourselves (the things in which we are interested may have changed). There is, there can be, no economic theory which will do for us everything we want all the time'.

Hicks (1975) cited in Schabas (1995, p. 183)

1 Introduction

It is often claimed, with some justification, that the difference between classical political economy and neoclassical economics is that one has social and historical content whilst the other does not and is universal in application. Indeed, critics and proponents of neoclassical economics point to its universal, ahistorical and asocial character as deficiency and strength, respectively. The purpose of this chapter is to attach some theoretical flesh to the bones of social and historical specificity. In what way, in particular, do Smith, Ricardo and Marx deploy a historical, and hence social, content to their theory, and what difference does it make? The focus will be on the historical, especially in the economy and classes peculiar to capitalism as a stage in history. But this inevitably carries with it a social content as well.

Debate over the relationship between economics and the historical has often been focused, not surprisingly, on the relative emphasis to be placed upon historical specificity as opposed to theoretical generality, not least in the *Methodenstreit* of the second half of the nineteenth century and the broader debates that preceded, and followed, the marginalist revolution, for more on which see Chapter 5. With the subsequent emergence of mainstream neoclassical economics, the balance has swung heavily in favour of the theoretical at the expense of the historical. This, however, leaves open two broad issues.

The first is to examine the shifting content of the historical and the theoretical, and not just the balance between the two. Clearly, pure theories can be very different from one another, despite sharing a lack of historical content, for example by appealing to marginal utility as opposed to distributional conflict. By the same token, theory-less narratives can differ from one another by virtue of their chosen focus for description – whether it be technology, production, consumption, standard of living, trade or finance.

The second issue concerns the question of whether there is necessarily a trade-off between theory and history: must one always be at the expense of the other? Or, to put it another way, must theory always be universal or general and, in this sense, ahistorical? Such is the basis for the parodied polar extremes in the *Methodenstreit*, with one side accusing the other of lacking historical specificity and the other riposting with a charge of lack of theory. As the quotation that opened this chapter indicates, even a leading neoclassical economist – albeit one with a strong sense of history – thinks otherwise. Yet it has become commonplace to observe that neoclassical economics is both universal and ahistorical, so much so that close consideration of what this means and what might be a different approach have been overlooked both by critics and proponents alike.

The purpose of this chapter is to reaffirm the possibility of economic theory with historical content, through selective appeal to elements in classical and Marxist political economy. To establish, despite frequent assertion to the contrary, that Marx and the classics offer historically rooted theory is far from immediate. For, broadly, there are two conventional interpretations of classical and Marxist political economy in terms of their contribution to, and dependence upon, the historical and social as well as economic analysis. One, and by far the most prevalent, reflects the division of social sciences into separate disciplines through each of which the classics can be fragmented and selectively read. This is most notable in the case of Marx, who can be incorporated successively or, more exactly, in parallel, into sociology, political science, anthropology, etc. to provide theories of class, the state, pre-capitalist society and the nature of contemporary capitalism as globalisation, imperialism, or otherwise.

The main exception to participation in this interpretative asset stripping of the classics of political economy is, by cruel irony, the discipline of economics. This is not because of its virtuosity and virtue in accommodating a rounded treatment of its precursors. On the contrary, it has shown scant and decreasing regard for the history of its own discipline. In what Coats (1969) reports as the first contribution in economics on the implications of Kuhn's theory of paradigms, normal science and scientific revolution, Gordon (1965, pp. 123, 126) posits and anticipates what has become a reality:[1]

> [Adam] Smith's postulate of the maximizing individual in a relatively free market and the successful application of this postulate to a wide variety of specific questions is our basic paradigm. It created a 'coherent scientific tradition' (most notably including Marx) and its persistence can be seen by skimming the most current periodicals ... I conclude that

economic theory is much like a normal science and that, like a normal science, *it finds no necessity for including its history as a part of professional training.* (emphasis added)

As reported by Davis (1997, p. 289), the history of economic thought has become a specialism that now falls outside its own disciplinary umbrella:

Since the [journal] *History of Political Economy* appeared nearly three decades ago, it seems as if most historians of economic thought have concluded that they no longer speak to other economists, and might accordingly focus entirely on thought that is no longer actively pursued by contemporary economists and on which history has closed the door.

Economics, consciously or otherwise, adopts the stance that whatever might be learnt from the past has already been incorporated and improved upon.

But – whilst possibly the main sufferer and, in a perverse way, the beneficiary of avoiding (false) interpretation, under this division of intellectual labour across the social sciences – Marx is by no means alone. Knowledge of the work of Adam Smith, for example, at least amongst economists, is mind-blowingly naïve, not least as revealed for both writers in Gordon's dismissal of the relevance of history of economic thought. Economists know that Adam Smith argued in favour of the free market, Marx against it, and it is (at most) enough to use their legitimising authority if this is where current analysis leads. It is no longer thought necessary to examine how and why Smith argued in favour of the market, nor indeed how he qualified his case. In effect, Smith's invisible hand has become a cliché, so much so that any case made for the market, from neoclassicals to neo-Austrians, can be perceived to be his case and to be invested with his trademark. So strong is the image of Adam Smith and the invisible hand that its veracity tends to be deployed by those who seek to argue against it, most notably in the idea of Chandler's (1977) *visible* hand of corporate capitalism and Amsden's (1989) getting the prices wrong in explaining the rise of East Asian newly industrialised countries (NICs). In any case, the idea of the invisible hand looks very different if it is interpreted by way of analogy with Darwinian evolution as opposed to mechanical equilibrium, Nadal (2004b, p. 197).

The second, and minority, approach to the classics is one that rejects the first and accepts, at least in principle, that they are interdisciplinary, that each individual system of thought forms an integral whole, and that it cannot legitimately be unpicked and distributed across, and sometimes within, the various disciplines. This approach is necessarily more scholarly in orientation, delving into texts, interpretations and context. It is far more intellectually demanding, and, in today's academic climate, suffers from the constraints imposed by interdisciplinary boundaries. To employ a hackneyed metaphor, both supply of and demand for rounded consideration of classical and Marxist political economy are in a spiral of decline, with the result that practitioners must pay a heavy price for their intellectual integrity – one that they are not always willing and able to bear.

But this is not the full picture: many of these general features of the classics of political economy equally apply to methodology. It is an issue that both straddles interdisciplinary boundaries and yet is treated as a matter of importance in research and teaching. Again, economics is a crucial exception where methodology has become a no-go area beyond marginalised specialists who, like historians of thought, are placed outside their parent discipline. Whilst not suggesting that either intra-disciplinary study or methodology are undemanding, one of the reasons why the study of the classics of political economy remains so limited across the social sciences is in part the intrinsic difficulty of sustaining an integral account of its various contributions. This is so in itself, and in light of the assaults from fragmented social sciences and economics in particular. In short, once making this first step, it is much easier to argue in principle that Smith and Marx are truly interdisciplinary than it is to demonstrate it is so in practice to those accustomed to asocial economics or social theory that excludes economics. Yet it can be done, even though attempts to do so are relatively rare in practice.

The next section makes a start on Adam Smith, demonstrating how his whole system of thought, including broad historical notions, informs his political economy. This is followed by an account of Ricardo, revealing how he lies at the opposite extreme to Smith in posing a political economy that is systemic but without systematic historical content. The result is to furnish a fascinating bundle of inconsistencies as the attempt to confront the realities of a specific historical period – that dominated by capitalism – with ahistorical theory comes unstuck. The account of Marx's value theory emphasises the role of dialectics in critically resolving the positive and negative aspects to be found in the works of Smith and Ricardo. In the concluding remarks, the marginalist revolution is assessed through the prism of its appropriating the limited deductive content of Smith and generalising it from Ricardo.

2 The invisible hand of history?

As a member of the Scottish Historical School, Adam Smith divided society by its various modes of providing subsistence. Further underpinning the organisation of these stages, and the transformation from one to another, are underlying human propensities – to truck, barter and exchange, and the moral conflicts between pursuit of self or social regard and self-interest.[2] Equally important for this discussion is that Smith's theory of value, confrontation with the most immediate and detailed aspects of the economy, is deeply embedded within his broader framework. For a number of reasons that will become apparent, this is well illustrated by contrasting his value theory for the rude and commercial societies.

For the former, Smith argues that value will be determined by labour time of production, as presented in his famous example of the relative prices of deer and beaver in reflecting relative hunting times. Whilst, as in mainstream economics, this might be simply interpreted as a cost of production theory with only one scarce factor, labour, and therefore of little interest, Smith's account differs, especially when placed in the context of more developed societies and the corresponding theory. For Smith's labour theory of value for the rude society is not simply an argument about the (labour) cost of production; it also concerns what orthodoxy would now term property rights. In the rude society, only labour has any command over output and so, according to Smith, only labour can enter as a constituent part of price.

The intent here is not to provide a full account of Smith's theory of history as successive modes of subsistence, each with a corresponding political economy. Rather it is to demonstrate the presence of the latter in principle. As a result, it is reasonable to jump ahead to the commercial stage in pursuing the case by way of extreme contrast. For the most advanced stage, Smith rejects the labour theory of value on the grounds that labour is no longer the sole form of property that commands a contribution from output, and must, therefore, make up a constituent part of price. Capital, labour and land all form part and parcel of the property relations of commercial society, and so the cost attached to each must be found in the price. This leads Smith to put forward a components theory of value or natural price – that it is made up of wages, profits and rents that contribute to it either directly, or indirectly through their influence on the cost of raw materials or other inputs.[3]

Now, as has been universally recognised, Smith's components theory is either wrong or a tautology (a price, or indeed anything, is made up of its constituent parts, although the way of making the division does have conceptual content). For the former, the problem is that all prices must increase if, for example, wages increase. Leave this, a point taken up by Ricardo, aside for the moment. Consider instead how Smith determines wages, profits and rents: he has a separate theory for each. In case of wages, his theory focuses upon the role played by a *growing* division of labour, as exemplified by the famous pin factory (for which dividing up the separate tasks involved in making pins leads to productivity increase). In such circumstances, the economy will be booming, and labour demand high and outstripping supply despite a wage level above subsistence.

Two points are important here. First, wage determination is tied to the *growth*, rather than the *level*, of the division of labour, and this is all bound up intimately in various ways with the totality of Smith's political economy and historical method. Most important is that the commercial stage of society enables a growing division of labour because of the extent of the market through which the underlying motive of self-interest can be expressed through productivity increase. In short, Smith's theory of wages is attached to his broader framework and is not simply a technical theory of supply and demand in the labour market. In particular, supply and demand are analytically constructed out of the way in which human attributes (self-interest and truck, barter and, ultimately, exchange) are coordinated in a specific historical stage, commercial society, and around a system governed by property rights in capital and land as well as labour.

Second, and highly relevant to later discussion as well as for illustration of the integral nature of Smith's theory of value, is to observe a remarkable feature of Smith's theory from the perspective of its absence in almost all subsequent thought, with the exception of Marx. This is that his theory of wages, and hence of price, is dependent upon how, in modern parlance, *technology* is changing. The wage *level* does not depend upon the level of the division of labour but upon whether it is growing or not. Again, translated into present-day terminology, Smith's theory is *dynamic* – how the economy is *changing*, not how it is at a given moment, is crucial for his theory of value. In contrast, whilst (dynamic) increasing returns to scale more generally (in which a growing division of labour might be interpreted through the filter of mainstream economics) have figured more or less prominently in economic theory since the time of Adam Smith, most notably in new growth theory today, they always do so in the absence of price or value theory, unless it be at some partial, microeconomic level. This assessment is stunningly confirmed by one of the leading and long-standing neoclassical economists who is, relatively rarely for such, prepared to address the issue. For Arrow (2000, p. 173):[4]

> The steady history of competitive equilibrium theory and the contrasting history of increasing returns theory are themselves conditions on the coherence of one theory and the lack of it in the other … Increasing returns arguments have been applied fruitfully … but one has to start again each time. In particular, what should be the core of any economic theory, a theory of value, is still not yet well defined.

This is two hundred years after Smith implicitly posed the problem and provided an answer of sorts in his own way!

More generally, at best, the mainstream (and often heterodoxy) has, if at all, tended to treat technical change (whether through increasing returns, division of labour or otherwise) in terms of comparative statics. How would prices alter in equilibrium if technology (choices) A prevails instead of technology B? Dynamics is treated separately, again if at all, in terms of the movement or stability of the economy. Does it move from A- to B-equilibrium? Absented is the treatment of the capitalist economy in which technical change is continuous, if irregular, with the new displacing the old as a process rather than as a movement from one equilibrium to another. In this respect, Smith has captured a fundamental feature of the dynamics of the capitalist economy. His analysis is in sharp contrast to the idea of allocation of scarce resources to competing ends, usually on the basis of given technology or at least one that is itself 'produced' by allocation of scarce resources to R&D or to 'human' capital.

Wage determination for Smith, then, runs from underlying propensities, through stages of society, to the growing division of labour governed by the extent of the market. These considerations also inform his theory of profits. Smith argues that, ultimately, as capital is accumulated (an attribute of the class of the owners of property other than land), it will exhaust the extent of the market and the potential for further growth in division of labour and productivity. As a result, profitability and prices will fall, which will dull the incentive to accumulate further, and lead to a stationary state, or long-run equilibrium state of rest in modern parlance. Substantively, Smith's theory is fundamentally flawed as his argument is intuitively drawn from a single sector of the economy, and assumes that others are not simultaneously expanding. For the more capital that is dedicated to a single sector, prices and profit are liable to be lower as long as other sectors remain the same in size and scope. But there is no reason why all sectors should not expand together, mutually serving one another with market opportunities. Nevertheless, Smith has raised a fundamental issue for the structure and functioning of the capitalist economy that corresponds to the sophistication of his theory of wages. How does the market coordinate supply and demand when their conditions are being transformed by the accumulation of capital and the growing division of labour? Again, the contrast can be drawn with the more limited approach to the (capitalist) economy of the allocation of scarce resources. Indeed, Smith's understanding is more sophisticated than the Keynesian view of the problem of deficient demand on the basis of given potential output (for which Keynes chooses Malthus' idea of demand created by parasitic landlords for his analytical precedent within the classics). Instead, Smith's concern is with deficient demand in the context of the potential to allow for productivity increase, and the extent of the market is qualitative (how extensive are *market relations*?) as well as quantitative.

Further, Smith's theory of profitability and the stationary state forges a close connection with his historical vision, not least in his theory of the invisible hand. For Smith, (far from absolute) commitment to laissez-faire has nothing to do with the Pareto-efficiency or otherwise of general equilibrium, nor even the freedom of the individual to benefit from the coordination of the market as suggested by neo-Austrians. Rather, Smith's support for the market is a consequence of his antipathy to feudal society, and his wish for it to be shattered asunder by the intrusion of the market. For him, the result will be the displacement of low-productivity, more or less self-contained economic enclaves, by commercial society in which the extent of the market expands and sustains the growing division of labour and wealth of nations.

In other words, Smith's theory of profitability, and the invisible hand, as an accommodation between growing division of labour and the extent of the market, are closely related to his views on what we would now term the transition from feudalism to capitalism. Indeed, Smith's theory is so closely connected to this issue that in subsequent debate over it between Dobb and Sweezy initially, and later in the (first) Brenner debate, Smith is used to denote one of the opposing positions, as neo-Smithian. This is that, following Sweezy for example, the market, and most notably the pressure arising from commerce that is *external* in origin, is the main lever in disintegrating the *internal* structures of feudal society.[5] For the moment, it suffices at the expense of pedestrian repetition to observe the integral nature of Smith's thought from the generality of his broad historical vision to the particularity (and peculiarity) of his value theory.

Significantly, Smith's broader vision is also brought to bear in his discussion of the stationary state and the prospects for commercial society. For, two hundred years before Fukuyama put forward his (now discarded) theory of the end of history or the triumph of capitalism, Smith takes a similar view. For him, underlying history is the need for social and economic organisation to resolve the tensions between the pursuit of self-interest and the desire for self and social regard. Capitalism delivers the goods both in *economic* and *moral* terms. It not only brings the stationary state in which the growing division of labour exhausts the market and reduces profitability to a minimum, but also, through the invisible hand, it can be argued that, within limits, pursuit of self-interest serves the common good. After all, it is the *absence* of benevolence on the part of the butcher and fellow entrepreneurs that delivers us our goods!

Finally, as the constituent element of price, consider rent. Most important here is that Smith recognises the presence of *differential* rent. One land will provide a higher rent than another because of, and in line with, its greater fertility. But Smith also subscribes to a theory of *absolute* rent. All land in use will yield a rent, whatever its fertility. This is because of both the presence of property over that land and its absolute level of fertility. Smith suggests that rents will be higher in those countries that produce crops that are more capable of supporting subsistence – rice over wheat for example. Essentially, Smith is recognising that capitalism does not bring an end to the role of landed property, and does not reduce it to one amongst a number of factors of production. Paradoxically, even perversely, he handles the specificity of landed property under capitalism only by treating it as if it were feudal property – able to command an absolute rent according to its absolute fertility (as opposed to the evolving relations between landed property and the accumulation of capital). Nonetheless, for reasons already laid out, Smith is determined that absolute rents should be absorbed into commercial society (rather than providing the feed for 'unproductive' retainers), the better to sustain the extent of the market and growing division of labour.

3 Ricardo with Smith as point of departure

As indicated at the outset, this partial overview of Smith's value theory has the intention of highlighting the integral nature of his thought. To do so, it has not been necessary to descend into great detail, although some of the limitations, even flaws, of Smith's arguments have been exposed. In this context, though, it is important to recognise that correcting Smith can do more harm than good. For, as argued, Smith's systemic approach to value theory raises questions (and points to economic and social processes, structures and relations) that can too readily be set aside. This is so, not least, for example, in the significance of productivity change for the theory of value and for the structure, functioning and historical and moral location of commercial society as the division of labour is coordinated through the market. By analogy, is it preferable to correct the mistakes in the vision portrayed by a Picasso painting by placing eyes and limbs in perspective until a photographic image is obtained? For Schabas (1995, p. 187), in uncritical vein for cartoon models:

> Most economic models, by focusing on a select number of salient features, necessarily distort. They are more like political cartoons than photographs with areas covered up. No single line of the face in the cartoon would correspond to a photograph of the statesman undergoing ridicule, but the overall picture has an uncanny resemblance and offers much insight.

Ricardo's contribution and critique of Smith can be viewed in this way. For, as already observed in Chapter 2, Ricardo's approach is profoundly abstract and asocial. He begins by demonstrating the flaws in Smith's rejection of the labour theory of value for commercial society. It is important to distinguish here between two different arguments, although they are closely connected and readily conflated. The first is whether Smith's case for rejecting the labour theory of value is correct. Ricardo argues, with justification, that it is not. There is nothing as such, leaving rent and land aside, in the division of net product between wages and profits, capital and labour, that means commodities no longer exchange at their (labour) values. More specifically, in critique of the components theory of price, Ricardo suggests that, for example, when wages rise, this will lead to a compensating fall in profitability, so that prices need not change at all. Indeed, for an economy with fixed conditions of production and commodity money, such as gold – thereby leaving aside the possibility of generalised inflation – if wages rise then so will the nominal (labour) costs of producing gold, as well as of everything else. So it will be a matter of how much each commodity's costs rise relative to those of the gold commodity. Put another way, Smith has made an elementary error, of treating the constituent parts of price as independent of one another. But, for example, if wages are determined at some level and then changed, profits cannot remain the same. They will move in the opposite direction to that of wages, possibly neutralising the wage effect on prices.

So the division between wages and profits (and rents) does not necessarily mean in and of itself that commodities no longer exchange according to labour time contained within them. Smith's argument as such is incorrect. But nor does this mean that prices do equal labour values, as is already apparent from the arguments of the previous paragraph. On this second question, Ricardo is caught on the horns of an analytical dilemma that he never resolves. On the one hand, he is committed (in typical asocial and ahistorical fashion) to use the labour theory of value as a tool or instrument to explain the exchange and other relations of the specifically capitalist economy. Unlike Smith, whose value theory is based on property relations and corresponding claims on output, Ricardo is convinced that value is, in all circumstances, a product of labour time. He uses this as a tool for understanding the capitalist economy just as Smith does, if only exclusively for the rude society.

As already argued, Ricardo's *instrumental* approach to value theory – how well does it serve in explaining the economy? – is the most significant step in substituting the deductive for the inductive method, see Pilling (1980). In a sense, value as labour time is speculatively invented, albeit on the basis of intellectual traditions, for analytical purposes, without reference to social and historical conditions. Essentially, the latter only enters in terms of what is to be explained, and not in the formation of the categories of explanation. The result is an inevitable contradiction between the theory and the realities of the capitalist economy as elements of the latter are (re)introduced to the categories that have been imposed upon them. Again, not surprisingly, there is a different sense in which Ricardo anticipates the deductive method of prospective mainstream economics. For, as is apparent in the passage from general equilibrium and the fundamental theorems of welfare economics through to the economic and information-theoretic approaches to the market and the non-market, there is a process of bringing back into the analysis what has been so rudely omitted in the first instance – whether it be the social, the historical, property rights, transaction costs, institutions, the state, path dependence or whatever, see Fine and Milonakis (2009).

In the case of Ricardo, the corresponding tension between deduction and induction assumes a more elementary and immediate form. For, whilst Ricardo argues against Smith's rejection of the labour theory of value, and despite his own undying commitment in favour of it, he finds himself questioning its veracity as soon as he investigates the simplest properties of the capitalist economy. Two of these are of profound importance, and each is examined in turn.

First, within capitalism, one principle of distribution is of profit earned in proportion to capital advanced. This is a consequence of the free flow of capital from one sector to another in pursuit of highest available return. The problem, for Ricardo, is that this violates the principle of exchange according to labour time of production. Those commodities brought to market at a slower pace (capital advanced for longer) or with a higher composition of capital (advances for inputs other than labour) will generally exchange at prices that exceed their labour values. Indeed, Ricardo is so impressed with this argument that he, perversely, uses it against Smith's components theory. For, if wages rise (and profits fall), Ricardo appropriately suggests that those with a higher turnover period or composition of capital will experience a *fall* in price. But Ricardo cannot have it both ways. If (relative) prices change with wages – some up and some down – relative labour values do not determine prices alone. He is forced to make concessions to his labour theory of value as revealed in the third edition of his *Principles*, published in 1821 following the first edition of 1817 and the second of 1819. He has a section IV, entitled 'The principle that the quantity of labour bestowed on the production of commodity regulates their relative value, considerably modified by the employment of machinery, and other fixed and durable capital', and a section V, 'The principle that value does not vary with the rise or fall of wages, modified also by the unequal durability of capital, and by the unequal rapidity with which it is returned to its employer'.

In his value theory, in which Ricardo again breaks with Adam Smith and the realities of capitalism, and also anticipates mainstream economics, in that his theory is static in the sense previously discussed. Conditions of production at any moment in time determine values. The way in which the economy changes, or is changing, does not otherwise enter into the value analysis. As a result, Ricardo's account of the prospects for capitalism is based on a sequence of outcomes derived from capital accumulation in which the *path* from one to the next is essentially irrelevant. For Ricardo, the capitalist economy is based on the allocation of available capital across industry and agriculture. The latter is essential for the subsistence of the working class, and output must grow in line with accumulation in order to provide food. But the agricultural sector is subject to diminishing returns, as ever worse land is perceived to be brought into cultivation as the better lands will already be in use. The value of corn, and hence the value of wages, must rise, and will inevitably lead to a decline in profitability, ultimately leading to the point where capital is not or can no longer be accumulated. The absolute limit, never reached, is where profits are zero since the average quality of land falls to a level that merely provides for subsistence wages.

For Ricardo, as well as for Smith, the fate of the capitalist economy is for it to experience a falling rate of profit and corresponding decline into a stationary state with no further accumulation. But there is a major difference between the two, in that Smith's case is based on the limitations of the market on the growing division of labour across the economy as a whole, whereas for Ricardo the decline of profitability in the sector of agriculture in particular is decisive.

For those acquainted with Ricardo's political economy, this account will appear, as is deliberately intended, to be unusual, and at odds with Ricardo's own exposition. The reason is that in his own presentation, falling profitability and the stationary state are intimately related to, and preceded by, his theory of rent. Consider the latter now as the second important example of Ricardo's difficulties in confronting the realities of capitalism with his deductive method. For the presence of land and of rent is inescapable – not least for Ricardo. He sought to deploy his rent and value theory in support of repeal of the Corn Laws and their protection of British agriculture in order to extend the extensive margin of cultivation overseas through foreign trade. The problem for Ricardo is that if commodities exchange at their values or labour time of production, with profit taking up the net product after the deduction of wages costs, then there is no room for the presence of rent.

Ricardo solves this problem by the simple expedient of changing his value theory, just as he does for prices, as previously discussed in case of the distribution of profit in proportion to capital advanced. For rent, the modification in deference to reality is dramatic. He simply adopts an entirely different value theory for agriculture (or more broadly in principle where land is perceived to have an impact on productivity). This is totally arbitrary, for a number of reasons to be explored later. For Ricardo, though, value in agriculture is determined by the labour time of production of the worst quality of land in use (presumed to be the last land brought into use).[6] Those lands of better quality, and higher productivity, which are already in use, will yield a surplus over and above wages and profits that exhaust output on the worst land. This gives rise to *differential* rent.

Now let us return to falling profitability and the stationary state. In Ricardo's presentation, as capital is accumulated, the total wage bill rises both in proportion to employment *and* with the rising value of corn, as ever less productive land is brought into cultivation. The same process also leads to rising rents, since those lands already in use increase their differential over the worsening marginal land being cultivated. So profits fall as the *value* of wages rises (although real wages in quantity of corn remain the same) as more land earns rent and each land already earning rent earns higher rents. Crucially, though, despite the benefits accruing to passive and parasitic landlords, neither they nor rents are the underlying cause of falling profitability or the stationary state, although they do hasten its arrival. For, even if landlords handed their rents over to capitalists as a boost to profitability, and these rents were reinvested, profitability would still decline and the stationary state would only be postponed. Stretching the point, suppose that all profits *and* rents were handed over to workers for reinvestment or as a support to wages. With Malthusian population growth, the stationary state still ultimately prevails at the point where *average* productivity over all lands equals the subsistence wage.

Put in familiar terms, then, Ricardo's theory of the stationary state, the demise of capital accumulation, is entirely ahistorical and asocial. It is simply a product of the iron laws of nature, and the inability of the land to support more than a certain level of population at a certain standard of living. The parallels with current, crude sustainability arguments are striking. For Ricardo's theory, though, addressing the conditions of capitalist production and the intervention of landed property can, at most, merely put off the inevitability of the stationary state.

The results of Ricardo's deductive value theory can be found not only in such grand historical questions over the fate of capitalism. Consider his rent theory more closely, not least in contrast with Smith's. Two closely related differences are striking. First, Ricardo relies exclusively on *differential* fertility to explain rent as opposed to Smith's inclusion of absolute fertility. It follows that Ricardo's theory of rent is remarkably ahistorical and asocial. Rent is solely a physical property of the land. All we need to know is the productivity on a strip of land by comparison with the worst land in use. Differential rent drops out, and the only role played by landed property is passive, in determining who is to be the fortunate beneficiary of this differential dividend. For Smith, landed property represents a feudal barrier to commercial society, and thereby appropriates an absolute rent.

Second, then, Ricardo, unlike Smith, has no theory of absolute rent. The worst land in use, whatever its productivity, pays no rent at all. Once again, such a posture on rent reflects a profound distance from the realities of the capitalist economy and, now, Ricardo is unable to change his value theory in agriculture to put this right, as he has already played this joker from the pack. The only way that zero rent on some land in use can be rescued is by treating absolute as monopoly rent, with the ownership of land as if it were a constraint on the free flow of capital into the sector. But land as monopoly in this sense is not specific to agriculture or to land itself, as monopoly prices and rents (if more likely to be designated as monopoly profits) could prevail in any sector or activity of the economy. Essentially, the *absence* of absolute rent and the *presence* of differential rent in Ricardo's value theory both reflect his failure to treat land (and relations around landed property) in their historical and social context, reducing them to a 'natural' condition of production. As Marx (1969b, p. 237) puts it by way of contrast with Europe where both capitalist agriculture, and in this respect, political economy, lagged far behind Britain:

> Both of them [Ricardo and his precursor Anderson], however, start out from the viewpoint which, on the continent, seems so strange: 1. that there is no landed property to shackle any desired investment of capital in land; 2. that expansion takes place from better to worse ... 3. that a sufficient amount of capital is always available for investment in agriculture.

It is hardly surprising that the divorce between theory and reality should so enrage the Historical Schools in the *Methodenstreit*, Chapter 5.

4 The dialectics of value

This is an appropriate point at which to examine the relationship between Marx and Smith and Ricardo, not only in their value theories but also in how they examine capitalism systemically and historically. More generally, observe initially that controversy has raged over Marx's labour theory of value from the time that it was first put forward.[7] The debate has exhibited two closely related aspects. One has concerned how value should be interpreted. Does Marx's theory differ from Ricardo's, for example, and, if so, how and why? Is it a matter of definition or of method? On the other hand, assuming agreement on the nature of Marx's value theory, there is the question of whether it is valid or not.

Here the debate has exhibited a paradox. For those who reject the labour theory of value often do so by appeal to exactly the same factors that endear it to its supporters, Fine (2003a). This is most notable in the so-called transformation problem, or equilibrium theory of prices as many would (falsely) have it. Critics of Marx suggest that the divergence between value and price, in the presence of wages and profits (and differing compositions of capital as understood by Ricardo), undermines the labour theory of value. But supporters argue that it is the very divergence between value and price that makes value theory essential. Not surprisingly, these differences reflect methodological and theoretical issues. But the paradox in the realm of debate is not accidental since the economy, and society more generally, evolve on a contradictory basis. As society becomes more developed and complex, does this undermine the validity and necessity for (labour) value theory, or does the latter remain essential as the abstract basis on which to reconstruct and comprehend increasingly complex and diverse outcomes? Deductivists reject the labour theory of value for its axiomatic failings; inductivists for its homogenising across historical and social diversity.

It is important to recognise that two separate, but closely related, methodological factors are involved here. The first is whether the features of the capitalist economy that are common across all of its history are amenable to explanation by reference to value theory – do we need the labour theory of value to explain wages and profits, or the course of economic growth and crises? The second issue is whether particular periods of capitalism, especially the more developed ones, reinforce or undermine the validity of value theory – as in monopolisation, for example, or the growth of unproductive labour in the 'service' and other (state) sectors. Whilst contributors to political economy and the value debate have always confronted each other across these analytical divides, it has meant that value theory has always been on the defensive. On the one hand, it is subject to continuing assaults for what are taken to be its underlying weaknesses. On the other hand, it is perceived to be inflexible in responding to historically new features of capitalism, both analytically and empirically. In short, is value theory, for example, appropriate at all as the basis for a theory of price and, if so, does it remain appropriate for monopoly pricing (or whatever)?

In this light, Adam Smith provides an excellent starting point for interrogating the methodological and substantive basis of Marx's value theory. Recall that Smith argues that the labour theory of value would hold, but only in the rude society, or primitive communism as Marx called it. Significantly, in view of the theme laid out above (does complexity undermine the labour theory of value?) as soon as the economy develops to allow for the presence of rents and, ultimately, profits, Smith argues against the labour theory of value and in favour of the dubious components approach.

From the perspective of Marx's value theory, Smith's contribution raises two crucial methodological issues. The first concerns the status of the argument in favour of the labour theory of value when Smith deems that it does hold. For, in a rude society, there would be no exchange. Whatever you want, you go out and hunt for it. This implies that there are no prices, so there is no need for a value theory at all! Quite clearly, Smith has gone through an inadvertent mental exercise. Suppose the rude society were like a capitalist society – would the labour theory of value hold? It is a totally meaningless question, and this implies there must be considerable doubts about the notion of value that Smith has constructed. It is purely instrumental and deductive, like Ricardo's, albeit less widely and differently applied in historical scope. Of course, it could be argued that there may be random disposal through exchange of more or less accidental surplus, or specialisation and skills in one activity rather than another. But this then raises the issue of who appropriates, controls and exchanges the surplus, and who gets to have one skill rather than another. The nature and terms of exchange can only be addressed on the basis of these prior questions, ones that are drawn increasingly into confronting the realities of a more complicated version of Smith's essentially imaginary rude society with its equally imaginary value and exchange.

There is in this context considerable difference between Smith and one aspect of Marx's own materialist method, one that is highly attractive in terms of its appeal to realism. For Marx depends upon justifying the use of particular concepts by demonstrating their correspondence, even if necessarily within the theory itself, with the realities of the society under consideration. From this perspective, concepts such as value and price are invalid if applied to the rude society, since the society does not systematically generate them itself. By whatever intellectual route that value has been derived as a concept, it is merely a general, mental, ahistorical and asocial construct for Smith. On his terms, it may or may not be useful in explaining exchange in the rude society (where the question is irrelevant) or in more developed economies where revenues also accrue other than to labour. In short, Smith has ideally constructed a labour theory of value as an instrument for understanding exchange in the (equally constructed) rude society where there is no exchange to explain, and has rejected the theory when it is transposed to societies where there is exchange. In contrast to such instrumentalism in the understanding and use of the labour theory of value, Marx's own approach can be understood by its first establishing whether value exists or not, see Pilling (1980). If not, it has no analytical status – as in Smith's rude society. When the answer, however, is in the affirmative, it leads to a number of subsequent questions: which labour counts towards value, by how much does it count and by what (social) mechanisms does it do so, and what are the relations between value and more complex economic and social outcomes?

The second methodological point that arises out of Smith's rejection of the labour theory of value is whether value, however defined and understood, and price should be seen as identical to one another or not – is value, for example, some sort of centre of gravity around which prices fluctuate? If so, certain factors determine value and others determine deviation from value. It is not clear where the boundary should be drawn between them unless some notion of equilibrium is to be deployed. More specifically, for Smith, it is a matter of whether value as labour time is identical to price or not. If not, value has to be amended until it does equal price, as in his components theory. Of course, such natural prices, as they are called, are perceived as the centre around which actual price fluctuations occur. This, in itself, involves the arbitrary division between those factors that determine the natural price and those that determine the deviations around it. In some sense, one set of factors is supposedly more fundamental than the other. This opens the way for any number of factors to enter the fundamental set, as is the case for price theory based on generalised theories of supply and demand.

Again, Marx's approach is different, and not arbitrary. Value as labour time is understood as an abstract and simple category derived from production. It cannot be directly observed as such, but is the basis on which the more complex exchange categories, such as price, are constructed both in reality and, correspondingly, in theory. In other words, the theory has an analytical structure or structure of abstraction in which more complex categories like price reproduce rather than displace the simpler categories like value. This reflects the previous methodological point in that, if the existence of value has already been established, it cannot simply be thrown away because of the complex forms that it assumes and which are its effects. If price is seen as the form taken by value in exchange, so the value/price nexus forges the relationship between producers as a relationship between buyers and sellers of goods. By analogy with the physical world, the element carbon can assume the form either of coal or diamonds, depending upon the way it is structured and worked upon by nature. But carbon does not cease to exist, nor to be of analytical relevance, simply because it can become, or become contained within, a number of different products.

In short, the value relationship is *quantitative* in terms of the labour time expended by individual workers but, *qualitatively*, it is much more besides. The existence of complicating factors, some of which are considered fundamental and some not – such as equalised profit and random or unsystematic factors, respectively – are by no means a reason for rejecting value theory, but rather the very basis on which it is constructed. It is perhaps unfortunate that the dialectical elaboration of this perspective, in terms of essence and appearance or substance and form, often expresses the second element of each couplet as *mere* phenomenal aspects (or forms and appearances). Whilst, in a sense, appropriate for a grand vision of fundamentals, it can lead to an unwarranted denigration of the importance of the critical features of the capitalist economy. If price is the *mere* form of value, is profit the *mere* form of surplus value, and the financial system the *mere* monetary form of capital? On the contrary, these are not symbols of the essence like the monarch on a banknote, but rather material relations with effects, even if they are derivative from the class relations between capital and labour. The important point is that value theory does not fall merely by virtue of the complexity through which it moves through the world of commodities, capital and otherwise.

Turn now to Ricardo as point of comparison with Marx. As previously seen, he takes Smith's instrumental approach to value as labour time and applies it to, rather than rejecting it for, capitalism. This creates the difficulties previously outlined, both in logical and historical terms, which lead many to reject what is taken to be *the* Ricardo/Marx labour theory of value, as Dobb (1973) dubs it even as a Marxist economist. But Marx's value theory is different from Ricardo's. First consider some of the methodological issues raised previously. The opening chapters of Volume I of *Capital* can be considered to establish that value does exist, but *only* in societies dominated by *commodity* production. The process of exchange necessarily forges an equivalence between the different types of labour that are used in production, although that equivalence is rarely, if ever, direct. Rather, the relation between (the labour of) producers is expressed as a relationship between commodities, as use values, in terms of relative prices. For convenience, it is assumed that commodities exchange at their relative values for, then, the qualitative distinction between value and price, as previously discussed, can be made prominent. By contrast, those unaware of this motivation, especially from a deductivist stance, see the abstraction merely as a simplifying assumption, as unjustified and as inconsistent with Marx's treatment of price of production in Volume III of *Capital*, the so-called transformation problem. Further, it becomes apparent in Volume I that value is most extensive, indeed predominant, only under the capitalist mode of production in which the proletariat joins the market, being both able and compelled to sell its capacity to work. Means of production and means of consumption are generally also brought into the orbit of exchange. The value relationship then, as for other modes of production where commodities are less pervasive, is not simply synonymous with the market. For it represents a set of entirely different economic relations between producers and those that command them, as well as differences in other socio-economic relations, such as access to consumption and, hence, social reproduction.

In establishing the nature of the value relation – as a relation between producers and not simply as quanta of labour time – Marx pinpoints the peculiar character of the money commodity. Initially, this is constructed on the basis of a particular use value, gold. But Marx, even at this early stage in his analysis, establishes that gold, as a general equivalent for other commodities, soon takes on a symbolic role – first of all with the debasement of the currency through wear and tear (and even clipping and filing), and eventually through paper symbols themselves. What this demonstrates is that the distinction between value and price is such that the one can be represented by the other even with the increasing displacement of commodity money from the process of exchange.

In short, Marx's theory of money is in part based upon the notion that commodity money is displaced by symbols of money and, hence, indirectly, symbols of value – although ratification of such symbols ultimately requires intervention by the state. Paradoxically, it is precisely this displacement in its most modern form, in which the functions of commodity money or gold are more or less confined to the reserves of central banks, which leads many to reject Marx's monetary theory – if they have genuinely considered it. How can a theory of commodity money, based on value theory, be of relevance when commodity money is no longer in use. In riposte, it can be argued that Marx's monetary theory implies the displacement of commodity money. How this occurs needs to be explored in its theoretical and empirical context, moving beyond the mere symbolic circulation of values as commodities to incorporate the symbolic, at times fictitious, circulation of surplus value. But this is to anticipate Marx's analysis of finance, although it does root consideration of the currently evolving financial system within the bounds of the production system on which it depends for its profitability, however much it might wish otherwise. Thus, without taking this further in detail or depth, Marx's theory of money, and of finance, is a neat combination of logical and historical/empirical analysis – examining how (surplus) value relations are expressed through money as a logical, practical and contingent process.

Although the abstraction that value equals price (in money form) draws the qualitative distinction between the two and establishes value as a social relation between producers specific to a commodity-producing society, the importance of this abstraction is arguably more important for another reason – the light that it sheds on class. For, throughout Volume I, once value is established as a legitimate category, Marx is primarily concerned with exchange to only a limited (but crucial) extent. His focus is solely upon the exchange between capital and labour, treating the economy, as it were, as if it were a single enterprise. On this basis, Marx initially addresses a single question: how is it possible that surplus value can be produced when every commodity exchanges exactly at its value? His answer is remarkably simple; the commodity labour power – the capacity to labour – is what is purchased by the capitalist but at a value itself that does not necessarily bear a quantitative relation as such to the quantity of labour performed by that capacity. Surplus value arises out of the ability of the capitalist to extract more working time, and hence value, than is required to purchase labour power. Interestingly, having answered this question *qualitatively*, the vast majority of Volume I is concerned both theoretically and empirically with the question of how capitalists extract surplus value *quantitatively*. By proposing the concepts of absolute and relative surplus value, Marx draws attention to the extensive (longer, harder work) and intensive (productivity increase through mechanisation) methods of production by which capital exploits labour. Each generally requires the accumulation of capital to proceed.

Marx's value theory, then, gives rise to (and ties political economy to) a number of notions: the classes of capital and labour are divided by a fundamental conflict over the production process – this is prior to distributional considerations, in contrast to Ricardian-type analyses of a trade-off between wages and profits; accumulation of capital is imperative for the capitalist system; and there are definite methods by which the expansion of surplus value is pursued, with Marx suggesting (to be breathtakingly brief) that productivity is systemically pursued through the relative displacement of workers from the production process as given amounts of raw materials are worked up into final products through the use of machinery, etc.

However much abbreviated, the account so far has touched upon, now to be highlighted at greater depth, five distinguishing features of Marx's value theory. First, methodologically, Marx's value theory is based on a dialectics in which the concepts employed are shown to have a correspondence to the reality under study both socially and historically, Harvey (1996). Further, abstract concepts are based on simple concepts such as value – itself derived from the notion of the two aspects of the commodity as exchange and use value – which are reproduced and not displaced by the emergence of more complex concepts such as price. This method is illustrated by the passage through the three volumes of *Capital*. In Volume I, Marx is concerned with establishing the nature of value and, then, how – as a category rooted in capitalist production – (surplus) value is produced. Qualitatively, surplus value depends upon the exchange between capital and labour. Its origins are revealed by stripping away, or abstracting from, all other forms of exchange. Quantitatively, it entails a thorough analysis of how the production process is directed towards both the intensive and extensive exploitation of labour. These are coupled to more or less direct consequences – in the accumulation of capital, the factory system, limits to the length of the working day, the emergence of a credit system, the formation of a reserve army of labour, etc.

In a sense, then, Volume I can be considered as being primarily concerned with the use value of that very unique commodity, labour power. The focus of Volume II is upon the exchange value of commodities more generally, and how, with the intervention of money, the accumulation and reproduction of the capital–labour relation can be sustained. This is not, however, simply a shift from one sphere of activity to another – from production to exchange – but rather a refinement of the concept of value itself. For Volume II is concerned to show how economic reproduction is simultaneously a balance between value magnitudes (as in the famous equations for economic reproduction) and a balance between use values across the sectors of means of production and means of consumption (with a further analysis, often overlooked, at the different ways in which these values circulate as revenues). This is far from being an analysis of equilibrium – at which word, all genuine Marxist scholars would reach for their critical red pen, ready to strike out.

In short, Volume II has nothing to do with equilibrium, although it can be interpreted in this way by those seeking analogies with various strands of orthodox theory. Rather, it reconstructs the concept of value, as understood in Volume I (and not just a quantum of labour time but the whole capital–labour relation as laid out there) in the more complex form of balance and movement, at whatever quantitative level, between sectors of the economy. Interestingly, there is, of course, the notion that use values are no longer simply defined by their physical properties, but that they take on a social content, peculiar to capitalism, of also being defined by their capacity to command money through sale.[8] In addition, the refinement of the concept of value allows a variety of more complex forms to be defined more rigorously and fully. Unproductive labour is that wage labour which is not engaged in the production of surplus value (because it is used for commerce or non-profit-making services); fixed capital is that part of constant capital which only releases its value into circulation over a number of periods of production, etc.

Volume III of *Capital* is concerned with the distribution of surplus value but not in the simple sense of who gets how much of the surplus value that has been produced, as for Ricardo. Note, however, that even this superficial interpretation presupposes – correctly in terms of Marx's method – that the surplus value has to be produced before it is distributed. If, though, the distribution is simply interpreted as a cake-division exercise, as in Ricardian interpretations, then the concepts of surplus value and profit collapse, and the former simply serves as a superfluous accounting exercise. In contrast, Marx deals with the distribution of surplus value as a refinement of the concept of value. The results of the previous two volumes are brought together and used to develop more complex and concrete categories in terms of the economic processes by which production and exchange are integrated in a society that accumulates capital and produces and distributes surplus value as profits, rent and interest.

Thus, the so-called transformation problem addresses the formation of prices of production. Whilst this has incorrectly been seen as an equilibrium theory of prices (and the rate of profit), a careful reading of how Marx understands the composition of capital – over which Ricardo's value theory falters – reveals that Marx's pre-occupation is entirely otherwise, and remains much more sharply if abstractly focused. It is concerned with the question of how the inevitable development of productivity at different paces across the different sectors of the economy allows for the tendency for capital to be equally rewarded according to the quantity of capital advanced. For, when the rate of change of productivity differs across sectors, profitability would change in favour of those performing better. Prices have to adjust, and capital move, for profitability to move towards equalisation. But the situation is more complex than this, in that productivity and corresponding price changes and movements of capital will have knock-on effects for the input costs of means of production and in the price of items of consumption.

This is an appropriate starting point for Marx's law of the tendency of the rate of profit to fall (LTRPF) – and counteracting tendencies – although the

LTRPF and the transformation problem have traditionally been treated separately, despite sharing in common the capacity to attract target practice for those seeking to reject Marx's value theory. This separation between the two 'problems' – what happens to prices and profits for given values and what happens to them when values are changing – has been almost universal, even amongst those sympathetic to, and supportive of, Marx. The approach adopted here is different. The LTRPF, is in Marx's hands, more complex than, and different from, an empirical prediction or mathematical proof of movements in the rate of profit. This is so for Smith, Ricardo, classical political economy more generally, and latter day interpretations of Marx in the deductive mode of mainstream economics. In contrast, Marx deals at a relatively abstract level with the co-existence of the consequences of accumulation, as laid out in Volume I, and the need for these to be coordinated through the mechanisms of exchange as detailed in Volume II. Quite apart from a host of socio-economic change attached to the accumulation of capital, such as monopolisation, urbanisation, the reproduction of a reserve army of labour, etc., the exchange system has to accommodate the shifting rates of productivity and profitability that are analytically laid out in the treatment of the transformation of values into prices of production. Marx draws the conclusion that this cannot always be done without the accumulation of capital being punctuated with crises from time to time.

Volume III does, however, go much further than this, by confronting the previously developed categories with capital more generally. Volume II has highlighted the need for commodities to be sold; this can itself become a specialised activity within exchange undertaken by merchant capital which tends to earn a rate of profit equal to that of industrial capital but without itself creating any (surplus) value. Volume II has also shown how money is continuously entering and leaving the circuits of capital, thereby creating a pool of idle money. Volume I suggests that capital prospers to the extent that it can command money-capital through the credit system. Through these insights, Marx forms the notion of interest-bearing capital, the borrowing and lending of money for the purposes of producing surplus value (upon and around which any number of other forms of credit and money-dealing can be incorporated or evolve), not least involving the finances of the state.

Volume III also considers circumstances in which there are potential obstacles to the accumulation of capital in the form of landed property. In contrast to Ricardian and most other rent theory that is its variant, Marx is concerned with how the presence of class relations on the land affects the access of capital to a vital means of production. The result is to modify the pace and nature of accumulation, quite apart from the rent that emerges as a consequence. For this reason, Marx's theory is organised around the potential for landed property to obstruct the free flow of capital onto the land, in part by sharing in the differential profitability that arises out of the accumulation of capital. The result is the presence of both differential and absolute rent, each of which is dependent upon historically and socially specific relations between capitalists and landlords.[9]

This long account of the first distinctive feature of Marx's value theory, its dialectics, will allow most of the others to be handled much more briefly. Second, then, the value theory incorporates a particular understanding of class, one based on the fundamental conflict between capital and labour over production. The increasingly complex way in which (surplus) value is reproduced has its counterpart in an increasingly sophisticated understanding of class and class relations. For there is the implication of differentiation of the capitalist class – by sector, productivity, by fractions across industrial, merchant and interest bearing capital – and also of the class of labour by the same factors, as well as by skill, employed or not, etc., Fine (1998). Once again, greater complexity induces a rejection or refinement of Marx's theory of class for a range of criteria deployed in finer or alternative forms of stratification. This is so even before considering the social reproduction of the capital–labour relation where political, ideological and other socio-economic relations become involved (as in gender, race, nationality, etc.). Whilst it is essential to avoid economic reductionism (the capital–labour relation as such cannot inform us any more about these issues than it can about the exact outcomes for prices and profits), for Marx, value as a class relationship is an essential foundation on which to examine other non-economic issues and especially politics, ideology and the state.

Third, Marx's value theory is attached to a particular understanding of socio-economic structures. This is not simply a matter of the basic class relations from which the logical possibility of other classes can also be derived by their divergence from the simple, but rather a fundamental dichotomy between capital and labour. The self-employed, for example, constitute a category that is neither proletariat nor bourgeois, but which is defined relative to the two. Such derivation of categories also applies to other socio-economic structures. As is apparent, capital defines a fundamental distinction between production and exchange, and also between economic and social reproduction, the latter comprising those relations that are conditioned by, but which are not incorporated within, the direct orbit of capital – the two most used examples are the non-economic interventions, nature and determinants of the state and the role of the family system (and domestic labour, for example). These can be identified but not filled out by an abstract analysis of capital alone.

Fourth, an important part of these analyses is to specify the socio-economic processes by which structures are reproduced and transformed. Like class relations, these are abstract and form the basis on which the more complex structures are reproduced (or not). Often, the underlying processes are mutually contradictory, as in the imperatives towards vertical integration and disintegration of capitalist production, for deskilling and reskilling of labour, and (of crucial significance in value theory) how productivity increase via the accumulation of capital is experienced both as a boost to profitability in the form of lower production costs and as a threat to profitability in the form of more intensive competition for markets. For equilibrium analyses, these processes interact harmoniously and, subject to rational choice by capitalists of least-cost production techniques and no upward adjustment in wages, must enhance profitability. In contrast to Marx's LTRPF, there is no attempt to understand how the forces generated by the accumulation of capital and productivity increase place enormous strains on the economic structures and processes of the value system, and the social formation within which it is embedded.

In this respect, Marx's value analysis is uniquely successful in the links that it forges between the theory of value and productivity *change*. As already observed, orthodox economics does not even address the issue, and has tended to use equilibrium analysis with given technology for its value analysis. By contrast, Smith contributes a much more penetrating, if chaotic, understanding, and can even be credited with having first addressed the issue of how to determine value as productivity is changing. Marx's theory of (surplus) value, and of productivity change, and their consequences, are one and the same, deriving from the historical specificity of the capitalist mode of production.

Fifth, this leads to the historical aspect of Marx's value theory, see Milonakis (1995). As already observed, its applicability is limited to those societies in which there is commodity exchange that only attains its peak with capitalism. This is not only to justify the use of value as labour-time on materialist grounds, but also an acknowledgement that value is a social relation between producers whose interaction with one another is through the system of exchange in complex and potentially historically variable ways. These elementary historical and social insights should suffice to recognise that the labour theory of value is not adequate, if based solely on the idea of value as a quantum of embodied labour. For then, of course, in a sense, we do not need to know anything about social relations at all in understanding value, as in its application to Smith's rude society, just as we do not need to know about other objects or substances if we only want to know how much iron is contained in them. Of course, the notion of the labour theory as labour embodied has been seen by critics from mainstream economics as arbitrary, and has led to parodies in terms of iron or energy theories of value.

5 Concluding remarks

The constructive rationale for the labour theory of value that has been out-lined is well established not only through Marx's own work but also, equally, through the value theory debates that have continued. The presence of value theory within economic and social theory (and history) has been much more muted; insights gleaned from Marx – for the state, class, power, finance, conflict, technology or whatever – are seldom rooted systematically within his thought as a whole nor his value theory in particular. In this respect, the various Historical Schools present an (often inadvertent) example of one extreme, with the emphasis on the social, the historical, the specific and the inductive at the expense of theory and deduction. At times, there is explicit reference to Marx for his historical analyses and his corresponding framework of determining factors, often as if these had no connection to his value theory.

On the other hand, mainstream economics stands at the opposite extreme, with deductive theory as the instrument through which history is a set of empirical outcomes to be explained statistically. Marx is seen (at most) as an erroneous or extremely special case of value theory, with no influence for demand (utility) and dependent upon uniform conditions of production across sectors. As Schabas (1995, p. 187) observes of Milton Friedman, for example, an unreconstructed instrumentalist and a Nobel prize-winner in part for his economic history of US monetary policy:[10]

> There is, I submit, a deep tension in cliometrics [econometrics applied to history] between instrumentalism and realism that results from the wedding of neoclassical models and historical practices. Whereas many economists readily purchase the instrumentalism of Milton Friedman, historians tend to be realists by bent, insofar as they avoid theoretical constructs ... Friedman's sort of instrumentalism is distinguished by deeming the theoretical constructs to be explanatory instruments with no commitment to their existence.

Indeed, Ricardo's deductivism *and* positivism are taken to the limit in mainstream economics, as with Friedman's (1953) instrumentalist methodology. Assumptions need bear no relation to reality; it can even be claimed that theory has greater purchase the more unrealistic its assumptions. And the historical only enters after the main *theoretical* event – as data for the purposes of verifiability and/or falsifiability. In short, neoclassical economics enters its own theoretical world, without regard to the social and historical except as ex post reality checks, something that can always be accommodated by appropriate statistical manipulation or model refinement.

There is, then, a striking parallel with Ricardo's mode of modifying, albeit at a grander theoretical level, his labour theory of value to be able to explain equalised profitability and the existence of ground rent. But, of course, the instruments deployed by mainstream economics have moved on from the labour theory of value, not least through the impact of the marginalist revolution of the 1870s. But there are affinities with the deductivism of both Smith and Ricardo, if none of the dialectics of Marx. Smith's components theory of price, arising out of the forms of property that he took to be characteristic of the commercial stage, has been stripped of all inductive specificity as, for mainstream economics, any productive factor can be an input. It has given rise to what has been described as a plethora of capitals – physical, natural, financial, human, personal and, in case anything has been left out by such an atomised methodology, social capital (as if all other capital were not social, just productive things).[11]

By the same token, Ricardo's value theory is perceived to be inductively arbitrary in seeking to distinguish industry and agriculture by mutually inconsistent theories of value for each, even if, however successfully, he thereby furnishes a theory of rent. One or other of the theories of value has to go and, not surprisingly, it proves to be his labour theory of value. Instead, values comes to be determined at the margin in all sectors. Thus, everything – and so nothing – becomes rent-like! This is explicitly acknowledged by Marshall, for whom the temporary *profits*, which superior capitals accrue in the short term before competition has eliminated them (only for them to recur elsewhere?), are termed quasi-*rents*. But, as everything becomes rent-like, so rent itself disappears altogether in all but name as a distinctly determined form of surplus and revenue. Value theory becomes a matter of productivity at the margin of whatever scarce resource contributes to output. And the location of the margin derives from demand, itself the result of the utility-maximisation of individuals, thereby forging a subjective theory of value. So, by comparison with classical political economy, out go property relations, classes, the historically-specific, value as cost of production, productivity change, etc.

5 Not by theory alone

German *historismus*[1]

'The idea that economic life has ever been a process mainly dependent on individual action, – an idea based on the impression that it is concerned mainly with methods of satisfying individual needs, – is mistaken with regard to all stages of human civilization'.

Gustav Schmoller (1897, p. 2)

1 Introduction

As seen already, by the late 1860s and early 1870s, classical political economy in general, and Ricardianism in particular, were suffering a deep crisis of confidence. It had become the object of increasing attack from three main quarters: Karl Marx, the German historicists and the marginalists. Having already examined the basic methodological and analytical principles of Marx's theoretical edifice in Chapter 3, in this chapter we concentrate on the writings of the members of the German Historical School before coming, in the next chapter, to the marginalist revolution and the clash over method between the representatives of these two schools, Gustav Schmoller and Carl Menger.

As elsewhere in the book, the relationship between the economic theory of the past and that of the present is more or less unavoidable in laying out what was previously involved, since it is from the present that we look back at the past. How have theories differed by method, theory, motivation and subject matter, and what light do they shed upon one another? Other than for the purpose of criticising the economic theory of today, such concerns appear to be only of academic interest, given that the Historical School has been relegated to the intellectual dustbin of history as far as the mainstream is concerned. But, for our purposes, the Historical School is of significance. Initially, it sought to distance itself from Ricardian political economy and, in doing so, exposed the latter's undue emphasis on the deductive method and a universal applicability that was deemed to be inappropriate, especially beyond the borders of Britain in general and to Germany in particular. Subsequently, the School found itself addressing identical problems of method in confronting the rise of marginalism. As a result, sandwiched as it was between a Ricardianism in decline and a marginalism on the rise,[2] the German historicists offer salutary insights into the relationship between economic theory and its social and historical content. These insights continued to exercise influence over 'early' and 'old' marginalists, including Menger and Marshall (Chapters 6 and 7), leading each in different ways to set limits on what could be achieved by marginalist economics.[3] Such reservations were increasingly set aside in the drive of mainstream economics to reduce theory to a set of axioms and deductions from them (to be tested against the facts). Paradoxically, today – as the mainstream has decided institutions, culture and history do matter – these are now being addressed once again, without regard to the Historical School that was so rudely set aside for its falsely presumed lack of theory. Nonetheless, the return to the historical and social in contemporary mainstream economics is crude and superficial by comparison with its earlier presence through the deliberations of the Historical School. It serves as a reminder of what we have lost and what has yet to be regained as far as economic orthodoxy is concerned.

First, then, the German Historical School is nowadays mostly remembered (if it is at all) by economists for Gustav Schmoller's role in the *Methodenstreit*. Second, related to this, its basic legacy in terms of its impact on subsequent developments is the decisive role it played, together with its British counterpart, in the emergence of economic history as a separate discipline, rather than the impact it had on the evolution of economic theory, see Chapter 7. At the same time, although this tradition was most prominent in Germany, it was not confined to it. The British Historical School, if such it was, was also notable, Chapter 7.[4]

Third, the Historical School is perceived to have been most concerned to compile empirical material and to be void of, if not hostile to, theory. Was this its fatal flaw that allowed deductivism to triumph and to usher in neoclassical economics as we know it today? Such a conclusion is at least a partial, if not false, picture for a number of reasons to be charted in this chapter. Although heavily favouring induction and the historical method, the members of this school were neither totally opposed to theory nor even atheoretical. To quote Schumpeter (1994, p. 507), 'the older Historical School ... while appreciating the importance of historical research, displayed no hostility toward "theory"'. Rather, as apparent in the *Methodenstreit*, their fiercest antipathy was reserved for *universal* theorising in general, and for Ricardo and marginalism in particular, as the leading examples of deductivism during the school's span. Members of the Historical School rejected purely deductive theory, with theory at most applicable in special circumstances that needed to be firmly rooted in reality, and qualified, across time, place and activity.

Fourth, the Historical School tends to be unduly homogenised in retrospect. It evolved over time, partly in response to its own internal dynamic, partly in response to external changes in the economic environment, as industrial capitalism increasingly took hold in Germany, and partly in response to the shifting intellectual environment and not least the shift from classical political economy to marginalism. By extinguishing the diversity of stances towards, and levels of acceptance of, the Historical School amongst marginalists, and those accepting marginalism with something more, the reservations and limitations as accepted by 'early' and 'old' marginalists themselves are also too readily overlooked. The consequences of this continue to be realised today, if unconsciously, within the discipline of economics.

In this chapter, we give an overview of the formation of the German Historical School in Section 2, followed by a brief encounter with its most important methodological foundations. The issue of the laws of historical development, which is perhaps its most important theoretical legacy, and the particular mixture of history and theory of the German writers with some attention to its diversity and dynamic are examined in Sections 4 and 5, respectively, before drawing some tentative conclusions in conjunction with a summary of the basic attributes of the School in Section 6. Underpinning all of this is an account not so much of the division between theory and history, between induction and deduction, as an illustration of the struggles to bridge these divides rather than to set them aside.

2 The making of the German Historical School

At the polar opposite extreme to the Ricardian abstract deductive type of economic theory was the German Historical School, with its unequivocal advocacy of the inductive/historical method long before the emergence of marginalism. Indeed, the School was born out of a reaction against classical political economy, and was in part politically motivated. Mises (2003, p. 7) puts the point eloquently, referring to the German rejection of classical political economy:

> The hostility that the teachings of Classical economic theory encountered on the European continent was primarily caused by political prepossessions. Political economy as developed by several generations of English thinkers, brilliantly expounded by Hume and Adam Smith and perfected by David Ricardo, was the most exquisite outcome of the philosophy of the Enlightenment. It was the gist of the liberal doctrine aimed at the establishment of representative government and equality of all individuals under the law. It was not surprising that it was rejected by all those whose interests it attacked.

To these sins against selective self-interest should be added the abstract formalism of Ricardian economics, its advocacy of the labour theory of value, and its abetting of socialism. So, as seen in Chapters 2 and 3, such methodological elements attracted criticism long before the marginalist revolution, although it strengthened on certain respects with the extremes of marginalist deductivism, as in the *Methodenstreit*, see next chapter. In 1875,

Cliffe Leslie (1875, p. 83), one of the founders of the British Historical School, writes:

> Two different conceptions of Political Economy now divide economists throughout Europe, of which, looking to their origin, one may be called English, the other German, though neither meets with universal acceptance in either England or Germany. English writers in general have treated Political Economy as a body of universal truths or natural laws; or at least as a science whose fundamental principles are as fully ascertained and indisputable, and which has nearly reached perfection. The view, on the other hand, now almost unanimously received at the universities, and gaining ground among practical politicians, in Germany, is that it is a branch of philosophy which has received various forms in different times and places from antecedent and surrounding conditions of thought, and is at a stage of very imperfect development. Each of these conceptions has its appropriate method; the first proceeding by deduction from certain postulates or assumptions, the second by investigation of the actual course of history, or the historical method.

Leslie, as will be seen in Chapter 8, not only points to this schism in methods but also deplores being driven to reliance upon either extreme.

The Historical School had a major impact on German political economy in the latter half of the nineteenth century, with a gestation and longevity extending its sway to cover the best part of a century. Generally, it is considered that the school began its long journey with the publication of Wilhelm Roscher's *Grundriss* in 1843, while the death of Sombart in 1941 signified its final eclipse, Hodgson (2001, pp. 57–9). Despite these credentials, it has been woefully neglected not least because its insights, and the issues it raises, are so unpalatable to the mainstream economics that has been, falsely as will be seen, presumed to have delivered it a decisive defeat, Grimmer-Solem and Romani (1999), Kobayashi (2001, p. 55) and Hodgson (2001, p. 59).[5]

Wilhelm Roscher (1817–94) is considered to be the founder of the Historical School in economics, and the 'Preface' to his *Outline of Lectures on Political Economy Following the Historical Method*, published in 1843, as 'the first clear note of the new movement ... a sort of manifesto ... for the future work of the historical school', Ashley (1894, pp. 99–100). At least four basic strands in this school of thought have been identified in the literature: the older German Historical School, the younger German Historical School, the youngest German Historical School and the British Historical School.[6] The members of the older German Historical School were Wilhelm Roscher, Bruno Hildebrand (1812–78) and Karl Knies (1821–98).[7] The most prominent member of the younger German Historical School is Gustav von Schmoller (1838–1917), while others include Georg Knapp (1842–1926), Karl Bücher (1847–1930) and Lujo Brentano (1844–1931). Arthur Spiethoff (1873–1957), Werner Sombart (1863–1941) and Max Weber (1864–1920) form the youngest branch of the German Historical School, Schumpeter (1994, pp. 807–820). Overall, the leading member of this historical tradition in economics is considered to be Gustav von Schmoller, the main representative of the younger German Historical School. With him, historical economics came closest to forming an alternative school. However, for some, historical economics as a whole is better thought of as a 'historical movement', Hutchison (1953, pp. 130–1), or a 'historicist critique rather than a historicist effort of building a new system of economic theory', Koot (1987, p. 2).[8] Although the better known German Historical School did try to construct an alternative historical economics, based on the inductive method and the principle of empirical and historical investigation, the same is not true of the British historical economists whose main concern, with the exception of Leslie and Ashley, was to promote the more inductive disciplines of economic history and applied economics, Coats (1954, pp. 143–53), Koot (1987, pp. 1–2), Lindenfeld (1997, p. 168), Tribe (1995, pp. 67–8), and Milonakis and Fine (forthcoming). The difference lay less in methodology and approach, and more in intellectual context and prospect for an economics other than that based on deductivism. Respectively, one faced a Ricardianism in decline whilst the other a marginalism attaining ascendancy, especially after 1890.

The two basic objectives of German historical economics were social reform, and the transformation of economics into a historical science. They rejected both capitalism as they lived it and the theory explaining it that was prevalent at the time (classical political economy). 'The common bond', says Betz (1988, p. 415), between the members of the German Historical School, 'should be seen in their attempts to reform economics as well as society; a reorientation in the scope, method, and purpose of economics would promote the ethical and moral conditions of man and the social organism of which he is part'. As Grimmer-Solem and Romani (1999, p. 334) put it:

> historical political economy was a policy-oriented empirical economics which viewed history as an essential source of data and knowledge and the national past as the principal inspiration for understanding patterns of change and for devising appropriate policies to accommodate that change.

The policy-oriented character of historical economics is reflected in the attempt to form a basis for an appropriate economic policy, aimed at promoting industrial growth, international competitiveness and social reform, something of crucial significance for what was then a latecomer in nation-forming and development. The structure of the German economy and society during the nineteenth century was very different from that of Britain, with Germany lagging behind in many respects. Following the Napoleonic wars, the primarily agricultural German society was weak and divided, competition and freedom of enterprises was restricted, mercantilist policies persisted, a large bureaucracy had developed, while the 'social question' was also acute.[9] Granted this, it was natural that nationalism, state interventionism, protectionism and social reform would find favourable grounds in which to flourish. The German Historical School had to adjust their intellectual postures to the pressing needs of the German economy and society relative to the more advanced British economy. The classical dogma of laissez-faire was not appropriate for a developing and divided country such as Germany of the early and middle nineteenth century, caught as it was in the process of catching up. This is one of the reasons they pressed for 'historically concrete' and 'nationally specific' analysis. It also explains their aversion towards general theories with universal validity and their adherence to the historical as opposed to the abstract method of analysis, Oser and Blanchfield (1975, pp. 199–200). As Mises (2003, p. 8) puts it, 'when the Germans started to study the works of British Classical economists' they soon found themselves in disagreement with 'the conclusions ... which had to be inferred for political action', so they started raising questions:

> Is not the experience from which the British authors derived their theorems different from the experiences that would have faced a German author? Is not British economics defective on account of the fact that the material of experience from which it is distilled was only Great Britain? ... Is there, after all, such a thing as an economic science valid for all countries, nations, and ages?

In short, the apparent lack of applicability of British theory to German conditions raised doubts over that theory *and* its accompanying method.

Schmoller, in particular, supported the policies of the conservative Prussian government by advocating state interventionism and a kind of corporatism. Throughout his life, he pleaded for a strong and effective government. The historicists rejected both what they considered to be the naive optimism of Smith's invisible hand and laissez-faire policies, and socialism – especially for its affinity with Marxism. 'No laissez-faire capitalism and no centralized despotism in the form of Marxist socialism', was Schmoller's proclamation, quoted in Balabkins (1988, p. 38). As Balabkins puts it, p. 47:

> Schmoller felt that the laissez-faire school of economics 1) was inadequate to cope with the pressing problems of the 1890s; 2) could not provide solutions for dealing with the emerging new forms of business enterprise; 3) could not deal adequately with the unintended consequences of competition; 4) was unable to explain the ongoing bitter trade rivalry all over the world among the major industrial countries, and 5) proposed no solution to problems faced by economically and demographically small countries of the world.

There is a striking parallel with the way in which the developed world today (as opposed to Britain then) advises neo-liberalism (as opposed to British political economy) to the developing world (as opposed to Germany), see Chang (2002).

At the same time, the historicists were themselves deplored by both the liberals (who first called them *Kathedersozialisten* or 'academic socialists' or 'Socialists of the Chair'), and by socialists and Marxists, such as Kautsky, who saw them as an instrument for government control of the working class. The German historicists were writing at a time when the social consequences of rapid industrialisation, such as growing inequality of income, were acute. In such conditions, they favoured a more just society, a sort of 'socialised capitalism'. This, however, according to Schmoller, should be brought about in a piecemeal way through social legislation to alleviate poverty and the suffering of the industrial masses. In this respect, he can be considered the intellectual founder of the modern welfare state in Germany, and its supposedly distinctive Bismarckian paternalistic character.[10] Schmoller's chief concern was to integrate the German industrial workers into the mainstream of German society, and to prevent the emergence of a Marxist 'centralised despotism', a term used by Schmoller and picked up by later neo-liberals. As Schefold (1987, p. 257) comments, 'Schmoller advocated a paternalistic social policy to raise the material and cultural standard of the working classes as the only means to prevent revolution, integrate the workers into the monarchic state, and keep the traditions of Prussia alive. He even envisaged an alliance between the monarchy and the working classes', see also Koot (1987, pp. 103), Kobayashi (2001, pp. 64–6) and Giouras (1992, pp. 128–31). The German historicists' advocacy of social reform is associated with their notion of social and economic justice. After having dealt with several different conceptions of justice, Schmoller (1893–4, pp. 1–3), declares that:

> The specific conception of justice, the one which principally interests us here, is that of justice in distribution … Is there a just distribution of economic goods? Or should there be? This is a question which is raised again to-day, a question which has been asked as long as human society and social institutions have existed … Whether a just distribution of goods exist or not … there is a general belief in it; this belief is speculated upon, and it has its practical consequences.

The other objective of the Historical School was to transform political economy into a branch of historical research. According to Roscher (1882a, p. 106) there are two ways of conducting scientific investigation: the 'idealistic' and the '(realistic) physiological or historical'. He identifies the former with the use of the abstract, deductive method, i.e. 'the *analytical* comprehension of reality', and the latter with 'the *descriptive* reproduction of reality in its full actuality', Weber (1975 [1903–6], p. 55). Of the two methods, he considers the historical as the most appropriate method for analysing social phenomena. He puts his view forward in no uncertain terms, Roscher, quoted in Hodgson (2001, p. 59):

we do not hesitate to declare economic science a pure empirical science. For us history is not a means, but the object of our investigations.

Further, Roscher (1882a, p. 91) also points to 'the close connection between politics and Political Economy', since, 'like all political sciences, or sciences of *national life*, it is concerned, on the one hand, with the consideration of the individual man, and on the other, it extends its investigations to the whole of human kind', p. 88. Last comes the organic analogy: 'As the physiologist cannot understand the action of the human body, without understanding that of the head; so we would not be able to grasp the organic whole of national economy, if we were able to leave the state ... out of consideration', pp. 91–2.

In other words, the Ricardian abstract/deductive method is rejected in favour of a purely inductive/historical, if not atheoretical, approach to political economy, that also incorporates a holistic stance, much closer to the method of Malthus than Ricardo as observed by Ashley (1894, p. 102). As Schumpeter (1994, p. 807) suggests:

> The basic and distinctive article of the historical school's methodological faith was that the organon of scientific economics should mainly consist in the results of and in generalization from historical monographs. The economist should first of all master historical technique. By means of this technique he should dive into the ocean of economic history ... And the only kind of general knowledge that is attainable in the social sciences would then slowly grow out of this work. This was the original core of what became known as the historical method in economics.

Ashley (1894, pp. 101–2), one of the leading British historicists, gives the following summary of Roscher's manifesto for the historical method. First, the basic aim of political economy is 'the representation of what nations have thought, willed, and discovered in the economic field', p. 101. Second, such a representation is only possible if undertaken in conjunction with, and in parallel to, the study of the history of law, the history of polity and the history of civilisation. Third, because the nation is not merely a mass of individuals, observation of current conditions is not enough. It has to be supplemented by the study of earlier stages of civilisation. Fourth is the comparison from an economic point of view of all nations from which something can be learned. The historical, collectivist, organicist, multidimensional and comparative elements of Roscher's approach are immediately obvious, and they became the canons of the historical method espoused by the historical movement, see below.

3 Methodological foundations

In many respects, the roots of the Historical School are to be found in nineteenth century German romanticism and nationalism, which was a reaction against eighteenth century Enlightenment, of which classical political economy was an offspring. As a result, the school is opposed to both individualism and rationalism, Shionoya (2001a, p. 7) and Screpanti and Zamagni (1993, pp. 91–2). Milford (1990, p. 17) describes the methodological position of the Historical School concisely. German economics, he says, adopts:

> A methodological and epistemological framework which embraced, apart from subjectivism, also inductivist, scientist, historicist, collectivist, and organicist theories. Its scientist and historicist theories committed the representatives of the Historical School to the idea that theoretical social science is some kind of theory of history; its collectivist theories committed them to the idea that nations, peoples, or other social institutions have to be perceived as real existing 'wholes'; and its organic theory committed them to the view of social 'wholes' as entities equipped with the spirit or will, which serve as the preconditions for individuals to act.

And for Koot (1987, p. 35):

> The German historical economists sought to create a body of economics which was national, organic, historical, and state centered as an alternative to what they called the cosmopolitan, individualistic, deductive, and laissez-faire British tradition.

That the historicists rejected methodological individualism is beyond reasonable doubt.

This raises the question, though, of how to reconcile the subjectivist element with the collectivist and organicist character of their method. Their subjectivism, on the one hand, refers to concern for the motives of individuals. This subjectivism, however, is radically different from the utility-maximising subjectivism and instrumental methodological individualism of the Marginalist School and of neoclassical economics more particularly, see next chapter. For the Historical School, individual behaviour is not motivated simply by self-interest and the desire for wealth as some classicals and the marginalists held. 'Man, in the eyes of the historical or realistic school' says Cliffe Leslie (1875, p. 92), talking about the German Historical School:

> is not merely an 'exchanging animal' … with a single unvarying interest, removed from all the real conditions of time and place a personification of an abstraction; he is the actual human being such as history and surrounding circumstances have made him, with all his wants, passions, and infirmities.

Also, for Roscher (1882a, p. 104):

> as our science has to do with men, it must take them and treat them as
> they actually are, moved at once by very different and non-economic
> motives, belonging to an entirely definite people, state, age etc.

And, for Schmoller (1893–4, p. 2):

> Even he who reduces all human impulses and actions to the feelings of
> pleasure and pain must admit that, as far as we know human nature,
> there are besides lower impulses, higher intellectual, aesthetic and moral
> ones. They give those ideal aims, from them grow those conceptions which
> accompany and influence all human life, all actions, all institutions, as
> ideal visions of what ought to be.

The individual, in other words, should be treated as an indivisible whole, a
complex organism with many different motives and desires. Thus, for example, Schmoller, in his search for causal explanations, considers the psychological (and moral) elements of prime importance since, according to him, all
economic activities are rooted in man's motives, feelings and needs, or his
psyche, Betz (1988, p. 422). In trying, however, 'to explain more fully the
psychological processes in question', Schmoller (1893–4, p. 5) suggests:

> the first step always seems to be to group in our conceptions a number
> of men into bodies of moral community ... The groups of persons into
> which our conceptions necessarily classify mankind are manifold. The
> members of the family, the bellows of a society and a community, the
> citizens of a State and of a federation, the members of a church and of a
> race, finally all humanity in a certain sense can be so grouped, but only in
> so far as they form a moral community and pursue certain common ends.

The holist and collectivist connotations of this statement are obvious. These
'groups of persons', be it the family, the Church or society at large, are
treated as something more than the mere aggregation of their individual
members, as autonomous entities with a real, actual existence. Indeed, for
the historical economists, the basic unit of analysis is not the individual, but
society or the 'national economy' as a whole. What is more, these social
entities represent integrated, organic wholes. 'Our task', declares Roscher
(1882a, p. 111), 'is ... so to speak, the anatomy and physiology of social or
national economy!'.

The organicist element of the historical approach means that each collective entity is treated as a living organism equipped with the will to 'pursue
certain common ends'. Hence 'the need to understand the social structure of
the economy and the relationships between its various components (families,
associations, corporations, the state, etc.) and the complexity of its common

purpose', Betz (1993, p. 335), and also Betz (1988, pp. 412–13). Treating social entities in an organicist way means that these social wholes are in a state of perpetual change, continually growing and developing. So the notion of development is a necessary corollary of the treatment of society as a living organism.

The combination of the subjectivist with the holistic and collectivist aspects of their approach means that, for the historicists, individual motivation is strongly influenced by 'the cultural intermediate structure of ethical-cultural intentions, morals and ethical norms of society', which act as causal influences on economic behaviour, Koslowski (1995, p. 5). So what also needs to be examined is the way in which these ethical-cultural value aspects intermingle with the economic utility aspects of human agency, p. 5. 'It is through this interrelation between the individual and society that the psychological develops into the ethical, a shared ethos and a hierarchy of goals as reflected in socio-economic and political institutions', Betz (1993, pp. 342–3). Hence, *homo economicus*, the economic man of theoretical economics, is substituted by *homo sociologicus*. This is related to the way in which the historicists define their subject matter, as Roscher (1882a, pp. 99, 111) puts it:

> Political Economy treats chiefly of the material interests of nations. It inquires how the various wants of the people of a country, especially those of food, clothing, fuel, shelter, of the sexual instinct etc., may be satisfied; how the satisfaction of these wants influences the aggregate national life, and how, in turn, they are influenced by the national life ... Our aim is simply to describe man's economic nature and wants, to investigate the laws and the character of institutions which are adapted to the satisfaction of these wants.

Schmoller himself calls his science historico-ethical, stressing the importance of the ethical element in his political economy, Schumpeter (1994, p. 812).[11] For him, quoted in Koslowski (2002, p. 150):

> The common element which relates each economic individual or nation is not only the state, but is something deeper: the common language, history, memories, morals, and ideas ... It is a common 'ethos' what the Greeks called the spiritual-moral sense of community, that is crystallized in the morality and law and that influences all human actions, as well as economic actions.

So human action is shaped by the institutional framework of the economy which consists of such ethical factors as customs, laws and morals. Granted this, 'economic life cannot be understood without a knowledge of the historical development of [these] three norms', Shionoya (1995, pp. 60, 71). Hence the centrality of the historical evolution of institutions in Schmoller's economics, which heralded what later came to be known as evolutionary or institutional economics, pp. 71, 78, see Chapters 9 and 10.

It is obvious that such analysis cannot be conducted in purely economic terms, but has to encompass all different aspects of social life. This is deemed necessary because, as Roscher (1882a, p. 88) puts it:

> national life like all life, is a whole, the various phenomena of which are intimately connected with one another. Hence it is, that to understand one side of it scientifically, it is necessary to know all its sides. But, especially, is it necessary to fix one's attention on the following seven: language, religion, art, science, law, the state and economy.

In similar vein, Knies, quoted in Kobayashi (2001, p. 56), argues that:

> the economic life of a people is so closely interwoven with other areas of its life that any particular observation can only be made if one keeps in view its relation with the whole, existing as a truth in the complexity of empirical reality ... Since political economy has to respect this context ... it is therefore enjoined to take its place with the moral and political sciences.

Roscher (1882a, p. 89) considers study of three aspects of national life, 'law, the state and economy, [to] constitute a family, as it were [both] apart and more closely connected. (The social sciences, in the narrower sense of the expression)'. In other words, an interdisciplinary approach to economic phenomena is needed. In Schumpeter's (1994, p. 812) words, 'the school professed to study *all* facets of an economic phenomenon; hence *all* facets of economic behaviour and not merely the economic logic of it; hence the *whole* of human motivation as historically displayed'. Indeed, for Schmoller, the essence of economic processes is lost if one treats the economy in isolation from its social and institutional context. Hence he advocates what would now be termed an interdisciplinary approach, that would combine psychological, sociological and philosophical aspects of economic problems, Schefold (1987, p. 157).

4 Laws of development

As seen already, the historicists' concern also lay in policy issues and their advocacy of social reform, for which abstract theory was (so they thought) of no use. For them, the task of social science is the establishment of evolutionary laws of historical change. Roscher (1882a, p. 87) defines political economy in exactly these terms: 'By ... Political Economy', he says, 'we understand the science which has to do with the laws of the development of the economy of a nation, or with its economic national life'. However, contrary to the representatives of the Classical School (if not Marx) who tried to discover general laws with some affinity to natural laws, no such laws exist for the historicists. Economic laws, to the extent that they exist, are relative to time and place. They are historically and geographically specific. Thus, for Knies, as Lindenfeld (1997, p. 185) observes:

> to be historical meant to be context-bound. Economic facts and theories must be interpreted in the context of the place and the time period of the society or people in question, not in the light of a larger developmental scheme or timeless causal law. This differentiated economics from other natural sciences.

This position forms 'part of the historical conception of "social" sciences that these were fundamentally different, in some sense, in procedure and criteria, from the "natural sciences"', Hutchison (1953, p. 131).

With this view prevailing over the various strands of the Historical School, Spiethoff (1952, p. 132), a member of the youngest Historical School puts the matter most clearly:

> Most economic phenomena are time conditioned and are rooted in specific geographic areas. They are subject to change over time and cannot be treated, therefore, with the help of concepts and theorems purporting to be of universal applicability. Economic theory can deal with those phenomena only by differentiating patterns of economic life, patterns which have come into being in the course of the historical process ... Every theory that deals with unique institutions and patterns subject to change in time is 'historical theory' ... Economic theory [then is] 'historical theory', that is time-conditioned theory.

As such, these laws cannot be discerned through the deductive method because of its abstract, non-empirical premises, which make it arbitrary in relation to the diversity and complexity of the real world. For the historicists, whatever economic laws exist, and these are mostly related to questions of economic development, can only be discerned through the detailed empirical study of the process of historical evolution. They are, in other words, historical laws. For, Schmoller (1897, p. 1):

> To pass judgment as economists upon a whole historical period necessarily involves a comparison of it with what preceded and what followed; it involves, that is to say, our understanding it as occupying a place in some larger movement of economic evolution ... In association with the tribe, the mark, the village, the town (or city), the territory, the state, and the confederation, certain definite economic organisms have been successively evolved of ever wider scope: herein we have a continuous process of development, which, though it has never accounted for all facts of economic life, has, at every period, determined and dominated it.

The attempt to provide a stages theory of economic development is characteristic of most members of the Historical School, including Roscher, Hildebrand and Schmoller. Where they differ is in the status they ascribe to these laws of development. Thus, although Roscher 'sought absolute laws of economic development', for most other members of older and newer German historical economists – including Hildebrand, Knies and Schmoller – where such laws exist, they are short-run relative laws, specific to the given type of society, and relative to time and space, Bostaph (1978, p. 9). This historicist doctrine which stresses the specificity and uniqueness of specific historical trajectories has its reflection, if not its roots, in the German Historical School of jurisprudence, Moore (1995, p. 71).

Hildebrand, for example, seeks to pinpoint what he considers to be the key features of the economy of his time, distinguishing between 'natural economies', 'monetary economies' and 'credit economies', laying emphasis on the institutions of money and credit, Hodgson (2001, p. 60). Schmoller's stages theory, on the other hand, differs in the emphasis he places on the interaction between economy and ethics as the motor behind institutional evolution. Through this scheme, he is able to identify the evolution of the institutions of community from tribal economy to village economy to city economy to national economy. He also offered a similar stages theory for the institutions of the family and the commercial firm, although for each he used a different organisational principle, Shionoya (2001a, pp. 14–15) and Giouras (1992, pp. 114–28).

Following upon this, it is obvious that the scientific claims of Schmoller's political economy are not confined to empiricist observations, as in the older Historical School. Rather, for him, the historical method 'aimed to gather materials to ultimately build a broader theory for the institutional framework of the economy and its historical stages', Shionoya (2001a, p. 11). He, in fact, distinguishes three basic levels of scientific research: first, observation and description; second, formation of concepts and classification of the facts; and, third, the search for and discovery of causes. So, for Schmoller, empirical observation only forms the starting point of scientific research, the basis for constructing a conceptual framework for explaining specific societies as a whole. At the same time, Schmoller, expressed his scepticism over the existence of economic laws generally, even if historically rather than theoretically derived. 'By cloaking propositions as "laws"', he contends, 'one gives them the appearance of necessity which they do not possess ... It is more justifiable to doubt whether today we can and ought to speak of historical laws', Schmoller, quoted in Hutchison (1953, p. 182), but see also Shionoya (2001a, p. 12), Giouras (1992, pp. 108–9), Screpanti and Zamagni (1993, p. 93), Roll (1992, p. 280), Hodgson (2001, ch. 4 and 5), Lindenfeld (1997, pp. 36–7) and Betz (1988, p. 422). But the problem for the Historical School, and for many more besides, is that to emphasise the limitations of theory in scope of (historical and social) application is to court the charge of being atheoretical, especially by those attached to universal theory with mainstream neoclassical economics, and often its precursors, in the lead.

5 History without theory?

Coming, then, to the charge that the school is without theory, close consideration of the quotations given above across the various phases of the school suggest that it is far from anti-theoretical and without theory. 'Even when they wrote descriptive economics', says Pearson (1999, p. 551):

> theory peeked through: in their ready recourse to 'ideal types' and other factual generalizations that enjoyed provisional validity across time and space, and in their repeated efforts to reduce diverse economic outcomes to the operation of the rational ... adaptation to variable environments or preferences or both.

At the same time, descriptive economics and historical monographs were not an end in themselves, but only preliminary work on the basis of which theoretical generalisations could be made. This is how Schmoller, translated in Small (1924, pp. 220–1), himself puts it:

> In the future there will come a new epoch for national economy. It will come, however, only through giving full value to the whole body of historico-descriptive and statistical material that is now being assembled, not through further distillation of the already hundred times distilled abstract theories of the old dogmatism ... It is by no means a neglect of theory, but a necessary substructure for it, temporarily to put prevailing emphasis in a science upon its descriptive phases.

Schmoller's own research efforts pay testimony to this. For about 25 years, between 1864 and 1887, he collected masses of material and wrote mostly statistical and historical monographs. He wanted to avoid premature generalisations, something of which he accused the older Historical School, and especially Roscher. From the mid-1880s, however, Schmoller decided to attempt to forge a theoretical synthesis of the material that he and his colleagues had gathered. This resulted in his *Grundriss*, the first volume of which was published in 1900 and the second in 1904, Balabkins (1988, pp. 54–5, 57). In this process, both deduction and induction are needed to disentangle the increasingly complex nature of economic causation.

Indeed, more constructively, the Historical School often discusses what sort of theory is appropriate, as well as condemning attempts at ahistorical theory, rather than rejecting theory as such. As Hayek (1942–4, p. 54) puts it:

> Their just dislike of any generalization about historical developments also tended to give their teaching an anti-theoretical bias which, although originally aimed only against the wrong kind of theory, yet created the impression that the main difference between the methods appropriate to

the study of natural and to that of social phenomena was the same as that between theory and history.

As Caldwell (2004, p. 69) records, Menger made the argument that even the Historical School must make some abstractions by selectivity, and hence, 'the prohibition against abstractions is contradicted by the practices of the historical economists themselves'. By the same token, it has to be accepted that the deductivists incorporate historical content in the concepts they use and the problems they address. But it is worthy of note that the Historical School's insistence upon realism of abstraction by reference to history has been turned into the accusation of lack of abstraction altogether. Having said this, it is still true that the German historical writers, and Schmoller in particular, were not interested in economic theory for its own sake. Rather, his concern was mostly to collect descriptive material and use it to motivate social legislation designed to raise the welfare of the industrial masses, Balabkins (1988, p. 45).

Streissler (1990) has recently tried to show that German writers exerted a great deal of influence upon Menger, something that the latter author himself acknowledges throughout his *Principles*, pp. 33–8, see next chapter. By looking at textbooks published by German authors between 1825 and 1875,[12] Streissler comes to the conclusion that subjective value theory was in German textbooks long before it was (re)discovered by Menger. Not only that, but the typical German textbook of this period offered a 'blend of the classical theory of growth and production ... with a theory of price ... governed by individual and utility', p. 46! This theory, says Streissler, 'was *neo*-classical in the sense of Marshall: half classical, half *neo*', p. 46. German economics, he concludes, was 'partial equilibrium analysis of demand and supply par excellence', p. 55. What the Germans were lacking, according to Streissler, were the 'theoretical underpinnings' which were later supplied by Alfred Marshall: the representative individual and competitive markets. The Germans simply 'did not delve very deep', reflecting their general stance, p. 55.

In closing this section, just to reinforce (and to refine) these points, it is only necessary to engage in a casual reading of Roscher's (1882a and 1882b) political economy, first published in 1854, to recognise how theoretical substance is present in the Historical School from the outset. To begin with, Roscher uses the notions of wants, goods, value and wealth, which are all of a subjectivist nature, as 'the *fundamental* concepts' of German economics, Streissler (1990, p. 49). There is discussion of different types of want and how they are either basic or created by individual and social development, Roscher (1882a, p. 52); of exchange as incorporating a range of potentially different underlying social relations, p. 58; attention to Adam Smith and the impact of division of labour on productivity increase, p. 186; a theory of the developmental gains attached to landed property, 'The anticipation of rent may render possible the construction of railroads, which enable the land to yield that very anticipated rent', Roscher (1882b, p. 38); a standard account of the supply of and demand for capital as a determinant of the rate of interest, 'The legitimateness of interest is based on two unquestionable grounds: on the real productiveness of capital, and on the real abstinence from enjoyment of it by one's self', p. 125; a rejection, with reference to Malthus, of Say's Law in light of the presence of money, pp. 208–9:

> The mere introduction of trade by money destroys as it were the use of the whole abstract theory. So long as original barter prevailed, supply and demand met face to face. But by the intervention of money, the seller is placed in a condition to purchase only after a time, that is, to postpone the other half of the exchange-transaction as he wishes. Hence it follows that supply does not necessarily produce a corresponding demand in the real market. And thus a general crisis may be produced, especially by a sudden diminution of the medium of circulation.

And, most remarkably, an anticipation of Keynesianism, pp. 212–14:

> The act of saving, if the consumption omitted was a productive one, is detrimental to the common good; because now a real want of the national economy remains unsatisfied. The effecting of savings by curtailing unproductive consumption may embarrass those who had calculated on its continuance. But its utility or damage to the whole national economy will depend on the application or employment of what is saved. Here two different cases are possible ... It is stored up and remains idle ... a commercial crisis of greater or smaller extent ... [or] If the saving effected be used to create fixed capital, there is as much consumption of goods, the same support of employed workmen, the same sale for industrial articles as in the previous unproductive consumption; only, there the stream is usually conducted in other channels.

In short, these snippets reveal that to deny the theory of even the earliest representatives of the Historical School is equally to deny what is later to be claimed to be the basis of much social theory as well as elements of mainstream economic theory itself! Yet it has to be accepted at this point that, although Roscher is considered by most as the founder of the German Historical School, his subsequent works do not appear to follow closely the historical method. According to Ingram (1915 [1888]), who was one of the chief members of the British Historical School:

> to the three writers ... Roscher, Hildebrand, and Knies, the foundation of the German historical school of political economy belongs. It does not appear that Roscher in his own subsequent labours has been much under the influence of the method which he has in so many places admirably characterized.

Similarly, for Schumpeter (1994, p. 508), Roscher:

> should be classified, so far as his analytic apparatus is concerned, as a
> very meritorious follower of the English 'classics', though a follower who
> happened to have a particularly strong taste for historical illustration.

To a large extent, then, the evolution of the Historical School involved discarding the theory to which Roscher was attached. But, on the other hand,
there is no evidence of an absolute loss of theory, more a shift in its content.
There is a growing acceptance, even anticipation, of some role for marginalist principles as part of an explanation for some phenomena. Of course,
much of this theory is surrounded by, if not buried beneath, a host of other
theoretical, empirical and historical commentary, some in pure form of historical narrative. This is all liable to test the patience of the modern reader
who is only interested in theory, and especially one seeking to deny the presence of theory within the Historical School(s) on the grounds of inductivism
rather than positively fishing for that theory.

6 Concluding remarks

To the extent that it is still acknowledged, the Historical School of economics is remembered for its standing on one side of the *Methodenstreit*, see next
chapter. Otherwise, it scarcely warrants a mention nowadays, even in history
of economics textbooks, these themselves lying outside of the orbit of the
mainstream economist. At most, the Historical School tends to be homogenised for the purposes of representing it as atheoretical, descriptive and,
thereby, readily vanquished (rightly or wrongly) by the deductivism of marginalism as antediluvian. However, although heavily in favour of the historical method and inductivism, historicism is better seen not so much as
having been conquered as cast asunder. First, was the Historical School
atheoretical and even anti-theoretical (with such attributes contributing to a
corresponding weakness in debate with marginalism and its powerful ally of
universal theorising)? As has been argued in this chapter, the general accusation of lack of theory across the Historical School is untenable. Some historicists of the older generation did, indeed, confine themselves mostly to
historical narratives. But others, as indicated, lay more emphasis on theoretical considerations – although not of the abstract, deductive type – and can
even be viewed as having converged upon marginalism, at least in the 'old'
form associated with Marshall, see Chapter 7. As Grimmer-Solem and Romani
(1999, pp. 338–9) curtly pose it, 'Recent scholarship agrees in regarding the
notion that historical economists dismissed theory as little more than
legend'. For opponents at the time, and commentators subsequently, it is
easy to level this false accusation by homogenising the school around those
works, or parts of works, and authors that were predominantly descriptive, suggesting no principles at all whilst at least implicitly meaning lack of

marginalist or universal principles. In this way, the Historical School's approach to, and not absence of, theory is precluded, since a common element within its principles is that theory should be specific to the circumstances under review rather than universal. A search for the latter is bound to lead to failure. Granted this, it is also true that the historical movement did not manage to pull together many generalisations out of their historical treatises and, as such, they did not leave behind a coherent body of theory. Their basic theoretical legacy of any worth is in terms of their stages approach to economic development.

Schumpeter (1967, pp. 176–80) sums up the position of the German Historical School as consisting of the following elements: 1) historical relativity rather than universality, 2) the unity of social life, 3) anti-rationalism based on a multiplicity of human motives, 4) a focus on evolution and development, 5) a concern with individual correlations rather than the general nature of events and 6) the organic rather than mechanistic nature of society. To these attributes can be added the empirical, fact-based nature of economic science and its policy-oriented, social reform character, Grimmer-Solem and Romani (1999, p. 335), Hodgson, (2001, pp. 113–14), Screpanti and Zamagni (1993, pp. 91–3), Roll (1992, pp. 276 and 281–2) and Betz (1988, pp. 412–13 and 421–4). Balabkins (1987, pp. 27–8) identifies six basic tools of analysis or 'viewpoints' employed by Schmoller. The first four – history, statistics, theory and 'what ought to be done' – had been identified by W. T. Mitchell, the leading institutionalist, see Chapter 10, to which Balabkins adds both psychology which, according to Schmoller, cited in Balabkins (1987, p. 28), 'is the key to all humanities and hence to economics', and 'awareness of the "spirits of the times" and its social, economic and political problems for the nineteenth century'. As we shall see in Chapter 11, this is very close to Schumpeter's (1994, ch. 2) list of the relevant fields of research which constitute the basis of economic science, and which include economic history, statistics, economic theory and economic sociology, indicating one possible liaison, among many, between the German Historical School and Schumpeter.

One basic attribute of this tradition in economics is that the writings of its members were so diverse that some scholars have suggested that they did not really form a distinct school. Hutchison (1953, pp. 130–1), for example, refrains from using the term 'school', preferring instead to refer to the 'historical movement', while, for Schumpeter (1994, p. 822), historical economists did not form a school, 'in the sense of a scientific party committed to fighting for a distinctive program'. Although we have treated the historical movement as a school, it was admittedly a heterogeneous school.[13] This heterogeneity, in part a consequence of its evolution, did not extend to its antipathy to Marxism, which was marked throughout its long life once Marxism itself became a viable alternative to deductivism. As a result, and to the extent that it did indeed incorporate theoretical substance, the Historical School was also going to prove a lame force in the opposition to the third reaction against classical political economy and Ricardianism, that of the marginalists – and for the debate with which the Historical School is nowadays mostly remembered, partially erroneously, as vanquished opponent. This is a result of the *Methodenstreit* between Gustav Schmoller and the marginalist Carl Menger, covered in the next chapter, an apparent beacon of methodological dispute in the history of economic thought.

Yet, the differences, as will be seen, between the Historical School and an emerging marginalism were not so great in principle but, across the deductive/inductive divide, they could not co-exist and persist in practice within economics as a separately defined discipline. The result for economics is well known with the triumph of marginalism in practice, but not, it is worth emphasising, in principle. For the Historical School can be adjudged to have enjoyed something of a Pyrrhic victory, or victories, of its own, spawning the separate discipline of economic history, the 'social economics' of Weber and Schumpeter (in which marginalist principles were accepted as appropriate in capturing the economic rationality of capitalist society as long as they were complemented by other principles reflecting capitalism more fully, and later to become economic sociology), and American institutionalism, see Chapters 8, 9, 10 and 11. But it is to the *Methodenstreit* itself that we now turn, and its bearing on the passage through the marginalist revolution.

6　Marginalism and the *Methodenstreit*

'[The] pure theory of economics is a science which resembles the physico-mathematical sciences in every respect'.

Walras (1954 [1874], pp. 71–2)

1　Introduction

The Historical School and the marginalists had a common point of departure: to reform political economy in order to rectify what they thought were the inadequacies of the classical school in general and Ricardianism in particular. However, although the historicists thought that one basic cause of the problems of classical political economy was the use of the Ricardian abstract deductive method, the marginalists thought this the most appropriate tool together with Bentham's utilitarianism, which could be used as the basis for the total reconstruction of political economy. Section 2 examines how the 'early' marginalists, especially the troika of William Stanley Jevons (1835–82), Léon Walras (1834–1910) and Carl Menger (1840–1921), grounded the approach in explicit breaks with classical political economy, each in his own way.[1]

For there were also differences amongst the early marginalists, both in substance and context. In particular, for Carl Menger, when the marginalists wrote their main works in the early 1870s, the German Historical School was dominant in German universities. Menger's *Principles of Economics* was published in 1871, and it received a mixed reception, Bostaph (1978, p. 5), Caldwell (2004, pp. 35–8) and Streissler (1990, pp. 38–40).[2] One somewhat cool, if not hostile, review was most probably by Gustav Schmoller (2004) [1873]. And this, in turn, may also help to explain why Menger thought it necessary to devote his energies to produce a book, his *Investigations*, published in 1883, with the singular aim of exposing the inadequacies of the Historical School. This book gave rise to one of, if not the most, famous of methodological debates in the history of economic thought, the so-called *Methodenstreit* or the 'Battle of Methods' between Carl Menger and Gustav Schmoller. This debate broke out in 1883, raged for some time, before gradually disappearing after serving as a token touchstone for relative commitment to induction or deduction, theory or narrative, universality or specificity, etc. This debate is the focus of Section 3. The substance of the debate across these issues is of less interest than its context and consequences. For the debate had the effect of both symbolising and consolidating differences of opinion across the virtues of abstract deductive theory *vis-à-vis* the historical approach. By doing so, it helped to propel and delineate the boundaries between the German Historical School and marginalism, and inaugurate the Austrian School of economics, Chapter 13.

Section 4 deals with the issues of the impact of the marginalist revolution on the developments taking place in social sciences, and the fate of the *Methodenstreit*. With the slow but steady rise to hegemony of the followers of the marginalist revolution, a home was no longer to be found within the discipline of economics itself for the social and the historical, as it became increasingly stripped of political economy.[3] Instead, political economy was broken up, thus contributing to the process of fragmentation of social sciences and the formation of new disciplines as we know them today. However, not all of political economy has been retained as the disciplines of sociology, economic history, etc. have taken on methods, dynamics and subject matters of their own. Specifically, the historical content of political economy has variously made its way into the long-lived economic history, Chapter 8, but also the short-lived social economics, Chapter 11, if now re-emerged as the new economic sociology.

Thus, whatever the causes of the marginalist revolution, and whether the Historical School was defeated or outflanked in the *Methodenstreit*, the consequences have been much broader and more mixed than simply establishing mainstream economics as it is today, as discussed in the concluding remarks. What exactly was thrown away by marginalism, and when and how it did or did not get to be used elsewhere, has proven to be a subtle and complex process, although the endpoint, as far as economics alone is concerned, has been particularly noticeable. Before the *Methodenstreit*, Jevons, for example, was too far ahead of his time in treating economics as a branch of the natural sciences. The same applies to Walras for other reasons, his general equilibrium only proved palatable once the principles of partial equilibrium had been fully established and accepted, and only then extended to the economy as a whole once more. And Menger's promotion of marginalism proved convenient in opposing historicism, but was less convenient in its more rounded understanding of subjectivism (the importance of both meaning and inventiveness to individuals). Thus, following the *Methodenstreit* and the rise of marginalism, interest in method declined, focusing more on the extent to which it did or did not conform to the latter's needs in theoretical and technical terms, discarding anything that did not so conform, and often blundering forward without regard to methodological implications. Initially, though, this could only be done by accepting the arguments of opponents, if only as reservations rather than concessions. In this respect, the lead was taken by Alfred Marshall, especially as far as principles were concerned, with John Neville Keynes handling the methodological side of things, as taken up in the next chapter.

2 Marginalism and the second schism in economic thought

If Marx thought of himself as providing a critical reconstruction of the Ricardian system, Chapter 3, the same does not apply to the marginalists. Despite major differences in their respective projects, to be discussed more fully below and in Chapter 7, Section 2, the self-conscious aim of the three main originators of the so-called marginalist revolution, Jevons, Walras and Menger, was nothing less than the total reconstruction of political economy. Although the reception of their ideas was only gradual, their aims were fully realised in the longer run. The marginalist revolution and the subsequent emergence of neoclassical economics brought about a great rupture in economic thought.[4] 'The combined achievements of Jevons, Menger and Walras', says Coats (1973a, p. 38), 'did constitute a significant intellectual breakthrough in the development of economic analysis and may be regarded as revolutionary in their implications, if not in their novelty or in the speed of diffusion'. It is now well established that the marginalist revolution was not a dramatic event that took place suddenly in the early 1870s, but more a sort of 'fundamental reconstruction', Black (1973, p. 99), which was the result of a long drawn out and intermittent process that started as early as the 1830s and did not culminate until the end of the century, with the (re)invention of the concept of marginal utility by Jevons, Walras and Menger in the early 1870s marking an important landmark in this process, Blaug (1973, pp. 6–7, 11) and Coats (1973b, p. 337).[5] As Meek (1973a, pp. 243–4) puts it:[6]

> The term 'revolution' here is something of a misnomer. The change in the general atmosphere was real enough, but the leading ideas of the 'revolutionaries' were by no means as novel as they sometimes like to contend. Many of these ideas had already been put forward – often in a surprisingly 'advanced' form – in the years before 1870, particularly in the course of the debates on the Ricardian theory which took place in the 1820s and 1830s.

Across their many differences, the marginalists did share many things in common. Here we concentrate mostly on the writings of Stanley Jevons and Léon Walras who, despite their differences, shared more in common than they did with Menger. As Walras (1954, p. 36) says, 'Mr Jevons' work and my own, far from being mutually competitive in any harmful sense, really support, complete, and reinforce each other to a singular degree'. Carl Menger will be dealt with in more detail in Section 3 below, in the context of the *Methodenstreit*, and in Chapter 13.

One common starting point of the marginalists was the rejection of what Jevons (1957 [1871], p. li) called 'the principal doctrines of the Ricardo–Mill economics', such as the wage fund theory, the cost of production theory of value and the natural rate of wages, pp. xlv–xlvi. He bluntly refers to Ricardo as, 'that able but wrong-headed man [who] shunted the car of Economic science on to a wrong line', p. xvi. 'The only hope of attaining a true system of Economics', says Jevons, p. xlv, 'is to fling aside, once and for ever, the mazy and preposterous assumptions of the Ricardian school'. The only way to do this, according to Menger, is through a thorough reform of political economy. Such a reform was necessary because of what he considers to have been the inadequacies of the Classical School which rendered it incapable of solving 'the problem of a science of laws of national economy satisfactorily', Menger (1985 [1883], p. 29). 'Even before the appearance of the historical school of German economists', he writes, 'the conviction grew more and more that the previously prevailing belief in the perfection of our science was false and that, to the contrary, the science needed thorough revision', pp. 27–8. The reform and revision of economic science became the leitmotif of the marginalists. For Menger (1985, p. 28) there are three ways open for the reform of political economy. 'Either a reform of political economy had to be attempted on the basis of the previous views of its nature and problems and the doctrine founded by Adam Smith ... or else new paths had to be opened for research', p. 28. One such new attempt at reform was delivered by the German historicists, but not to Menger's satisfaction, see Chapter 5 and Section 3 below. The marginalists offered a different option.

Despite the marginalists' aversion towards the classical doctrines, two of the pillars on which the marginalist revolution rested were actually handed down by classical writers. First is the abstract deductive method of Ricardo, Senior, Mill and Cairnes, and second is the utilitarianism of Jeremy Bentham. One of the basic aims of the marginalists was the transformation of economics from an art to a pure science. 'The main concern of the economist', says Walras (1954, p. 52), 'is to pursue and master purely scientific truths'. To do this, economic science should get rid of 'prescientific vestiges and survivals', Winch (1973, p. 60), such as the social, historical, philosophical, political and ethical elements. Unlike classical political economy (and the Historical School), it must become a value-free science in pursuit of pure truth and devoid of normative questions about what ought to be done. In other words, pure science should be clearly distinguished from what Walras, following Senior and Mill, calls arts or applied sciences and from ethics or moral sciences. Applied economics, according to Walras (1954, p. 60), deals with the question of 'what ought to be done from the point of view of natural well-being', leaving ethics or moral sciences with what 'ought to be done from the point of view of justice'.

To illustrate this point, Walras picks up Smith's definition of political economy. To begin with, he praises Smith for being the author of the first successful attempt, 'to organise the subject matter of political economy as a distinct branch of study', p. 51. What he finds wanting, however, is the way that Smith defines his object of study which, in Walras' view, has led his analysis in the wrong direction. According to Smith, political economy consists of two objects: 'first, to provide subsistence for the people ... and secondly, to supply the state or commonwealth with revenue sufficient for the public services', quoted in Walras (1954, p. 52). According to Walras, however, this is exactly what economics should avoid in order to become a pure science. 'The distinguishing characteristic of pure science', he says, 'is the complete indifference to consequences, good or bad, with which it carries on the pursuit of pure truth'. What Smith is describing with his definition of political economy is not the science of pure economics, but the art of applied economics, which deals with the production of social wealth, and the improvement of individual well-being, pp. 54, 60. Applied sciences should be kept strictly separate from pure economics, as should social economics (a moral science or ethics), which deals with questions of property, justice and distribution, pp. 76–80. Arts, says Walras, pp. 61–2, 'advises, prescribes and directs', whereas science 'observes describes and explains'. Applied and moral sciences deal with human phenomena ('the operation of the human will'), while 'the operations of the forces of nature constitute the subject matter of what is called *pure natural science* or *science*', p. 61.

So Walras identifies pure science with natural science. If economics is to become a pure science, it must be constructed as if it were a natural science. He made his intentions clear by adding the adjective 'pure' in the very title of his book, *Elements of Pure Economics*. For Walras, economics can become a pure science by shifting attention away from the processes of growth and distribution to the process of exchange and the determination of prices – another basic transformation brought about by the marginal revolution. '*Pure economics* is, in essence, the theory of the determination of prices under the hypothetical régime of perfectly free competition', says Walras, p. 40. With marginalism, the theory of exchange not only becomes the focus of attention, but also the very template of the whole economic science, p. 44:

> The theory of exchange based on the proportionality of prices *to intensities of the last wants satisfied* (i.e. to *Final Degrees of Utility* ...) which was evolved almost simultaneously by Jevons, Menger and myself ... constitutes the very foundation of the whole edifice of economics

Since, however, all things obtain their value from scarcity, value in exchange 'partakes of the character of a natural phenomenon', p. 69. A thing has to be scarce in order for it to have any value in exchange. So the problem of scarcity and choice is being introduced as part, if not the chief part, of the subject matter of economic science. Not only that: since value in exchange is a magnitude that is measurable, and the object of mathematics is to study magnitudes, it follows naturally that 'the theory of value in exchange is a branch of mathematics', p. 70. For Jevons (1957, p. vii, xxi),[7] since economics 'deals throughout with quantities, it must be a mathematical science', so much so that 'all economic writers must be mathematical so far as they are scientific at all', see also opening quote by Walras.[8] For economics to become a pure science, then, it must be treated as a natural science, and since it deals with quantities it must become a branch of mathematics.[9] Granted this, it becomes obvious that all classical political economy and the Historical School automatically fall outside the realm of pure science and become either an art, a moral science or both. So, with the marginalists, the quest for a value-free economic science on a par with natural sciences is embarked upon; this journey had, to some extent, been initiated by Senior, Mill and Cairnes, and was further consolidated with the methodological treatises of John Neville Keynes in 1890 and Lionel Robbins in 1932, see Chapters 7 and 12, respectively.

Alongside this change in the definition of what constitutes a pure economic science, and the change in emphasis that accompanied it from macro-dynamic to micro-static issues, the marginalists adopted the abstract/deductive method, which is associated with the other great divide in economic thought (see Chapter 2), in its putative use as the exclusive scientific method of economic investigation. In this, once again, they follow in the footsteps of Ricardo, Mill and Cairnes. 'I think', says Jevons (1957, pp. 16, 17), 'that John Stuart Mill is substantially correct in considering our science to be a case of what he calls the Physical or Concrete Deductive method'; this view is 'almost identical with that adopted by the late Professor Cairnes'. Much like Mill, however, Jevons qualifies his use of the deductive method by invoking the need for verification through the empirical method. Only such verification is extremely difficult due to lack of appropriate data, pp. 21, 22:

> I do not hesitate to say ... that Economics might be gradually erected into an exact science, if only commercial statistics were far more complete and accurate than they are at present ... The deductive method of Economics must be verified and rendered useful by the purely empirical science of Statistics ... But the difficulties of this union are immensely great.

These difficulties, however, do not diminish the value of deductive theory per se. Jevons gives the example of free trade to illustrate this point. Although, he says, the benefits from free trade to all parties involved cannot be proved a posteriori, through the use of empirical data, this does not deprive them of their validity. They are true just by virtue of being proven logically through the deductive method. As Jevons puts it, 'they are to be believed because deductive reasoning from premises of almost certain truths leads us confidently to expect such results', p. 19. Walras (1954, pp. 71–2), on the other hand, defends the deductive method pure and simple. No recourse to empirical verification is necessary. All true 'physico-mathematical' sciences, including economics, he says, 'abstract ideal-type concepts which they define, and then on the basis of these definitions they construct a priori the whole framework of their theorems and proofs. After that they go back to experience not to confirm but to apply their conclusions', p. 71.

Jevons simply saw economics as a branch of application of general scientific laws. Schabas (1995, p. 198) makes the point for Jevons by quoting from a lecture of 1876 on 'The Future of Political Economy':

> The first principles of political economy are so widely true and applicable, that they may be considered universally true as regards human nature ... I should not despair of tracing the action of the postulates of the political economy among some of the more intelligent classes of animals.

Thus, economics is not only universal for Jevons as an expression of human nature, it is also to be based on the animalistic nature of human beings.

This prompts Leslie (1879a, p. 3), leading representative of the British Historical School of economics, to lampoon:[10]

> Mr. Jevons, though favourably disposed by philosophical culture and tastes towards historical investigation in economics, has urged, on behalf of deduction from the acquisitive principle, that even the lower animals act from a similar motive, 'as you will discover if you interfere between a dog and his bone'. A bone fairly enough represents the sort of wealth coveted by a dog, who has a comparatively simple cerebral system, and few other objects. Yet you cannot predict the conduct even of dog from his love of bones, or not one would be left in the butcher's shop. The dog has a regard for his master and a fear of the police, and he has other pursuits.

In other words, Jevons is inadequate as a theorist of the dog and his bone, let alone of humans and economy as if dog- and bone-like.

As suggested already, the macro-dynamic view of the economy espoused by classical political economy gives way to static equilibrium analysis. The basic vehicle in this transformation, in addition to the exclusive use of the deductive method, was the concept of marginal utility, which became the keystone on which the whole neoclassical edifice has been erected.[11] As Schumpeter (1967 [1912], p. 181) puts it, 'the concept of marginal utility was the new ferment which has changed the inner structure of modern theory into something quite different from that of the classical economists'. One of the chief implications of the adoption of this concept is that the subject matter of economic science shifted from the investigation of the causes of wealth and its distribution, to the interrogation of the economic behaviour of individuals, especially in the form of the principle of (utility) maximisation. 'I have attempted to treat Economy as a Calculus of Pleasure and Pain', says Jevons (1957, p. vi), in typical Benthamite, utilitarian fashion. In this way, the objective theory of value of classical political economy (which took the form of the labour or cost of production theory of value) gives way to a subjective theory based on individual utility maximisation. Indeed, such was the importance attached to the concept of marginal utility by Jevons that, according to Jaffé (1976, p. 517), he 'looked at his differential coefficient as the lethal weapon with which to strike down forever the classical theory'. And for Schumpeter (1967, p. 190), 'the theory of marginal utility accepts value in use as a fact of individual psychology'. It is important, however, to be aware that the use of 'subjectivity', just like Schumpeter's more broadly based 'individual psychology', as the basis of value is itself open to shifting interpretation and content, and is by no means confined to the familiar given utility function of present-day neoclassicals. Indeed, the process of reducing subjectivity, and utility, to such narrow concerns is part and parcel of the making of the mainstream in its current form.

So the adoption of pure deduction as a basic methodological guide to a pure economics, was accompanied by another methodological rupture. Concern with economic aggregates, such as classes or the national economy, gives way to what Menger called 'atomism' – what later came to be known as methodological individualism. As seen in Chapter 2, the latter refers to the method of explanation whereby the whole is explained in terms of the properties of its individual parts (members). For Menger (1985 [1883], p. 93) only individuals have interests. No collective body, such as the national economy, can be analysed in its own right without reference to its constituent individual members. In marginalist hands, and later on with neoclassical writers, methodological individualism takes the specific form of what has been called 'psychological individualism', in which the individual is simply considered as a rational agent driven by some psychological (utilitarian) motive, to maximise own benefit, Zouboulakis (2002, p. 30).

The concept of marginal utility also proved instrumental in two other respects. First, being a mathematical concept, it gave a great impetus to the mathematisation of economics. As Hutchison (1953, p. 16) has appropriately put it in the extreme, 'what was important in marginal utility was the adjective rather than the noun'. Second, it gave a rationale for narrowing the scope of economic investigation to the study of the problem of allocation under scarcity and the determination of prices, by focusing on market relations treated in isolation from their social and historical context, 'Thus a different and much "purer" economics originated', Schumpeter (1967, p. 188), but also 'a very contracted science', Black (1973, p. 106). Hence the change from political economy to economics, symbolically reflected in the title of the classic magnum opus of the new neoclassical economics, *Principles of Economics*, authored by Alfred Marshall, but see Chapter 7.[12] With the excision of the political, out also went the social and the historical. Paradoxically, this *narrowing* of scope permitted the *expansion* of its boundaries historically to an almost unlimited degree: 'the first principles of Political economy are so widely true and applicable, that they may be considered universally true as regards human nature', Jevons (1876, p. 624) and Zouboulakis (1997, pp. 16–17). As Winch (1973, p. 69) puts it:

The chief merit of the reconstructed science was that it demonstrated both the unity and universality of the laws of choice in economic situations. By defining *the* economic problem as one of allocating scarce means between alternative uses ... the proponents of marginalism stressed the universal application of the laws of human choice.

What Jevons and the other marginalists were looking for was a general theory with universal applicability, valid in all social systems, de Vroey (1975, p. 426).

We have so far concentrated on what the marginalists shared in common and how they have jointly affected the course of events in the evolution of economic ideas. However, there are also important differences which have increasingly become the focus of attention. Although the literature has focused mostly on Menger, who is the most diverse of the three, see Section 3 and Chapter 13, there are also important differences between Jevons and Walras. We have already encountered a methodological one. Although Walras is in favour of the abstract/deductive method pure and simple, without any recourse to empirical verification, the latter is an important supplement to abstract reasoning in Jevons' 'complete inductive method', Black (1973, p. 110). However, there are also major differences so far as their substantive analyses are concerned.

For Jevons, the import of Benthamite utilitarianism into his theory is the point of departure as well as the most pervasive element of his whole analysis, p. 23:

> The theory which follows is entirely based on a calculus of pleasure and pain; and the object of Economics is to maximize happiness by purchasing pleasure, as it were, at the lowest cost of pain ... I have no hesitation in accepting the Utilitarian theory of morals which does uphold the effect upon the happiness of mankind as the criterion of what is right and what is wrong.

His main aim was exactly 'to use utilitarianism to build an exact science of the theory of value in exchange', Jaffé (1976, p. 518). As he puts it, '*value depends entirely upon utility*', Jevons (1957, p. 1). Hence he starts his analysis with an examination of the theory of pleasure and pain and the theory of utility, which he regards not as an intrinsic aspect of an object, but as a subjective valuation of the pleasure gained through the use of an object by an economic agent. Then he goes on to discuss the theory of exchange by examining the case of two individuals exchanging two commodities. The basic conclusion he reaches, 'the keystone of the whole Theory of Exchange and of the principal problems of economics', as he says, is the following, p. 95:

> The ratio of exchange of any two commodities will be the reciprocal of the ratio of the final degrees of utility of the quantities of commodity available for consumption after the exchange is completed.

Then Jevons considers labour by using the same utilitarian apparatus, while his theory of rent closely follows the classical (Ricardian) theory of diminishing returns from the extensive margin of bringing increasingly inferior land into cultivation.

Coming to Walras, his general equilibrium system, which is his chief contribution to economic science, is a sort of prototype of a universal abstract theory. The aim of his analysis is similar to Jevons: to find the conditions of equilibrium in exchange. But the route he follows is the opposite, and the means he employs is different. What differentiates Walras' analysis from Jevons' is his focus of attention, his general equilibrium system, which is depicted as a set of interrelated markets and is expressed in mathematical form as a set of simultaneous equations. Granted this, his main objective is to prove mathematically that the attainment of equilibrium in all markets is possible, by solving this set of equations with regard to the relevant prices and quantities. In equilibrium, two chief conditions must be satisfied: first, all economic agents maximise their utility; second, aggregate quantity demanded in each market equals aggregate quantity supplied. Mathematically, the condition of maximum utility is achieved when 'the *raretés* of these commodities are proportional to their prices upon completion of the exchange', Walras (1954, p. 45). This is the condition also arrived at by Jevons, but through an entirely different route. As Jaffé (1976, p. 515) has persuasively shown, *rareté* (Jevons' 'final degree of utility' or marginal utility), rather than being the point of departure for the elaboration of a theory of consumption, as in Jevons' theory, is simply used by Walras to close his previously derived general equilibrium system. Despite his use of utility functions to close his system, Walras was not a utilitarian and, in contrast to Jevons, Bentham's name does not appear once in his entire book, p. 518, nor indeed in his *Correspondence*. As Jaffé (1976, p. 518) puts it, 'Walras peremptorily and nonchalantly ... postulated a measurable marginal utility theory without more ado, for the sole purpose of rounding out his previously formulated catallactic theory of price determination'. And he adds, p. 522, 'Léon Walras felt that his construction of an overall simultaneous equations bound together by the marginal utility principle had proved that *rareté* is the cause of value'.

Thus, Walras' system is 'rigorously static in character ... [and] is applicable only to a stationary process', the latter referring to 'a process which *actually* does not change of its own initiative', Schumpeter (1937, pp. 165–6). With Walras' general equilibrium system, economic science reaches its apogee with regard to its static nature and its abstract, mathematical content which is totally divorced from reality, hence satisfying his dictum that 'the scholar has the right to pursue science for its own sake', pp. 71–2. It is a theoretical system that is both 'institutionally empty' and 'institutionally neutral', Kaufman (2007, p. 10):

> It is empty because institutions either do not exist (e.g. money has no theoretical role, firms are technologically determined production sets) or are passive and exogenously given background factors ... It is also

institutionally neutral in that the predicted outcomes are independent of both property rights assignments ... and the form of ownership ...

Institutions and, one should add, history, simply do not matter in the Walrasian frictionless, perfectly competitive world.

Despite their great emphasis on pure theorisation, both Jevons and Walras also displayed an interest in more practical matters and policy issues. Only, for them, the latter, which dealt with normative issues, is a separate task to be totally distinguished from the quest of pure science dealing with positive questions. On policy matters, both Jevons and Walras were supporters of a combination of laissez-faire with moderate reforms in the form of legislation for issues such as child labour and health and safety conditions in factories (Jevons) or land taxation and nationalisation of natural monopolies (Walras). Walras, this 'rationalistic optimistic French radical reformer' as Hutchison (1953, p. 216) described him, went so far as to call himself a socialist, but in essence his political position was a 'mixture of traditional liberalism and the doctrine of state intervention', Screpanti and Zamagni (1993, p. 170) and Oser and Blanchfield (1975, pp. 233–4).

3 Carl Menger and the *Methodenstreit*

By contrast to the skirmishes in Britain and the resistance to Jevons, see Chapter 7, the controversy around marginalism in Germany was intense. The presence and strength of the Historical School inevitably brought it into conflict with marginalism, not least because the latter had adopted Ricardian deductivism that had already been rejected by the Historical School. The ensuing conflict reached its climax in the *Methodenstreit*, or the 'Battle of Methods', which took place in 1883–4 between Carl Menger and Gustav Schmoller. So what did this battle involve? Having introduced the general principles of marginalism through the work of Jevons and Walras, and having had a close look at the Gistorical School and Schmoller in the previous chapter, the next step is to introduce the other protagonist in the debate, Carl Menger, by locating him both within marginalism and with respect to the Historical School. Menger is an interesting and pivotal figure in many respects. He is considered by many as the 'odd man out' of the marginalist revolution, Blaug (1997, p. 290).[13] He is usually remembered as one of the originators of the concept of marginal utility, and as the initiator of the *Methodenstreit*, Schneider (1985, p. 1). At the same time, however, he is also considered as the father of the Austrian School which, in its neo-Austrian version (represented mostly by Mises and Hayek), despite its strong subjectivism, is totally opposed to both marginalism and neoclassicism. The development of the Austrian School will be scrutinised in Chapter 13. Here we concentrate on Menger and his role in the *Methodenstreit*.

Menger's *Principles of Economics* is his sole book on economic theory, and is considered to be the *locus classicus* of the Austrian School of economics,

Streissler (1990, p. 33n). In this work, Menger's basic objective was to provide the scientific foundations for economic theory. For him, the basic object of economic theory is the investigation of 'the practical activities of economizing men', Menger (2004 [1871], p. 48). Hence the focus of economic theorising should be 'the conditions under which men engage in provident activity directed to the satisfaction of their needs'. Moreover, this involves:

> Whether and under what conditions a thing is *useful* to me ... whether and under what conditions it is an economic good, whether and under what conditions it possesses *value* for me and how large the *measure* of value is for me, whether and under what conditions an *economic exchange* will take place between two economizing agents and the limits within which a *price* can be established if an exchange takes place.

Menger wanted to uncover the laws governing economic phenomena which, according to him, and much like the other two marginalists, resemble the laws of nature, and are independent of human will, p. 48. The *basic principles* on which his work rests are, first, what Menger (misleadingly, by today's terminology) calls the 'empirical method', but what he was later more conventionally to call 'the analytic-composite method'. 'In what follows I have attempted to reduce the complex phenomena of human economic activity to the simplest elements that can still be subjected to accurate observation ... and ... to investigate the manner in which the more complex phenomena evolve from these elements according to definite principles', Menger (2004, pp. 47–8). Second, these 'simplest elements' are none other than the 'economizing individual', in accordance with the principle of methodological individualism. As Ikeda (2006, p. 7) argues, Menger was committed to methodological individualism from an early stage. Indeed, this is the basis for a scathing critique of both Adam Smith and the Historical School, not least in believing that there is a national economy independent of the 'individual economies' that constitute it:[14]

> Adam Smith and his school have neglected to reduce the complicated phenomena of human economy in general, and in particular of its social form, national economy, to the efforts of individual economies, as would be in accordance with the real state of affairs. They have neglected to teach us to understand them theoretically as the result of individual efforts. Their endeavours have been aimed, rather, and, to be sure, subconsciously for the most part, at making us understand them theoretically from the point of view of the national economy fiction. On the other hand, the historical school of German economists follows this erroneous conception consciously. It is clear, however, that under the sway of the fiction discussed here a theoretical understanding of the phenomena of national economy adequate to reality is not attainable. Also, the slight value of the prevailing theories of economics finds its explanation in no

small measure in the above erroneous basic view of the nature of the present-day social form of human economy.

This is not to deny the existence of national economy, only that, in a remarkable inversion of Marxist political economy, the national economy is seen as a (real) illusion underpinned by individual economies, despite appearances to the contrary.

Last, and as a corollary, is Menger's principle of subjectivism, by which is meant that, 'the subjective valuations placed by individuals on things that they believe will satisfy their needs are the origin of all economic activity', Caldwell (2004, p. 25). These subjective valuations also refer to the meaning that individual actors attach to their actions, a notion that was later developed by Mises (1996) in his concept of human action, Chapter 13, and by Max Weber through his conception of understanding (*Verstehen*), Chapter 11. This is how Hayek (1973, p. 8) puts the matter:

> Menger believes that in observing the actions of other persons we are assisted by a capacity of *understanding* the meaning of such actions in a manner in which we cannot understand physical events. This is closely connected with one of the senses in which at least Menger's followers spoke of the 'subjective' character of their theories, by which they meant, among other things, that they were based on our capacity to comprehend the intended meaning of the observed actions. 'Observation', as Menger uses the term, has thus a meaning that modern behaviourists would not accept; and it implies a *Verstehen* ('understanding') in the sense in which Max Weber later developed the concept.

For Menger, then, individuals both make and *interpret* actions.

On the basis of these principles, the *basic themes* analysed in the *Principles* are, first, the subjectivist theory of value in contrast with the cost of production or the labour theories of value of the classical school. Second is the *process* of price formation as opposed to the Walrasian price determination, Moss (1978, p. 17). If, for Jevons and Walras, the problem was to find the properties of equilibrium prices in exchange, Menger was more interested in explaining 'the process by which that set of prices is attained and changes', in other words the process of price formation, Wagner (1978, p. 66). Third is the emergence of institutions, which are considered to be the unintended consequences of economising individual action, and their role in economic development. However, whilst Menger is committed to methodological individualism and institutions as the undesigned result of individual actions, he is firmly opposed to a parallel between the evolution of human society and natural organisms, and social as natural science. This is because social development reflects natural mechanisms only partially, because human action is purposeful in pursuit of creating ends, even though these may not turn out as intended, Ikeda (2006, pp. 8–9). Menger's analysis proceeds in a step by step fashion, starting with the analysis of goods, then going on to economic (scarce) goods, then in his Chapter 3 to the analysis of value, which offers the basis for his theory of exchange and price, before in the final chapter coming to the explanation of the emergence and nature of one specific institution, money.

The first skirmishes between Menger and the German Historical School appeared immediately after the publication of his *Principles*. This happened despite the fact that Menger dedicates the book to Roscher, and praises the Historical School for furnishing the ground on which his own work would rest, 'the reform of the most important principles of our science here attempted is therefore built upon a foundation laid by previous work that was produced almost entirely by the industry of German scholars', Menger (2004, p. 49). Gustav Schmoller, however, thought otherwise. In a short review of the *Principles* published in 1873, he attacked Menger's textbook for being one-sided, and its method for being 'reminiscent of Ricardo rather than the tendencies reigning today in German scientific circles', Schmoller (2004 [1873], p. 407). What Schmoller rejects is Menger's abstract method, the results of which are not of great use, since 'they amount to no more than new formulations of abstract conventional topics rather than actual solutions of real problems', p. 407. He also criticises the author's unsuccessful attempt to emulate the method of natural sciences and to discover social laws with affinities to natural laws and independent of human will, p. 408:

> Is not the psychological basis of economic life ever changing, according to people and era? Is the author not herewith reviving the old, slanted English fiction, namely that economic life could be properly derived from the constant basic driving force of the abstract average man? Are not herewith all economic problems becoming for him merely and purely private considerations? The natural sciences have done their precise research with scales and microscopes; the approaches that correspond to them in economics are the historical, the statistical, etc.; if the natural sciences wanted to proceed, as Dr. Menger does in economics, they would have to abstractly explore the concept of the cell, the chemical element, and the like and derive their arguments therefrom. This too has its worth and its justification, but it is not so much exact method as speculation about concepts.

The prelude to the *Methodenstreit* had already been signalled. What sparked it off, however, was the publication ten years later, in 1883, of Menger's (1985 [1883]) treatise *Investigations into the Method of the Social Sciences with Special Reference to Economics*. In this, he makes a passionate plea for the reform of political economy because of what he considers to be the inadequacies of the classical school. One such new attempt at reform was delivered by the German historicists, but not to Menger's satisfaction. Indeed, he sees the main task of this book as being a critique of the doctrines (aims and methods) of the Historical School which was the then prevailing orthodoxy in German universities, p. 32:

> I was guided by the thought of making research in the field of political economy in Germany aware of its real tasks again. I thought of liberating it from the one-sided aspects harmful to the development of our science, of freeing it from its isolation in the general literary movement, and thus preparing for the reform of political economy on German soil, a reform which this science so urgently needs in the light of its unsatisfactory state.

Parallel to this task is Menger's 'positive exposition of the nature of theoretical analysis', Hayek (1934, p. 79). Indeed, says Hayek, the *Investigations* 'did more than any other single book to make clear the peculiar character of the scientific method in the social sciences', p. 79. The last contribution of this book is the opportunity it gave Menger for 'an elucidation of the origin and character of social institutions', p. 79.

This is how Menger sums up his position in the first book of his *Investigations*: 'in the preceding book we have set forth the essential difference between the historical, the theoretical, and the practical sciences of economy. We have particularly pointed out the errors of those who see a "historical" science of political economy', p. 97. Perhaps the most pervasive element of this part of the book is Menger's effort to clarify the difference between theory and history. He makes continuous and strenuous efforts to make as clear as possible the distinctions between the individual and the general, the historical and the theoretical, 'full empirical reality' and 'exact theoretical knowledge', etc. According to Menger, there are two different ways of analysing social phenomena: the individual and the general. The former refers to 'concrete phenomena in their position in time and space and in their concrete relationships to one another', while the latter to 'the empirical forms recurring in the variation of these, the knowledge of which forms the object of our scientific interest', p. 35. Corresponding to these two different points of view, there are two different types of scientific knowledge. On the one hand is what he calls 'the realistic-empirical orientation of theoretical research', which refers to the investigation of social phenomena in their '"full empirical validity", *that is, in the totality and the whole complexity of their nature*', p. 56. On the other hand, there is 'exact theoretical knowledge', referring to 'the determination of laws of phenomena which ... should be designated by the expression "exact laws"', p. 59. Indeed, the search for 'exact laws' as the main task of economic science, became the leitmotif of Menger's work on methodology. Historical analysis is closer to the first type of knowledge, since it refers to the investigation of the individual processes of development of an economic phenomenon, p. 43, while theoretical economics is closer to the second type of scientific knowledge since it deals with 'the general nature and general connection (laws)' of economic phenomena, p. 39. History, says Menger, examines '*all* sides of *certain* phenomena', while exact theories '*certain* sides of *all* phenomena', p. 79.

Granted all this, the main problem with German economics is 'the confusion of the historical and the theoretical understanding of social phenomena on the one hand, and the one-sided conception of the theoretical problem of the social sciences as an exclusively realistic one on the other', pp. 74–5. Menger also reacted strongly to the collectivist and organicist aspects of the Historical School, by firmly reasserting the individual as the basic unit of analysis, which is the basis of what he called 'atomism' (or what nowadays would be called 'methodological individualism'). For Menger, only individuals have interests. No collective body such as the national economy can be analysed in its own right without reference to its constituent individual members, p. 93. On the contrary, collectivities such as institutions or nations are themselves the underlying result of individual action, p. 93:

> the phenomena of 'national economy' are by no means direct expressions of the life of a nation as such or direct results of an 'economic nation' ... Rather the phenomena of 'national economy', just as they present themselves to us in reality as results of individual economic efforts, must also be theoretically interpreted in this light.

The difference with the methods and motives of the Historical School are clear.

On the question of individual motivation, Menger recognises the existence of other motives, such as 'public spirit, love of one's fellow men, custom, feeling for justice', p. 84, as well as self-interest. What prompts him, however, to base his theoretical investigations exclusively on the motive of self-interest, is the need to build an exact science of economics based on abstraction and the method of isolation. As he puts it, the exact theory of political economy 'does not have the task of teaching us to understand generally and in their totality social phenomena ... It has only the task of affording us *the understanding of a special side of human life, to be sure, the most important, the economic*', p. 87. Having isolated the economic sphere from other social spheres, the task of 'the exact orientation of theoretical research' is to reduce 'human phenomena to the expressions of the most original and the most general forces and impulses of human nature', p. 86. Of all such human impulses, Menger picks up the satisfaction of well-being, which is the chief manifestation of 'human self-interest' in the economic and material sphere, and by far the most important.

Based on the preceding analysis, Menger identifies three different groups of sciences of the economy: first, 'the *historical* sciences and the statistics of the economy'; second, '*theoretical* economics', both of which we have already encountered; third, 'the *practical* sciences ... with the task of investigating and describing the basic principles of suitable action ... in the field of national economy', p. 38. In his definition of political economy, Menger includes only the latter two, leaving historical investigation totally outside the scope of political economy: 'By *political economy*' he says, 'we will understand that totality of the theoretical-practical sciences of national economy (theoretical economics, economic policy, and the science of finance)', pp. 39–40. Thus, deliberately, and possibly provocatively, he moves his position as far away from the historicists as possible, and excludes much of their endeavour from lying within the orbit of political economy at all.

In sum, Menger in 1883 reacted to the historicists' inductivist claims by firmly reasserting the abstract deductive method in economic inquiry and the individual as the basic unit of analysis. According to him, the deductive approach is the only truly scientific method. Pure induction based on mere observation cannot be the basis for scientific inquiry. The economic individual based on the principle of self-interest becomes the cornerstone of Menger's economic analysis. The methodological collectivism of much of classical political economy and the Historical School gives way to methodological individualism, and the economising aspects of human behaviour become the primary focus of Menger's economic inquiry. Yet one of the principal preoccupations of Menger's political economy, lost in the wake of the marginalist revolution and its aftermath, was the question of the origins and nature of social institutions. This became attached to non- or even anti-marginalist schools of thought (the Historical School, old institutionalism, neo-Austrian School). Last, although substantively Menger called for a reform of political economy away from the doctrines of classical political economy, methodologically and with regard to the proper way of theorising in economic affairs, especially as far as the use of deduction is concerned, his views, much like those of the other marginalists, were very close in some respects to classical writers such as Senior, Mill and Cairnes, Hutchison (1973b, p. 27).

Schmoller's reaction was quick and sharp. In his review of Menger's *Investigations* published in the same year (*Zur Methodologie der Staats und Sozialwissenschaften*) his starting point, i.e. the urgent need for reform of the classical doctrine, is the same as Menger's, but for very different reasons.[15] 'The marrow of its strength', he says, translated in Small (1924, p. 221), 'dried up, because it tried to compose its results excessively into abstract schemes which lacked all reality'. So, rather than simply changing the substance of the old doctrine while keeping the abstract method, as Menger wished, what was needed was a totally new beginning, 'by looking at things from a new angle'. Such a new epoch, however, could not come through the recycling and further refinement of more and more abstract theories but, rather through the collection of more and more descriptive, historical and statistical material. This amounts to a powerful reassertion of the need for induction as the vehicle for the reform of (classical) political economy, because general theories, to the extent they exist, have to be firmly grounded in reality. 'Descriptive science', he says, 'furnishes the preliminaries for general theory ...

Every complete description is thus a contribution to the establishment of the general character of the respective science', p. 220.

Menger's reply in *The Errors of the Historical School* (*Die Irrtümer des Historismus*), published in 1884, yields no ground to his opponent. He essentially recapitulates the arguments of his *Investigations* by criticising the German scholars for their one-sided emphasis on historical and statistical studies and towards 'particularistic investigation', for their failure 'to make sharp discrimination between the theoretical and the practical divisions of economic science', and for undervaluing the need for theoretical economic investigation, translated in Small (1924, pp. 221–2). Once again he makes a sharp distinction between the empirical method and the 'method of isolation ... [whose] aim is to enable us to comprehend social phenomena not "in their complete empirical validity," but so far as their *economic side* is concerned'. And, although he recognises the usefulness of the 'history of public thrift', he considers it not part of political economy but as an auxiliary to it, pp. 225, 227, see also below.

To begin with, both Menger and Schmoller, and their followers, 'locked horns' and stuck to their initial positions, Balabkins (1988, p. 45). However, about a decade later, the rivals already started softening their positions with respect to one another. Thus Schmoller in his *Grundriss* called attention to the importance of abstraction for any meaningful observation while, writing in 1911, accepting the need for an economist to use both induction and deduction, pp. 45, 57. Similarly, for Menger writing in 1894, quoted in Hutchison (1973b, p. 35):

> If the German historical economists were often described ... as representatives of the inductive method, and the Austrian economists of the deductive method, this does not correspond with the facts ... Both recognize that the necessary basis for the study of real phenomena and their laws is that of experience. Both recognize, – I may well assume, – that induction and deduction are closely related, mutually supporting, and complementary means of knowledge.

Böhm-Bawerk (1890, p. 249), on the other hand, one of Menger's immediate followers and disciples, writing in 1890, suggests that:

> the question is not whether the historical method or the 'exact' method is the correct one, but solely whether alongside of the unquestionably warranted historical method of economics, we shall not recognize the 'isolating' method. Many, I among them, maintain that it should be so recognized.

A mood for reconciliation, then, soon took over from the resilient earlier stance of both sides, vindicating, from the point of view of the protagonists of this debate, Schumpeter's dictum regarding the 'wasted energies' that this theoretical battle entailed.

4 The aftermath

As has already been argued, the increasing reliance on the deductive method by the marginalists, in conjunction with the change in the subject matter of economic inquiry and a corresponding emphasis on individual maximisation and the principle of utility, were instrumental in narrowing the scope of economic investigation. It confined economics to problems that could be solved by applying the process of logico-mathematical reasoning, pushing economic science away from immediate confrontation with the real world. At the same time, the use of marginal analysis (an essentially mathematical tool) and the concept of equilibrium (borrowed from statical mechanics) made economics more susceptible to mathematical analysis, pushing economic science further down the road of abstraction and formalism, Deane (1978, pp. 83–6, 95), Pheby (1988, p. 18) and Mirowski (1989b).

The transformation in the scope and method of economic inquiry signified by the triumph of marginalism encapsulated a triple reductionism. First is an individualist reductionism, through which collective economic agents are replaced by individuals as the basic unit of analysis, and the economy is treated as the mere aggregation of its individual members. Second is an asocial reductionism, where the economy is treated in isolation from its broader social context through the total exclusion of all social (other than market) relations from the analysis. Last is an anti-historicist reductionism, through which economic science is totally divorced from history, Screpanti and Zamagni (1993, p. 149). One major consequence of this huge transformation in economic science is the emergence of the disciplines of sociology and economic history, based on the prior divorce of economics from society and history, respectively.

The move from political economy to economics heralded the separation of the latter from other social sciences. The anti-social and anti-historicist reductionism of marginalism gave economic science a rationale for developing independently of other social disciplines, Deane (1978, p. 75). As has been shown, this is *not* simply the result of the triumph of marginalism. Instead, it was the result of a long drawn out process, whereby each of these elements (the collectivist/holist, the historical and the social) was gradually taken out of economic analysis. Thus the historical element had, to a large extent, already been excised from the deductive analysis of Ricardo, Senior and Cairnes. Methodological individualism, as we have seen, was already partially present in both Smith and Mill, and wholly in Bentham's utilitarianism, whereas – a separate but crucial point – the social element in the form of class analysis was the last to be overthrown.

Indeed the major stumbling block for this evolving reductionism has been and remains the analytical location of class. For capitalism and its theorists unambiguously and inevitably make reference to class – a collective attribute – through the unavoidable recognition and analysis of the most immediate categories of wages, profits and rents. The displacement of substantive class analysis, and the corresponding movement from political economy to economics, needed to wait upon the triumph of marginalism towards the end of the nineteenth century, which established the vast majority of the principles of mainstream economics as we know them today. Significantly, the idea of class still prevails in diluted form after the marginalist revolution, even amongst its ardent proponents, not least in the theory of distribution. The idea that the wages, profits or rents are simply a price like any other – that distribution is simply a corollary of price theory rather than its precondition – proved hard to swallow, and this element of the classical tradition persisted. In a sense, the lingering attachment to class in marginalist economics, not least through Marshall's use of partial as opposed to general equilibrium, represents a fingernail hold over historical and social specificity as political economy gives way to economics, Fine (1980c) and Chapter 7.

In addition to the deathblow delivered to class by methodological individualism, what is distinctive with marginalism and neoclassical economics is, first, the introduction of the concepts of equilibrium and marginal utility – not least because both are historically empty concepts – thereby facilitating a mathematical content. Second is the combination of all three forms of reductionism within the same analytical apparatus. In this sense, the triumph of marginalism gave a further and decisive boost to the process of the separation of economics from the other social sciences, a process that had already started before the marginalists offered their treatises.

Economics was now to confine itself to the analysis of the economy, considered simply as the market process, by focusing on the economic aspects of behaviour in abstraction from any other social influences. Space was thus created for the emergence of other social sciences, which would fill the gaps induced by the desocialisation of economics. Two important features are crucial in the removal of the social from the economy. First, the focus of analysis not only shifted to the individual but also to the particular form of optimising behaviour through utility maximisation (with profit maximisation by firms or entrepreneurs as a corollary) or psychological individualism of a special and limited type. Second, the economy became identified with the market, with broader social and political relations fading into the exogenously given background, to be studied by other social sciences. In other words, the economy as market relations was constituted as a distinct object of study, with the discipline of economics to undertake the task. There was, as Hicks (1976) has called it, a change of attention from 'plutology', or the production and growth of wealth, to 'catallactics', or the allocation of resources, itself ultimately reduced to a logic of individual choice, see also Zafirovski (2001).

It is no accident that the establishment of neoclassical orthodoxy, with its narrow, asocial and ahistorical vision of the economy and of what constitutes the object of its inquiry, was soon followed by the emergence of sociology and economic history as separate disciplines. The birth of economic history as a separate discipline will be dealt with in Chapter 8, and Milonakis and Fine (forthcoming), while the appearance of sociology as a distinct field of study will be examined in Chapter 12.

For the time being, suffice it to say that the birth of economic history as a separate discipline can be attributed to two parallel developments. First is the failure in the long run of the Historical School to establish itself as an alternative school of economic thought and theory; second, the separation of neoclassical economics from history through the narrowing of its scope, vacating space for the new field or discipline to emerge. The one episode that was a catalyst in this process, by bringing to the fore all the major differences between the historical method and abstract deduction, was the *Methodenstreit*.

In short, whilst historical economists tried to make history the object of economic investigation, they were besieged or, more exactly, outflanked by the totally ahistorical nature of marginalism, based on the use of the deductive method and the concept of equilibrium. With the benefit of hindsight, with whatever relative intellectual merits, the marginalists eventually won a decisive victory in the *Methodenstreit*. This is so in practice, at least as far as the discipline of economics is concerned. The historicists' approach to economic investigation is generally considered to have suffered from two major weaknesses. One was their apparent unwillingness to abstract in order to isolate the basic causal factors in economic analysis. As Schumpeter (1994, p. 812) describes it, talking about Schmoller in particular, 'nothing in the social cosmos or chaos is really outside of Schmollerian economics'. This unwillingness is considered to be related to another, even more serious, limitation of historical economics – their aversion to abstract theory. This, according to Schumpeter (1967, pp. 172–3), is 'the most important scientific cause' of the reaction against the Historical School. Even Schmoller, who explicitly accepted the need to theorise, failed to provide an adequate theoretical framework. In short, the failure of historical economics to establish itself as an alternative school in economics is mostly attributed to its lack of theory and coherence, Hodgson (2001, ch. 6).

Such an assessment, however, does not represent the whole picture, and as such is not entirely accurate. First, the content and interpretation of the Historical School(s) has been heavily influenced by its debate with 'economics', with its weaknesses exaggerated and its strengths overlooked. Hence, for example, as seen in detail in Chapter 5, historical analysis is not and cannot be entirely theoryless.

According to Pearson (1999, p. 551):

> practicing members of the 'younger' GHSE [German Historical School of Economics] felt no particular obligation to eschew generalization. Some of them worked on relatively 'pure' theory, like Knap (monetary theory and the economics of transportation), Bücher (industrial organization), Lujo Brentano (wage theory), and even Schmoller himself (taxation

and insurance) ... By the time the 'youngest' GHSE rose to prominence with Weber and Sombart, the association of German economics with curational obscurantism was altogether untenable.

In similar spirit Shionoya (2001a, p. 11) argues that:

> even for Schmoller the historical method was not simply directed to the accumulation of historiography and historical monographs; rather, it aimed to gather materials to ultimately build a broader theory for the institutional framework of the economy and its historical changes.

Throughout, the Historical School(s) were not theoryless nor anti-theory. What they opposed very strongly was the universal type of theory valid in all places and for all epochs, of the type practised by the marginalists and later by neoclassical economics, as well as the speculative type of abstract theory which is not firmly anchored in reality. At the same time, however, the extent to which they used theory varied between different writers in the tradition, with a tendency, at least as far as the German branch is concerned, to become more and more theoretical.[16] This trend reached its climax in the works of the members of the youngest branch (mostly Weber and Sombart), who were primarily theorists, see Chapter 11.

Second, the true issues behind the *Methodenstreit* were not simply methodological, but also (and mostly) epistemological and substantive. Epistemologically, according to Bostaph (1978), the differences between Menger and Schmoller were far greater than they themselves may have realised. To treat them simply as involving the question of induction versus deduction, as is usually done, is to miss the point of the debate, pp. 14–5. Bostaph contrasts Schmoller's nominalist with Menger's Aristotelian position.[17] For Schmoller as a nominalist, 'the essence [of specific phenomena] was to be obtained by a summarization over entities of all their characteristics, rather than the apprehension or perception of a central and defining characteristic', p. 10. This involves a descriptive type of causality where, following David Hume, 'the explanation of the causal relation [is perceived] as merely uniformity in succession', rather than 'any intrinsic or necessary connections uniting these events', p. 10. As a result, because the empirical context is always different, the search for universally applicable concepts and absolute laws is bound to fail, p. 11. Menger's Aristotelian essentialism, on the other hand, considers all phenomena as having some essential properties that underlie their nature, and searches for causal relations among the individual elements of these phenomena through the method of abstraction and isolation, pp. 11–12:

> Menger sought the 'simplest elements' of everything real, the essences, the nature (*das Wesen*) of the real. In his exact approach, he used the process of abstraction from the individual phenomena of the empirical

world to discover their essences, to isolate them, and then to utilise the 'simplest elements' so obtained to deduce 'how more complicated phenomena develop from the simplest, in part even unempirical elements of the real world'.

Because these 'simplest elements', which, of course, are none other than the essential characteristics of the individuals, are derived from empirical reality, Menger's method, according to Bostaph, cannot be called a priori. At the same time, substantively, the *Methodenstreit* referred to real problems: analysis of utility and price through the abstract/deductive method for the neoclassical economists, versus the issue of institutional evolution and development of national economies dealt with through the historical and ethical method for the historicists, Hutchison (1973, pp. 34–5) and Shionoya (2001a, p. 11). As Menger himself puts it in his obituary tribute to Roscher in 1894, quoted in Hutchison (1973b, p. 35):

> The differences that have arisen between the Austrian school and some of the German historical economists were by no means ones of method in the proper sense of the word ... The real foundation of the differences, which are still not completely bridged, between the two schools is something much more important: it relates to the different view regarding the *objectives* of research, and about the set of tasks, which a science of economics has to solve.

So something more, even other than method, lay at the heart of the *Methodenstreit*, as suggested by one of its own protagonists.

Third, and of great importance in the *Methodenstreit* and its outcome, was the general political stance of each of its participants towards the established order. Mises (2003, p. 15), the leading neo-Austrian economist and a champion of liberalism, in his characteristic style, puts this point in no uncertain terms. 'The British free trade philosophy triumphed in the nineteenth century in the countries of Western and Central Europe', he says. And, he continues:

> But very soon the government of Bismarck began to inaugurate its *Sozialpolitic*, the system of interventionist measures such as labor legislation, social security, pro-union attitudes, progressive taxation, protective tariffs, cartels, and dumping. If one tries to refute the devastating criticism leveled by economics against the suitability of all these interventionist schemes, one is forced to deny the very existence – not to mention the epistemological claims – of a science of economics ... This is what all the champions of authoritarianism, government omnipotence, and 'welfare' policies have always done. They blame economics for being 'abstract' and advocate a 'visualizing' mode of dealing with the problems involved. They emphasize that matters in this field are too complicated to be described in formulas and theorems. They assert that the

various nations and races are so different from one another that their action cannot be comprehended by a uniform theory ... The political significance of the Historical School consisted in the fact that it rendered Germany safe for the ideas, the acceptance of which made popular with the German people all those disastrous policies that resulted in the great catastrophes. Schmoller and his friends and disciples advocated what has been called state socialism; i.e. a system of socialism – planning – in which the top management would be in the hands of the Junker aristocracy. It was this brand of socialism at which Bismarck and his successors were aiming.

In other words, for Mises, the anti-theoretical stance of the German Historical School is explained by the fact that the theoretical economics of the day provided the scientific ground for the legitimation of free trade policies and against interventionism that they championed. The triumph of the latter in Bismarck's Germany offers an explanation of the success this school enjoyed in Germany for the best part of a century. Its close association with what Mises misleadingly calls 'state socialism', however, also determined their fate in the longer run. Schumpeter (1967, pp. 172–3) hints at this when he writes that the latter 'had associated itself with political trends in the same way in which the classical economists had done in their time. And like the latter they now had to pay the price for this'.

Although both Schumpeter's and Mises' views expressed above should be taken with a grain of salt because of their own strong liberal political views, which sometimes 'clouded their perception of the history of their subject', Streissler (1990, p. 40), they certainly, in this case, contain a strong element of truth. The political and ideological elements, as we have seen, played a decisive role in the development of economic ideas. Schmoller himself is absolutely conscious of this fact. As he puts it, quoted in Koslowski (2002, p. 151):

Today's political economy represents an ethical and an historical conception of state and society rather than one determined by realism and materialism. From pure theory of the market and of exchange, a kind of 'cash nexus economics', which was once a class weapon of the rich, has once again become a great moral-political science. It analyses not only the production but also the distribution of goods, the value-adding processes as well as economic institutions, and it puts man instead of goods and capital in the center of scientific endeavour.

Schmoller's critical attitude towards the capitalist system (and that of the Historical School in general), and advocacy of government intervention and social reform, is to be contrasted with the Austrians' generally Panglossian approach, where, in truly liberal tradition, the human condition is presented as the best of all possible worlds, and where social harmony and eudemonia are feasible objectives within the given context. As Mises (2003, p. 16) would put it later on, 'every new generation will add something to the good accomplished by its ancestors. Thus mankind is on the eve of a continuous advance toward more satisfactory conditions. To progress steadily is the nature of man ... The ideal state of society is before us, not behind us'. Having said this, recent scholarship seems to be divided on the question of Menger's political predisposition. This misty picture is partly the result of the fact that Menger himself wrote precious little on questions of policy. According to one view, which seems to predominate, what evidence there is seems to suggest that he was most probably an 'uncompromising champion of laissez-faire', Kirzner (1990, pp. 94–7) and Streissler (1990).[18] Other scholars, however, consider Menger more of a social democrat, who sympathised with the weak and the poor at the expense of the aristocracy, and point to other evidence which suggests that, contrary to the conventional wisdom, Menger was an advocate of government intervention, Wagner (1978, pp. 1–2) and Boehm, cited in Kirzner (1990, p. 94).

5 Concluding remarks

The causes of the success of the marginalist revolution are multifaceted. Prominent are the problems faced by classical political economy itself, which led to the crisis of Ricardian economics in the late 1860s and 1870s. According to Hutchison (1978, p. 58), 'in the space of a few years in the late 1860s and early 1870s the classical structure of "theory" underwent a remarkably sudden and rapid collapse of confidence, considering how long and authoritative has been its dominance in Britain'. This crisis was reflected at the dinner, held in 1876 to honour the hundreth anniversary of the publication of the *Wealth of Nations*. It revealed that the consensus built around Mill's popularisation of Ricardianism had evaporated. It became apparent that there were deep divisions among the participants concerning every single aspect of political economy (method, role of history, state intervention, distribution, free trade, etc.). This prompted Bagehot, quoted in Hutchison (1953, p. 6), to comment that, political economy 'lies rather dead in the public mind'. At least, the crisis served the function of clearing the ground for the emergence of the new orthodoxy – but no more. The crisis of a given paradigm is one thing, and what should replace it quite another. And, as we have seen, there were three main contenders, Marxism, historicism and marginalism, Hutchison (1953, pp. 1–6 and 1978, p. 1) and Koot (1987, pp. 10–14).[19]

The success of marginalism is also associated with the professionalisation of economics, which took place in the last quarter of the nineteenth century and helped to establish it as an academic science. This professionalisation was intimately connected with the further acceptance and consolidation of marginalism as the basis of the 'new' economic science, which did not really take place until the end of the century, Howey (1973, p. 25). 'For nearly two decades', says Hutchison (1973a, p. 185), 'there was in Britain a somewhat confused interregnum'. Other landmarks in this process of consolidation were the adoption of the concept by such major writers as the Austrian followers of Menger, Wieser and Böhm-Bawerk, and the Swede Wicksteed in the 1880s. Neoclassical economics, however, did not really shoot to prominence until well after the publication of Marshall's magnus opus, *The Principles of Economics*, in 1890, Howey (1973, p. 25 and 1960, chs 26, 27), Blaug (1973, p. 14), Stigler (1973, pp. 310–20), Winch (1973, p. 60), Khalil (1987, p. 119), and Chapter 7.

In this light, was the Historical School defeated, and, if so, with what immediate and longer-term effects? In retrospect, the obvious answer would appear to be a resounding affirmative to defeat, in view of the unambiguous triumph of deductive marginalism, at least within economics. But the record of the debate itself suggests otherwise, with the telling and even valued points of the Historical School at least partially accepted in principle by its opponents (e.g. the need to combine deduction with induction) but increasingly disregarded in practice as marginalism experienced its own imperatives and dynamic. In this respect Jacob Viner (1991, pp. 238–9), cited in Hutchison (2000, p. 359) strikes the right chord in his eloquent assessment of the fate of the *Methodenstreit*:

> My fellow theorists tell me that the theorists won a definitive victory in this battle when Carl Menger, in the 1880s demolished Gustav Schmoller. I cannot agree. I believe that the battle was mostly a sham one, and that while Schmoller certainly carried off no laurels, the ones that have ever since been bestowed on Menger for his victory in this battle are tinsel ones ... The real challenge which Menger should have faced was not that of justifying in principle recourse to abstraction by economists, but justifying the particular extent and manner in which he and his fellow theorists practiced it.

Defeated by marginalism or not, one thing is certain. The effects of the marginalist revolution, and of the *Methodenstreit* in particular, were long lasting and far reaching. One particular effect to which the *Methodenstreit* partly, if indirectly, contributed was the birth of the Austrian School of economics, which was consolidated and became increasingly marginalist through the influence of Menger's followers and disciples, Böhm-Bawerk and Wieser. Later on, however, through the influence of Mises and Hayek which gave the school its neo-Austrian flavour, the marginalist element was lost, although still remaining increasingly individualist and subjectivist, see Chapter 13.

A second effect was the detachment of theoretical economics from policy issues. Contrary to the Historical School, whose main aim was to construct a historical economics in service of social reform in order to meet the pressing problems of the day, while stressing the ethical dimension of political economy, the marginalists sought to construct a value-free economic science based on exact laws in fashion similar to natural sciences. This trend in economic thinking was not new. Ricardo, Mill and Senior were all adherents to this approach. What marginalism did was to help in consolidating the distinction between positive and normative economics, with scientific economics being confined to the former. This consolidation was made explicit by John Neville Keynes' treatise on method, *The Scope and Method of Political Economy*, published in 1890, see next chapter. The debate over the desirability or not of a value-free economic and social science was given a further twist through the publication of Weber's essay on 'Objectivity in Social Science and Social Policy', where he stood firmly on the side of a value-free social science, see Chapter 11, Section 3. This article gave rise to another prolonged methodological debate. In economics, the call for a positive, value-free economic science achieved the supreme position it continues to enjoy to the present day following the publication of Robbins' book, *An Essay on the Nature and Significance of Economic Science*, published in 1932, more than 40 years later, Balabkins (1988, pp. 63–4) and Chapter 12. Hence there occurred a shift from political economy to (positive) economics, first proclaimed by Jevons and explicitly depicted in the title of Marshall's magnus opus *The Principles of Economics*.

Last, and related to the above, was the separation of economics from the social and the historical. Building an 'exact' science of economics meant isolating the economic sphere from other social spheres. This narrowing of the scope of economics created the space for the emergence of other social sciences, including sociology, to deal with the non-rational aspects of human behaviour, Chapter 12, and economic history as at most an auxiliary to economics, Chapter 8. Thus, Max Weber, himself a member of the youngest German Historical School, who was so instrumental in the birth of sociology as a discipline, is also interesting as one writer who found himself caught between the extremes of the Historical School and the newly emerging marginalism. He attempted to reconcile the two sides through mutual convergence. In this light, Weber can be seen as representing the extreme end of evolution and conciliation, as far as the Historical School is concerned, and a leading representative of the new order in seeking to add the social to economic rationality. The result was a short-lived stab at social economics, to which we turn in Chapter 11, itself ultimately signifying the demise both of the Historical School from which it derived in part and also the 'old' marginalism of Marshall that it had hoped to promote as a core component part, see next chapter.

As is apparent and generally accepted, Marshall's role in promoting marginalism is central. This is not because he was single-mindedly in favour of its principles – quite the opposite. For, whilst he was fully aware of the *Methodenstreit*, he prevailed in the context of a different intellectual milieu, albeit one that incorporated affinities with the German Historical School in its opposition to marginalism. Marshall's main adversaries were to be found amongst the British Historical School, in relation to whom Marshall wavered between compromise and conflict. Either way, the result was to witness the forward march of marginalism. Whatever his own reservations, Marshall's goal was to establish marginalism in principle as the core standard in a professionalised economics. He himself provided that core, tempered by concessions to the importance of other factors, giving rise to old marginalism. The latter, though, has given way to new marginalism – neoclassical economics as we know it today – with the nagging intellectual conscience furnished by the Historical Schools having faded into oblivion. That is within the discipline of economics itself. Whilst the residue of the German Historical School survived, however fitfully, as social economics and American institutionalism, Chapters 9–11, in Britain, the idea that economics needed something other than marginalism found expression in other forms. It gave birth to economic history as a separate discipline (and as the progeny of the British Historical School), Chapter 8, and in the emergence of macroeconomics as distinct from microeconomics, Chapter 14.

7 The Marshallian heritage

'Much of pure theory seems to me to be elegant toying'.

Marshall (1996, vol II: p. 178), cited in Hutchison (2000, p. 357)

'[John Neville] Keynes' *Scope and Method* and Marshall's *Principles of Economics* proceeded side by side, with each author reading and criticising the other's chapter drafts and proofs ... [Keynes' book] was accepted by a majority of reviewers as being the definitive methodological text for the new political economy (in Britain identified with Marshall's *Principles*), and as ending the long and tedious *Methodenstreit*'.

Deane (1983, pp. 3–4)

1 Introduction

Alfred Marshall's (1842–1924) *Principles of Economics*, first published in 1890, is the most revealing of watersheds in the evolution of economic theory and in marking the passage from classical political economy to neoclassical economics. This is because so much finds its way into the making of the book, from the past and what lay in the future. If we look back from the book, economic theory looks entirely different than if we look forward. This is because, more than any other economist, Marshall both engaged with the political economy of his predecessors and established the economic principles of his followers.

These assertions are established in Section 2, where we examine the shifting intellectual context attached to the preparation, appearance and impact of Marshall's *Principles*. This paves the way in Section 3 for an account of Marshall himself and the tensions in his own writings between establishing marginalist principles to stand at the core of economics as a discipline, and retaining a more rounded, realistic and practical stance on economic analysis and policy. Such tensions are characteristic of 'old' Marshallian marginalism, as opposed to 'early' marginalism of Jevons, Walras and Menger, and their immediate followers. They apply to a generation or two after Marshall, but are progressively shed in favour of pure and universal principles as old becomes new marginalism, or neoclassical economics. The tensions involved are most apparent in the contributions of both Marshall and John Neville Keynes. The latter's methodological contributions, outlined in Section 4, complemented Marshall's *Principles*, essentially arguing for a methodology of deductivism and universal principles plus something else to account for other factors and variations across history, but with the possibility of establishing a positive as opposed to a normative economic science. This soon allowed Lionel Robbins to go even further, confining the definition of economics to the study of the allocation of scarce resources between competing ends, see Chapter 12. The concluding remarks point to the (in part intentional) consequences of Marshall having prevailed within economics – the emergence of a core of deductive, universal principles. Whilst there may have been disagreements between Marshall and J. N. Keynes over how far these could be applied and with what they needed to be supplemented, these differences, as well as the issues they raise, were soon to become irrelevant as deductive marginalism was increasingly embraced as sole sovereign in the discipline of economics.

2 Setting the scene: dehomogenising marginalism

In a nutshell, as seen in Chapter 6, what the early marginalists shared in common boils down to the employment of the abstract/deductive method (which in the case of Jevons and Walras takes the physico-mathematical form), the use of a subjective theory of value and marginalist principles. This common core is their shared legacy, which is also the most important part of their contribution. This was the picture of the early marginalists, prevalent among economists until the early 1970s. As seen already, however, beyond this common core, they shared little in common. From the early 1970s, a process of re-evaluation and dehomogenisation, as Jaffé (1976) has called it, of the writings of the troika has proved fruitful in untangling the different contributions of each individual writer, see Black (1973), Streissler (1973), Jaffé (1973 and 1976), Hicks and Weber (eds) (1973), Caldwell (ed) (1990) and Chapter 6. For White (2004, p. 262), Robbins is responsible for having homogenised Jevons, Menger and Walras in order to be able to deploy them to inaugurate 'the analytical framework ... subsequently characterized as the science of "Modern Economics"'. He continues by citing Blaug's (1997, p. 278) judgement that:

> With the publication of these three [one each from the troika] postclassical texts, 'for the first time, economics became the science that studies the relation between *given* ends and *given* scarce means that have alternative uses for the achievement of those ends'.

Yet, White observes 'That neat linear account is, however, misleading ... no Robbins-type statement can be found in Walras's *Elements* ... and the link to Menger appears "distant and diffuse"'.[1] Only with Jevons, 'the later definition of economics can find a clear precedent'. In this respect, Coase's (1994,

p. 211) citation of the LSE Calendar description by Robbins of his course on comparative economic theory is stunningly revealing:[2]

> The course will deal mainly with the economic theories of earlier generations, but it will attempt to exhibit these theories, not as so much antiquarian data but as the raw material out of which by a process of refinement and elimination the economic theories of today have been evolved. That is to say, its ultimate purpose will be to provide a negative preparation for modern analysis.

Coase perceptively comments 'That is, in this course, Robbins examined the work of earlier economists not so much to learn from them as to understand what had to be given up or changed in order to reach the economic analysis of today. The latest was the best', p. 212.

These differences within the troika, eliminated by Robbins, are important because of the role they played in their respective individual influences on subsequent developments, outside economics as it was to become, or on its borders with other disciplines. As Jaffé (1976, p. 522) puts it, 'The seeds of the subsequent developments in economic theory found in Menger are very different from those found in Jevons and Walras'. Blaug (1973, pp. 13–14), in contradiction to his linear view expressed above, possibly conflating individual and national contributions, has gone as far as to talk about distinct if inter-related developments:

> the three interlocking 'revolutions' that characterised the last two decades of the nineteenth century – the marginal utility revolution in England and America, the subjectivist revolution in Austria, and the general equilibrium revolution in Switzerland and Italy – [which] continued well into the twentieth century.

Jevons (1957, p. 21) describes his theory as 'the *mechanics of utility and self-interest*'. In addition to the import of Benthamite utilitarianism, he perceives the rational economic agent as an application of universal mechanical principles, Maas (1999 and 2005a) and White (2004). Walras' general equilibrium system was concerned to model the economy as a whole, through a set of simultaneous equations, for which he raised the issues both of the existence of equilibrium and the dynamics around it, Walker (1987). And Menger believes that the origin of all economic activity lies in subjectivism, while also focusing on the emergence and evolution of economic institutions as the unintended consequence of individual action, Caldwell (2004, pp. 23–7), see also Chapter 6.

Marginalism was not consolidated until the end of the nineteenth century – as Howey (1973, p. 25) puts it:

> Marginalism as a recognised part of economics did not originate until supporters were found and acceptance achieved ... The further history

of the development of marginalism, from 1873 through most of the 1880s, was the history of the search for acceptance and support of marginal utility.

Such acceptance and support was provided by Wieser in 1884, who was also the first to use the word marginal (*Grenznutzen*) in German, and Böhm-Bawerk in 1886, both supporters of Menger and co-founders of the Austrian School of economics, Howey (1973, p. 26) and Chapter 13. In English, the word marginal was introduced by Wicksteed, see Chapter 6, footnote 11, but the second major book to include the word was Marshall's *Principles*, pp. 31–2. Slowly but surely, the latter became the new bible of economic science and the most important landmark in the establishment and consolidation of marginalism. Such was its influence that what survived of the work of the early marginalists was whatever found its way into *Principles*. Jevons' utilitarianism made it in, but the trajectory of the utility concept was one of curtailment, gradually diminishing in its journey from cardinal utility, to ordinal, to revealed preference, Chapter 14. What did not make it into Marshall's *Principles*, on the other hand, soon fell into oblivion, including Walras' general equilibrium system, which by 1900 had been largely forgotten, only to resurface in the 1930s through Hicks, Allen, and Lange (the latter in the context of the socialist calculation debate), and later on through Samuelson, and Arrow and Debreu, Blaug (1997, p. 290).

Another contribution discarded in the passage from early marginalism is Menger's preoccupation with the emergence of social institutions. By the 1930s, very few economists knew of Menger's work directly. He was mostly remembered for his part in the *Methodenstreit*, and for his non-mathematical treatment of marginal utility. The substantive themes of Menger's work were only rediscovered in the 1930s and 1940s by Hayek, Vaughn (1990, p. 379). Indicative of this late rediscovery of the views of both Walras and Menger was the fact that Menger's *Principles* was only first translated into English in 1950, and Walras' *Elements* only in 1957. This time, however, rediscovery of Walras and Menger led to very different outcomes. Walras was celebrated as part of the hard core of the mainstream tradition, reaching its apogee in Arrow and Debreu's (1954) and Debreu's (1959) work on general equilibrium theory. As such, Walras is the main precursor of the new revolution in economic science associated with model building, formalism and excessive mathematisation, see Chapter 14. With the re-emergence of general equilibrium theory, Jevons and Walras could be seen and used, however wittingly, as a single body of thought, and a crude synthesis of their differing approaches could be adopted. Jevons' principles are more attuned to the mechanics of the economic system, with a corresponding attachment to the underlying pursuit of self-interest and the prospect of measuring it or its effects. This had its later counterpart in the emergence of econometrics. Indeed, as Black (1973, p. 112) suggests:

We have lived through another revolution in economics in the last twenty years; and if we were asked to say in what that revolution consists, we would probably point to the increasing rigor of theory and to the stress on econometric testing of it. If Jevons could be called upon to give his opinion of the economics of 1971, I suspect that he would only express surprise that it has taken us so long to get so far; for are we not now applying those lessons of the need for logic and measurement which he taught? I would contend that here more than any statement of marginal utility theory, are the true hallmarks of his originality and the true sources of the contribution which Jevons the scientist made to the foundation of modern economic science.

Menger, on the other hand, was embraced as part of a new research programme, taking the form of what came to be known as neo-Austrian economics, and falling entirely outside the mainstream tradition, see Chapter 13.

It would be easy, then, to see each of Jevons, Walras and Menger as having anticipated, respectively, the economics imperialism of Gary Becker, see Fine and Milonakis (2009), the general equilibrium of Arrow and Debreu, and the neo-Austrian School. But the lines of intellectual descent would have to be traced, if possible, and there are hurdles along the way – not only to be knocked aside but also to be picked up and used elsewhere. Indeed, the differences between neoclassical economics following the Second World War and the classical political economy of the nineteenth century are so great that there are many different ways of reading how one (if it is such) became the other, and why. Hodgson (2001), for example, has read it in terms of the way in which economics forgot history, a theme that is important for this book. For Yonay (1998, p. 185), the passage between the two marked the triumph of 'the three components of the winning coalition: mathematical economics, econometrics, and Keynesianism'. He cites Debreu's Presidential Address to the American Economics Association to the effect that, in 1940, 'less than 3 percent of the refereed pages ... [of the *American Economic Review*] include rudimentary mathematical expressions ... [but by 1990] nearly 40 percent ... display mathematics of a more elaborate type', p. 194. Similarly, for Hutchison (2000, p. 191), the shift marks a formalist revolution, one accompanied by the passage from the UK to the USA in leadership of the discipline of economics and the rapid growth in economists and economics students, see also Blaug (1999, 2001 and 2003). This is only possible, however, because economics is constituted as a separate discipline – one set apart from the other social sciences in subject matter and method. In other words, as emphasised by Maloney (1976 and 1985), the marginalist revolution and its aftermath represented the professionalisation of economics. Indeed, for Maloney (1985, p. 65), 'the automatic adherence to the neoclassical paradigm of anyone who could handle it is the most disquieting aspect of the *professionalisation* of economics' (emphasis added).

For many, including Hutchison and, most recently, the Critical Realism School of economics,[3] that disquiet centres on what he dubs ultra-deductivism. The most obvious symbol of the latter is the excessive formalism associated with the heavy reliance upon mathematics. Distinct from it came the theory of the optimising individual, especially as utility maximising subject to constraints, following Samuelson's pioneering work, *Foundations of Economic Analysis*, published in 1947. This also required a fundamental shift in approach. As Ingrao and Israel (1990, p. 47) indicate in their history of general equilibrium theory, a major problem arises in the transition from classical political economy, that of reconciling 'the need to construct a science possessing *objective* value with the intimately *subjective* nature of the material to be dealt with'. Indeed, how can you have natural-type laws concerning equilibrium by analogy with mechanics when 'the material to be investigated is composed of subjects whose actions stem from free and autonomous choice'? Significantly, his absolute and influential rejection of the mathematisation of social science was 'pushed by Say almost to the point of the idiosyncratic rejection of mathematics *tout court*', p. 60. Yet, perversely, Say is now mostly remembered for his law of markets – that supply creates its own demand and the impossibility of general gluts – propositions that are most readily expressed in the mathematics of supply and demand in aggregating across all markets.

Our own focus in this volume is on the shifting social and historical content of economics, and its corresponding methodological conundrums. But this is not offered as an alternative or complementary reading to that of others. Rather, our approach is to highlight the evolving tensions *between* the various changes in approach, and their subject matter, that were taking place, and how they were, or were not, resolved only for such tensions to reappear in other forms or to be replaced by others. Otherwise, if of interest, the passage from one school of economic thought to another becomes interpreted as an inevitable teleology, whose telling is dictated by the outcome. The before and after differ, it is just a matter of how one became the other. But could things have been different, and why did one become the other and not something else altogether, however minimally different? And who opposed, or sought to qualify, the changes taking place, and why and how did they or did they not have an effect? All of this is what makes Marshall so revealing. Much, if not all, that went before is reflected through the prism of his work.

Thus, because mainstream neoclassical economics in its current form has now become so dominant, it is difficult to imagine that it could have been otherwise. Yet the fact of the matter is that it *was* otherwise, and alternatives or qualifications to its claims have been well-established until relatively recently, even amongst those who have played a leading role in promoting it to prominence. In this respect, the most appropriate starting point is Alfred Marshall and his *Principles of Economics*. As Michie *et al.* (2002, p. 351) suggest, 'Yet even one of the founders of neoclassical economics, Alfred Marshall, would barely recognise nor accept what is today presented as economic analysis, ignoring as it does the key industrial and organisational detail underlying production'. And the command of Marshall's *Principles* over the emerging discipline of economics persisted well into, if not beyond, the inter-war period.

In some sense, then, Marshall looked over (and overlooked) the past, as well as making the future. He was very much the product of his age, drawing extensively from most traditions in economics that were prevalent at the time. These included the classicals and especially J. S. Mill, the Germans like Rau, Hermann and Thünen, and, of course, the marginalists, especially Jevons, although with protestations to the contrary. He did more than anybody to establish economics as an academic discipline, but at the same time he was very interested in real economic problems. His mind was synthetic and his mood conciliatory. He tried to fuse a classical cost of production theory with demand theory based on the principle of marginal utility in his partial equilibrium analysis.

Significantly, Marshall differed from each of our troika of early marginalists in more than one respect. He was more rounded than Jevons in his view of individual economic agents (and established a framework based equally on supply and demand). He was committed to partial rather than general equilibrium, in contrast to Walras. And he was more even-handed than Menger when it came to the *Methodenstreit*, committing himself much more and openly to a mixture of deductive and inductive methods. Indeed, he tried to forge economic theorising with a historical sense, and with his eyes on the need to tackle economic problems, to combine theory with reality. Despite being a trained mathematician, he was suspicious of the use of mathematics in economics – much like Menger, if less so, although the latter lacked any mathematical training, Schumpeter (1994, p. 827) and Blaug (1997, p. 279). The first edition of the *Principles* even incorporated a couple of chapters of descriptive economic history, although these were dropped from later editions. These compromises allowed Marshall to command widespread support for the use of marginalism within economic theory – as was his purpose. His was one of the last attempts within mainstream economics to keep the link between theory and history alive, compromised though it was by the wish to establish marginalist theory.

But even he had, in the end, to succumb to the marginalists' unanimous urge for subdivision in economic science, reflecting the developments taking place in and around economics at the turn of the twentieth century (not least the emergence of economic history as a separate discipline). This perhaps offers a partial explanation for why he decided to drop the first two historical chapters from the *Principles* in subsequent editions. Of significance in this respect was his continual battle with the historical economist William Cunningham, which reached a climax in their bitter exchanges in the British '*Methodenstreit*', and his support for the theoretical economist Pigou against the historicist Foxwell as his successor at Cambridge.[4] By then, the split between theory and history as far as mainstream economics is concerned was complete. The last theorists who tried to forge a link between theory and history all lie outside mainstream economics, and include the likes of Max

Weber and Joseph Schumpeter, see Chapter 11, and the American institutionalists, Chapters 9 and 10, see Hodgson (2001, ch. 8), Koot (1987, ch. 7), Backhouse (2002b, p. 179) and Chapter 8.

Not surprisingly, then, as revealed in the next section, there were considerable, often explicit, tensions within Marshall's work and the man himself. Consider Groenewegen's (1995, p. 788) conclusions from his extensive biography:

> as a neo-classical in the manner that the word was coined by Veblen ... [he] was never anti-classical in the sense that Jevons and, to a lesser degree, Menger and Walras opposed the older economics of Mill, Ricardo and Smith ... supply and demand for Marshall were more than functional relationships. He saw them as two fundamental categories by which to analyse the dialectically related opposites of production and consumption, wants and activities ... [and] evolutionary emphasis within his economics made him invariably conscious of change, of dynamics, of progress and time ... He would have staunchly opposed the obfuscation inherent in the distinction between micro- and macro-economics as both narrow and simplistic ... because it treats too many essential factors as exogenous from principle rather than from pragmatic analytical necessity ... and leaves too much of what is important to other disciplines ... Marshall likewise rejected the positivism underlying so much of contemporary micro-economics, though not the quest for scientific detachment ... Marshall also placed his economics firmly within the social sciences, ever aware of its crucial associations with politics and history especially.

These characteristics sit uncomfortably alongside a commitment to the principles of marginalism. The corresponding tensions within Marshall were largely and increasingly resolved by his successors, in the token way of setting them aside as inconveniences to be ignored. Priority lay in the discovery of, and adherence to, a common set of core (microeconomic) principles. However, reservations around such principles were especially prompted by the inability of marginalism to address adequately the functioning of the economy as a whole. Within the UK, this led to the emergence of Keynesianism, Chapter14; in the USA to the strengthening of what is now known as 'old institutionalism', Chapter 8. In retrospect, Coase (1978, p. 207) put it well:

> The view that economics is a study of all human choice, although it does not tell us the nature of the economic theory or approach which is to be employed in all the social sciences, certainly calls for the development of such a theory.

Let economics as choice be studied, but without allowing it to exhaust economic theory as a whole. Such is the spirit of Marshall's old marginalism, reflecting both his intellectual context and goals, and its limitations.

3 From soaring eagle ...

At the time that Marshall's *Principles* first appeared in 1890, Mill's *Principles of Political Economy* still remained the most important text. As John Maynard Keynes (1925, p. 19) put it in his obituary – incorrectly and no doubt to emphasise but not exaggerate Marshall's impact – 'When Marshall began, Mill and Ricardo still reigned supreme and unchallenged'. Nonetheless, mathematisation of economics was in the air of both the natural *and* the moral sciences, p. 20, and Marshall and his *Principles* brought such prospects down to earth. His text was to run to eight editions and to remain the single most important contribution to the discipline until after the Second World War. Not surprisingly, Keynes deemed Marshall to be 'the father of Economic Science as it exists in England to-day', citing Foxwell's judgement as early as 1888, that 'Half the economic chairs in the United Kingdom are occupied by his pupils, and the share taken by them in general economic instruction in England is even larger than this', p. 59.[5]

Keynes explicitly lists six analytical elements that had marked Marshall's fathering of economics and, remarkably, they continue to stand the test of time some 80 years later. In abbreviated form, they are, pp. 41–6:

1 Bringing cost of production and demand together (as opposed to the one-sided emphases of Ricardo and Jevons, respectively).
2 Hence supply and demand curves, intersecting at equilibrium, each in turn aligned to the margin, substitution and, putting these together, substitution at the margin.
3 The element of time and the distinction between short and long runs, together with the idea of quasi-rent and representative firm.
4 Consumer surplus and an analytical breach with the necessary virtues of laissez-faire.
5 The significance of monopoly, increasing returns and external economies.
6 Elasticity as a tool of analysis.

To a greater or lesser extent, these remain bread and butter techniques and concepts for the modern economist 100 years and more after Marshall first formulated them. It certainly is an achievement for Marshall to have promoted them all in a single text. But Keynes adds a seventh contribution, pointing to Marshall's historical treatment, which 'led him to attach great importance to the historical background as a corrective to the idea that the axioms of to-day are permanent. He was also dissatisfied with the learned but half-muddled work of the German historical school', p. 46.

Apart from bearing no relationship to modern concerns, nor to the other six, Keynes' observation signifies Marshall's and his own emphasis on addressing the relationship between the formal apparatus of economics and its historical content, see also Chapter 14. More personally, as Keynes (1925, p. 12) puts it, 'the master-economist must possess a rare *combination* of gifts.

He must reach a high standard in several different directions and must combine talents not often found together. He must be mathematician, historian, statesman, philosopher ... Much, but not all, of this ideal many-sidedness Marshall possessed'. This all points to a major tension within Marshall's endeavours. Certainly, he was mightily gifted across the qualities that Keynes deemed to be necessary. His *Principles* begins with references to Herbert Spencer and Hegel. He also indicates that the subject matter of economics should include the forming of character, the degradation attached to poverty, the significance of religious motives, the inevitability of lower classes and the greater deliberation of choice rather than its debasement to purely economic motives. But it is also apparent for Marshall that, in order to establish economics as a discipline, it is necessary that it be underpinned by a set of principles however much these might need to be qualified by historical circumstances.

Indeed, in his inaugural lecture upon appointment at Cambridge in 1885, Marshall (1925a) refers to such principles as an 'organon', as yet in the process of being discovered and formulated. It does not contain universal truths, but is rather a tool for investigating concrete circumstances, in which its principles are modified by context and by appeal to analogy with the theory of mechanics. Such reservations should not be taken to the point of denying universal principles altogether in deference to atheoretical, historical specificity – his reason for antipathy to the Historical School. Further, whilst the organon might ultimately be presented in entirely formal terms, this is best set aside for the moment whether to aid investigation or, possibly, acceptability. Indeed, for Marshall (1925a, p. 159), 'While attributing this high and transcendent universality to the central scheme of economic reasoning, we may not assign any universality to economic dogmas. For that part of economic doctrine, which alone can claim universality, has no dogmas. It is not a body of concrete truth, but an engine for the discovery of concrete truth, similar to, say, the theory of mechanics'.[6] Yet there is a danger that, pp. 159–60:

> impetuous people would rush to the conclusion that there was no universal organon of mechanical reasoning. This is exactly the mistake ... made by the extreme of the "real" or historical school of German economists. Ultimately part of this organon will no doubt be presented as a perfectly pure or abstract theory. But at present, while we are feeling our way, it seems best to sacrifice generality of form to some extent, and to conform to the modes of expression adopted by the older economists.

Further, in his *Principles*, Marshall emphasises that the virtues of economics as an exact social science leads to a trade-off between that exactitude and its applicability, which can only be settled on a case-by-case assessment, p. 643:

> Economics has made greater advances than any other branch of the social sciences, because it is more definite and exact than any other. But every widening of its scope involves some loss of this scientific precision;

and the question whether that loss is greater or less than the gain ... is not to be decided by any hard and fast rule.

The putative trade-off between scope and exactitude of marginalist principles is crucial to the understanding of 'economics imperialism' currently taking place in and around economics, see Fine and Milonakis (2009), in taking the trade-off in favour of scope far beyond what Marshall could have envisaged, let alone allowed. But to make that trade-off at all, the principles had first to be put in place and to be accepted as legitimate with some degree of applicability – the task that Marshall set himself.

Thus, two important conclusions can be drawn from Marshall's *Principles*. On the one hand, he wished to posit these as part and parcel of establishing economics as a discipline with an analytical, as opposed to a historical, content. On the other hand, and equally important, such principles were qualified by a thicket of caveats. For the use of mathematics, for example, Marshall could hardly be accused of being inadequately trained as he finished in second place in his degree in mathematics at Cambridge. His reading of Mill's *Principles* is annotated with the attempted mathematical representation of his propositions, Groenewegen (1995, p. 147). As Keynes (1925, p. 34) observes, Marshall was committed to the use of mathematics, but only when it was grounded in reality.[7] Significantly, the vast majority of the mathematical treatment in the *Principles* is deliberately assigned to appendices or footnotes, and Marshall was committed to the idea that arguments in economics should be able to be formulated in common language, not least as a 'reality check'.

In part, this reflects the tension between the perceived excessive relativism of the German Historical School and the excessive formalism of Jevons (1957, pp. vii, xxi) and Walras (1954 [1874], pp. 70, 71), for whom economics resembles the physico-mathematical sciences, leading Jevons to conclude that Mill and Cairness are correct in using the abstract/deductive method, pp. 16, 17, see also Chapter 3, Section 2. In contrast, for Marshall (1925b, p. 309), there needs to be an inextricable balance between deductive and inductive methods:[8]

> Each study supplements the other: there is no rivalry or opposition between them; every genuine student of economics sometimes uses the inductive method and sometimes the analytical, and nearly always both of them together. There is a difference in proportion between different students; as one may eat more solid food and another may drink more fluid: but every one must both eat and drink under pain of starving or dying of thirst.

Further, in his *Principles*, he asserts that 'It is obvious that there is no room in economics for long trains of deductive reasoning; no economist, not even Ricardo, attempted them', p. 644.[9]

Interestingly, despite Jevons' position on economics as a deductive science, Hutchison (2000) does not assign him to the camp of the 'ultras'. This is because the principles in Jevons' *Theory* are deemed to be concerned with what we would now term microeconomics, and that he was far more inductive in his contributions on macro, as in the identification of, and explanation for, major aggregate economic fluctuations. Apart from resolving the tension between induction and deduction in this way (an artificial separation between, and assignment to, macro and micro, respectively), this highlights the same issue for Marshall. His own *Principles* never move beyond the micro; they are partial equilibrium par excellence.[10] This is despite his intentions otherwise – a second volume was projected to deal with macro issues in the broadest sense, but it never materialised. As Groenewegen (1995, p. 430) reports:

> In a resumé of the twenty years which followed first publication of the first volume, Marshall explicitly abandoned his proposed second volume, suggesting by way of replacement, more or less independent volumes on *National Industries and Trade* and *Money, Credit and Employment*. In recognition of this change of policy, the Volume I was removed from the spine where it had featured for the previous five editions, and the scope of the work was explicitly re-defined as a self-standing volume of foundations.

Indeed, 'Marshall reserved questions of the state, money, international trade, combinations and trusts for his second volume, [and] he invariably reminded readers of his completed first volume that all the solutions presented were provisional in the absence of that discussion', p. 788. The failure to move to complete that second volume does not necessarily reflect the obsessive preoccupation of a genius in refining his existing *magnus opus*, Groenewegen (1995, p. 437) drawing on Stigler. The reason is surely the difficulty, if not impossibility, of Marshall turning such shaky foundations into a completed structure, if remaining committed to his analytical principles. As Hutchison (2000, p. 277) reports, *none* of Menger, Walras and Marshall was able to complete works shifting from micro to macro (simply incorporating money, for example, surely a minimal concession to realism).

In these respects, the tensions between micro and macro go far beyond the 'aggregation problem', the term by which they would primarily be addressed in today's mainstream economics. For, first, the core focus on an individual maximising a given utility is too narrow a compass for Marshall. There are other motives and, although some may be appropriately examined under economics, not all can be, and nor can their interaction – see Marshall (1925a, pp. 161 fwd), for example, where he takes economics to be the study of those motives measurable against money. Second, there is the issue of what falls under the scope of economic analysis. Whilst, in principle, economic motives and behaviour can apply to all goods and actions, the analysis in practice tends to presume that it is merely commodities or the market to which they are applicable. Third, as already recognised, these are different examples of the trade-off between general principles and applicability. To the extent that the scope of economics is limited, it cannot be readily and legitimately translated into an analysis of the functioning of the economy as a whole because of the inevitability of intervention of non-economic behaviour and factors.[11]

In this light, Marshall's choice of title of his *Principles* is symbolic, as he replaces political economy with economics, as he did to public notice in his inaugural lecture of 1885. Jevons (1957, pp. xiv–xv), for example, who retained the political if only in name, in his own *Theory*, writes in the Preface to his second edition that 'Among minor alterations, I may mention the substitution for the name Political Economy of the single convenient term *Economics*. I cannot help thinking that it would be well to discard, as quickly as possible, the old troublesome double-worded name of our Science ... It is thus to be hoped that *Economics* will become the recognized name of a science ... Though employing the new name in the text, it was obviously undesirable to alter the title-page of the book'. By contrast, Marshall's excision was intended to dissociate the subject from party-political considerations: 'It was never intended as a means to narrow the scope of the subject or to divide it artificially into an "art" and a "science"', Groenewegen (1995, p. 761). Nonetheless, and revealing the tensions in Marshall's approach to establishing economics as a discipline, 'This is not to deny that ... Marshall was ambivalent in his aims and, occasionally, particularly when it suited his argument, could support the position of economist qua economist'.

Fourth, but now focusing on tensions within economic analysis itself in moving from micro to macro, there is the problem of distribution (into wages, profits and rents). As made apparent by Clark (1891), not least in communication and dispute with Marshall, Groenewegen (1995, p. 418), one of the implications of marginalism is that wages, profits and rents are determined in exactly the same way, just like the price for any other good. They are all rents at the margin of use. As Fine (1983, p. 139) puts it:

> One crucial logical implication of the marginalist system is that the different sources of factor income are conceptually distinguishable only in so far as the conditions governing supply and demand are differentiated. This is why Hobson (1891) refers to the 'the law of the three rents' and Clark (1891) sees 'distribution as determined by a law of rent' ... This involves what Fetter (1901) termed 'the passing of the old rent concept'.

In short, everything becomes rent-like and so rent (and land) becomes indistinguishable from wages (labour) and profits (capital). As Marshall (1892, p. 512) indicates in terms of his differences with Ricardo:[12]

> Ricardo's teachings on rent do not appear to him [Cunningham] to have the same general import as they do to me. For I regard them as containing a living principle applicable, with proper modifications, to the income derived from almost every variety of Differential Advantage for production: and applicable also under almost every variety of rights as

to property, dues, and freedom of action, whether those rights be upheld by law or by custom: while he regards them as applicable only to the rents of farms.

This then goes against the classical tradition and, it should be added, the common sense realism that labour, capital and land are significantly different from one another. Accordingly, wages, profits and rent should be determined by different principles or, at least, by principles that recognise their differences in a substantive fashion. Marshall, then – somewhat unfairly in view of his own failings in this respect – finds little in Jevons to advance his own thinking, especially with respect to distribution theory, with which he 'was experiencing real difficulties', Groenewegen (1995, p. 159). To some extent, Marshall escaped this conundrum by remaining at the level of partial equilibrium. The market for labour was hardly going to be reducible to a physical input as far as he was concerned. Rent corresponded to a fixed factor of production, capital to one only temporarily so. Nonetheless, it was in part, rent-like, commanding by way of compromise a 'quasi-rent' (a term invented by Marshall) in the short run. In short, Marshall's principles did not allow him to deal with distribution, a significant issue within political economy at his time of writing. And, whilst he did emphasise the passage of time as an economic factor, not least with the idea of a quasi-rent, both a focus upon (partial) equilibrium and otherwise unchanging conditions of supply and demand rendered any serious treatment impossible, apart from in appeal to those factors that fall outside his putative organon.

There is little doubt that Marshall was determined to establish analytical principles for the professionalisation and application of economic theory, especially in the context of market society. Such analysis might be able to stand alone and trump the apparent intervention of other explanatory factors. As he puts, it in the case of India, Marshall (1996, p. 209) cited in Mirowski (2000, p. 923):

My information has been got gradually, a great deal of it from conversation; I have crossexamined people (normally conversant with India) who have started by saying that prices & wages in India were ruled by custom & have got them to admit that the custom always changed in substance, if not in outward form, whenever there was any considerable Ricardo-economic reason why it shd.

It is, perhaps, though, to go too far in concluding, as does Mirowski that, pp. 922–3:

Contrary to his usual public image, Alfred Marshall serves conveniently to reveal the extent to which 'custom' and 'culture' were to be relegated to the status of epiphenomena in the conceptual hierarchy of neoclassical causal principles.

For Marshall was acutely aware of the limitations of such an exercise of reduction to the economic. In case of consumption, for example, he advises in his *Principles* that:[13]

> The higher study of consumption must come after, and not before, the main body of economic analysis; and though it may have its beginning within the proper domain of economics, it cannot find its conclusion there, but must extend far beyond.

Thus, the study of consumption through marginalism is partial *and* at a lower level. Paradoxically, Marshall's strongly and frequently stated reservations over a purely deductive, mathematical approach, without realism, insisting upon a more rounded individual and a sense of the historical, had the effect of smoothing the way for such a pure notion of economics as a science to be adopted. As it were, Marshall offers an organon complemented by the traditional concerns of political economy and historical considerations, so it should be accepted in view of his authority and his reservations over substance and scope. Further, Yonay (1998, p. 35) draws on Jha (1973) to observe that the neoclassical economics of the decades around the turn of the century were supportive of trade unions and state intervention, especially in the context of unemployment and poverty. Marshall more than followed suit, and was selected to preside, for example, over the annual congress of the co-operative movement, Groenewegen (1995, p. 455). Marshall's genuinely held postures in these respects rendered more acceptable the promotion of what was to become standard microeconomics, precisely because he allayed the fears of those who shared his methodological concerns.

Pearson (2004) points to the strength of attention to motives other than self-interest at the time of the marginalist revolution, especially amongst the marginalist themselves. This is so for Marshall, pp. 34–7, but also for Walras, for example, who complements the psychology of self-interest in his *Studies in Social Economy*: 'with love, with amity, with the affection that joins us to kin, with charity, with enthusiasm for the homeland and for humanity', p. 31. And, for Taussig, who edited the *Quarterly Journal of Economics* from 1896 to 1936, and whose *Principles of Economics* was the main textbook in the USA in parallel with Marshall's *Principles*, and in print from 1911 to 1945, nothing but self-interest reigned within it. In other writings, however, he referred to the altruistic impulse, philanthropy and public spirit, the instinct of devotion, duty and social solidarity, pp. 37–8. As Maloney (1985, p. 93) puts it, with the exception of Edgeworth:

> Some of the English marginalists identified themselves with utilitarianism; others opposed it. But all saw modern economic theory as freed from its methodological limits and ... from its ideological grip.

In other words, in contrast to the original or 'early' marginalists (Jevons, Walras and Menger), the 'old' marginalism gathered around Marshall was one that recognised and accepted its own limitations. Yonay (1998, p. 48) adopts a particularly strong position in this respect, suggesting that marginalism in the UK and the US was well 'aware of the complexities of human nature and of the major role that institutions play in shaping human behavior. It saw historical studies as an integral part of economic science'. Indeed, this is so much so that he concludes that it is wrong to see today's neoclassicals as the natural outgrowth of the old, Marshallian marginalism, and more as a departure from it.[14] The same does not apply to the early marginalists – especially Jevons and Walras – whose works can certainly be considered precursors, albeit in different ways, of recent, postwar developments in neoclassical theory, see Section 2 above.

4 ... to vulgar vultures?

Marshall, then, set an analytical agenda of discovering and formalising economic laws as the way of establishing economics as a discipline distinct from others. The subsequent passage from old marginalism, as Yonay (1998) would have it, to modern neoclassical economics is easily read and traced as one with two fundamental, separate but closely related, characteristics: one is the reduction of such economic theory in its conceptual content; the other is to become oblivious to the limitations of, and reservations over, the applicability of such theory. In other words, the theory first becomes an object of analysis in its own right, and then is applied without regard to its weaknesses gathered in pursuit of that object

In this light, consider the contribution of John Neville Keynes (1852–1949), Maynard's father, whose methodological treatise *The Scope and Method of Political Economy* (1997) appeared in 1890, the same year as Marshall's *Principles*. Whilst, at least in part an unwilling protégé to Marshall, Maloney (1985, p. 60) and Groenewegen (1995), Marshall read (if not vetted) Keynes' text that is adjudged by Hutchison (2000, pp. 4–5) to have been the only book on the methodology of economics to be published before 1970. Such a conclusion depends on what counts as a book exclusively on methodology.[15] But it is indicative both of the extent to which methodological questions were either ignored for being too uncomfortable for the direction being taken by economic theory, or else considered to be settled, subject to a few minor details. It is an appropriate coincidence, though, that both books should appear in the same year – Marshall offering the principles and Keynes the underlying methodology, although not without tension between the two of a complex nature. For whilst Keynes seems to go beyond Marshall in pushing for the scope of application of the latter's principles with weaker if continuing qualifications, Marshall seems to have exhibited a greater commitment in practice to have those principles established.

Keynes' definition of the scope of political economy or economics remains broad, concerning 'substantive *wealth*' and activities around its creation, appropriation and accumulation, and corresponding institutions and customs, p. 2. A sharp distinction is drawn between two methods – the positive, abstract and deductive, as opposed to the ethical, realistic, and inductive, pp. 2–3. But this is more a matter of principle than of practice, for 'It should be distinctly understood that this sharp contrast is not to be found in the actual economic writings of the best economists of either school', p. 10. Indeed, the deductive method is not entirely speculative or oblivious to the real world, since 'observation guides the economist in his original choice of premises', p. 228, and the Historical School necessarily draws upon deductive inferences, Chapter IX; it is also necessary to assess approximation to reality in *ceteris paribus* assumptions, p. 230, and for the economist to use 'observation in order to illustrate, test, and confirm his deductive inferences', p. 232.[16] Critics of political economy as a goal in itself commit 'the single error ... of mistaking a part for the whole, and imagining political economy to end as well as begin with mere abstractions', p. 118. Rather, realism is necessary in the sense of developing theory appropriate to the relevant causal factors, which are generally interdependent across the social sciences. But this is not to deny separate disciplinary treatments, in order that they can complement one another in their interdependence, p. 135ff. Further, the idea of pure self-interest is rejected, since non-economic motives enter into consideration, such as love of country and public spirit, as well as co-operation and solidarity amongst the labouring classes, pp. 131–2.

Whilst this is all consistent with Marshall, there is more besides that pushes further in pursuit of an abstract economics (as it was to become). Thus, it is asserted that the possibility of political economy without passing ethical judgements seems to be a 'truism', p. 40. Keynes points explicitly to the distinction between positive and normative economics that came to be a core component of economic methodology over the next century. This is significant in itself, as well as in pushing the particular form of positive economics associated with marginalism and its universal principles.

Keynes, then, in trying to assert the necessity of building an independent science of political economy, takes one step towards – or is it just one step away from? – accepting the necessity and not just the possibility of a purely deductive, economic approach. For 'whilst the study of economic phenomena cannot be completed without taking account of the influence exerted on the industrial world by social facts of various kinds, it is nevertheless both practicable and desirable to recognise a distinct systematized body of knowledge, which is primarily and directly concerned with economic phenomena alone', p. 114. It is even suggested that such an approach is closely related to the strength of economic as opposed to other motives, so that it serves as an approximation that can be very close to reality as in the study of stock markets, p. 120. This is surely a proposition with which his son was to reveal profound disagreement, in view of his own treatment of waves of expectations and their impact upon macro-functioning.[17]

Thus, the father draws 'the distinction between abstract and concrete economics', p. 299, with the latter based on the former, taking account of specific circumstances. The abstract is the '*instrument* of universal application ... principles that are universal in the sense of pervading all economic reasoning', p. 300, see also p. 311. This includes 'the fundamental conceptions of the science, such as utility, wealth, value, measure of capital, and the like'. Thus, Jevon's 'law of the variation of utility ... is of the greatest importance in the whole theory of distribution', and 'the aid which a unit of labour ... can afford to capital ... diminishes as the number of units is increased. The truth of this elementary principle is quite independent of social institutions and economic habits', p. 311. And Ricardian rent theory 'may even be said to hold good in a socialistic community, for the differential profit does not cease to exist by being ignored or by being municipalised or nationalised', although 'the actual payments made by the cultivators of the soil, is a relative doctrine'.

Not surprisingly, then, current economic theories are applicable to earlier periods of history, p. 302, and so '*the undesirability of limiting political economy to the theory of modern* commerce', p. 306. More specifically, 'the laws of supply and demand' have 'a very wide application indeed. These laws work themselves out differently under different conditions, and in particular there are differences in the rapidity with which they operate. Their operation may, however, be beneath the surface even in states of society where custom exerts the most powerful sway', p. 314. It is not clear whether this involves some underlying notion of long run equilibrium but, if so, it would beg the question of the stability of the powerful customs over the time taken to get there!

This all places economics in a particular relationship to the historical and economic history, for: 'The propositions of economic history are accordingly statements of particular concrete facts; economic theory, on the other hand, is concerned with the establishment of general laws', p. 268. Economic theories can be illustrated by history, and the latter be used to question and even to suggest economic theories. But, by contrast, because of its abstract concepts, such as utility, value and capital, economics is universally applicable. Indeed, the historical approach to economics is rejected because of its failure to accept the possibility of universal laws, and because it has not in any case provided a historically specific economics of its own, Chapter IX. Ultimately, Keynes accepts that the premises of deductive political economy are not fixed but for a few *exceptions* such as the law of diminishing utility, Appendix 4. And, by the same token, in his entry for the Palgrave on the Principle of Relativity in Political Economy (or lack of universal truths as postured by the Historical School), Keynes concludes that 'relativity cannot be extended to the ultimate analysis of the fundamental conceptions of the [economic] science', Appendix 5.

Keynes gives examples of what must be interpreted as Marshall's organon, 'the universal in the sense that they pervade all economic reasoning'. Thus, there is 'the law of variation of utility with quantity of commodity, and the principle that every man so far as he is free to choose will choose the greater apparent good'. These 'may be given as examples of fundamental economic principles, which, in the words of Jevons, "are so widely true and applicable that they may be considered universally true as regards human nature"'. Similarly, 'the LAW OF SUBSTITUTION in the form that where different methods of production are available for obtaining a given result, the one that can do the work the most cheaply will in time supersede the others'. And, drawing as before on the universal appeal of Ricardian rent theory, it is claimed that 'the theory of economic rent in its most generalised form ... [has] no limitation to its applicability'. And last but by no means least, there are on offer the general, universal and abstract principles that underpin 'the laws of SUPPLY AND DEMAND', Appendix 5.

Here, then, Marshall's principles are paraded as universal truths. Whatever their validity, there is the striking claim for universal application of those principles that are clearly drawn from perusal of a far from universal (capitalist) market economy, and to which, in some instances such as supply and demand, they can only really apply. There is equally confusion over the distinction between profit and rent. Considering their lightness, it is hardly surprising that Marshall himself should have been disappointed with the results of his principles in being able to address the economy as a whole. As Maloney (1976, p. 450) reports:

> One might say with hindsight that marginalism has not lived up to the expectations placed upon it. In particular, the hopes that it might come to provide an improved scientific basis for macroeconomic policy have been frustrated; and we have it on the authority of Marshall's nephew, C. W. Guillebaud, that this was the greatest single disappointment of Marshall's professional career.

We will take up the issue of disappointment in the context of macroeconomics in Chapter 14, but, as Maloney concludes, the diminishing returns to such propositions in understanding the economy had rapidly become secondary, relative to 'helping or hindering the transformation of economics into a science. To have the right aims counted for more than success in achieving them'. These aims were taken up with a vengeance, not least by Lionel Robbins, see Chapter 12. And such was possible because of the settling of accounts with opponents, the British Historical School, for example, and in the time-honoured fashion of accepting their points and then discarding them, see Chapter 8.

5 Concluding remarks

The differences between Marshall and Keynes can be exaggerated relative to what they share in common – the wish to establish universal deductive principles, qualified by other factors and other methods but with a scope extending beyond contemporary economies. This was all-important, both to be distinctive from the Historical School (and those antagonistic to theory) but also not to alienate those who recognised the latter's worth and that of historical study of specifics. Yet, as Coase (1994, p. 167) suggests, 'John Neville Keynes's references to Marshall in his diaries are uniformly hostile', quoting him as follows: 'Marshall's long disquisitions are very tiresome'; 'Marshall said a good many silly things', and 'I really have not time to be on a Board of which Marshall is a member'.[18] And Marshall clearly perceives himself at odds with Keynes, for, after considerable correspondence between the two on his book, Coase quotes Marshall, 'I find we differ more than I thought', p. 168. Coase identifies the source of their differences as Marshall's greater eclecticism and his not basing himself on a dualism between induction and deduction. Indeed, citing Marshall, 'I take an extreme position as to the *methods & scope* of economics. In my new book I say of *methods* simply that economics has to use every method known to science', p. 168. And, 'You make all your contrasts rather too sharply for me. You talk of the inductive and the deductive methods: whereas I contend that each involves the other, & that historians are always deducing, & even the most deductive writers are always implicitly at least basing themselves on observed facts', p. 169. But possibly most revealing of the differences in approach between Marshall and Keynes is to be found in a letter from Marshall to – of all people – the historical economist Foxwell,[19] to whom he suggests that Keynes departs too far from the Historical School! He writes, 'Most of the suggestions which I made on the proofs of Keynes's *Scope and Method* were aimed at bringing it more into harmony with the views of Schmoller. Some were accepted. But it still remains true that as regards method I regard myself midway between Keynes+Sidgwick+Cairnes and Schmoller+Ashley', pp. 170–1.

In this light, it would be all too easy to interpret Keynes' methodology and universal principles as pushing beyond what was acceptable to Marshall. But the situation is more complicated because, in practice, Marshall was determined to have his principles accepted as the pre-condition of a more rounded approach. Nor was this some academic matter alone, since it affected the appointment of Marshall's successor, with Marshall successfully favouring Pigou at the expense of Foxwell, for whom Marshall even blocked the endowment of a new Chair. Coase (1994, p. 152) reports that 'Marshall apparently did everything in his power to ensure that Pigou was selected'. Also, 'Marshall did not share Foxwell's antipathy to theory or his enthusiasm for the historical approach in economics. Foxwell's specialty, the history of economic thought, was to Marshall a subject of secondary importance', p. 158. Most revealing of the dissonance between method in principle and in practice is Marshall's letter to Keynes, on the proposal that a Chair be endowed for Foxwell, in which he quotes the following extract of a letter to someone who may have helped to bring it about: 'Keynes has perhaps a higher opinion of the importance of Foxwell's specialty to Cambridge than I have', p. 161. And Marshall goes on with the heaviest of criticism of Foxwell for holding back youth, imposing judgements rather than developing skills, and changing his own views to the opposite every six months.[20]

In the sweep of the history of economic thought, these paradoxes and tensions reflect intellectual and personal features unique to Cambridge, and are of lesser importance than observing the dual impact of Marshall and Keynes together on economic principles and economic methodology, whatever their own disagreements and reservations in principle and practice, all of which were soon to be discarded in favour or universal, deductive principles, etc. Marshall, with Keynes as his foil, was a considerable analytical acrobat, balancing classical political economy with marginalism, deduction with induction, mathematical methods with less formal discourse, the economic with the non-economic, the historical with the universal, partial and general equilibrium, micro and macro, etc. In all of this, then, it is appropriate to acknowledge that Marshall recognised the strength of argument of the Historical School(s) but that he was also committed to establishing a core of deductive principles. As he told Edgeworth, 'theory alone was empty, while empirical investigations without theory were suspect; hence only the interweaving of theory and evidence constituted "economics proper"', Sutton (2000, p. 13) cited in Ekelund and Hébert (2002, p. 209). For Hodgson (2005, p. 123), this means that he 'tried to steer an intermediate position between deductivism and empiricism'. But as a description of Marshall himself, and certainly of his influence, it is more appropriate to see him as seeking to hold to both (or more) positions simultaneously. This made it all the easier for his followers to discard the empirical and historical side of his approach in deference to his deductivism, without due regard to his own reservations, let alone those of others – especially the Historical School and 'the näive empiricist views in their midst', p. 122. In this light, there is some validity to the conclusion drawn by Ekelund and Hébert (2002, p. 212), that 'The Marshallian method, which combined inductive theory and deductive empiricism, was ultimately the impetus to the development of econometrics and to the modern practice of economics'.

But it is misleading if these later developments are only seen as perfecting Marshall rather than also breaking with him, as will be seen in later chapters, as the inductive gave way more or less in an absolute way to the deductive within the discipline of economics. With the deductive increasingly attached to the empirical evidence through econometrics, as a putative way of testing theories, economics wedded itself to a particular form of positivism. Theoretically, the result is apparent in the corresponding reliance upon economics as choice, and upon economic rationality in its own right, independent of qualification by other motives and the non-economic. In this way, Marshall's organon becomes a toolkit without qualification, the now familiar technical apparatus of utility and production functions. Indeed, not only does the organon become detached from history, but, following the cliometrics revolution of the 1960s, it is also enabled to do history, ironically alongside or in place of the economic history that emerged in parallel with Marshall's

marginalism, both in opposition to that marginalism and in correct anticipation of what it was liable to become in application to economic history.
Referring to Robinson Crusoe's choices over what to take from the ship-
wreck, the latter day cliometrician, McCloskey (1996, p. 158), concludes that:

> It goes without saying that political issues are raised when the historian
> reaches for the choice-as-economics tool. The tool is of course shaped by
> ideology. But then it would be naïve to claim that some other tool is not.
> Carefully handled the tool can inscribe good history, without injuring
> the writer or reader. The neoclassical theory of choice is a sweet little
> saw and hammer set, just the one to take for many historical uses, like
> the tools that rational Crusoe chose to take in his few, scarce hours on
> the wreck.

But this is to anticipate the reduction of the market, and the non-market
(looting the wreck), as well as of the historical, to the economic rationality of
the isolated individual. This gives rise to economics imperialism in general,
Fine and Milonakis (2009), and its application to history in particular (following the cliometrics revolution of the 1960s) to be covered in Milonakis
and Fine (forthcoming). In the mainstream economics of today, Marshall's
old marginalism is to be found only in the form of a reductionism that he
was himself careful and committed to reject.

8   British historical economics and the birth of economic history

'The success of the historical economists in creating a discipline of economic history removed them from being considered economists. Instead of revolutionizing all economic study, the historical economists subdivided the subject. The critic of economic theory who fails to offer a satisfactory alternative theory is soon forgotten in the history of the subject. Those who subdivide a field are honored as founders by the adherents of the subdivision, but are often relegated to obscurity within the core of the subject'.

Koot (1987, p. 187)

1 Introduction

As already argued, classical political economy in general, and Ricardianism in particular, were already in decline by the time of the marginalist revolution, and different schools strived to replace them. Whilst, within economics, marginalism emerged triumphant, and correspondingly dominates the telling of the history of economic thought as the passage to its inevitable victory, this is to overlook the contribution of others and their continuing influence outside economics as a discipline as such. In particular, in the UK, as in Germany, there emerged a Historical School that opposed Ricardian deductivism and, not surprisingly, its marginalist pretender to the crown of political economy.

Mill's attempted reconciliation, Chapter 3, substantively between the objective and subjective theories of value and price, and methodologically between deduction and empiricism, tended to exacerbate the crisis rather than resolve it. Indeed, it was partly Mill's eclectic methodological stance which allowed two of his closest disciples, John Elliot Cairnes and T.E. Cliffe Leslie, to follow radically different approaches in their political economy, thus heralding what might be termed the British *Methodenstreit*. Cairnes, as seen in Chapter 3, was one of the most strident supporters of the abstract/deductive method, whereas Leslie was, after Jones, one of the two originators of the inductive and historical research on the British Isles, Koot (1975, pp. 322–4).

It is against the perspective provided by the developments discussed in Chapter 7 that we turn to the debates around which Marshall was engaged prior to the publication of his *Principles*. In this, muted on his side in typical English fashion, his main protagonists were provided by the British Historical School.[1] The members of the latter include T. E. Cliffe Leslie (1827–82), John Kells Ingram (1823–1907), James Thorold Rogers (1823–90), Arnold Toynbee (1852–83), William Cunningham (1840–1919), Herbert Foxwell (1849–1936) and William Ashley (1860–1927). Of them, Cliffe Leslie can be considered as the leading light of the school, while William Ashley was its most prominent member and its most probable leader, if there was to be one. The British *Methodenstreit*, which endured from the 1860s until 1914, Moore (1999, pp. 53–4n), started with the opposing approaches of Cairnes and Leslie, was continued through the exchanges between Leslie and Jevons in the 1870s, and culminated in the battle between Marshall and Cunningham. In Section 2, we elaborate on Leslie's antipathy to deductivism and marginalism in general, and Jevons in particular (with whom he was on cordial terms). His arguments are entirely reasonable from a Marshallian perspective (not wedded to pure deductivism), but are most significant for providing support to a more historical approach to economics and economic history. This itself comes into direct confrontation with Marshall through the personage of William Cunningham, Section 3. Their debate, as always, remained unresolved, other than allowing each, and their followers, to do their own thing. For Marshall, it was to give birth to economic theory without history; for Cunningham it allowed for economic history without theory. The defeat of the British Historical School *within* economics heralded the emergence of economic history as a discipline separate from it. We conclude this chapter with a brief discussion of the first steps of economic history proper in the British Isles.

2 British historicism: T.E. Cliffe Leslie

Cliffe Leslie's main objective, much like the representatives of the German Historical School, was the search for solutions to the pressing problems of England and Ireland. In the 1860s, he concentrated on more inductive studies of wages and prices, while in the 1870s his focus switched to methodological issues and the history of economic thought. At the time of Leslie's writings, both England and Ireland were facing a rapidly deteriorating situation, reflected in the occasionally decreasing living standards of English wage-labourers and Irish cottiers. Ireland, an English colony at that time, was still a backward agrarian society, dominated by small plots and short leases, with subsistence existence of agricultural labourers, and marked by massive emigration to America and a stagnant industry. Under these conditions, Leslie pressed for social reform which included the free transferability of land and security of tenure, and a more balanced economy between agriculture and industry, while emphasising the role of the home market and of the demand side. The vehicle of successful social reform, so he thought, was inductive and historical research. He was guided in this by the more inductive and historical side of both Adam Smith and John Stuart Mill, and by the historical jurisprudence of Sir Henry Maine, Koot (1975) and Moore (1995).[2]

Leslie is considered to have laid 'the foundation of historical economics in England', and his 1876 article, 'On the Philosophical Method of Political Economy', to be its 'classic methodological foundation', Koot (1987, pp. 41, 53). As such, he can be used to dispel myths about the Historical School. This article represents a vehement attack on all aspects of classical political economy, and resembles in many respects similar attacks by the German historicists. On the methodological front, according to Leslie, 'the abstract and a priori method', as exemplified by Cairnes and used especially by Ricardo, 'yields no explanation of the laws determining the nature, the amount, or the distribution of wealth', which represents the basic problem of (classical) political economy, 1876, pp. 15.

As will be apparent, this was not some antediluvian dogma, for he commanded a sophisticated position on the relative merits of induction and deduction, and was certainly not wedded to a purely descriptive approach. Indeed, he seems to have enjoyed an amicable dispute with Jevons on these matters, even if no punches were pulled.[3] We appear to have consulted Jevons' own copy of Leslie (1879b) as a slip, 'From THE AUTHOR', is bound into the volume together with a letter from Leslie to 'My dear Jevons', from 'Union Club, Trafalgar Square, SW', dated 12 June, year not given. It reads, with heavy sarcasm, 'Our notes crossed, as you will have perceived. I shall be very glad if the Spectator gives me and the rest of the world the benefit of your criticism'.[4] Less anecdotally, in print, Leslie (1879c, p. 72) makes it clear that not only does he favour a mix of induction and deduction but that he, and the Historical School, have been falsely interpreted as otherwise by Jevons, who has himself at least in part been persuaded of the need for this.

Thus, Leslie's opposition to Ricardian deductivism does not mean that he was against theorising in general and deduction as such in particular. He makes this clear in reply to Jevons, where he accuses him of misinterpretation of his and the Historical School's views, Leslie (1879c, p. 72):

> The order which the evolution of human wants follows is one of the inquiries that await a rising historical and inductive school of economists, which happily has no opposition to encounter from Mr. Jevons. But with respect to the deductive method, Mr. Jevons does not quite fairly represent the view of that school when he says, 'I disagree altogether with my friend, Mr. Leslie; he is in favour of simple deletion; I am for thorough reform and reconstruction'. We are, it is true, for deletion of the deductive method of Ricardo: that is to say, of deduction from unverified assumptions respecting 'natural values, natural wages, and natural profits'. But we are not against deduction in the sense of inference from true generalizations and principles, though we regard the urgent work of the present as induction, and view long trains of deduction with suspicion.

Leslie has no problem with theory as long as it is relevant to the object of study.

However, such a theory must be anchored in reality and be driven by incorporation of the relevant factors rather than by abstract deduction from 'unverified assumptions', Leslie (1879a, p. 10):

> Political economy is thus a department of the science of society which selects a special class of social phenomena for special investigation, but for this purpose must investigate all the forces and laws by which they are governed. The deductive economist misconceives altogether the method of isolation permissible in philosophy ... To isolate a single force, even if a real force and not a mere abstraction, and to call deductions from it alone the laws of wealth, can lead only to error, and is radically unscientific.

Substantively, Leslie (1875) illustrates the limits of the abstract/deductive method as used by Ricardo by attacking the way in which he tackled what he considered as the basic problem of political economy, i.e. the problem of production and distribution of wealth. The way classical theory deals with this problem, he maintains, is 'illusory' and 'throws ... hardly any light on the nature of wealth'. At the same time, Mill's and Senior's *homo economicus*, i.e. the depiction of man as driven mostly by the principle of 'the desire to possess wealth', also comes under heavy fire. 'Closely connected with the illusory exposition of the nature of wealth', says Leslie, 'is the doctrine of abstract political economy, that the mental principle which leads to its production and accumulation "is the desire for wealth"'. This, however, represents a gross oversimplification of reality, since Leslie (1880, p. 142) is aware of the relativity of economic doctrines, suggesting:

> Economic theories and systems may be regarded in several different lights: (1) in reference to their causes, as the products of particular social, political, and physical conditions of thought; (2) in reference to their truth or error; (3) as factors in the formation of public opinion and policy.

Such an approach would surely have inculcated a healthy scepticism towards the universal truths being peddled by the deductivist approach to economics. Economic analysis for Leslie is contextually influenced.

Far, then, from being anti-theoretical, Leslie as one of the chief representatives of the British Historical School can be deemed to have been in defence of theory in two respects. First, the school accepted theory, but only as long as it was rooted in reasonable assumptions for the object of study. Second, as we will see, it defended such theory against appropriation and misinterpretation as purely deductive reasoning. Why, then, is the Historical School considered to be purely or primarily descriptive and without theory? One reason is because of the long tracts that they offer on the movement and history of prices, and the geography and national conditions influencing production. These would surely test the patience of any reader seeking to tease out analytical principles. But these contributions need to be considered with some sensitivity. They reflect not only an older tradition within political economy itself, but also an attachment to the mode of investigation and presentation associated with Adam Smith as opposed to David Ricardo. Thus Leslie (1870, p. 148) in his defence of 'The Political Economy of Adam Smith', opens by citing the interpretation that:

> Political Economy belongs to no nation; it is of no country. It is the science of the rules for the production, the accumulation, the distribution, and the consumption of wealth. It will assert itself whether you wish it or not. It is founded on the attributes of the human mind, and no power can change it.

The quotation is from Robert Lowe in a speech delivered in support of the Irish Land Bill. The reference is returned to frequently by Leslie in his writings, in order to demonstrate how the political economy of Adam Smith is being misrepresented and is also thereby being used as a prop for universalising economic theory.[5]

In short, for Leslie, Adam Smith and political economy more generally is being interpreted as 'a body of necessary and universal truth, founded on invariable laws of nature, and deduced from the constitution of the human mind'. Although this refers *back* to how Adam Smith is being interpreted and abused, it also reflects a remarkable anticipation of the direction being taken by marginalist economics. Leslie, on the other hand, asserts:

> I venture to maintain, to the contrary, that Political Economy is not a body of natural laws in the true sense, or of universal and immutable truths, but an assemblage of speculations and doctrines which are the result of a particular history, coloured even by the history and character of its chief writers; that, so far from being of no country, and unchangeable from age to age, it has varied much in different ages and countries, and even with different expositors in the same age and country.

Thus, not only do economic causes change across history, so do interpretations of them, so that all must be treated with caution.

The best way of doing this is by what might be termed a reality check – of following empirical movements and the proximate causes for them. Leslie (1873, p. 378), for example, questions the standardised assumptions concerning the equalisation of wages and profits by competition on such terms:

> Economists have been accustomed to assume that wages on the one hand and profits on the other are, allowing for differences in skill, and so forth, equalized by competition, and that neither wages nor profits can

anywhere rise above 'the average rate' without a consequent influx of labour or of capital bringing things to a level. Had economists, however, in place of reasoning from an assumption, examined the facts connected with the rate of wages, they would have found, from authentic statistics, the actual differences so great, even in the same occupation, that they are double in one place what they are in another.

This displays not only that Leslie is aware of the arguments concerning the role of competition, but also that its operation and impact, in conjunction with other factors, needs to be investigated empirically prior to making assumptions.

As far as his own positive contribution is concerned, Leslie's focus of attention is once again the issue of evolution and development. He treats social progress, through the succession of 'the hunting, pastoral, agricultural, and commercial states', as a process involving all its multi-faceted aspects: the economical, moral, intellectual, legal and political, Leslie (1876, p. 190). 'Tradition, custom, law, political institutions, religion and moral sentiment' all play a crucial role in the process of social evolution. In other words, what Leslie calls for is a political economy of the evolution of social institutions. For this reason, the 'philosophical method of political economy must be one which expounds this evolution'. In other words, it 'must be historical, and must trace the connexion between the economical and the other phases of national history'.

And, from his writings, it is also apparent that Leslie studied available political economy extensively and in depth, in order to deploy theory in its proper context. He not only defends Adam Smith against false interpretations, but also provides surveys of political economy in other countries, such as Germany and the USA, Leslie (1875 and 1880, respectively). The latter, for example, is distinguished by four features: a rejection of Malthusianism, a heavy presence of preacher-economists (or religious content to economic studies, and an ethical pre-cursor to American institutionalism), an absence of long chains of deductive reasoning, and (significant for what follows) a close attention to the dynamic of industry and its wide variations across time and place, with corresponding effects on the price level. Discussion of theory is never far from the facts and circumstances to which it is attached.

Inevitably, this all reflects and is bound to deeper methodological issues, somewhat crudely compartmentalised at times by Leslie into an opposition between induction and deduction, for which he sees Adam Smith as the original source, see Chapter 2, Section 3. For Leslie (1870, p. 151):[6]

> The peculiarity of Adam Smith's philosophy is, that it combines these two opposite methods, and hence it is that we have two systems of political economy claiming descent from him – one, of which Mr. Ricardo was the founder, reasoning entirely from hypothetical laws or principles of nature, and discarding induction not only for the ascertainment

of its premises, but even for the verification of its deductive conclusions; the other – of which Malthus in the generation after Adam Smith, and Mr. Mill in our own, may be taken as representatives – combining like Adam Smith himself, the à priori and the inductive methods, reasoning sometimes, it is true, from pure hypotheses, but also from experience, and shrinking from no corrections which the test of experience may require in deductions. Of the two schools, distinguished by their methods, the first finds in assumptions respecting the nature of man, and the course of conduct it prompts, a complete 'natural' organization of the economic world, and aims at the discovery of 'natural prices,' 'natural wages,' and 'natural profits.'

Significantly, in contrast to a pure method of deduction, there is no place in Leslie's account for a pure method of induction. Apart from anticipating natural organisation (equilibrium) and prices, wages and profits, there is also an anomaly in so far as Adam Smith himself put forward a theory of natural price, etc.

This, however, points to a further reason for the presentation of economic statistics. As Fine (1982) argues, especially in the context of Smith's value theory, any such theory of natural or equilibrium price tends to divide causal factors into those that count in determining it, and those that do not. The latter then become included as factors determining the deviation of equilibrium from its supposedly 'natural' level, see also discussion of Veblen in Chapter 9. But what is the basis for the division between those factors that count towards natural price and others that count towards deviation from it? In the case of Smith, the systematic components derive from a historical understanding of commercial society, one based on the full complement of revenues comprising wages, profits and rents. But, on a reality check, the impact on prices of other factors can be much greater and more long-standing. This is especially true of war and taxation, and the role of the state more generally. Of course, in retrospect, any such factors can be rounded up into a theory of supply and demand in the short to long run. But this itself would involve reductionism to the market of nation and culture, etc., that would hardly be accepted by the Historical School. In short, as Leslie (1876, p. 226–7) eloquently puts it, offering a sensitivity to gender issues:

> The real defect of the treatment by economists of these other principles is, that it is superficial and unphilosophical; that no attempt has been made even to enumerate them adequately, much less to measure their relative force in different states of society; and that they are employed simply to prop up rude generalizations for which the authority of 'laws' is claimed. They serve, along with other conditions, to give some sort of support to saving clauses, – such as 'allowing for differences in the nature of employments,' 'ceteris paribus,' 'in the absence of disturbing causes,' 'making allowances for friction' … A theory surely cannot be

said to interpret the laws regulating the amount of wealth, which takes no account, for instance, either of the causes that make arms the occupation of the best part of the male population of Europe at this day, or, on the other hand, of those which determine the employments of women.

Thus, in short, p. 227:

The truth is, that the whole economy of every nation, as regards the occupations and pursuits of both sexes, the nature, amount, distribution and consumption of wealth, is the result of a long evolution in which there has been both continuity and change, of which the economical side is only a particular aspect or phase. And the laws of which it is the result must be sought in history and the general laws of society and social evolution.

In short, for the British Historical School, and Leslie in particular, no universal laws, but laws (and corresponding methodology and theory) nonetheless.

3 The birth of economic history

Both analytically and professionally, Marshall's concern was to establish economics as a science, albeit complemented by other ingredients and reservations that were subsequently discarded whatever Marshall's own intentions and hopes. The qualifications aside, this inevitably placed him in conflict with the British Historical School, with a simmering debate ultimately coming to a head. Marshall's opposition to William Cunningham – a former student, Cambridge colleague and rival for his chair, committed to the historical approach and strongly opposed to utilitarianism and marginalism in all its forms – is well documented. Maloney (1985, p. 92) suggests 'It can be presumed that no one dared remind Marshall, on his retirement in 1908, that to date Cunningham had written more works of political economy than all other Cambridge dons, living and dead, put together'. Public dispute between the two arose out of Marshall's (1925a) inaugural lecture of 1885. In this, he lavished praise on the Historical School, but in the *past* tense, 'in a decidedly obituary tone', but added the criticism of its lack of theory in the *present* tense, Maloney (1985, p. 99).

Cunningham's (1892b, p. 493) response was to lay out explicitly what he thought to be the stance of the emerging economic principles, especially with respect to their implications for economic history:

The underlying assumption against which I wish to protest is never explicitly formulated by those who rely on it; but it may, I think, be not unfairly expressed in some such terms as these. That the same motives have been at work in all ages, and have produced similar results, and that, therefore, it is possible to formulate economic laws which describe the action of economic causes at all times and in all places ... If this assumption were sound, it would seem to follow that these economic laws could be most conveniently studied in the present, under our own eyes, as it were; but that when once recognised and stated, they serve to explain the past.

Cunningham denies that there is any such 'royal road' to economic and social history, p. 491.[7] And Marshall (1892, p. 507) essentially refuses the challenge to provide one, suggesting that he has been misinterpreted in presuming otherwise. But this is only because other factors are also at work. Otherwise, Marshall is at pains to suggest that economic motives of self-interest may be more applicable than previously thought, as illustrated by the earlier discussion of Ricardian rent theory and, for example, his idea that customary behaviour may reflect or be worked around by it.[8] The main reason, however, for Marshall's response to Cunningham – a rare occasion of his reacting publicly to criticism – is made clear, p. 518:[9]

Thus, his endeavours to interpret me to other people are almost as conspicuous for their industry as for their incorrectness. Some of them may be read by foreign historical economists and others who do not know my views at first hand; and the facts that he is a colleague, and was formerly ... a pupil of mine might reasonably suggest to such readers that he could not fail to have entered into my point of view ... For these reasons I have broken through my rule of not replying to criticisms.

In short, Marshall sought both to put forward his principles and to have them accepted by historical economists other than those who, such as Cunningham, would deny them as a legitimate object of study. This seems to have been the main substantive issue between the two, clouded though it was by other matters, personal and professional, Hodgson (2005, p. 124). As Collini *et al.* (1983, p. 267) conclude:

In the course of the 1880s ... Cunningham became more aggressive still in his criticisms of political economy. He realised that one possible implication of post-Jevonian marginalism was a broadening of the scope of the subject; no longer confined to industrial societies or even to a competitive market, it could arrogate to itself the study of all measurable motives. Cunningham wanted to insist that the price of this increase in theoretical ambition was to reduce even further its purchase on practical problems. 'Political economy in its new-fashioned form gets beyond the old limitations, but only by becoming more and more of a formal science, the relations of which with actual life are more vague and indefinite than ever'. He accordingly confined the science to the purely logical enterprise of deducing a series of timeless relations between axioms, denying altogether that it was appropriate to speak of 'causes' in political economy any more than it was in geometry. Thus gelded, the pure science could be put out to pasture, stripped of its authority to pronounce even upon problems of economic policy.

Methodologically, other than in the belief that there would be some useful irreducible core of economic theory that could be deployed for practical purposes in light of other considerations, there is not too much with which Marshall would disagree. Cunningham underestimated the sway of marginalism, no doubt because of the weaknesses that he identified, which he was sure would limit its influence, and its non-mathematical representation that he perceived as more acceptable, Maloney (1985, p. 115). In any case, his main pre-occupation was to defend a specialised economic history rather than to attack pure deductivism within economics.

His goal was to be realised. In part, this was a consequence of push factors derived from the changing nature of economics as a discipline. The separation of mainstream economics from the historical is closely connected with the birth of economic history as a separate discipline. It was borne out of necessity – as a result of the ahistorical path taken by economics which was symbolised in the aftermath of the *Methodenstreit*. Indeed, separating out economic history seems to have been a deliberate choice on the part of the marginalists, as a response to the critiques expressed by the members of the Historical School against their abstract theorising. Thus, Jevons' (1957, p. xvii) proposed solution in 1879, even before the *Methodenstreit*, was to call for a division of economics. 'Subdivision is the remedy', he proclaims. This is necessary because, pp. xvi–xvii:

> the present chaotic state of Economics arises from the confusing together of several branches of knowledge ... We must distinguish the empirical element from abstract theory, from the applied theory, and from the more detailed art of finance and administration. Thus will arise various sciences, such as commercial statistics, the mathematical theory of economics, systematic and descriptive economics, economic sociology, and fiscal science.

Further, p. 20:

> instead of converting our present science of economics into an historical science, utterly destroying it in the process, I would perfect and develop what we already possess. And at the same time erect a new branch of social science on an historical foundation.

Despite the difference in terminology, Jevons' proposal is similar to Walras' subdivision into pure economics, applied economics and social economics, and Menger's identification of three different branches of the science of the economy (the historical, the theoretical and the practical), Chapter 6. What the three marginalists are calling for is the segmentation of economic science into economic theory or abstract deductive theorising of economic phenomena: applied economics, which would employ the statistical and the historical method in order to apply economic theory to particular conditions, and which would be used as a guide to economic policy; economic history or economic sociology, which would devote itself to the investigation of the laws of economic development; and social economics which would deal with moral issues such as distribution and justice, see also Koot (1987, p. 27).

The marginalists' intent is clear enough, and is made even clearer by Menger in reply to Schmoller. This is offered in his pamphlet *The Errors of the Historical School* (*Die Irrtümer des Historismus*), published in 1884, five years after Jevons' suggestion. It calls for a strict separation of theory from history and statistics. Menger recognises 'the usefulness of the history of public economy as an aid in understanding economic phenomena ... No reasonable person denies the importance of historical studies of research in the field of political economy', translated in Small (1924, p. 225). Be that as it may, Schmoller is wrong to believe that economic history is 'the *descriptive* division of political economy', p. 225. On the contrary, 'his history is not a division of political economy at all, but an auxiliary to economics ... a useful, an indispensable auxiliary, but still an auxiliary', p. 227.

Within a few decades, the marginalists' desire was to materialise.[10] As far as history is concerned, at the beginning of the previous century, the historical economics of the Historical School gradually gave way to economic history proper. This transformation mostly took shape in the British Isles. The British historical economists (Leslie, Ingram, Rogers, Toynbee, Cunningham, Foxwell and Ashley) played the leading role in the birth of economic history as a new discipline in Britain. The last members of the British Historical School, who presided over the transformation of historical economics into economic history, were Cunningham, Foxwell and Ashley.

Following in the footsteps of the German Historical School, and Schmoller in particular, what the members of the British Historical School stood for is a more historical and inductive form of economic science, geared towards practical purposes. But, as seen already in Chapter 5, whilst the trend with the German Historical School was to become more and more theoretical, reaching its theoretical climax in the works of the members of its youngest branch (mostly Weber and Sombart, see Chapter 11), the trend in the British Isles was in the opposite direction. In the work of Rogers and Cunningham, the empiricist drift of the British historical tradition came to a head. Following Leslie's lead, what British historicists target is effectively the economic and social history of institutions in the service of social reform. If the 'national' and the 'social' questions are the prime policy target of the younger German Historical School, the social consequences of the Industrial Revolution became the leitmotif of their Anglo-Irish counterparts, following Toynbee's lead. This was certainly the case with Cunningham's work. His

The Growth of English Trade and Commerce, published in 1882, became the *locus classicus* of the writings of the British Historical School, as well as the foundation stone of economic history as a discipline. Indeed, 'both critics and supporters of William Cunningham agreed that the archdeacon's volumes on English economic history laid the foundation of the discipline in England as an academic field of study', Koot (1987, p. 135). Rogers, on the other hand, although he considered himself an historical economist, was perhaps the first economic historian proper in Britain. In his voluminous *A History of Agriculture and Prices in England*, he concentrated his efforts chiefly on the history of wages and prices. Although at first he believed that his research into the history of prices would lead him to some theoretical generalisations, he was later on to drop this belief, in order to concentrate simply on 'the presentation of the quantitative facts of economic history', Koot (1980, pp. 183–4)

Rogers and Cunningham were instrumental in the emergence of economic history as a separate discipline in other respects as well. With Cunningham's adoption of an ultra-empiricist stance, where facts are supposed to speak for themselves, the drift between historical economics and economic theory became even more pronounced. The reconciliatory stance of both Schmoller in the *Methodenstreit* and Ashley subsequently (see below), and their plea for a combination of the historical method with abstract theory was left behind, and a more hostile approach to economic theorising was adopted. Cunningham's extreme empiricist position in this battle helped to marginalise him further and, with him, the Historical School in general in British academia, Hodgson (2001, p. 111, ch. 8). Marshall played an important part in this process both academically and institutionally, both directly and indirectly through his wide influence and recognition. Although Marshall's stance on the British *Methodenstreit*, as engaged in dispute between him and Cunningham, was generally conciliatory, his own position was firmly on the side of allowing for a separate, abstract theory. His own *Principles* pays testimony to this – hedged though it is with reservations that are easy to overlook – and despite the amount of historical material included especially in the first edition of his book, see previous chapter.

Ashley's academic trajectory is highly symbolic of the role played by historical economics in the British Isles in the birth of economic history as a new discipline. If Cunningham's book became the *locus classicus* of British historical economics, Ashley is appropriately designated as the most prominent member of the school, and the most likely leader, if one is to be identified. Between them, as Price (1900, p. iii), quoted in Harte (1971, p. xxvi) puts it, Cunningham and Ashley 'created Economic History for English students'. Ashley, in particular, became the first professor of economic history in the world in 1892, at Harvard, Koot (1987, pp. 106, 112). Ashley (1893, p. 7) was closer to Schmoller both in his more conciliatory stance in the *Methodenstreit*, ('it is surely time to cry a truce to controversy') as well as in his more general approach, which was more theoretically inclined. He believed that the role of historical inquiry in the work of Schmoller and his followers was to discover generalisations 'as to the character and sequence of the stages of economic development'. The studies of the school, he believed, were collectivist and institutional, and 'the "laws" of which they think are "dynamic" rather than "static"; and they aim at presenting the "philosophy" of economic history'. In other words, in Ashley's view, the basic aim of the school was to build a 'philosophical' type of history, based on the laws of economic development.

As far as the consequences of the *Methodenstreit* are concerned, the prevailing view at the time was that the abstract theorists had won the argument. 'The "methodological" arguments of the orthodox', he says, 'may seem to have gained an easy victory', p. 4. Ashley, however, takes a different view. The historical movement, he writes, three years after the publication of Marshall's *Principles:*

> has performed a work of vital importance. It has been no mere aberration, passing away and leaving no trace; ... [to the contrary] it has changed the whole mental attitude of economists towards their own teaching. The acceptance of the two great principles ... that economic conclusions are *relative* to given conditions, and that they possess only *hypothetical* validity, is at least part of the mental habit of economists. The same is true of the conviction that economic considerations are not the only ones of which we must take account in judging of social phenomena, and that economic forces are not the only ones that move men.

Hence, contrary to the view prevalent at the time, Ashley thought that the historical movement had left a clear mark on the thinking and teaching of 'theoretical' economists. He picks up Alfred Marshall, among others, as a typical example of this influence, p. 5:

> Professor Marshall so clearly realizes that the understanding of modern conditions is assisted by a consideration of their genesis that he introduces his work by two chapters on 'The Growth of Free Industry and Enterprise', and by another chapter on 'The Growth of Economic Science'.

And Ashley goes on to list a host of other examples from Marshall's *Principles* (such as his discussion of population, his treatment of industrial organisation and his theory of rent and distribution) where historical reflections and illustrations are used as component parts of his analysis. So, for Ashley, not only did the historical movement have an impact, but this impact is more pronounced than even those influenced by it themselves realise or would admit.

Be that as it may, Ashley also believed that the main result of the *Methodenstreit* on the historical movement was the transformation of historical economics into economic history. Thus, Ashley could proclaim as early as 1893 that 'the historical movement has pursued its way, and is now settling down into a channel of its own. This is none other than the actual investigation of economic history itself', p. 6. More than 30 years later, in the first issue of the newly launched *Economic History Review*, Ashley (1927, p. 1) defined economic history as 'the history of actual human practice with respect to the material basis of life. The visible happenings with regard ... to "the production, distribution, and consumption of wealth" from our wide enough field'. Historical economics in Britain thus gave way to a new discipline, economic history.

4 Concluding remarks

Historical economists, having failed to make the historical the object of economic inquiry, saw their own research becoming transformed into a branch of historical research, see opening quote from Koot. The relative reluctance with which British historical economists received this new development is evident in the words of their leading member, who was to become the first president of the newly founded Economic History Society in 1926, Ashley (1927, p. 4):

> The theoretical economists are ready to keep us economic historians quiet by giving us a little garden plot of our own; and we humble historians are so thankful for a little undisputed territory that we are inclined to leave the economists to their own devices.

How long that plot was to remain undisturbed is a moot point with the emergence of a less than humble cliometrics a couple of generations later, to be addressed fully in Milonakis and Fine (forthcoming).

The first steps of economic history proper bore all the birthmarks of its long drawn out process of gestation. Both the historical trend in economics and the muted British *Methodenstreit* left their imprints on the writings of the first generation of economic historians proper, and gave rise to two opposing traditions within economic history itself. Coleman (1987, ch. 5) aptly describes them as the 'reformist' and the 'neutralist' traditions.[11] Tawney and the Hammonds are the main representatives of the former group, while Clapham is the founder of the latter tradition, to be followed by Ashton.[12] All members of the 'reformist' tradition come from the historians' camp, and write in the spirit of the historical economists. The basic legacies that historical economists bequeathed to them are an empiricist and institutionalist orientation, coupled with a general hostility towards economic theory, a concern for the (negative) social consequences of the industrial revolution and an advocacy of social reform, pp. 63–5. Whether in the form of the mixture of 'religious theory' (such as Christian ethics) with the 'growth of individualism' and 'the triumph of economic interests', as in Tawney's (1938 [1922]) *Religion and the Rise of Capitalism*, or in the comprehensive account of the effects of the industrial revolution on the standard of living of working people, as in Hammonds' (1911) *The Village Labourer*,[13] the first 'reformist' economic historians wrote first and foremost descriptive, narrative-type social history, based primarily on qualitative sources. In the writings of Tawney, but also of Unwin, economic history took a markedly sociological turn, Tawney (1932, p. 104) and Court (1970, p. 142). A social history emerged, set in a wider philosophical framework, Harte (1971, p. xxviii), and informed by categories such as class and industrialisation that are far from methodologically and theoretically neutral (as, indeed, would be their absence).

Clapham, on the other hand, was the founder of the 'neutralist' trend in economic history, a tradition that was later continued by Ashton. Being 'a historian who turned toward economics', and a student of Marshall, he was to initiate a wholly new tradition in economic history, Court (1970, p. 143). In direct contradistinction to Toynbee's and the Hammonds' 'catastrophic' interpretation of the consequences of the Industrial Revolution, one basic attribute of Clapham's work is his insistence on a balanced and neutralist (hence Clarke's and Coleman's label) interpretation. But one of the chief characteristics of this tradition is the mostly quantitative nature of both its style and the type of sources used, coupled with some (limited) appeal to economic theory. As Clapham, quoted in Coleman (1987, pp. 77–8), puts it, 'every economic historian should have acquired ... the habit of asking in relation to any institution, policy, group or movement the questions: how large? how long? how often? how representative?'. Be that as it may, Clapham's use of economic theory remained limited and implicit, and mostly took the form of general assumptions of Marshallian-type neoclassical theory. This may in fact be a dissatisfaction with the limited historical applicability of the economist's abstract tools, which in 1922 he attacked as 'empty economic boxes', Clapham (1922a and 1922b). It was Ashton, in fact, who more than any other economic historian to his time, 'made economic history the economists' history' by extending Clapham's quantitative type of history and making use of Marshallian type economics more explicit, Coleman (1987, pp. 77–87) and Koot (1987, ch. 9). In this sense, if Clapham can be considered an early precursor of the 'cliometrics revolution' in economic history in the 1960s, Ashton's work represents the crucial link between the early atheoretical type of economic history and the 'new economic history' based on neoclassical economic theory and quantitative analysis, Milonakis (2006).

The birth of economic history as a separate discipline, and its separation from economics proper, can be seen as an offspring or direct result of two parallel and interrelated processes. The first is related to the first great divide in economic thought between abstract deductive theorising and more inductive empirical work, a process that, as we have seen, started with the debate between Ricardo and Malthus over the relative virtues of the two approaches, and was continued through the methodological and other works of Senior, Mill and Cairnes, on the one hand, and Jones and the various strands of the German and the British Historical Schools, on the other. The second is related to the second schism in economic thought that was brought about by the marginalist revolution, which further exacerbated the differences between the two camps. The eruption of the *Methodenstreit* between Menger and Schmoller in the 1880s represented the culminating point of these two parallel and interrelated processes, and brought the differences between the two camps to the fore. Despite attempts at reconciliation and calls for the use of both methods, the end result of this 'deep cultural divide' was a split into two separate disciplines, in which each group could concentrate its efforts uninterrupted on what its members thought was the best way of investigating the facts of social and economic life. Judging in retrospect, one major consequence of this separation, and of the absence of any interaction between the two disciplines, was the relative impoverishment of both.

9 Thorstein Veblen

Economics as a broad science

'An adequate theory of economic conduct, even for statical purposes, cannot be drawn in terms of the individual simply – as is the case in the marginal-utility economics – because it cannot be drawn in terms of the underlying traits of human nature simply'.

Veblen (1909, p. 242)

1 Introduction

Friedrich Hayek was the first major Central European economist to visit the United States after the First World War, according to his own recollection, Hayek (1963, pp. 34–8). This visit took place in the early 1920s, and Hayek had the opportunity to meet most of the leading economists, including J.B. Clark, Seligman, Seager, Mitchell, T. Carver, Irving Fisher, Jacob Hollander, W.C. Mitchell and Thornstein Veblen. This is how Hayek summarises his first impression of his visit: 'I must confess', he says, pp. 35–6:

> From my predominantly theoretical interest the first impression of American economics was disappointing. I soon discovered the great names which were household words to me were regarded as old-fashioned men by my American contemporaries, that work on their lines had moved no further than I knew already, and that the one name which the eager young men swore was the only one I had not known until Schumpeter gave me a letter of introduction addressed to him, Wesley Clair Mitchell. Indeed business cycles and institutionalism were the two main topics of discussion ... And one of the first things the visiting economist was urged to do was to go to the New School for Social Research to hear Thornstein Veblen mumble sarcastically and largely inaudibly to a group of admiring old ladies – a curiously unsatisfactory experience.

Personal comments aside, what Hayek is describing in his own lucid style is a situation totally different to the one he had left behind in Europe, where marginalism had become the new orthodoxy, and was reigning supreme. Instead, what he finds in the United States is an intellectual environment where neoclassical economists such as Clark and Fisher never gained a secure hold, and where institutionalist economists such as Mitchell and Veblen had taken the upper hand. The paths of economic science in Europe and America at that time could not have been more diverse. This was the golden age of institutionalism in America, reaching its zenith during the inter-war period, with six of the American Economic Association presidents, from 1925 to 1944, being institutionalists, twice the number of neoclassicals, Yonay (1998, p. 57). How did this state of affairs come about?

To trace the roots of American institutionalism, German historicism is a necessary starting point. In his recent article, Pearson (1999) argues that the adjective 'historical' is a misnomer for the writers of the German Historical School, and that the terms 'evolutionary', 'institutional' or, even better, 'cultural' would describe the essence of their work more accurately. Although it is arguable whether the adjective 'historical' should be dropped when describing this group of writers, Pearson strikes an appropriate chord when he underlines the evolutionary, institutional and cultural aspects of their work. Evolution, according to Pearson, captures the centrality of the theory of stages in the school's agenda, while the institutional element is evident throughout their writings as in their concern for, p. 553:

1   showing how various rules and customs impinge upon economic activity,
2   explaining those institutions, preferably in terms of economic structure,
3   asking which social and political constitutions best succeed in cultivating functional institutions.

Last, the term 'cultural' is even more appropriate, because it has 'the added advantage of a gesture toward tastes and ethics alongside rules and customs'.

Despite the appeal of Pearson's observations, we concur with Caldwell (2001, p. 650) that the conclusions he draws from them are too strong. As we have argued at length in Chapter 5, it is inappropriate to deny the existence of historical economics as a distinctive school, even if it can be situated as 'one component of a larger "evolutionary", or "institutional", or "cultural" tradition in economics'. Nonetheless, on this account of the basic attributes of the Historical School, there is no doubt that if this school spawned a successor, it is to be found not in Europe but in America. For at the same time that historical economics was losing ground in Europe, inductivism and empiricism were winning a new lease of life across the Atlantic in the form of American institutionalism.

At that time, America was a rapidly expanding country, much like Germany at the time of the historicists, and, as such, the issues of long-run development and institutional change were high on the agenda. In addition, Marxism did not get a hold on this part of the globe as much as it had in various parts of Europe, thus leaving ground for a heterodox and critical school such as institutionalism to flourish without a serious rival, Hodgson (1994, p. 375). Its heyday lasted from the 1880s until the Second World War, and the first to use the term is considered to be Walton Hamilton (1919) in his article 'The Institutional Approach to Economic Theory'. The writings of Thornstein Veblen (1857–1929), Wesley Mitchell (1874–1948), John Commons (1862–1945) and Clarence Ayres (1891–1972), despite their many differences, can be considered as a continuation of the historicist school of thinking. For American institutionalism served as an offspring of European historical movement in economics in more than one way. It also had many affinities with Weber's and Schumpeter's notion of social economics, although it placed its emphasis on *inter*-disciplinarity rather than *multi*- (or *trans*-) disciplinarity, as for Weber's and Schumpeter's programme of *Sozialökonomik*, see Chapter 11.

This chapter begins in the next section by teasing out what elements can be found in common across the American institutionalists. It does so in order, in part, to emphasise their differences, as is revealed in the successive treatment in subsequent sections of this chapter, and in the next chapter of its leading representatives, Veblen, Mitchell, Commons and Ayres. In retrospect, three features stand out as far as the school's place in the history of economic thought is concerned. First, especially through reference to institutions, is an implacable hostility to exclusive reliance upon orthodox neoclassical economics, as it was then, in the process of further consolidation. The second, despite this, is the degree of support and respect that it commanded. Third, this was all to prove short-lived. These themes are revisited in the concluding remarks.

2 Institutions, evolution and history

From before the First World War, many American students went over to Germany for their postgraduate studies, returning with historicist influences, Dorfman (1955), Rutherford (2001, p. 177n) and Hodgson (2001, p. 138).[1] According to Biddle and Samuels (1997, p. 291), the two schools share in common:

> emphases on a broad conception of the economic system, an empirical rather than strictly deductive apriorist approach to knowledge, the importance of institutions, the conduct of case studies, and the deep sense of the historicity of the economic system and of economics as a discipline.

Thus, despite Veblen's (1898a) early critique of the German Historical School for its non-evolutionary character, excessive empiricism and lack of theory, the institutionalists had much in common with the historicists.

Veblen (1901, p. 254) himself, in a critique of Schmoller, makes a sharp distinction between, on the one hand, the writings of 'the elder line of the historical school [which] can scarcely be said to cultivate a science at all, their aim being not theoretical work', but the confinement of economics to 'narrative, statistics and description', p. 256; and, on the other hand, Schmoller's approach (especially in his later writings), which, 'differs from that of the elder line of historical economics in respect to the scope and character' of economic theory, as well as 'in ulterior aim which he assigns to science', p. 264. The distinguishing characteristic of Schmoller's work, according to Veblen, is its Darwinian character, and 'it is "historical" only in a sense similar to that in which a Darwinian account of the evolution of economic institutions might be called historical', p. 265.[2] As we shall see below, however, this is a defining characteristic of the institutionalists for whom social institutions are seen as the foundation for economic activity. Despite Veblen's protestation against excessive inductivism and empiricism, and his insistence on the need for adequate theorisation, the institutionalists' impact on theoretical economics was short-lived, their basic, immediate legacy to economics being a contribution to applied economics. This parallels the historicist basic legacy which was mostly in economic history rather than in economic theory.

Despite their differences, institutionalists did share much in common. First and foremost is their concern with institutions as providing the template for all economic activity. Second, given the impure nature and non-economic aspects of most institutions, this alone suffices to render their science interdisciplinary in nature. They drew inspiration for their economics from other social sciences – chiefly from psychology, anthropology and sociology. This is in sharp contrast to the neoclassicals, and Weber and Schumpeter, for whom a strict separation of social sciences is possible (although, the two theorists of *Sozialökonomik*, as we will see in Chapter 11, strongly emphasise multi-disciplinarity or the need for close cooperation between separate and distinct social sciences in analysing economic phenomena). Institutionalists are, in this respect, more in line with Marx's and the historicists' more holistic approaches, for which the boundaries between different social sciences are not and cannot easily be drawn. As Perlman and McCann (1998, p. 516) conclude, 'In effect, the school succeeded in showing that Pareto's dictum – that rational (economic) and nonrational (sociologic) disciplines must be distinct and separate – simply did not and could not hold'.[3] Third, for them, economics is a historically specific science that studies economic relationships in their historical context. Unlike neoclassical economics, they are against the use of universal concepts and categories. Mitchell (1910b, p. 204) argues that:

> The theorist commits an error ... when, in accounting for the current situation, he treats the concepts which modern men have gradually learned to use as if they were a matter of course, an integral part of man's native endowment, something genetically human.

Clearly, there is a close connection between these three aspects – institutionalism, interdisciplinarity and historical specificity.

Fourth, the institutionalists were against any brand of methodological individualism, since the explanation of social phenomena cannot be found within the abstract individual. 'There is no isolated, self-sufficing individual', Veblen (1898b, p. 33) proclaims. Further, 'All production takes place in society – only through the co-operation of an industrial community', p. 34. Granted this, Veblen (1909, pp. 242–3) concludes:

> The wants and desires, the end and aim, the ways and means, the amplitude and drift of the individual's conduct are functions of an institutional variable that is of a highly complex and wholly unstable character.

So, whilst some attention should be paid to individuals, it needs to be historically, socially and institutionally located.

Not surprisingly, and more specifically as a corollary of the previous point, fifth is their shared critique of the neoclassical assumption of rational economic man, what Veblen (1898a, p. 389), in his famous phrase, called 'the hedonistic conception of man', which he ridiculed as a 'lightning calculator of pleasures and pains'. Instead of this 'isolated, definitive human datum', they focused their attention, much like the historicists, on the social (or institutionalised) individual, whose behaviour is conditioned by the social environment. 'Man is a social animal', Veblen (1909, p. 242) declared. This is so, since:

> the response that goes to make up human conduct takes place under institutional norms and only under stimuli that have an institutional bearing; for the situation that provokes and inhibits action in any given case is itself in great part of institutional cultural derivation.

As is apparent, attention to institutions is the driving force behind both the critique of orthodoxy and the construction of an alternative.

Sixth, they also favoured a dynamic approach, as opposed to static equilibrium analysis. Veblen (1898a, p. 378) astutely observes and anticipates of orthodoxy that equilibrium will always be subject to 'normal' or 'natural law', with disturbing non-natural, not least social, factors set aside as secondary (or random shocks in modern parlance):

> When facts and events have been reduced to these terms of fundamental truth and have been made to square with the requirements of definitive normality, the investigator rests content. Any causal sequence which is apprehended to traverse the imputed propensity in events is a 'disturbing factor'.

Instead of using the mechanical metaphor, as in Jevons and neoclassical equilibrium analysis, the institutionalists drew their inspiration from Darwinian evolutionary biology (Veblen) or from historicism (Commons) or both. For them, economics is first and foremost an evolutionary science that focuses on institutional change, which is considered to be the subject matter of economic theory, see Hamilton (1919, p. 314).

Despite these common elements of the institutionalist paradigm, the approaches of individual writers of this school differed widely. Much like the Historical School, or indeed marginalism and any other school, institutionalism did not form a unified school of thought, sharing mostly an antipathy to the emerging or emerged orthodoxy and a concern with institutions. As Ayres (1962, p. xi), one of the last of the major American institutionalists, observed as late as 1962:

> even today there is no clearly defined body of principles on which institutionalists are generally agreed and by which they are known. But if there is anything that all institutionalists have in common it is dissatisfaction with orthodox price theory.

Yet, one of the most important lacunae in institutionalist thought is exactly the absence of a theory of price, or value theory.

3 Veblen versus marginalism, Marx and the Historical School

Veblen is generally considered to be the founder of institutional economics. His aim was to build an evolutionary science along the lines of Darwinian evolutionary biology. From this vantage point, he launched a relentless critique of the then prevailing economic theories, mostly the marginalist/neoclassical, the historical, and the Marxian, for their non-evolutionary nature, albeit for different reasons. First, building an evolutionary economics is impossible within the marginalist/neoclassical framework. On the one hand, 'hedonistic economics' cannot deal with the phenomena of growth and cumulative change that accompanies the dynamic aspects of economic phenomena (in terms of 'genesis, growth, variation, process') and, as such, is unlike other modern sciences, 'except so far as growth is taken in the quantitative sense', Veblen (1908, p. 192). On the other hand, 'the hedonistic conceptions concerning human nature and human action', which underline much of modern economic theory, take human nature for granted and do not allow any space for the formation of 'a theory of the development of human nature', Veblen (1898a, p. 78). This is only possible through an evolutionary approach that can provide a theory of the development of human nature 'in terms of a cumulative growth of habits of thought'.

Veblen's critique of Marxism takes a different form. Institutionalists generally, and Veblen in particular, thought highly of Marx's work, which they considered to be both institutionalist in content and evolutionary in approach. According to Mitchell (1924, p. 363), Marx 'saw the central problem of economics in the cumulative change of economic institutions', while for Veblen (1906a, pp. 409–10), he came close to meeting the requirements of Darwinian evolutionism without, however, quite grasping all of its prerequisites. For Veblen, Marx's system, which 'draws on two distinct lines of antecedents – the materialist Hegelianism and the English system of Natural rights ... is characterized by a certain boldness of conception and a great logical consistency'. This Hegelian pedigree gives the Marxian system its evolutionary character. As Veblen (1906a, pp. 413–14) puts it, the reliance of Marx's materialist conception of history on the Hegelian dialectic, 'throws it immediately and uncompromisingly into contact with Darwinism and post-Darwinian conceptions of evolution'. But what lies behind the failure of the Marxian system fully to meet the test of Darwinian evolutionism, is its tele-ological, goal-directed character, which it derives from its Romantic, neo-Hegelian roots, and the distortion of its properly materialist character through the infusion of conscious class struggle as the basic motor of social change, Veblen (1906a, pp. 417–18 and 430, and 1907, p. 436). Veblen (1906a, p. 417) considers the latter to be non-Hegelian in nature but 'of utilitarian origin and of English pedigree ... a piece of hedonism ... related to Bentham rather than to Hegel'. This is taken to be the result of the influence on Marx's thought of the liberal–utilitarian school which was prevalent in England in his lifetime, Veblen (1907, p. 431). As such, 'it proceeds on the ground of reasoned conduct, calculus of advantage, not on the ground of cause and effect', which is characteristic of Darwinism, p. 441. Only through the exclusion of conscious class struggle as an explanatory variable in Marx's schema could his materialist dialectic have led 'to a concept of evolution similar to the unteleological Darwinian conception of natural selection', and to the iden-tification of social progress as a process of cumulative causation, p. 416. In addition, Marx's political conclusions were deemed responsible for its relatively minor influence on contemporaries who were 'too much scandalized ... to profit by his methods', Mitchell (1924, p. 363).

Last, the evolutionary project cannot be attained through the utilisation of the historical method as practised especially by the elder generation of his-torical economists. Contrary to the historicists' tendency to content them-selves with 'an enumeration of data and a narrative account of industrial development', an evolutionary science is a 'close-knit body of theory ... a theory of a process, of an unfolding sequence', Veblen (1898a, p. 58). It is a process that traces the evolution and development of institutions, from their genesis to their demise. Thus, 'A Darwinistic account of the origin, growth, persistence, and variation of institutions, in so far as these institutions have to do with the economic aspect of life either as cause or as effect', Veblen (1901, p. 256). For Veblen, a 'Darwinian account' refers to an evolutionary process carried forward by a process of natural selection through the identi-fication of causal mechanisms, Hodgson (2004, p. 149). This is how Veblen (1898a, p. 77) defines evolutionary economics:

> An evolutionary economics must be the theory of a process of cultural growth as determined by the economic interest, a theory of cumulative sequence of economic institutions stated in terms of the process itself.

Indeed, for Veblen, the investigation of the whys and hows of this cumulative process of institutional evolution forms the subject matter of economics: 'It is this cumulative process of development, and its complex and unstable outcome, that are to be the economist's subject matter', Veblen (1901, p. 267). This conception of cumulative causation is open-ended and non-teleological, since in it 'there is no trend, no final term, no consummation', Veblen (1906a, p. 416 and 1907, p. 436). Yet this leaves the institutionalists, like the Historical School before it, open to the (generally false) charge of being atheoretical. This is especially so for the orthodoxy that increasingly fails to recognise as theory anything that is not subject both to formalism and equilibrium as an organising concept. Yet it remains a moot point how and how well the institutionalists managed to blend together their own historicist and evolutionist elements with well-grounded theory of whatever species.

4 Veblen's evolutionary scheme

Crucial in Veblen's theory of institutional change and in his formulation of Darwinian cumulative causation is the concept of 'habits of thought'. These are induced in human beings by their material circumstances, be it 'hereditary bent, occupation, tradition, education, climate, food supply' or what have you, Veblen (1907, p. 438). Veblen (1990, p. 239) defines institutions as, 'settled habits of thought common to the generality of man'.[4] He considers habits of thought to be a substitute for the hedonistic rationality of marginalism, and the rationality of conscious class-conflict of the Marxian scheme, Veblen (1907, p. 438). Human action is guided by habits of thought rather than material interests, and is considered a result of the response to stimuli, pp. 441–3. Through this concept, Veblen was able to overcome one of (what he considers to be) the deficiencies of both Marxism and the Historical School, by identifying the mechanism through which institutions affect preferences and tastes. He thus builds a bridge between the institutional structure of society and human conduct, Hodgson (2001, p. 150).

Generally, the investigation of human nature and conduct plays a crucial role in Veblen's (1898c, p. 85) theoretical scheme – 'Man's life is activity; and as he acts, so he thinks and feels'. Despite, however, his sharp critique of the psychological–hedonistic conceptions of human nature, and his overwhelming emphasis on the role of institutions in shaping human conduct, he also derives human behaviour as driven by fixed basic human propensities and instinctive drives. 'Man is a creature of habits and propensities', he proclaims, p. 85, for 'He is endowed with a proclivity for purposeful action ... The impulse itself is a generic feature of human nature', p. 80. He devoted the third of his early books, *The Instinct of Workmanship*, first published in 1914 – which he considered his best Hodgson (2004, p. 143) – to the investigation of these human propensities or impulses. In his quest, he was guided by the propositions of instinct–habit psychology.[5] He identifies three basic drives or instincts that govern human behaviour: the instinct of workmanship or the impulse to work in order to 'turn things to human use', Veblen (1898c, p. 84); the instinct of idle curiosity, referring to the propensity to understand and explain the external world through the use of imagination; and the instinct of parental bent, stressing human interest in the welfare of others, Veblen (1964b [1914], pp. 85–91, 1906b and 1898c).

Of these human impulses Veblen (1975, p. 270) picks up the instinct of workmanship as the primordial and 'more generic, more abiding trait of human nature'. Guided by this 'proclivity for turning the material means of life to account', Veblen (1898c, p. 80), and the drive of idle curiosity, people strive to improve the conditions of their lives and to satisfy their basic needs as best they can. In these human propensities lies the secret behind both technological advance and the onset of modern industry, and the process of social change and evolution more generally, Veblen (1906b, p. 13). Here, Veblen offers a theory of economic development rooted in human nature, Zingler (1974, p. 326). What is more, he also suggests at one point that this process of technological advancement, resulting from these basic human propensities, lies behind institutional change and changes in the habits of thought, Veblen (1906b, p. 17):

> In the modern culture, industry, industrial processes, and industrial products have progressively gained upon humanity, until these creations of man's ingenuity have latterly come to take the dominant place in the cultural scheme; and it is not too much to say that they have become the chief force shaping men's daily life, and therefore the chief factor shaping men's habits of thought. Hence men have learned to think in the terms in which the technological processes act.

Passages such as these, and the influence of Ayres' (1962 [1944]) work (see next chapter), have given rise to a technological–determinist reading of Veblen's work, where technological improvements are thought to be the root cause of all social change, while 'institutions are static and tend to resist change', Walker (1977, p. 220) and Zingler (1974).

Subsequently, however, this view has been challenged by several commentators, on the grounds that, although Veblen did use 'the idea of technological change leading to new habits of thought', this alone does not suffice to give a complete picture of his scheme, since it ignores many other elements of his analysis of institutional change, Rutherford (1984, p. 331), Brette (2003) and Hodgson (2004, ch. 17). First, it ignores the social and institutional basis of technological development in Veblen's writings. For Veblen (1898b, p. 34), 'There is no technical knowledge apart from an industrial community'. Second, it ignores the 'human factor' which is also essential in Veblen's theory of economic development, Brette (2003, pp. 462–3). Veblen (1898b, pp. 71–2) concludes:

> The changes that take place in the mechanical contrivances are an expression of changes in the human factor. Changes in the material facts breed further change only through the human factor. It is in the human material that the continuity of development is to be looked for;

and it is here, therefore, that the motor forces of the process of economic development must be studied if they are to be studied in action at all.

Thus, not just technology but the relation between instinctive drives and habits of thought, and the role of institutions in shaping human behaviour, are of particular importance in Veblen's work and recur throughout his writings.

A prime example is his first book, *The Theory of the Leisure Class*, first published in 1899, where Veblen analyses what he calls 'the institution of the leisure class ... [which is] by custom exempt or excluded from industrial occupations, and are reserved for certain employments to which a degree of honour attaches', p. 1. First, he gives an historical account of the emergence of the leisure class as an offspring of what he calls the 'barbarian culture', and which, in his view, 'coincides with the beginning of ownership', pp. 1, 22. Veblen (1906b, p. 10) uses the term 'barbarian or predatory culture' to denote all societies based on 'a settled scheme of predaceous life, involving mastery and servitude, gradations of privilege and honour, coercion and personal dependence', which includes the modern 'pecuniary culture', see below, as opposed to the earlier 'savage culture' which involved a peaceful life.

Second, the main concepts he uses to analyse the institution of the leisure class are those of 'conspicuous consumption' (including 'conspicuous leisure' and 'conspicuous waste') and 'pecuniary emulation' ('pecuniary culture'). Here, we first encounter one of Veblen's famous dichotomies between 'conspicuous consumption', which is culturally determined through habitual appropriation, conventions etc., p. 23, and (subsistence) consumption, which is determined by basic human needs. A crucial concept is that of 'emulation'. Conspicuous consumption refers to the portion of goods bought not in order to increase the welfare of the individuals involved, but rather in order to 'retain their self-esteem in the face of the disesteem of their fellows' – in other words, to 'emulate' the consumption patterns of 'others with whom he is accustomed to class himself', pp. 30–1. Conspicuous consumption is therefore culturally determined, the result of the predatory or barbarian culture. In Veblen's analysis, the institution of ownership and the motive of pecuniary emulation become 'the material and psychological foundations of the leisure class', Bowman (1998, p. xix).[6]

Following Veblen's use of the principle of emulation, which has negative connotations, some commentators distinguish between what they call constructive or positive instincts, and destructive or negative instincts which are presumed to have equal status in Veblen's work, Dowd (2002, pp. 41–4), Ramstad (1994, p. 366). The former includes the three basic instincts referred to above (workmanship, idle curiosity and parental bent), while the latter comprise the predatory proclivities such as the propensity for emulation and 'the antipathy to useful effort', Veblen (1898c, p. 82). However, although all these proclivities are present in Veblen's work, they do not share the same status. Thus, for example, he considers the instinct of workmanship as 'more fundamental, of more ancient prescription, than the propensity for predatory emulation', while the emulative principle is a 'special development' of the former, following the emergence of predatory life, and the predominance of self-interest over solidarity, Veblen (1975, p. 270 and 1898c, p. 87). In other words, the instinct of workmanship, which is an innate human impulse, under the influence of the institutions and habits of thought associated with predatory culture, can realise itself through the emulative principle. Indeed, Veblen (1964b, pp. 142–51) considers the latter and pecuniary exploit as a 'self-regarding sentiment', derivative upon the pecuniary culture, rather than a basic human instinct as such, on a par with the instinct of workmanship, etc. Similarly, he considers the 'antipathy to useful effort' to be a habit of thought that is derivative of predatory culture, Veblen (1898c, pp. 82–5). More generally, Veblen considers self-interested impulses as culturally derived. However, Veblen nowhere provides an explanation of the mechanisms or processes by which habits of thought are affected by instincts, and how instinctual propensities that are thought of as good humanly inclinations (such as workmanship) give rise to predatory habits of thought, such as pecuniary emulation, Walker (1977, p. 219). It is more a matter of guilt by institutional association, via ownership of property, membership of the leisure class, etc.

Similarly, the instinct of idle curiosity gives rise in the savage period to dramatised myths and legends. But, in the modern era, and under the influence of new institutions and habits of life related to machine technology, it takes the form of 'the scientific spirit', Veblen (1906b, pp. 7, 12 and 15). Hence, under the impact of technology and its associated institutional structure, the balance and realisation of the basic human instincts changes drastically. Idle curiosity gradually gives way to workmanship, which, in modern times, can find expression either in the predatory emulative impulse or in scientific discovery and technological advance based on matter-of-fact knowledge, pp. 13–16. As Bowman (1998, p. xii), puts it, for Veblen:

> Instinctive behavior was shaped by social norms, customs, and habits. Consequently, even though human instincts are innate, the way in which the instinctive ends of life were worked out would depend upon a host of cultural factors.

This is another indication of the complex relationship between instinctive drives and habits of thought in Veblen's work, which he did not always succeed in clarifying.

The subject matter of his first book, then, was the institutional basis of the formation of tastes and the consumption habits of the leisure class in modern times. In his next major work, *The Theory of Business Enterprise* (1958 [1904]), he switches his attention to the anatomy of the 'capitalistic system' or the 'modern industrial system'. In particular, he wanted to uncover the material basis of modern civilisation. This he did through his second – and justly famous – distinction between business enterprise and industrial process, which became one of his main analytic tools, and which is considered by many scholars to be Veblen's major contribution to economics and social science more generally, through what later came to be known as the Veblenian dichotomy. Between them, these two institutions are 'the two prime movers of modern culture', p. 178. Veblen (1958, p. 7) considers modern civilisation, including law and politics, as resting to a large extent on these material forces:

> The material framework of modern civilization is the industrial system, and the directing force which animates this framework is business enterprise ... This modern economic organization is the 'Capitalistic System' or 'Modern Industrial System', so called. Its characteristic features, and at the same time the forces by virtue of which it dominates modern culture, are the machine process and investment for profit.

This line of reasoning closely resembles Marx's scheme of base and superstructure in his materialist conception of history, see Chapter 3.

Business enterprise refers to the activity of making money, and is associated with pecuniary and business employments (the modern leisure class), whose basic drive is pecuniary gain through investment for profit. For 'The motive of business is pecuniary gain, the method is essentially purchase and sale. The aim and usual outcome is an accumulation of wealth', p. 16. The industrial process, on the other hand, concerns the business of making goods, which is the work of the class of 'efficiency engineers' and other 'industrial and mechanical employments', dominated by the values of workmanship and serviceability. Mechanical efficiency is their chief habit of thought, and technological advance the outcome of their labours, p. 147. The industrial process 'enforces the standardization of conduct and of knowledge in terms of quantitative precision, and inculcates a habit of apprehending and explaining facts in terms of material cause and effect', p. 37. The relation between the two institutions is not one of peaceful coexistence, but of continuous strife and conflict, leading to the evolution of the modern business system. And, despite the role of industry in promoting technological advance, it is not industry and the engineers with their workmanlike attitudes and motives that drive the capitalist economy, but capitalists and business enterprise, governed by their pecuniary habits of thought and the 'all-dominating issue ... of gain and loss', p. 45. Indeed, p. 8:

> The business man ... has become the controlling force in industry because, through the mechanism of investments and markets, he controls the plants and processes, and these set the pace and determine the direction of movement of the rest.

For this reason, the theory of the modern capitalist system must be first and foremost 'a theory of business traffic, with its motives, aims, methods, and effects', p. 8. Further, not only the capitalist economy as such, but modern civilisation more generally (including law and politics) is governed by these business motives and aims, ch. VIII. This is despite the work of these 'captains of industry' having adverse consequences for industry, since their motives almost always and everywhere militate against the industrial process, p. 62. For 'The modern businessman is necessarily out of effectual touch with the affairs of technology as such and incompetent to exercise an effectual surveillance of the process of industry', Veblen quoted in Dugger and Sherman (2000, pp. 150–1). Indeed, business enterprise lies behind most phenomena associated with the modern capitalist economy, such as 'crises, depressions, hard times, dull times, brisk times, periods of speculative advance, "eras of prosperity"', p. 88.

Be that as it may, what differentiates the modern situation from earlier times is 'the intrusion of new technology ... with its many and wide ramifications', Veblen (1958, p. 144). This is the result of 'the mechanical process [which] pervades modern life and dominates it in a mechanical sense', p. 146. What is distinctive about the new habits of thought associated with the machine process is their impersonal nature of cause and effect, which throws out more 'anthropomorphic' habits of thought, associated with tradition and custom, such as dexterity and diligence, p. 148. At the same time, the advance of machine technology brings about an ever-widening and deepening divergence in the habits of thought of the two basic classes: business people and the efficiency engineers. The pecuniary habits of the business class have a more conventional blend, based as they are on the institutions of natural rights, ownership and property, which contrasts with the workmanlike habits of thought of the industrial classes, based on matter-of-fact knowledge and material cause and effect, p. 151. This institutional, conventional basis of their pecuniary culture, and the vested interests to which it gives rise – especially the continuous receipt of income without work through what Veblen (1964a, pp. 152, 180) later called absentee ownership – renders the business classes a conservative force. In contrast, the industrial classes, through the formation of trade unions following the industrial revolution, have come to challenge the 'received natural rights dogmas', and the institutions of property and free contract, pp. 156, 158. Although the direction of the general cultural movement – whether towards 'a more conservative, conventional position', or towards 'a more iconoclastic, materialist direction' – cannot be forestalled, the cultural drift during modern times, according to Veblen, has been towards more matter-of-fact habits of thought, which penetrates both opposing classes, thus undermining the more conventional habits of thought, pp. 164, 180–1, 189. Granted this, as Veblen puts it, 'the machine discipline acts to disintegrate the institutional heritage ... on which business enterprise is founded', p. 177, thus leading to the disintegration of the pecuniary culture with its predatory and servile institutions, p. 188.

Although via a different route, Veblen reaches a similar conclusion to both Marx and Schumpeter, regarding the disintegration of the capitalist order and its associated institutions. His analysis depends upon the Veblenian dichotomy discussed above between business and industry, between pecuniary gain and industrial efficiency, between accumulation of wealth and technological advance. On the basis of these complex analytical distinctions, Veblen offers a theory of the dynamics of modern economy with affinities to Marx's class analysis, albeit with many differences. One such has to do with how he treats the 'institution' of class, with his emphasis being on the type of occupation – between industrial and pecuniary employments – rather than on the possession or non-possession of means of production or wealth possessed, as with Marx. Consistent with his overall approach, for Veblen, 'It is a question of work because it is a question of habits of thought, and work shapes the habits of thought', p. 165, and industrial employment comprises functional work as opposed to the activity of the leisure class. In his *Instinct of Workmanship*, for example, he identifies three classes, the upper predatory, the middle business, and the lower industrial class, Veblen (1964b p. 184):

> the upper being typically that (aristocratic) class which is possessed of wealth without having worked or bargained for it; while the middle class have come by their holdings through some form of commercial (business) traffic; and the lower class gets what it has by workmanship. It is gradation of (a) predation, (b) business, (c) industry; the former being disserviceable and gainful, the second gainful, and the third serviceable.

In contrast, for Marx, what different parts of the capitalist class share in common is their functioning for the accumulation and reproduction of capital and/or the appropriation of surplus value in the process, irrespective of important distinctions between such fractions and corresponding impact on the pace and rhythm of accumulation.

5 Method and history in Veblen's work

It is difficult to categorise Veblen methodologically. He sits uncomfortably in relation to the usual dichotomies between deduction and induction, between methodological holism and methodological individualism. The guiding element in his work is Darwinian evolutionism. Throughout his critical and methodological essays, he emphasises that modern science should be guided by the principle of cumulative causation and should search for causal relations. For as soon as the scientist asks the question 'why', he says, 'he insists on an answer of cause and effect', Veblen (1898a, pp. 60–1) and Rutherford (1994, p. 11). And it is transparent that he considers 'economics' to be unable to address problems of cause and effect because of its dependence upon both the natural and equilibrium, thereby precluding dynamic, evolutionary understanding. These general methodological principles aside, however, Veblen did not stick to any particular set of methods, which is why he is open to differing methodological interpretations. What is sure, however, is that Veblen uses both cause and effect and historical types of reasoning throughout his writings. Induction, however, in the form of generalisations from empirical studies, as in the case of the Historical School and of the later generation of institutionalists, particularly Commons and Mitchell (see next chapter), did not form an essential part of Veblen's methodological toolkit. Neither did pure deductivism of the type used by neoclassical economics. For Veblen (1898a, p. 80), the deductive method, with its failure to deal genuinely with causal factors and causation itself, will only lead to a theoretical cul-de-sac and serve to frustrate those engaged in productive activity and accustomed to other modes of thought. For:

> to men thoroughly imbued with this matter-of-fact habit of mind the laws and theorems of economics, and of the other social sciences that treat of the normal course of things, have a character of 'unreality' and futility that bars out any serious interest in their discussion. The laws and theorems are 'unreal' to them because they are not to be apprehended in the terms which these men make us of in handling the facts with which they are perforce habitually occupied.

Veblen, true to his evolutionary scheme, continuously searches for abstract causal relations as the basis for empirical outcomes. His instinct theory of human action is of this cause and effect type. Hence, in imputing instinctive drives derived from human nature, he follows a similar line of argument to that of Adam Smith. And the same applies to his imposition of the propensity to 'truck, barter and exchange' as a chief (economic) motive behind human action and, through the latter, the chief motor behind economic development, although Smith's self-interested drives have been substituted for by the instincts of workmanship and of idle curiosity. But, for Veblen, this is not attached to a deductive approach, but rather is open-ended around the nature of cause and effect, with particular antipathy to the 'natural' as an outcome in general and to equilibrium in particular. Veblen's (1898a, p. 382) broad reservations over classical political economy, and especially over Adam Smith, concern the appeal to 'laws of the normal or the natural, according to preconception regarding the ends to which, in the nature of things, all things tend'.

Yet, as he was a methodological eclectic, one can find in Veblen several of the dualities present in Smith's work. Throughout his writings, in his quest for causal relations, Veblen intermingles psychologism with class analysis, and individualistic argumentation with relativist and collectivist modes of reasoning. What binds all these modes of analysis together is the conception of institutional evolution and development – which, as we have seen, plays a pivotal role in his work. Because institutions are multi-faceted social entities, interdisciplinarity cannot be escaped. At the same time, Veblen's treatment of institutions as habits of thought transmits into them a dual ontology. They involve both social and psychological dimensions – a collectivist (collective habituation) as well as an individualistic element. All these components pervade the whole of Veblen's intellectual output, although the emphasis shifts according to the topic under investigation.

Thus, in *The Instinct of Workmanship*, Veblen's analysis is conducted in individualistic and psychological terms. He substitutes the rationalistic and hedonistic psychology of marginalism with the more rounded and realistic conceptions of instinct and habit psychology. This has led Rutherford (1984, p. 344) to charge Veblen with making concessions to psychologism. However, both in his *Theory of the Leisure Class* and *The Theory of Business Enterprise*, Veblen switches to more collectivist types of reasoning, where class becomes the basic unit of analysis, and different types of institutions (leisure class, business enterprise, industrial process, etc.) come to occupy centre-stage in shaping human behaviour. If his work is treated as a whole, we agree with Hodgson (2004, p. 179) that, despite the presence of both individualistic and collectivist arguments in his work, overall Veblen has avoided reductionism in either direction. Thus, the individual is neither the sole source of all economic and social change, nor are they fully determined by their institutional surroundings. What we find in Veblen's work, taken as a whole, is a continuous interplay between instincts and habits, between the social and the psychological, between the collective and the individualistic, all attached to an evolutionary approach based on a process of cumulative causation. In other words, in Veblen's work 'individuals and social structure are *mutually constitutive*', p. 179.

Veblen's evolutionary scheme, however, also forms the background for another attribute of his methodological disposition: his extensive utilisation of the historical mode of presentation. What Veblen offers in the three books scrutinised above – especially in *The Theory of Business Enterprise* and *The Instinct of Workmanship* – is a theory of economic development and change, based on the dynamic interplay between human instincts, technological advance and institutional change (alterations in the habits of thought), all attached to a process of cumulative causation. This dynamic, under the modern capitalist system, finds expression in the mutual interaction between the two poles of the Veblenian dichotomy, between business enterprise driven by the pecuniary motive and the industrial process dominated by the instinct of workmanship. Veblen did not place so much explicit emphasis on the relation between economics and history as did the historicists. Instead, he chose mostly to relate economics to other social sciences (psychology, anthropology, sociology) and biology. His focus on economic development and institutional change through the utilisation of the Darwinian conception of evolution, however, offered ample space for historical narrative to enter the analysis. His observation regarding Schmoller's work, referred to above, to the effect that the latter's work 'is "historical" only in a sense similar to that in which a Darwinian account of the evolution of economic institutions might be called historical', applies with even greater force to himself. As Rutherford (1994, p. 11) correctly observes, 'Veblen's own work is almost always a blend of theory with a discussion of the related historical sequence of events' and, as seen, there are countless examples of such in Veblen's work.

Veblen, then, throughout his work, makes use of the historical approach in order to explain the emergence of most of the institutions he analyses, be it the leisure class, the institution of ownership, conspicuous consumption or the split between business and industry. Underlying the historical explanation of the emergence of all these institutions is a stages approach to historical evolution. Following the long tradition of many classical, evolutionary and historicist writers – from Adam Smith to Karl Marx and Gustav Schmoller – Veblen's utilisation of a stages approach is pervasive in most of his writings. He identifies two basic stages in the history of mankind: the early primitive savage era and the predatory or barbaric phase. The latter is subdivided into three further sub-phases: the early stages of barbarism, the handicraft era and the modern industrial phase. The borderline between the two main phases is drawn by the passage from hunting and gathering to settled agriculture. The communities of the early savage era are characterised by the absence of a leisure class and of class differentiation more generally, and of the institution of ownership. They are small groups, normally 'peaceable ... sedentary [and] poor', with a simple primitive structure, Veblen (1975, p. 7). At this early phase in the evolution of mankind, the instinct of workmanship and the sense of solidarity dominate over men's self-interested proclivities. This is necessary for the survival of the group, given the primitive level of technical advance, Veblen (1898c, p. 87).

For man's self-interested propensities to come to the fore, the passage to predatory life is necessary. This passage from primitive savagery to barbarism is associated with the emergence of the leisure class and the beginnings of the institution of ownership. Indeed, Veblen considers these two institutions as simply 'different aspects of the same general facts of social structure', since they 'result from the same set of economic forces', Veblen (1975, p. 22). Both become possible only once technology has advanced to such a degree as to render the production of a surplus above the subsistence of the group, possible, Veblen (1898c, p. 87), for 'The transition from peace to predation therefore depends on the growth of technical knowledge and the use of tools', Veblen (1975, p. 20). The passage to predatory life is also marked by the tendency of the self-interested propensities of men to come to the fore and take the upper hand from the other-regarding proclivities of individuals. The most pervasive characteristic of the predatory culture is 'the element of exploit, coercion, and seizure', Veblen (1898b, p. 44). This tendency reaches its climax with the principle of pecuniary emulation, characteristic of modern pecuniary culture. At the same time, the form of manifestation of the basic human instincts also changes under the influence of new institutions. Thus, as already seen, the myths and legends of the savage period give way to the 'scientific spirit' of the modern era, as manifestations of the instinct of idle curiosity.

The transition to the barbaric stage is also marked by the emergence of another major division in the social structure of these societies: the separation between industrial and non-industrial employments (such as war, government, sports, etc.), p. 43. Again, this differentiation reaches its apogee during the transition from the handicraft era to modern industrial production, with the emergence of the modern business class (as distinct from the industrial classes), with its own pecuniary motives that, as seen already, have come to dominate modern culture. This, again, is the result of technical advance and the appearance of machine technology, Bowman (1998, pp. xxiii–xxiv).

One last instance of the use of the historical method by Veblen is his historical account of the development of conspicuous consumption in his *The Theory of the Leisure Class*. Although unproductive consumption was present in the earlier phases of the predatory culture, it was 'primarily ... a mark of prowess and a prerequisite of human dignity', p. 69. This changes with the onset of modern culture, where conspicuous consumption becomes 'honorific' and 'a means of reputability to the gentleman of leisure', pp. 74, 75.

Overall, historical narrative is marked by a continual appearance in Veblen's writings, and plays a key role in the development of his evolutionary scheme. It can even be argued that, despite his stated antipathy to the Historical School, his own historical/institutional grasp constrained his theoretical reach. The observation of a leisure class (and corresponding and other dualisms) in his own society fuelled a desire to root out their historical and instinctive origins in earlier, barbaric, societies. It no doubt gave him pleasure and critical satisfaction to place these below savage society in realisation of positive as opposed to negative human propensities.

6 Concluding remarks

Despite the incisiveness, originality and profundity of Veblen's work, he never really managed to achieve what he most admired in Marx, which is his 'boldness of conception and great logical consistency', Veblen (1906a, p. 409). Although guided by the same general principles throughout his writings, Veblen did not produce a unified and robust theoretical framework as did Marx. Instead, what he left us are works covering different (although related) ground, with the methodological emphasis switching according to the topic under investigation. This, coupled with his overall methodological eclecticism, are signs of both strength and weakness; but overall, they have combined to produce opaque theoretical fragments. This is reinforced by vagueness in the way Veblen treats his concepts, coupled with several inconsistencies and lacunae in his work, to some of which we have referred above. The result of 'his failure to build a systematic theory' is that, as Hodgson (2001, p. 151) puts it, 'Veblen aided and abetted the empiricist drift among institutionalists that was present at the time ... Veblen's theoretical corpus is one of sporadic brilliance but systematic deficiency'. In the hands of Commons, and especially Mitchell, institutional economics became increasingly inductive and empiricist, both in substance and in outlook, and, to some extent, even sought a compromise with the science of choice. It is to these writers, together with Ayres, that we turn our attention in the next chapter.

10 Commons, Mitchell, Ayres and the *fin de siècle* of American institutionalism

'Social patterns are not the logical consequents of individual acts; individuals, and all their actions, are the logical consequents of social patterns'.

Ayres (1951, p. 49)

'I have never been able to think of the various social sciences as separate fields of history, political science, economics, ethics and administration. What we need is some way of working through the whole complex of problems that grow out of this fundamental struggle'.

Commons (1950, p. 118)

'It is not merely "curious and interesting" but extremely suggestive and valuable for any student of economic phenomena. By economists ... it must be read sympathetically, and without criticism on grounds of the absence of clear argument, for a clear position or coherent analysis, either of economic principles or economic institutions. But if they take it in the right spirit, minds trained in orthodox economic theory and devoted to clarity, definiteness and "system" are the very ones to read it with great profit'.

Knight (1935, p. 805) in review of
Commons *Institutional Economics: Its Place in Political Economy*[1]

1 Introduction

By the 1920s, the intellectual climate was changing rapidly. The pillars on which the Veblenian theoretical corpus was erected were going out of favour. Positivism was rapidly gaining ground in philosophy, see Chapter 12, Section 5, while Darwinism was becoming more and more controversial within biology. In psychology, on the other hand, behaviourism was rapidly supplanting an instinct–habit nexus, Hodgson (2004, ch. 12). It was natural that these new intellectual trends would influence developments both within economics in general, and institutionalism in particular. Perhaps the greatest influence on institutionalism was the 'empiricist drift' that is evident in the work of most latter-day institutionalists such as John Commons and Wesley Mitchell.

As seen in the previous chapter, Veblen focused his attention on 'the evolution of institutions and their impact on human conduct', Rutherford (1994,

p. 10). As shown in Section 2, Commons places emphasis on the study of the legal institutional framework of the economy, while Mitchell directs his intellectual efforts to applied research and the amassing of statistical data, Section 3, and Ayres to the exploration of the fundamentals of human progress, Section 4. Finally, some tentative conclusions are drawn in Section 5.

2 Commons' compromises

Commons was a student of Ely, who was by turn a student of Knies, a member of the older German Historical School. The traces of this intellectual pedigree are evident throughout his contributions. Most of his earlier work consists of historical monographs with little interest in developing theoretical concepts. In these, the emphasis is on the history of law and property rights, the evolution of the state and the impact of trade union organisation and collective bargaining. His later (post-1924) work followed a period of empirical investigations of US collective bodies such as labour unions, the US Industrial Commission, and the Industrial Revolution Commission. Commons' mature work is represented by his three major books, *Legal Foundations of Capitalism* (1924), *Institutional Economics* (1990a and 1990b [1934, originally one volume]) and *Economics of Collective Action* (1950, published posthumously). The most pervasive element in Commons' work is the role of *legal* institutions in economic activity. And at least three prominent themes underpin his brand of institutional economics. One is the history of law, and especially in its impact on property rights. Another is the history of economic thought, and the incorporation of its insights into his thinking. The third is to draw from his own experiences as investigator, policy maker and trade union representative, Commons (1990a, ch. 1), Rutherford (1990) and Chamberlain (1963, p. 68).

The basic elements of Commons' theoretical corpus are presented neatly in summary form in Commons (1931). According to him, (institutional) economics is behaviouristic, since it investigates the behaviour of individuals in transactions. He places great emphasis on the volitional aspects of human activity. In this light, institutional economics requires an institutional, negotiational or behaviouristic psychology, as opposed to Veblen's instinctive psychology. He defines economics as the science of economic behaviour which 'requires analysis into similarities of cause, effect or purpose, and a synthesis in a unified system of principles', p. 648. Arguing in similar vein to neoclassical economics, Commons (1990a, p. 6) considers the common characteristic of all human economic activity to be that of choosing between alternatives, which in turn is the result of scarcity: 'I start, like economists, with scarcity, as universal for all economic theory'.

Commons, then, builds his theoretical corpus around three basic concepts: scarcity, conflict of interest and collective action. Property rights in scarce resources give rise to conflicts of interest: 'I make "conflicts of interests" predominant in transactions', p. 6. The latter are held in check through collective action. He uses the notion of collective action as roughly equivalent to that of institutions. In the latter, he includes both unorganised custom and what he calls 'organised going concerns', such as the family, the corporation, trade unions, and the state. Collective action and the institutional structure mould and shape individualist thought and action, Rutherford (1983, p. 732).

He defines an institution as 'collective action in control, liberation and expansion of individual action', where collective action takes the form of a taboo or prohibition or sanctions on individual action, Commons (1931, p. 649). Institutions, on the other hand, lay down working rules that are the rules of the game determining economic relationships. These working rules involve collective sanctions, the analysis of which requires the investigation of the relationship between economics, law and ethics, giving Commons' economics a distinctly interdisciplinary flavour. This is especially marked in the relationship between economics (material properties) and law (property relations), for 'analytic economics has to do solely with the function of scarcity, just as analytic jurisprudence has to do solely with the function of force', Commons (1990b, p. 696). For Commons, the economy cannot be understood without considering of the force of law. 'Hence, ownership becomes the foundation of institutional economics', Commons (1990a, p. 5).

For Commons, the basic unit of analysis for institutional economics is the transaction which he describes as 'the smallest unit we can find which permits the analysis of all dimensions of the human will in action, with the correlated social relations', Commons (1950, pp. 118–19). His method for proceeding is to focus on five simplified elements, which are identified as sovereignty, scarcity, efficiency, futurity, and custom – each notably universal and lacking historical specificity. Nonetheless, they are chosen 'for the purpose of attaining systematic interpretation and understanding in a world of diversity. They are devices for investigation. The validity of such assumptions is found through the fruitfulness of their uses', p. 73. Transactions are also divided into three types: bargaining, managerial and rationing, p. 57. The first involves market transactions between buyers and sellers, and is presumed to take place between legal equals (possibly by persuasion and even coercion), whereas the latter two involve hierarchy, command and obedience – one relating to the production of wealth within enterprises, the other to its (re)distribution through government. Each transaction involves three social relations: conflict of interest, dependence on each other and working rules creating order. So, for Commons, social relationships necessarily involve notions of power and conflict, Marangos (2006, pp. 56–7). Thus, he concludes, 'conflict, dependence and order become the field of institutional economics, builded upon the principles of scarcity, efficiency and futurity ... but correlated under the modern notions of working rules of collective action controlling, liberating and expanding individual action', p. 656. Thus, although Commons starts with neoclassical notions such as scarcity and efficiency, he gradually builds a system where collective action, and hence power and conflict, assume central importance.

One fundamental distinction Commons draws is between two ways of looking at the commodity – as a use value or physical object, or as attached to particular property relations. Thus, he refers again and again throughout his work 'to the two contradictory meanings of a commodity – the material thing and the ownership of the material', Commons (1990a, p. 393) for example. Whilst law, and governance and custom, etc. settle the ownership side of things in terms of conflict of interest and exercise of power between contracting parties, economics as a discipline has placed varying and different emphases on these two aspects. For Commons (1990b, ch. X), the significance of the contradiction comes to the fore in modern (US) capitalism. Significantly, it is dubbed the Banking System in deference to the power of finance, and in contrast to Communism and Fascism. Borrowing from Veblen, the 'intangible' assets associated with finance are paramount. These no longer represent material substance, but rather claims on future profits (and hence emphasis on futurity on which see below). But, for Commons, there is a deeper significance, as the discussion is situated in a chapter of more than two hundred pages, entitled 'Reasonable Value'. This reflects an abiding concern, analytical and ethical, of how the prices of goods are determined relative to their material properties (supply and demand) and the property rights attached to them, itself closely related to but separate from the pursuit of individual self-interest as opposed to collective action.

As is apparent from this cursory overview, Commons' economics is highly idiosyncratic. Further, far from being theory-less – as is the common charge against the old institutionalists – Commons is prepared to accept more or less any economic theory as potentially having some relevance. For his reading of the history of economic thought is made through the prism of the contradictory commodity, with different contributors perceived as emphasising one or other of its aspects. This leads to a greater or lesser correspondence to the economies studied, in terms of their mode of balancing individual against collective action in theory and practice.

One can identify several basic attributes of Commons' political economy through difference with Veblen. According to Hamilton (1953, p. 50):

> the difference between [Veblen and Commons] is largely one of approach. Commons came to his theory through long years of research among labor unions, cooperatives and government agencies. Veblen approaches the economic problem from anthropology and a long study of culture.

As Commons (1990a, p. 1) himself puts it in the opening remarks of his *magnus opus, Institutional Economics*:

> My point of view is based on my participation in collective activities, from which I here derive a theory of the part played by collective action in control of individual action.

His method was one of going from observation and experience to concept building. He was an inductivist whose concepts were firmly grounded on reality and empirical observations. Following his teacher Ely, he helped to establish the importance of field investigation, Chamberlain (1963, pp. 90 and 92). However, Commons was certainly no crude empiricist. Because, according to him, 'not all history is relevant to economic theorizing. Hence the economist must abstract from the empirical data of history only so much as is needed ... to construct an all-round ideal type for the particular phase of history which, as economist, he is concerned with', Commons (1990b, p. 722). Here he uses the Weberian ideal type concept as a way of combining Menger's 'exact science of diminishing and marginal utility' with Schmoller's 'historical evolution of customs, laws and institutions ... in a comprehensive unit of a single reality that should be both theoretical in Menger's deductive sense, and empirical in Schmoller's historical sense', Commons (1990b, p. 721). Through this concept, according to Commons, the antagonism and dualisms between 'the deductive and historical schools, between economics and ethics, between theory and practice, between science and arts' is transcended.

A second basic characteristic is Commons' wide use of the historical method. This is clearly evident in his earlier works, which consist mostly of historical monographs, but also in his later more theoretical work. As Biddle and Samuels (1997, p. 292) put it:

> Commons was unequivocally historicist if by historicism is meant a focus on both the reality of change and the ongoing process of *becoming*. For Commons the historicist the meaning of anything resides in its history, its process of becoming what it is at any point in time, and not solely either generalized ahistorical, ideal type, conception of it or what it is (hypothesized to be) at a point in time.

A supreme example of Commons' historicism is his *Legal Foundations of Capitalism*. In this work, he explores the emergence and evolution of capitalism by focusing on the legal history as the foundation of capitalism. The exploration of the 'legal–economic nexus', in turn, lays the template for analysing the process of social change under capitalism, pp. 293–4. This is not without a cost, however, since incorporating the historical dimension adds to the complication of any theoretical endeavour. At the same time, however, as Marangos (2006, p. 54) puts it:

> while the incorporations of history makes the science of economics more complex and unmanageable, it simultaneously makes economic science less dogmatic and less irrelevant; economics becomes more investigational, more workable and, very likely, as Commons (1950: 237–8) points out, more conciliatory.

Third, as seen already, for Commons, economics is a behavioural science based on a volitional conception of human behaviour, as opposed to Veblen's instinctive theory, Zingler (1974). Indeed, he considers this volitional aspect of human action – 'the concerted but conflicting action of human wills' – as the basic demarcation line between social and physical sciences, Commons (1990b, p. 719). Fourth, and again unlike Veblen, he did not totally reject neoclassical theory, but he rather thought to supplement it with the theory of collective action. 'The problem', Commons (1990a, pp. 5–6) says:

> is not to create a different kind of economics – institutional economics divorced from preceding schools, but how to give collective action, in all its varieties, its due place throughout economic theory ... This collective control of individual transactions is the contribution of institutional economics to the whole of a roundabout theory of political economy.

For Kaufman (2007), Commons does not reject marginalism, but rather considers it needs to be supplemented by those considerations that it omits. And he concludes that, p. 38:

> The key concepts of institutional economics, as suggested by Commons and more fully and clearly developed by other economists, are bounded rationality, property rights, working rules, institutions and transactions. Its most important theoretical tools, in turn, are positive transaction costs and incomplete contracts.

In this way, Commons becomes one of the main precursors of new institutional economics of Coase and Williamson, see Fine and Milonakis (2009).

Fifth, as is obvious from the above summary of his theory, Commons' focus of attention was on individual decision makers. Unlike Veblen, Commons was a methodological individualist, but not of a neoclassical, psychological kind, Rutherford (1983, p. 732). Instead, he looked at the individual as part of the wider institutional structure, as an 'Institutionalised Mind'. His emphasis was on the relationship between human and human, rather than between human and object. For Commons (1990a, pp. 73–4), individual action is controlled and sanctioned by institutions and collective action giving rise to 'collective human will'. He was an 'individualist who was in love with collective action', Chamberlain (1963, p. 90). Hence Rutherford's (1990, p. xviii) label of his method as 'institutional individualism'. What Commons (1990a, p. 1) sought was 'a reconciliation with the individualist and collectivist theories of the past two hundred years'. And, he adds, 'It is not needful to repudiate the older theories of individual economics when all that is needed is to adjust them to the newer theories of collective economics', Commons (1990b, p. 680). In short, for Commons, individuals never existed in a prior vacuum from which they begin to trade. Rather, they are institutionalised from the outset.

What is important is the nature of those institutions, and how much they allow for collective action both to benefit from and to correct the excesses of freedom of individual action, p. 874:

The theory of reasonable value may be summarized in its pragmatic application, as a theory of social progress by means of personality controlled, liberated, and expanded by collective action. It is not individualism, it is institutionalized personality. Its tacit or habitual assumptions are the continuance of the capitalist system based on private property and profits.

The alternatives to such enlightened capitalism are various forms of Communism and Fascism which offer guarantees of security at the expense of suppressing freedoms and originality, Chapter XI. Commons' preference is for a reformed and reforming capitalism, laced with fears of the alternatives should this not materialise through enlightened and collective action. In this, he is close to Keynes' adherence to a reformed capitalism. Indeed, Kaufman (2007, p. 9) notes support of Keynes for Commons, citing a personal letter from the one to the other: 'There seems to be no other economist with whose general way of thinking I feel myself in such genuine accord'. And, for Marangos (2006, p. 51), Commons 'was just as persistent as Keynes in proclaiming that laissez-faire must be abandoned if capitalism was to be saved'. It is no accident that Commons, much like Keynes, see Chapter 14, considers Malthus rather than Ricardo to be his predecessor. Indeed, Malthus's empiricism and emphasis on institutions is more akin to institutional economics, as opposed to Ricardo's deductivism, which was to be embraced so fully by neoclassical economics, Kaufman (2007, pp. 8–9).

In sum, Commons was an idiosyncratic writer who implicitly adopted a reconciliatory stance in the *Methodenstreit*, as is obvious from above discussion, arguing for the need for both theory and observation, deduction and induction, on top of historical analysis in the development of an adequate economic science. He believed there to be a close association between the evolution of the economy and the law. Hence he lays overwhelming emphasis on the evolution of legal institutions as the framework for the emergence and functioning of capitalism.[2] For Commons, institutions involve social relations in the form of collective action and, for completeness, their analysis also requires historical investigation. The incorporation of both social relationships and history make the notions of power and conflict indispensible for the analysis of institutions. However, although Commons was a great concept builder moving from cases to concepts, he was not a theory or system builder of the same calibre, Chamberlain (1963, pp. 63, 88). Much like Veblen before him, and even more so, he failed to leave behind a comprehensive theoretical system. As Frank Knight (1935, p. 805) was to comment in review, tongue firmly in cheek, from the perspective of the enlightened orthodoxy of the time:

The positive task which the author sets himself is that of giving a *theory* ... of negotiation and of collective action. There will again be difference of opinion as to the wisdom of this course, in comparison with a possible adherence to direct, realistic description of courses of events. The reviewer, after going through the book, could not give a statement of the author's 'theory'. His treatment runs in terms of a long list of general concepts, such as scarcity, efficiency, futurity, liberty, security, equality, conflict, interdependence, *etc.*, coming to a climax in 'fair value'. I have expended much honest effort over a number of years (being one of those who saw earlier mimeographed versions of the more general parts of the work) in trying to make out what Professor Commons means by such terms, and have had to give up; and I have heard numerous others rated as economists make a similar admission.

This contrasts with Commons' own view of the prospects for his theory, which he believes is soon to triumph.

3 Mitchell's empiricism

Wesley Mitchell considered himself as part of the evolutionary tradition in economics – what he calls 'a more scientific type of economic theory – one that looks at its material from the evolutionary view-point', Mitchell (1910b, p. 216), in which he includes 'the work of Schmoller and Sombart in Germany, of the Webbs in England, and of Veblen in America', Mitchell (1910a, p. 112). His writings can be divided into two groups: those consisting of articles chiefly devoted to appraising existing economic doctrines; and his more empirical writings mainly comprised of monographs. Being a student of Veblen, his teacher's intellectual mark is clearly visible in all his theoretical writings. First is his critique of orthodox economic theorising, and especially the notion of economic rationality which he considers not as mistaken but as 'inadequate to explain the facts', such as 'the work of rank and file in industry and business' or 'the activities of consumption', Mitchell (1910b, pp. 200–1). For Mitchell, there is, p. 210:

> a need to reveal the institutional and partial character of human rationality. The man created by the imagination of economists is indeed a thin and formal character in comparison with their heir of all ages, with his rich racial inheritance of instincts, his dower of social concepts, and his wealth of habits. His rationality gets its character from the institutions under which he is reared.

Neither individualism in itself and rationality as its form will suffice.

Second, for Mitchell (1924, p. 369), economics is first and foremost a science of human behaviour. However, the evolutionary character of economic theory necessarily implies that human behaviour is heavily influenced by the institutional context. For Mitchell (1910a, p. 111):

> In [evolutionary] type of economic theory, human nature is conceived, not as a ready-made something taken over from the outset, not as a *postulate* whose consequences must be developed, but as itself the chief

subject of investigation. When economic activity is studied in this fashion, great importance is found to attach to institutions, because the latter standardise the behaviour of individuals.

Hence economics should focus attention on the crucial role that social concepts and institutions play in shaping human action and economic activity more generally, what he considers to be the leading problem to be addressed by economic theory, Mitchell (1910b, p. 216):

> To account for the actual human types which are found in every nation, by tracing the processes by which habits and institutions have grown out of instincts, and by examining the fashion in which the new acquisitions and the old traits combine in controlling economic conduct.

'Social concepts', he says, 'are the core of social institutions'. Following Veblen, he defines institutions as 'the prevalent habits of thought which have gained general acceptance as norms for guiding conduct', p. 203. This conception of economics calls for close cooperation between economics and other sciences of human behaviour, thus forging a link between them, especially between economics and psychology, Mitchell (1924, p. 369).

Thus, third, in a fashion similar to Schumpeter, Chapter 11, Mitchell also calls for a close cooperation between different branches of economics, such as economic theory, economic history and applied economics. These different branches have 'close organic relations' and, as such, should cease to be treated separately, but should 'become organic parts of a single whole', p. 369.

Fourth, any scientific economic theory has to be historically specific to the situation under consideration. As we have seen above, according to Mitchell (1910b, p. 204), human behaviour and humanly devised concepts are not the result of some innate attribute of human beings, but rather are institutionally determined. Mitchell (1924, p. 371) considers pecuniary concepts and the institution of the money economy as the chief moments shaping human conduct and modern culture more generally. These pecuniary concepts and institutions are the product of the modern age, the result of a long drawn out historical process of gestation, Mitchell (1910b, pp. 108–9):

> During the long centuries that men have been gaining a subtler mastery over the use of money, pecuniary concepts have been gaining a subtler mastery over men ... The pecuniary concepts constitute a system which is measurably beyond the control even of society and which ever again produces consequences which no man willed.

As is apparent, the evolution of money and corresponding modes of thought lead them to wield power over society and its individuals.

Despite the significance of these broad theoretical contours in Mitchell's intellectual trajectory, his main legacy and originality have been in terms of his more empirical writings. Throughout his career, Mitchell placed great emphasis on the need for economic theory to have strong empirical foundations. However, in his later work, he went further than this, in stressing the overwhelming need for more empirical work and more use of quantification to inform economic theory. Because 'it is mass behavior that the economist studies', he argues, 'the institutions that standardize such behavior of men create most of the openings for valid generalizations', Mitchell (1924, p. 375).

To study this behaviour, the method that the economist and all other social scientists should follow is 'the quantitative analysis of behavior records', Mitchell (1925, p. 27). As more quantification becomes possible, so economic theory will change and become more objective as more credible generalisations become possible, pp. 32–3. Thus, Mitchell (1924, pp. 375–6) concludes:

> A much more dependable set of generalizations can be attained as rapidly as objective records of mass behavior become available for analysis. The extension and improvement of statistical compilations is, therefore, a factor of the first consequence for the progress of economic theory. Gradually economics will become a quantitative science. It will be less concerned with puzzles about economic motives and more concerned about the objective validity of the account it gives of economic processes.

In other words, economic theory will be more concerned with relationships between objective quantifiable variables than with qualitative analysis based on the motives of imaginary individuals. So more observation, more statistical figures, more measurement and more quantification provide the route for the attainment of a more objective economic science. 'Indeed, qualitative work itself will gain in power, scope and interest as we make use of wider, more accurate, and more reliable measurements', Mitchell (1925, p. 36). As this happens, the breach between economic theory and applied economics through statistical analysis will be narrowed, p. 28. He devoted the latter part of his career to this task, and was one of the founders of the National Bureau of Economic Research, which produced many empirical studies on business cycles and price movements, and pioneered a whole range of new statistical series on economic aggregates such as national income. Indeed, according to Mirowski (1989b, p. 307), Mitchell, along with others, invented the notion of national income, thus paving the way 'for Keynes' decision to base the *General Theory* upon it'. In this respect, he is also considered a precursor of Keynes' *General Theory* and of modern macroeconomics, see also Hodgson (2004, ch. 14).

Mitchell focused his attention on the empirical investigation of business cycles, his two major works being *Business Cycles* (1913) and *Business Cycles: The Problem and Its Settings* (1927). Based on these, Mitchell promoted a policy of counter-cyclical public measures in order to alleviate the excesses of the cycle. This is how Kuznets (1963, p. 103), that other champion of empirical and quantitative economics and one of Mitchell's students, sums up his teacher's contribution in these two works:

> The concentration of these studies on money, prices, and business cycles, their unity in treating, with depth of observation, mastery of detail, and skill in organization, those aspects of the money economy that must be understood in gauging properly its short-term responses to long-term potentials is evident; and has been much commented upon. They are models of the kind of study that Mitchell saw as providing a basis for a realistic and useful discipline of economics.

The same author identifies Mitchell's basic contributions to economic science as being, first, the new light that his empirical studies shed on the actual functioning of money, business cycles and the aggregate performance of the US economy. Second is the vast extension of basic statistical compilations generated by Mitchell's and his colleagues' work on prices, business cycles and national income. Third is the quickening impact that his empirical studies had on economic theory by sharpening some of its concepts. Fourth is his insistence 'on the kernel of empirical content that every theory must contain', p. 110. Finally, there is the importance of his more objective quantitative analysis as the basis for policy prescription, pp. 107–11.

It is obvious from Kuznets' summary of Mitchell's basic contributions that they are all related to his empirical work. This certainly has to do with Kuznets' own personal academic inclinations, but it also has a large amount of truth as an overall assessment of Mitchell's work. Mitchell's heavy insistence on empirical work has led Schumpeter (1950, p. 254), who also produced a major treatise on business cycles by combining economic theory with historical and statistical analysis, see Chapter 11, to charge his two major works with 'lacking effective conceptualization'. However, Schumpeter goes on, the aim of his work on business cycles was 'to make the phenomenon stand up before us and by so doing to show us what there is to explain', p. 256. This is how Burns and Mitchell (1946, p. 4), cited in Koopmans (1947, p. 162), themselves, put the matter:

> Whatever their working concepts ... all investigators cherish the same ultimate aim – namely, to attain better understanding of the recurrent fluctuations in economic fortune that modern nations experience. This aim may be pursued in many ways. The way we have chosen nations is to observe the business cycles of history as closely as we can before making a fresh attempt to explain them.

This heavy emphasis by Mitchell on empirical investigation has led Koopmans (1947) to charge him with being a champion of 'measurement without theory'. This is the conclusion he reaches in a review of the above mentioned book, p. 172:

The book is unbendingly empiricist in outlook. Granted this basic attitude, it shows great perseverance and circumspection on the part of the authors in handling a vast amount of statistical data ... But the decision not to use theories of man's economic behavior, even hypothetically, limits the value to economic science and to the maker of policies, of the results obtained or obtainable by the methods developed.

In this light, there is no doubt that the empiricist drift within institutionalism came to a head with Wesley Mitchell.

4 Ayres' Veblenian themes

It was left to Clarence Ayres, the last of the major institutionalists of his generation, to redress the balance with theory by clarifying and further delineating the relation between institutionalism and empiricism. Writing in 1951, he considers empirical studies as complementary to institutionalist theory. They provide the groundwork of institutionalist theorising, but they are by no means identical to it. 'Simply to identify institutionalism with empiricism is a mistake. Descriptive studies are the spadework of institutionalist thinking; but they do not produce a body of theory by spontaneous generation', Ayres (1951, p. 55). His own work pays testimony to this view.

For Ayres was Veblen's closest disciple. Hence the label Veblen–Ayres tradition has been used to differentiate the work of these two institutionalists from the work of the other two major figures of this tradition, Commons and Mitchell. There is no doubt that the former duo share more in common than the latter. The basic focus of Ayres' mature work, *The Theory of Economic Progress* (1962 [1944]), as the subtitle of the book itself suggests, is the 'study of the fundamentals of economic development and cultural change'. 'Economic theory', he suggests, 'has always been – since long before the time of Adam Smith – a theory of economic development', Ayres (1951, p. 12). The roots for the explanation of this process cannot be found within the motives of the abstract individual, as had been sought by much economic theory. He considers the abstract individual of standard economic theory a myth. Instead, for Ayres, as with most institutionalists, 'human nature is itself a social phenomenon', p. 49. Granted this, explanations for economic development must be sought in the social forces in operation, and not in terms of universal human wants or natural scarcity. Following in Veblen's footsteps, he considers the interplay between institutions and technology as a source of 'the basic analytical principles' for the study of the economy. Between the two, however, it is technological progress that provides the basic motor of social change, including economic development, pp. 50–2.

Unlike Veblen, however, he does not consider human instincts and proclivities as lying behind technological progress. For Ayres (1962, p. vii), technology 'includes all human activities involving the use of tools'. Following Veblen, he considers tool-using in an instrumental way as 'physically productive, a creative process that underlies all the achievements of mankind', Ayres (1951, p. 52). On the other hand, he identifies social institutions with ceremonialism. The latter refers to the type of behaviour shaped by status and social stratification, social conventions, ideology, systems of indoctrination and sacred ceremonies, Ayres (1962, p. viii). Pushing the Veblenian dichotomy to its limits, Ayres considers technology to be the sole agent of social change, the chief dynamic factor shaping modern civilisation. This contrasts sharply with Schumpeter's and others' notion that modern culture is the result of the institutional structure of capitalism, or the modern capitalist spirit or the leadership of great men, Walker (1979, p. 521). This does not, however, mean that technology is an external force. It is internal both to social structure and human behaviour, Ayres (1951, p. 51). For Ayres (1962, p. 176):

> The history of the human race is that of perpetual opposition of these forces, the dynamic force of technology continually making for change, and the static force of ceremony – status, mores, and legendary belief – opposing change.

As such, social institutions inhibit rather than facilitate technological progress.

This contrasts with Veblen's more subtle approach. As Keaney (2002, pp. 92–3) suggests of Ayres:

> this sharp dualism contrasts with Veblen's more sophisticated recognition of the simultaneous instrumentality and ceremonialism inherent in social institutions ... Veblen saw instrumentality and ceremonialism as organically related and even mutually supportive, as well as conflicting.

Ayres' scheme is closer to (some readings of) Marx's analysis of the basic motors of history in his preface to *Critique of Political Economy*, see Chapter 3. Ayres' dichotomy between technology and institutions parallels Marx's dichotomy between forces and relations of production. And his overwhelming emphasis on the role of technological progress in social change corresponds to the technological determinist reading of Marx's passage. According to the latter, Marx considers the development of what he calls productive forces as the basic motor of history, which at some point comes into conflict with the existing production relations and brings about a transformation in the social structure, see also Hodgson (2004, pp. 373–6). However, as we have argued in Chapter 3, for Marx, the emphasis lies in the contradictory unity of the productive forces and the relations of production. As is evident from his analysis in *Capital*, the role of production relations in his scheme is active in shaping and energising the development of productive forces. Thus, for example, he considers the unprecedented growth of productive forces witnessed in modern bourgeois society as the result of the capitalist social structure: 'The bourgeoisie cannot exist without constantly revolutionising the instruments of production, and thereby the relations of production, and with them the whole relations of society', Marx (1848, p. 38). Even so, at certain points, Ayres does allow for a more flexible role for institutions. Hence, for example, the role that western institutions played in the rise of western civilisation was permissive, if not dynamic. It allowed the industrial revolution to occur, but did not otherwise facilitate its occurrence, Ayres (1962, p. 177–8).

With Ayres, Veblenian dichotomies took an extreme form, and leaned heavily towards a mutually exclusive form. Veblenian institutionalism was offered with a technological determinist twist and a more schematic form, and its dualistic structures came to the fore. At the same time, Ayres' focus on 'the fundamentals of economic development and cultural change' made possible, if not inevitable, the extensive utilisation of historical material and the historical method. For the alternative was also opened of reducing development to modernisation, itself having separate if interacting elements in terms of economy and culture.

5 Concluding remarks

After the Second World War, institutionalism witnessed a sharp decline both in terms of its appeal and influence and in terms of its prestige. Leading present-day institutionalists agree on the most important causes of this degeneration of American institutionalism, some of which are external and others internal. One important factor was the rapidly changing environment in the social and other sciences referred to above. The decline of the influence of Darwinian evolutionism in biology, coupled with the rise of behaviourism at the expense of instinct and habit psychology, undermined the foundations of Veblenian institutionalism. At the same time, the new trends in psychology could not provide a clear foundation for the further development of the theoretical framework of institutional economics, which was thus left stranded where it was left by Veblen and Commons. This failure of institutionalism to develop a coherent body of theory that could rival other existing theories including neoclassicism and Marxism, is an important factor in its decline.

But other developments in mainstream economic theory and methods also played an important part. Thus, the rise of Keynesianism provided a more concrete and robust theoretical corpus for the explanation for, and cure of, the most pressing problem of the inter-war period, unemployment, and as the basis for reform. Similarly, the rise of econometrics, and the extensive use of quantitative methods by mainstream economics, meant that another area where institutionalists played a leading part in developing economics (and its historical content) could no longer be regarded as their privileged terrain. Other developments within mainstream economics – such as the theories of imperfect competition and market failures, and the increasing formalisation of economic theory after the Second World War – also played a part in the increasing marginalisation of the institutionalist movement within economics,

Rutherford (2001, pp. 182–5) and Hodgson (2004, ch. 18). Increasingly, the institutionalist tradition served as a corrective to the deficiencies of the mainstream – in answering the big questions of economic and social change, and in accounting for missing factors or the economic impact of those non-economic factors that were studied predominantly within the other social sciences. Subsequently, and inevitably, this proved a recipe for marginalisation, neglect, amnesia and – ultimately, should all these fail – contempt for alien methods and supposed lack of (rigorous) theory.

Most institutionalists were social reformers with a radical and progressive stance from the perspective of Cold War ideology. Further, American institutionalism is the last major school of thought where the historical, the social and the psychological all find refuge as constituent elements in economic theorising. All these features were also central to the historicist movement in Germany. It is no accident, then, that both schools suffered similar fates, although to a different degree. They have been set aside as atheoretical, thereby neglecting both their critical and constructive aspects, even though these were generally recognised at the time they were put forward by those inspiring different, if less extreme, directions than their followers.

It may help the modern reader to situate and understand American institutionalists by casual comparison with current, critical attempts to pin down (economic) globalisation. Treatments of the latter are equally amorphous and diverse, and gain their insights by an eclectic and incoherent juxtaposition and combination of empirical and historical insights, and the deployment of theoretical and methodological fragments. The literature has come to distance itself from economic orthodoxy, not least for its failure to deal with 'globalisation' systematically and systemically in light of its formal and individualistic methodology. By the same token, the American institutionalists sought to grapple with the continuing and evolving features of (especially) American capitalism as they themselves experienced it, selecting more or less appropriately across empirical and theoretical material as best they could against the swell of marginalist thought.

Stretching this parallel to breaking point (as similarities can always be found in one way or another between heterodoxies) two further affinities can be noted. First is the heavy ethical as well as political content of the American institutionalists. They were sharply dissatisfied with capitalism as it was evolving, and sought, at the very least, to see it tempered and reformed. Further, Veblen's is an undisguised contempt for the parasitism of the leisure class and all to which it was connected, across his dualistic understanding of capitalism and how it both drew upon negatively formed instincts and also obstructed more fundamental virtues of human nature. Much the same is true of a range of anti-capitalist feeling today, from the green movement to those who oppose globalisation from a range of perspectives.

Second is the remarkable optimism with which the American institutionalists viewed their own prospects. This no doubt partly reflected their status at the time, but it also symbolised a faith in the possibility, if not power, of reason and common sense to prevail. We have already seen this in case of Commons. For Veblen (1898b, p. 396), to what he presumed to be a sympathetic audience, deploring the failure of economics yet to have become an evolutionary science, it seemed just a matter of time before this would be corrected. This is because of the previously noted failure to get to grips with the reality of American society, i.e. to develop 'knowledge of the brute facts which is shaped by the exigencies of the modern mechanical industry'.

In this light, he concludes:

> Provided the practical exigencies of modern industrial life continue of the same character as they now are ... it is only a question of time when that (substantially animistic) habit of mind which proceeds on the notion of a definitive normality shall be displaced in the field of economic inquiry by that (substantially materialistic) habit of mind which seeks a comprehension of the facts in terms of a cumulative sequence.

Clearly, in principle and in practice, this view of the relationship between economic life and economic thought, as with Commons, is seriously wanting, as the gap between the practical exigencies of modern industrial life and the animistic habits of mind within economics have not only opened but ranged over a wider terrain.

This is of relevance in assessing the current revival of (the new) institutional economics (with little or no such prospect for any new historical school). The rediscovery that institutions matter within orthodox economics inevitably leads to some revisiting of the old institutionalists. Inevitably, the latter's own intents and insights are observed more in the breach by those seeking to extend neoclassical principles to pastures new (or should that be old and forgotten?) through the process of economics imperialism, analysed in detail in Fine and Milonakis (2009).

11 In the slipstream of marginalism

Weber, Schumpeter and *Sozialökonomik*

'The social process is really one indispensable whole. Out of its great stream the classifying hand of the investigator artificially extracts economic facts ... A fact is never or purely economic; other – and often more important – aspects always exist'.

Schumpeter (1961 [1934], p. 3)

1 Introduction

During the first decades of the twentieth century, the separation of economics from the social and the historical was becoming increasingly pronounced. There were some dissenting voices, however, that tried to keep the relationship between economics, sociology and history alive, even if as separate disciplines. They came from two of the last specimens of the species of good old classical European intellectuals: Max Weber (1864–1920) and Joseph Alois Schumpeter (1883–1950). Each is highly significant for the theme of this book, but also highly symbolic both of the developments taking place around economics at their own time and also for later developments. They both had extensive training, as well as wide-ranging intellectual, social and political interests, and they were greatly influenced by contemporary theoretical trends while remaining two of the most original thinkers of our times.[1]

Marx, the Historical School and marginalism each played an essential part in the formation of their thought, although they also diverged in important ways from each of these theoretical currents. It is no accident that Weber (1949, p. 65) considers Marx and Roscher as the founders of social economics. For his general liberal stance, but also for the shear breadth and scope of his theoretical contributions, Weber has been characterised as a 'bourgeois Marx', Therborn (1976, p. 270),[2] while Schumpeter has been labelled a 'bourgeois Marxist' – again for his liberal views, but also for borrowing and reworking some central themes of Marxist political economy, Catephores (1994) – although he was also highly critical of some aspects of Marx's work. At the same time, despite their valiant attempts to hold to a broader view of economic science, they ended up symbolising the division of social sciences into separate disciplines, with Weber being classified as sociologist, Schumpeter as economist. Although Weber's contribution to economic theory per se was non-existent, most of Schumpeter's work dealt with economic theory. Yet, despite theoretical compromises, he was cast aside as far as his continuing contribution to the evolution of economic theory is concerned. Although Weber became one of the founders of sociology, Schumpeter, despite his prominence in his own time, did not play any major role in subsequent developments in economic science.

Two questions immediately arise. First, since Weber is considered a member of the (youngest) German Historical School, why treat him separately; and, second, why include him, when generally perceived as a sociologist, in the same breath as Schumpeter, generally recalled as an economist? The answer to the first question is that, although Weber and the other members of the youngest branch of the Historical School are generally thought to belong to this tradition, he also had some important differences with it, as will be charted in this chapter. In particular, Weber and Sombart dealt extensively with historical issues, although they were theoreticians reflecting the fate of the *Methodenstreit* first and foremost. At the same time, both of them were strongly opposed to the ethical dimension in political economy, and argued instead for a value-free economic science, while, unlike most historical economists, Weber (but not Sombart) was at least in part a methodological individualist.

With regard to the second question, what brings Weber and Schumpeter together is their common quest for a broader scope for economic science, and their conciliatory stance in the *Methodenstreit*. Both Weber and Schumpeter were, in one way or another, directly or indirectly exposed to most trends in economics that were prevalent at the time. Weber was a student of Knies, one of the founders of the Historical School, and his work on economic theory should be seen both as arising out of this tradition, but also as a reaction against it. The 'Battle of Methods' which took place in 1883–4, when Weber was still a university student, also left its imprint on his thought, Swedberg (1999, pp. 4, 9, 10). Schumpeter, on the other hand, was a student of Böhm-Bawerk and Wieser, both of them belonging to the Austrian wing of the marginalist tradition. At the same time, he was also exposed to Marxism through his participation in a seminar where heated debates took place between the Austrians and the Austro-Marxists, Otto Bauer and Rudolf Hilferding. Last, he was also acquainted with the ideas of the Historical School, not only through his association with Weber but also through his appointment at the University of Graz, which, at the time, was dominated by historical economics, Caldwell (2004, p. 91) and Swedberg (1991a, pp. 7–12).

Following in the footsteps of Karl Marx and the Historical School, both writers stood for an economics of broad scope, with a strong historical sense and an equally strong social dimension. Unlike Marx and the Historical School, though, they were in favour of a separation of economics from other social sciences. The influence of marginalism and the Austrian School, on the other hand, is obvious in their adoption of methodological individualism, albeit of a different sort to that of the marginalists, even if accepting of the concept of marginal utility of Menger, Wieser and Böhm-Bawerk.

In what follows, we begin in Section 2 by examining the meaning that Weber and Schumpeter attach to the notion of social economics. In Section 3, we assess the views of these writers on the role of values in economic theory and their basic methodological principles. In Section 4, their attempts and those of Sombart to construct a 'reasoned history' of capitalism are examined, before concluding the chapter in Section 5.

2 Constructing social economics or *Sozialökonomik*

If the final result of the *Methodenstreit* was the total victory of the narrow, ahistorical, asocial type of theoretical economics prevailing over historical economics, then Weber and Schumpeter are the two individuals who more than any others of prominence tried to keep the broader scope of economics alive. Both of them adopted a more conciliatory stance in the *Methodenstreit*. 'There cannot be any serious question', wrote Schumpeter (1994, p. 814), 'either about the basic importance of historical research in a science that deals with a historical process or about the necessity of developing a set of analytic tools by which to handle the material'. This is why, according to him:

> in spite of some contributions toward clarification of logical backgrounds, the history of this literature is substantially a history of wasted energies, which could have been put to better use.

The strict separation of theory from history and of induction from deduction associated with the *Methodenstreit* is, in other words, superficial and untenable. According to Schumpeter (1967 [1912], pp. 167–74), both protagonists of the *Methodenstreit* admitted as much in what he calls the last phase of the debate. Menger 'recognized ... the necessity of an historical basis', p. 170, while Schmoller emphasised 'the causal and theoretical task of social science', p. 171. Schumpeter's and Weber's work represent the last major attempts at bridging what Weber (1949, p. 62) described as 'an apparently unbridgeable gap' between the '*two* sciences of economics' created by the *Methodenstreit*. But their syntheses go well beyond the mere integration of the theoretical with the historical in economic science, for they encompass the whole universe of social science. Because 'economic and noneconomic facts *are* related', Schumpeter (1994, p. 13) proclaimed, 'the various social sciences *should* be related'.

Significantly, Weber considers both the hypothetico-deductive method and the historical approach as inappropriate for social theory. In his essay on Roscher and Knies, Weber (1975 [1903–6], pp. 65–6) concludes:

> It obviously does not make sense to suppose that the ultimate *purpose* of concept formation in the historical sciences could be the deductive

arrangement of concepts and laws ... under other concepts and laws of increasingly general validity and abstract content.

The discovery of 'a complex of regularities' in the form of '*lawlike relations*' or the establishment of correlations between economic or other social phenomena cannot and should not be 'the ultimate goal' of social (or any other) science, since 'these generalizations would have no causal status', pp. 60, 63.

At the same time, unlike Schmoller and the historicists in general, for Weber, the vehicle for a broader scope for economics cannot be the historical approach, which he identifies with 'the intuitive reproduction of the total reality of economic life', p. 58. Instead, the notion of what Heinrich Dietzel[3] (1857–1935) first termed *Sozialökonomik*, or social economics, is proposed as the platform for bringing the various social sciences together: 'the term, wider than "institutional economics" and less inclusive than "sociology", enabled him to encompass all relationships of economy and society', Roth (1968, p. lxiii). Weber was not simply one of the first to use the term, but he also devoted much of his intellectual energy to developing its substance. 'The word was Social Economics, *Sozialökonomie*', says Schumpeter (1994, p. 21f), 'and the man who did more than any other to assure some currency to it was Max Weber'. This is reflected in his undertaking to edit Weber's *Grundriss der* Sozialökonomik (*Outline of Social Economics*). This was a huge collection of works within economics, and took almost two decades to collate (between 1914 and 1930). It was only completed after Weber's death. His intention had been to provide a broad perspective for the study of economics. It should include the interaction between economic and non-economic phenomena such as social institutions, the state etc., and the use of different approaches such as economic history, theoretical economics, economic geography and population theory.[4]

Although Weber's own overall contribution differs from Schumpeter's in important ways, what unites their endeavours is the common quest for a broad-based economics or *Sozialökonomik*. It was to prove an ambitious mission, and, despite Weber's and Schumpeters's best efforts, was never to be fully realised. Eventually, like the fate of the Historical School that it was designed to succeed, it has sunk into obscurity. Nowadays, it too hardly warrants a mention even in histories of economic thought, Swedberg (1991b).

Weber's views on *Sozialökonomik* are to be found in his most famous methodological article, 'Objectivity in Social Science and Social Policy', originally published in 1904, and reprinted in Weber (1949), while the approach in his mature economic thought appears in the second chapter of his *Economy and Society* ('Sociological Categories of Economic Action'). Neither he nor Schumpeter, however, gives a clear definition of the subject matter of social economics. Swedberg (1998, p. 192) summarises Weber's complicated definition as follows: 'social economics deals with those phenomena that are scarce, that are necessary to satisfy ideal and material needs, and that can only be provided through planning, struggle, and in cooperation with other people'.

So Weber, unlike Schumpeter, and in accordance with mainstream economics, points to 'the scarcity of means' as the 'fundamental social-economic phenomenon' and, as such, the *raison d'être* of social economics.

Weber (1949, p. 68) also makes clear that what he tries to achieve through the notion of *Sozialökonomik* is a *multi-disciplinary* approach to economic phenomena. The need for such a multi-disciplinary approach is motivated by the idea that 'the boundary lines of "economic" phenomena are vague and not easily defined', p. 65. This is because, for Weber, much as for Marx, the Historical School and American institutionalism, the economy does not exist in a social vacuum, but rather is part of society at large. According to Weber (1949, p. 67), the central aim of social economics is 'the scientific investigation of the *general cultural significance of the social-economic structure of the human community* and its historical forms of organization'. The substantive analysis of his version of social economics is contained in the second chapter of his *Economy and Society*. It focuses on the relation between the economy and other parts of society. As he puts it, 'the connections between the economy ... and the social orders [such as law, politics, and religion] are dealt with more fully [in this work] than is usually the case. This is done deliberately so that the autonomy of these spheres vis-à-vis the economy is made manifest', quoted in Smelser and Swedberg (1994, p. 10). The emphasis here is on the social aspects of economic action, including the role of power, and the meaning attached to them by economic actors.

The same fluidity over the boundaries of the economy, according to Schumpeter (1994, p. 10), applies to the frontiers of the individual social sciences, which are correspondingly 'incessantly shifting'. This, indeed, is one of the main reasons why 'the science of social-economics since Marx and Roscher ... is concerned not only with economic phenomena but also with those which are "economically relevant" and "economically conditioned"', Weber (1949, p. 65). 'Economic phenomena', according to Weber, refer to institutions such as the stock exchange and banking which are '*deliberately* created or used for economic ends', p. 64. On the other hand, 'economically relevant phenomena' include institutions such as religion which, although not economic in themselves, may have economic consequences. Lastly, 'economically conditioned phenomena' refer to social phenomena that are influenced by economic factors. Yet Weber also makes clear that his intention is *not* to create a 'general social science'. This is partly the result of his liberal political convictions. As Holton and Turner (1989, p. 58) put it, 'Weber's resistance to a general theory of society clearly stemmed in large measure from his liberalistic objections to organicism and holism'. Instead, both he and Schumpeter, unlike Marx's and the Historical School's holistic approach, and in line with Jevons' and Menger's separatist proposals, advocate a strict separation of the different social sciences. Given, however, the multi-faceted and impure nature of economic phenomena, and that these are necessarily related to non-economic events and institutions, a broad-based, multi-disciplinary approach to economic science is sought, which would draw upon different social sciences in the context of *Sozialökonomik*. In sum, '*Sozialökonomik* meant primarily two things: (1) that economics should be broad in scope and include a historical as well as a social dimension; and (2) that economics should draw on several distinct social science disciplines in its analyses', Swedberg (1999, pp. 11–12).

According to Schumpeter (1994), this broad vision of economic science which he also calls 'scientific economics' or 'economic analysis', p. 21, consists of 'an agglomeration of ill-coordinated and overlapping fields of research', p. 10. These include economic history, statistics, economic theory and economic sociology, Chapter 2. Of these four fields, he picks up *economic history*, referring mostly to descriptive, institutional type economic history as 'by far the most important', p. 12. This is a result of the very nature of the subject matter of economics, which is 'a unique process in historic time', and as such necessitates 'an adequate amount of historical sense', pp. 13, 14. At the same time, the nature of economic history itself makes this field multi-disciplinary in character, p. 13:

> Historical report cannot be purely economic but must inevitably reflect also 'institutional' facts that are not purely economic: therefore it affords the best method for understanding how economic and non-economic facts are related to one another and how the various social sciences *should* be related to one another.

The latter virtue makes this field an indispensable, if not the most important, part in Schumpeter's *Sozialökonomik*.

Economics in the narrow sense (or 'economics proper' or economic theory or 'pure' economics) deals with 'pure' economic phenomena or economic mechanisms, such as the market mechanism, Schumpeter (1949b, p. 293 and 1994 [1954], p. 21). It consists of 'simplifying schemata or models' comprising a set of hypotheses or axioms, together with the concepts used and the relations between these concepts. 'It is the sum total of these gadgets ... which constitutes economic theory'. Schumpeter (1994, p. 15). *Statistics* or statistical series of figures are of vital importance 'not only for explaining things but in order to know precisely what there is to explain', pp. 13–14.[5]

Economic history supplies the institutional framework for the functioning of the 'schemata of economic theory'. However, it is not only economic history that renders this service to economic theory, p. 20. If the dynamic nature of economic processes makes historical research indispensable to a broad-based economic science, the multi-faceted nature of economic phenomena calls for a new discipline to deal with the 'economically relevant phenomena'. This field is *economic sociology*, which denotes 'the description and interpretation of economically relevant institutions, including habits and all forms of behavior in general, such as government, property, private enterprise, customary or "rational" behavior', Schumpeter (1949b, p. 293). All these institutions represent 'social facts that are not simply economic history but are a sort of generalized or typified or stylized economic history', Schumpeter (1994, p. 20). In contradistinction to economic theory, which deals with how individuals behave and with their economic consequences (economically conditioned phenomena), economic sociology addresses the social institutions that affect human behaviour (economically relevant phenomena), Schumpeter (1994, p. 21 and 1949b, pp. 293–4). In sum, as Shionoya (2001b, p. 139) puts it, economic sociology is 'the generalization, the typification and the stylization of economic history by means of institutional analysis'. This is synonymous with what Schumpeter elsewhere calls 'reasoned history' or '*histoire raisonée*'. In opposition to economic history proper, which refers to descriptive, institutional-type history, Schumpeter uses the concept of 'reasoned history' to denote a 'conceptually clarified' or 'systematized' or 'rationalized' history. In other words, an economic history with a strong theoretical and analytical content, Schumpeter (1982 [1939], vol. I, p. 220, 1987, p. 44 and 1994 [1954], p. 818) and Shionoya (2001b, p. 139).

Schumpeter, in his essay on Schmoller, selects the latter's work as the prototype of economic sociology. Indeed the historical method, especially as applied by Schmoller, is the means through which a 'universal social science' could be built, cited in Shionoya (1995, p. 67) and Shionoya (1991, p. 193). Schumpeter (1987, p. 10) also considers Marx's economic interpretation of history as 'one of the greatest intellectual achievements of sociology to this day'. At the same time, as seen in Chapter 3, he also praises him for being 'the first economist of top rank to see and to teach systematically how economic theory may be turned into historical analysis and how the historical *narrative* may be turned into *histoire raisonée*', p. 44. In opposition to his own and Weber's research objectives, however, Marx's objective was to construct a 'unitary social science', Schumpeter (1994, p. 441). Schumpeter (1987 [1943], p. 44) claims that Marx 'set the goal for the historical school of economics', even though the latter's work was independent of Marx's suggestion, and the 'organon' used in each case was also to be very different. For the Historical School, then, the prime aim was the construction of a unified social science through the application of the historical method to economic phenomena. For Marx, it was the elaboration of a universal political economy where the economic is chemically integrated with the social and the historical. But for Weber and Schumpeter, as emphasised, the aim was to build a broad-based social economics that would draw on several distinct social sciences (mostly economic theory, economic history and economic sociology). This implies a separate discipline for 'pure economics', but also a 'social economics' or 'economic analysis' that incorporates the insights of other social sciences. Even so, Weber did not write any work on theoretical economics, although his scientific aspirations and research interests were very broad indeed, and extended well outside the socio-economic sphere to include analyses of law, politics, religious movements, etc., Aron (1970, pp. 185–6) and Shionoya (2001b, pp. 149–50).[6]

3 From value neutrality and ideal types to methodological individualism

As seen already, Weber is considered (with Sombart and Spiethoff) to be one of the last members of the (youngest) German Historical School. Despite this, his work (and Schumpeter's) differ from Schmoller's and the Historical School's contributions in important ways. As far as their views of what constitutes 'scientific economics', they were strongly influenced by the early marginalists, and Menger in particular. Hence Schumpeter (1994, p. 21) makes a distinction between nineteenth century 'political economy', which is mostly concerned with public policies, and what he calls 'scientific economics' that is devoid of any political connotations. Weber (1949), on the other hand, in his essay 'The Meaning of "Ethical Neutrality" in Sociology and Economics', first published in 1917, vigorously attacks Schmoller's tendency to mix science with value judgements, being strongly opposed to the ethical and normative dimension of Schmoller's political economy, p. 13. Instead, he argues for ethical neutrality and a value-free economics and sociology. Hence he pleas for a strict separation, between 'purely logically deducible and empirically factual assertions ... and practical, ethical or philosophical value-judgments', p. 1.

Schumpeter (1949a, p. 273), in his 'Science and Ideology', also argues that such a separation is possible: 'to investigate facts or to develop tools for doing so is one thing; to evaluate them from some moral or cultural standpoint is, in *logic*, another thing, and the two need not conflict'. Despite these claims, however, neither Weber nor Schumpeter managed fully to uphold this principle for two reasons. First, in Weber's research, for example, 'the evident intentionality of objectivity and the implicit assumption of values is mixed' and, second, the creation of concepts in social sciences necessarily involves values, Crespo (1997, pp. 34–5). Hence Schumpeter (1949a, pp. 274, 277, 286) warns against the dangers of the 'ideological bias' that results from the scientist's preconceptions about the economic process. These he calls the 'prescientific' or 'preanalytic cognitive act' or 'vision', which, however, by supplying 'the raw material for the analytic effort', also forms an absolutely indispensable template of any scientific endeavour, see also Schumpeter (1994, p. 41).

Second, despite their strong interest in, and acquaintance with, history, and in opposition to the goals of the Historical School, neither Weber nor Schumpeter saw economics as a branch of historical investigation. They were both, first and foremost, social *theorists*, albeit, as will be seen, of a different kind. Despite Schumpeter's comment, quoted above, to the effect that economic history is more important than economic theory, and in direct contradistinction to the monographs of the Historical School, most of his and Weber's work is theoretical in character, even if endowed with great historical depth, Aron (1970, p. 17). After all, this was a time in which economic theorising was winning the upper hand in its battle with the historico-empirical method following the *Methodenstreit*. According to Schumpeter (1967, p. 172):

a new generation – even of supporters of the historical school – no longer intended to continue with the mere collection of facts, while in the meantime economic theory had gained new life. There could no longer be any question of overcoming the latter.

So, for Schumpeter, reflecting the climate of his times, theory was an absolutely indispensable part of the long and complicated path to (economic) science.

The resultant heavy emphasis on theory was one of the most important features of the youngest Historical School (Spiethoff, Sombart and Weber) and sets it apart from the work of the earlier historical economists. Weber (1949, p. 106), for example, considers the use of the historical-inductive method in the social sciences as 'a preliminary task necessitated by the imperfections of our discipline'. Taking this as a point of departure, the goal of social science is to construct 'a system of concepts' through 'the construction of hypotheses, and their verification, until finally a "completed" and *hence* deductive science emerges', p. 106. His definition of economics follows closely along this path. In the footsteps of the marginalists, Weber (1949, pp. 43–4) takes one form of action, what he calls 'instrumental rationality', see Chapter 12, Section 2, as the main preoccupation of economic inquiry: 'Economic theory', he says:

> is an axiomatic discipline ... [It] utilizes ideal-type concepts exclusively. Economic theory makes certain assumptions which scarcely ever correspond completely with reality but which approximate it in various degrees and asks: how would men act under these assumed conditions, if their actions were entirely rational? It assumes the dominance of pure economic interests and precludes the operation of political or other non-economic considerations.

So Weber identifies economics as a separate, purely theoretical discipline, which deals with ideal types and covering only one specific aspect of human behaviour: rational action governed by material interests. So, for Weber, both ideal types and rational action play a pivotal role in identifying the subject matter of economics.

Weber defines his famous notion of 'ideal types' as 'unified analytical constructs' formed by an '*accentuation* of [the] essential tendencies' of social phenomena, pp. 90–1. Weber is at great pains to emphasise that ideal types are 'thought patterns' or 'mental constructs', 'the relationship of which to the empirical reality of the immediately given is problematical in every individual case', p. 103. As Schumpeter (1994, p. 819) puts it, ideal types 'are abstractions in that they possess only essential and lack non-essential properties: they are *logical* ideals'. His own definition of economic theory follows Weber's ideal typical path closely: 'economic theory', he says, consists of 'simplifying schemata or models that are intended to portray certain aspects of reality and take some things for granted [what he calls hypotheses or axioms or postulates or assumptions] in order to establish others according to certain rules or procedures', p. 15. The difference between this conception of economic theory and Weber's ideal types is that, as Weber (1949, p. 90) writes, the ideal typical concept is 'no "hypothesis" but it offers guidance to the construction of hypotheses'. In other words, as Hodgson (2001, p. 122) puts it, it is 'an attempt to interpret and to categorise, and thereby begin to explain, a complex reality, rather than to dig down and discover its allegedly fundamental building blocks'. At the same time, an ideal type represents a 'value reference', or, in other words, a theoretical construct based on subjective evaluations, which determine what is chosen for inclusion and what is not. It is a 'utopia ... formed by the one-sided *accentuation* of one or more points of view', Weber (1949, p. 90).

If ideal types represent one side of the coin of Weber's doctrine, the other side is reserved for the concept of *understanding (Verstehen)* or *interpretation of meaning*. This refers to the meaning attached by the actors themselves to their actions. Cultural phenomena have specific traits that differentiate them from natural phenomena. All human action is meaningful, and, as such, it has to be interpreted or understood: 'As regards the interpretation of human conduct', Weber (1975, p. 125) says:

> We can also attempt to '*understand*' it: that is, to identify the concrete 'motive' or complex of motives 'reproducible in inner experience,' as a motive to which we can attribute the conduct in question with a degree of precision that is dependent upon our source material. In other words, because of its susceptibility to a meaningful *interpretation* ... individual human conduct is in principle intrinsically less 'irrational' than the individual natural event.

In other words, for Boudon (1997, p. 9), '*explaining* the actions, beliefs, attitudes of an actor means "understanding" them; understanding them means *reconstructing their meaning to the actor*'. Unravelling this meaning and understanding the 'cultural contents' of action is what differentiates social sciences from natural sciences. '*Verstehen*', then, becomes the demarcation line between natural and social sciences, Therborn (1976, pp, 291–2). Hence, for Weber (1975, p. 65), the main purpose of social science should be 'to *understand* reality' by untangling 'the *meaningful* and essential aspects of concrete patterns'. Hence the label 'Interpretative Sociology' is given to Weber's social theory, Schumpeter (1994, p. 818).

Neither Weber nor Schumpeter accepted the organic and holistic aspects of the historical approach. Instead, they both accorded causal efficacy to the individual. Much like Menger and the marginalist school more generally, their scientific approaches had strong individualistic and subjectivist elements. Schumpeter was even the first to coin the phrase 'methodological individualism' in 1908, Machlup (1978, p. 472) and Blaug (1980, p. 49). Much like Schmoller's subjectivism, however, Schumpeter's individualism is more complex, and differs in fundamental ways from the methodological individualism of mainstream economic theory – unlike Weber's which, at times, takes a more instrumentalist character. For one thing, according to Schumpeter (1961, pp. 92–4), individual economic action is not simply governed by the hedonistic motive. Instead, a multiplicity of incentives is allowed to enter human motivation in addition to hedonism: 'the impulse to fight, to prove oneself superior to others', 'the will to found a kingdom' and the 'joy of creating, of getting things done'. Further, although the individual is the basic explanatory variable in social theory, individual behaviour itself is affected by the social environment, being in many respects shaped by it, a more or less inevitable (analytical) consequence of appeal to purposeful and meaningful action. At times, Schumpeter (1931, p. 286) even seems to be arguing contrary to his overall individualistic stance, in stressing the importance of the social milieu on individual action: 'We know that every individual is fashioned by the social influences in which he grows up. In this sense he is the produce of the social entity or class and therefore not a free agent'. The resemblance of this passage with Marx's (1976, p. 92) treatment of individuals as 'personifications of economic categories, the bearers of particular class relations and interests', is striking, see also Chapter 3, Section 3. What is more, although Schumpeter considers that, in the analysis of pure economic phenomena, such as the market, 'there is no choice but to start with the individual', which is by no means universally the case, 'In some problems of sociology or political life ... we have no choice but to start from the social whole', Schumpeter (1931, p. 287).

Be that as it may, Weber, at one point at least, takes a more extreme position, arguing in favour of methodological individualism even within sociology. 'If I have become a sociologist', he says, quoted in Swedberg (1998, p. 214):

> It is mainly in order to exorcise the spectre of collective conceptions which still linger among us. In other words, sociology itself can only proceed from the actions of one or more separate individuals and must therefore adopt strictly individualistic methods.

On a par with mainstream economics, Weber also considers (pure) economic theory as dealing exclusively with rational behaviour of individuals, and devoid of other (social) influences, as captured by the concept of 'instrumental rationality' in a world of perfect knowledge, see also Chapter 12, Section 2. At other points, however, Weber (1976, p. 54) points to the strongly social roots of individual action, in talking for example about the behaviour of individuals conforming to 'capitalistic rules of action', see also below. In reality, people are driven not only by the pursuit of their own self-interest, but also by a host of other motives and desires. Related to Weber's individualist approach to the social sciences, and the place of economics within it, is his rejection of the value theory of the classical school and of socialism, and his acceptance of the marginal utility theory of Menger and Böhm-Bawerk,

Swedberg (1998, pp. 185–6), Hodgson (2001, pp.117–28), Sumiya (2001, pp. 128–33), Bottomore (1992, pp. 18–20) and Lewis (1975, ch. 5).

4　Constructing *histoire raisonée*: Sombart and Weber

The previous section has dwelt upon the similarities between Schumpeter and Weber in some aspects of the ways in which they approached economics itself, and its relations to the other social sciences. But it is equally important to recognise how these two differed from one another. Whilst both were predominantly theorists, the directions taken by their research diverged. Weber is first and foremost a sociologist. 'Indeed', says Schumpeter (1994, p. 819), 'he was not really an economist ... His work and teaching had much to do with the emergence of Economic Sociology in the sense of an analysis of economic institutions'. Weber's main concern is to build a theory of economic sociology through a multi-disciplinary approach, by bringing together the economic, social, political and religious dimensions of social events, Swedberg (1998). His main contribution to *Sozialökonomik* is to be found in his voluminous *Economy and Society*, first published in 1922, his main work in economic and general sociology. The first part of this book is devoted to the development of his sociological concepts and 'categories of economic action', as he calls them, while the second part explores the connections and linkages between the economy and other moments of the social order such as religion, law and politics.

For our purposes, what is of more interest is his more historical work and especially his classic, *The Protestant Ethic and the Spirit of Capitalism*. It presents his analysis of 'the origins and likely course of evolution of industrial capitalism', Giddens (1976, p. 3). In Schumpeter's terms, it is a *histoire raisonée* of the emergence of the Western world, a subject of concern shared with Marx and Weber's own contemporary, Werner Sombart. Weber's contribution has aroused considerable controversy. Its substance and significance is, however, more readily assessed by first considering the contribution of Sombart.

Sombart was one of the last political economists to attempt to construct a reasoned history of capitalism. It is no accident that Schumpeter (1994, p. 818) picks up his *magnus opus, Modern Capitalism,* as a prototype of reasoned history: 'it is *histoire raisonée*, with the accent on the reasoning, and systematized history with the accent on system'.[7] Sombart is interesting for the themes of this book, not least because in his writings he combines elements drawn from the Historical School and from Marx, while on other matters he sides with Weber. As one commentator puts it, he 'successfully stood on the shoulders of Schmoller, at least with one leg, the other one being supported by Marx', although he was also critical of many aspects of their work, Betz (1993, p. 332). As a member of the (youngest) German Historical School, and a student of Schmoller, he was still strongly opposed to the ethical dimension of the latter's work. Much like Weber, he made a clear separation between value judgements and economics as a science, Lenger (1997, pp. 147,

155 and 166). At the same time, he considered Schmoller's work and that of the Historical School more generally as atheoretical. In this, he was strongly influenced by Marx: 'What separates me from Schmoller and his school', he wrote in his *Modern Capitalism* (vol. 1, p. xxix, quoted in Roth (1978 [1968], p. lxxi)):

> Is the constructive element in the ordering of the material, the radical postulate of a uniform explanation from last causes, the reconstruction of all historical phenomena as a social system, in short, what I call the specifically theoretical. I also might say: Karl Marx.

Much like Schumpeter, Sombart was an admirer of Marx's materialist conception of history, although he was also a severe critic of other aspects of his theory and method, such as dialectics and value theory. What he most valued were the theoretical aspects of Marx's historical work and, in particular, his analysis of the historical evolution of capitalism and of economic systems more generally, Betz (1993, p. 350). This is what Lenger (1997, p. 152) has aptly described as 'theoretical historism', before concluding that 'Sombart clung to the historism taught by his teacher Schmoller although he wanted to reconcile this historism with theory'.

At a time when history was mostly empirical, Sombart was strongly in favour of combining theory with history. 'No theory – no history!' he says. 'Theory is the prerequisite to any scientific writing of history', Sombart (1929, p. 3). Indeed, he sees his main work, *Modern Capitalism*, as a contribution to both theory and history, and as an attempt 'to end the baseless hostility prevailing between economic theory and economic history', p. 19. Further, the historian, he says, p. 2:

> whether he is dealing with the conduct of an individual, or a political situation ... he is concerned not with isolated facts but with connected systems ... Only as parts of a greater whole, and in relation to that whole, do they acquire any meaning ... The historian, then, must bear in mind that he has to deal with complex 'wholes' and with the causal connections in which the actual facts of history have taken shape.

So, contrary to Weber's and Schumpeter's methodological individualism and in true historicist spirit, Sombart adopts a holistic approach to historical questions.

At the same time, his method leans more towards induction than deduction. As Mitchell (1929, p. 276) observes:

> Sombart's methods differ from the methods employed by a writer like Marshall much as Marshall's methods in *Industry and Trade* differ from Marshall's methods in the *Principles of Economics*. In the superficial jargon that we ought to banish, 'induction' plays the stellar role that is usually assigned by theorists to 'deduction'.

In this light, the task Sombart sets himself in *Modern Capitalism* is to give 'a systematized historical account of European economic life in its entirety, from the beginnings to the present day', p. 17. He considers the biggest obstacle in this quest to be the absence of a body of theory suitable for the special requirements of economic history. This is the result of the 'unreal, abstract world' that economic theorists have constructed, focused as it is on the 'exchange operations of "economic men"', the loss of 'all historical sense' implied by the concept of equilibrium drawn from the natural sciences, and the seeking of 'universal and uniform' laws, applicable under 'every variety of conditions', p. 8. Following Marx and many members of the Historical School, for Sombart, the (economic) historian is mainly interested in 'differentiating between economic epochs, in emphasising their concrete and specific features, and in determining their place in history', p. 9.

Sombart tried to fill the theoretical gap left by the 'unreal and abstract' nature of economic theory through the concept of the 'economic system', which he uses in order to 'distinguish, describe and correlate economic phenomena', or, in other words, for both descriptive and classification purposes, pp. 13–14. Much like Schmoller's notion of 'national economy', the concept of 'economic system' illuminates the collectivist aspects of Sombart's method. In contrast to Schmoller, however, in Sombart's hands, this concept becomes the vehicle for the combination of theory with history, pp. 16–17 and Betz (1993, p. 223). Sombart defines an economic system as 'the mode of providing for material wants', which is very close to Marx's notion of a 'mode of production', although Sombart adds that this is, pp. 13–14:

1 'animated by a definite spirit' or geist;
2 'regulated and organised according to a definite plan'; and
3 'applying definite technical knowledge'.

Of these, he considers the *capitalist spirit* to be by far the most important determining factor of the genesis and evolution of capitalism, thus turning Marx's schema of base and superstructure on its head, and paving the way for Weber's famous thesis in his *Protestant Ethic and the Spirit of Capitalism,* see below. Preceding this was the handicraft spirit and before that the feudalistic spirit, Commons and Perlman (1929, p. 79). This spirit, according to Betz (1993, p. 347), is:

> the sum total of the intellectual influences on economic activity, comprises of all the values, norms and maxims which govern the behaviour of individuals and shape their collective institutional arrangements.

Lenger (1997, p. 159) appropriately concludes as follows:

> The relationship between ideas and reality ... was among the basic problems Sombart wanted to solve in his *Modern Capitalism*. Sombart's

solution gave considerable weight to the independent role of ideas as can be seen in his genealogy of the acquisitive spirit. Whatever one may think of his solution it remains Sombart's merit to have posed the problem of mediating structural processes and ideal factors quite clearly.

Indeed, it is a merit that reflects, in principle, the themes of nineteenth century political economy and its historical aspects.

According to Sombart, in practice, for each economic system there is a period during which it reaches its climax and achieves its relatively pure form. Before this climax is reached, however, all economic systems pass through an 'early epoch', a sort of transitory period between the present economic system and the previous one. After the climax comes the decline. On this basis, he offers a periodisation of the capitalist economic system into early, full or high and late capitalism, Sombart (1929, p. 16). Again, the affinities between Sombart's and various Marxist periodisations of capitalism are plain.

In his *Modern Capitalism*, Sombart traces the rise of capitalism from its beginnings in the Middle Ages to its full development in the nineteenth century.[8] 'Early capitalism' refers to the era before 1760, whereas the age of 'high capitalism' spans the entire epoch from the beginning of the Industrial Revolution to the outbreak of the First World War (1760–1914). Sombart, in a way closely resembling Schumpeter's theory of entrepreneurship and innovation (see below), considers the capitalist entrepreneur or business organiser, driven by the desire for gain, power and action to be the force underpinning high capitalism. He also considers the modern state and technical progress as the two other pillars of this stage of capitalism. What impressed him most was the extraordinary number of inventions witnessed during this epoch. And he offers a whole host of objective and subjective factors to explain this unprecedented process of innovation. These include anything from scientific advance, to research laboratories, to the motives for invention (desire for gain, pleasure in inventing, interest in the results of inventions for whatever reason, etc.). He does, however, single out gain from profits as the chief end of the activities associated with high capitalism. As he puts it, quoted in Michaelidis and Milios (2005, p. 35), capitalism:

> has a mania for innovations … Either through elimination of competitors by the establishment of new enterprises based upon them, or – primarily – through introducing new, more profitable processes, [it] soothes its innermost desire: to make an extra profit!

According to Mitchell (1929, p. 276), Sombart's basic concern in *High Capitalism* is 'to find what features differentiate high capitalism from other forms of economic organisation, how these features got their present form, and how they function'. And he concludes his review by saying that perhaps the best service of this book is to help us to see 'how much an economic historian needs to be a theorist, and how limited is the theoretical grasp of an economist who neglects history', p. 278.

Now Weber, in his *Protestant Ethic,* shared similar concerns to those of Sombart. In particular, his main preoccupation is with the causes of the genesis of capitalism. 'The capitalism of to-day', he says, 'which has come to dominate economic life' and 'the manner of life' associated with it, 'had to originate somewhere ... This origin is what really needs explanation', Weber (1976, p. 55). In his quest, Weber, much like Sombart, directs attention to an element of Marx's superstructure, to the world of ideas and the pursuit of profit as the 'spirit of capitalism' and the primary factor in its emergence, p. 68:

> It was not generally ... a stream of new money invested in the industry which brought about this revolution ... but the new spirit, the spirit of modern capitalism, had set to work. The question of the motive forces in the expansion of modern capitalism is not in the first instance a question of the origin of capital sums which were available for capitalist uses, but, above all, of the development of the spirit of capitalism.

Indeed, Weber considers his study as 'a contribution to the understanding of the manner in which ideas become effective forces in history' p. 90. Once again, this represents a direct reversal of Marx's causal schema of base and superstructure, where emphasis is laid on the economic and materialist forces of this transformation. Weber directly attacks what he calls the 'naïve historical materialism', according to which 'such ideas originate as a reflection or superstructure of economic situations', p. 55. Weber is here referring more to the version of historical materialism prevalent among the Marxists of his age than to Marx himself, whom he had read first-hand. As for Marx's own version of historical materialism, Schumpeter (1987, pp. 10–11) gives a reasonably accurate reading: 'the economic interpretation of history', he says:[9]

> does *not* mean that men are, consciously or unconsciously, wholly or primarily, actuated by economic motives ... Marx did not hold that religions, metaphysics, schools of art, ethical ideas and political volitions were either reducible to economic *motives* or of no importance. He only tried to unveil the economic *conditions* which shape them and which account for their rise and fall.

Weber would not have accepted this explanation for the rise of capitalism, nor its ethic, as a logical and historical consequence.

So what, for Weber, is the origin of this new ethos or set of new ideas if not the material conditions of social life? After all, as he puts it at another point, 'Capitalist acquisition as an adventure has been at home in all types of economic society which have known trade with the use of money', Weber (1976, p. 58). 'The spirit of capitalism', says Weber, was present 'before the capitalist order ... [but] had to fight its way to supremacy against a whole world of hostile forces', pp. 55–6. Chief among these was what he calls 'traditionalism', by which he means the 'type of attitude and reaction to new situations', and which includes 'the traditional manner of life, the traditional rate of interest, the traditional amount of work, the traditional manner of regulating the relationships with labour', etc., pp. 58–9, 67. 'Its entry on the scene was not generally peaceful. A flood of mistrust, sometimes hatred, above all of moral indignation, regularly opposed itself to the first originator', p. 69.

So the crucial question for Weber now becomes what is the factor that lay behind the new spirit's ascension to supremacy. This he finds in the changes taking place in religious beliefs. In effect, what Weber sets out to do in this work is to clarify 'the influence of certain religious ideas on the development of the capitalist spirit, or the *ethos* of an economic system', p. 27. His main aim is, 'to clarify the manner and the general *direction* in which ... the religious movements have influenced the development of material culture', pp. 91–2. Chief among the changes involved is the emergence of what Weber calls the 'Protestant ethic' or Protestant asceticism. This is related to Luther's conception of the 'calling', which 'expresses the value placed upon rational activity carried on according to the rational capitalistic principle, as a fulfillment of a God-given task', Weber (1927, p. 157). Further, for Weber (1976, p. 172):

> The religious valuation of restless, continuous, systematic work in a worldly calling, as the highest means to asceticism, and at the same time the surest and most evident proof of rebirth and genuine faith, must have been the most powerful conceivable lever for the expansion of that attitude toward life which we have called the spirit of capitalism.

So a work ethic is involved, and it is complemented by a legitimised acquisitive ethic.

Before Protestantism, for most religions, the acquisition of money was considered a sin. According to the Protestant ethic, however, it was possible to serve God and at the same time to make a profit. This is achieved through hard labour, which results in a principled way of life. At the same time, profits made through hard labour and saving are channelled to productive use, rather than dissipated on individual consumption and pleasure. 'When the limitation of consumption is combined with this release of acquisitive activity', Weber (1976, p. 172) says, 'the inevitable practical result is obvious: accumulation of capital through ascetic compulsion to save'. Hence the Protestants' greater tendency vis-à-vis the Catholics towards economic rationalism, p. 40. This created a whole new culture on the part of believers which, once diffused into the wider economic and social sphere, helped to create the ideological context for the domination of the capitalist spirit, Swedberg (1999, pp. 22–4). So, for Weber, in Schumpeter's (1994, p. 817) words, 'the religious revolution from which Protestantism emerged was the dominant factor in the molding of the capitalist mind and thus of capitalism itself'.

As Weber makes clear on several occasions, however, this new 'spirit of capitalism' is not the only factor that contributes to the genesis of western capitalism, and 'ascetic Protestantism' is not the only agent of this new capitalist spirit. As he puts it, 'it is not my intention to substitute for a one-sided materialistic an equally one-sided spiritualistic causal interpretation of culture and history', Weber (1976, p. 183). He also makes clear that he has 'no intention whatsoever of maintaining such a foolish and doctrinaire thesis as that the spirit of capitalism ... could only have arisen as the result of the Reformation', p. 92. True to the spirit of the Historical School, Weber is against mono-causal explanations in history and in favour of more pluralistic approaches to historical and social phenomena. What Weber offers in this work is a sort of systematised history, its main theoretical aim being the analysis of the causal factors in the rise of capitalism. It is, in other words, a sort of reasoned history or *histoire raisonée*. Weber also constructs an economic sociology of the genesis of the western world, by pinpointing an economically relevant phenomenon (religion) as the chief factor in its emergence, Swedberg (1999, p. 22).

Weber's, then, is not a one-way, unidirectional system. Although religious beliefs are a chief factor in the genesis of the capitalist spirit, the latter gives rise to a whole constituted economic system, which 'no longer needs the support of any religious forces', Weber (1976, p. 72). The capitalist system, once established, assumes an autonomous existence, and tends to impose its own rationalistic logic on individual action. It shapes and constrains human behaviour. As he puts it, p. 54:[10]

> The capitalist economy of the present day is an immense cosmos into which the individual is born, and which presents itself to him, at least as an individual, as an unalterable order of things in which he must live. It forces the individual, in so far as he is involved in the system of market relationships, to conform to capitalistic rules of action ... Whoever does not adapt his manner of life to the conditions of capitalistic success must go under, or at least cannot rise.

It must have been intellectually pleasing to have discovered the origins of capitalism in the rise of the Protestant ethic, especially as it is liable to be buried once capitalism has established itself.[11]

As mentioned, *The Protestant Ethic* proved to be one of Weber's most prominent, and controversial, works. One of the many critics of his contentious thesis was Schumpeter (1994, p. 80), for whom there was:

> no such thing as a New Spirit of Capitalism in the sense that people would have to acquire a new way of thinking in order to be able to transform a feudal economic world into a wholly capitalist one. So soon as we realize that pure Feudalism and pure Capitalism are equally unrealistic creations of our own mind, the problem of what it was that

turned the one into the other vanishes completely. The society of the feudal ages contained all the germs of the society of the capitalist age. These germs developed by slow degrees, each step by step teaching its lessons and producing another increment of capitalist methods and of capitalist 'spirit'.

In other words, the capitalist spirit as an external causal factor in the explanation of the genesis of capitalism is required because of Weber's use of two purely abstract and unrealistic concepts of feudalism and capitalism. With more realistic conceptions of these societies, it would become obvious that capitalism was born in the womb of feudalism in a gradual fashion. Capitalist methods, in turn, once in place, give rise to the capitalist spirit which thus becomes an endogenous and dependent factor.

Assuming that pure feudalism and pure capitalism represent Weber's ideal types in his discussion of the emergence of capitalism, it is then obvious that, in essence, what Schumpeter (1994, p. 80, n. 4) criticises here is the (mis)use of this concept by Weber himself. 'Unfortunately', he says:

> Max Weber lent the weight of his great authority to a way of thinking that has no other basis than the misuse of the method of Ideal Types. Accordingly, he set out to find an explanation for a process which sufficient attention to historical detail renders self-explanatory.

As Bottomore (1992, p. 119) correctly observes, these remarks by Schumpeter lend themselves to a crude empiricist reading of historical questions. However, Schumpeter's own main works on the question of capitalist development, *The Theory of Capitalist Development* and *Business Cycles*, pay testimony to the contrary. They are both mostly theoretical in character. After all, Schumpeter himself is first and foremost an economic theorist, although not of the conventional type, Swedberg (1991b, p. 38). For him and Weber, economics and sociology are mostly analytical rather than empirical or historical sciences.

The main aim of these two works, as Schumpeter (1937, p. 165) makes clear in his Preface to the Japanese edition of *The Theory*, is the construction of a 'theoretic model of the process of economic change in time'. He makes this point by reference to the two economists he admired most – Walras and Marx. The Walrasian system, according to Schumpeter, is not only static but also only applicable to a stationary process. By the latter, Schumpeter means 'a process which *actually* does not change on its own initiative', p. 166. This means that the causes of change are actually exogenous to the Walrasian system so that 'economic theorists ... cannot say much about the factors that account for historical change'. Schumpeter considered this to be wrong, since he strongly felt that 'there was a source of energy within the economic system'. This internal dynamic is the second element of Schumpeter's theory, which he derives from Marx: 'a vision of the economic evolution as a distinct process generated by the economic system itself', p. 166, and Schumpeter

(1961, p. 60, n. 1). Granted this, it becomes possible to derive 'a purely economic theory of economic change' which is the *raison d' être* of his analytical discourse, Schumpeter (1982, p. 220).

This dynamic element of his vision is another point of divergence from
Weber. The latter's theory of capitalism is more static in nature, and his
model of change is that of comparative statics, as for example in the change
from a traditional society to capitalism, Macdonald (1966, p. 378) and
Bottomore (1992, p. 128), although in his works one can also find scattered
pieces of dynamic analysis (e.g. in his *Outline of Economic History*). Contrary
to Weber, Marx's quest for an internal dynamic of capitalism is one source of
Schumpeter's admiration of his work. He praises Marx for what he calls a
'truly great achievement', meaning, Schumpeter (1987, p. 43):

> the fundamental idea ... of a theory, not merely of an indefinite number
> of disjoint individual patterns or of the logic of economic quantities in
> general, but of the actual sequence of those patterns or of the economic
> process as it goes on, under its own steam, in historic time, producing at
> every instant that state which will of itself determine the next one.

But this dynamic attribute of Marx's economic theory is itself a consequence
of its not being confined to economic considerations alone.

Marx's 'sociological' writings are the other source of Schumpeter's admiration for his work, as seen already. 'The so called *Economic* Interpretation of
History', he says, (1987 [1943], p. 10), 'is doubtless one of the greatest
achievements of *sociology* to this day', (emphasis added). Schumpeter, however, was also a severe critic of Marx's work, especially his economic theory.
He variously describes his labour theory of value as 'unsatisfactory', 'dead
and buried' or simply 'untenable', pp. 23, 25, 32 and ch. 3. He also expressed
doubts as to whether a synthetic method such as the one used by Marx, i.e.
'the coordination of economic and sociological analysis with a view of
bending everything to a single purpose', is always superior to a more 'narrow'
approach to social phenomena, p. 46:

> A valuable economic theorem may by its sociological metamorphosis
> pick up error instead of a richer meaning and vice versa. Thus, synthesis
> in general and synthesis on Marxian lines in particular might easily issue
> in both worse economics and worse sociology.

In other words, Marx's whole may be less than the sum of the individual
parts.

Schumpeter started his own *Theory* with a description of the leading
characteristics of the 'circular flow of economic life' of conventional economic theory, ch. 1. This is a static model *à la* Walras, which 'does not change
"of itself"', and which 'describes economic life from the standpoint of the
economic system's tendency towards an equilibrium position', Schumpeter

(1961, pp. 9, 62). This model, on its own, however, hardly suffices for the analysis of a system (capitalism), which is 'by nature a form or method of economic change and not only never is but never can be stationary', Schumpeter (1987, p. 82). Hence Schumpeter uses the model of circular flow simply as a point of departure for his dynamic analysis of economic development, which follows in the second chapter of his book. According to Swedberg (1991b, p. 40), although Schumpeter's more dynamic theory might have been originally conceived as a complement to the Walrasian circular flow, 'as the analysis progresses ... it increasingly came to *replace* it'. This is only natural for a theorist whose main preoccupation is economic change and development. The latter, according to Schumpeter (1961, pp. 63, 64) refers to:

> such changes in economic life as are not forced upon it from without but arise by its own initiative, from within ... It is spontaneous and discontinuous change in the channels of the flow, disturbance of equilibrium, which forever alters and displaces the equilibrium state previously existing.

What Schumpeter is describing here is an economy in perpetual change. What is more, this change comes from within the system. In his quest for the source of this internal dynamic, Schumpeter, much like Marx, turns his attention to the production process. The basic vehicle of this change is the continuous process of innovation: 'this historic and irreversible change in the way of doing things we call "innovation" and we define: innovations are changes in production functions which cannot be decomposed into infinitesimal steps', Schumpeter (1935, p. 138).

Unlike Marx, however, and given his adherence to methodological individualism, Schumpeter (1961, p. 65) focuses on the *individual* as the initiator of economic change. The fundamental attribute of this agent that elevates him into the basic motor of change is the carrying out of 'new combinations of means of production', which he describes as 'the fundamental phenomenon of economic development', pp. 66, 74. This concept, according to Schumpeter, covers five cases, p. 66:

1 The introduction of a new good;
2 The introduction of a new method of production;
3 The opening of a new market;
4 The conquest of a new source of supply of raw materials; and
5 The carrying out of the new organisation of any industry.

Schumpeter calls this function 'enterprise' (the setting up of 'a concern embodying a new idea'), as opposed to management (heading 'the administration of a going concern'), and the person responsible he calls the *entrepreneur*, Schumpeter (1947, p. 223). In this way, Schumpeter (1949d, p. 259) forges a link between enterprise and innovation, while identifying the entrepreneur with the 'business leader' or the 'innovator'. The latter's defining character-istic is simply 'the doing of new things or the doing of things that are already being done in a new way (innovation)', Schumpeter (1947, p. 223), as opposed to the manager or industrialist or capitalist, 'who merely may operate an established business', Schumpeter (1961, p. 758). The entrepre-neur's function consists of 'breaking up old, and creating new tradition', and as such s/he personifies 'the creative response in business', Schumpeter (1947, p. 222). In fact, Schumpeter (1949d, p. 259) defines *entrepreneurship* as essen-tially consisting of 'doing things that are not generally done in the ordinary course of business routine; it is essentially a phenomenon that comes under the wider aspect of leadership'. In this way, entrepreneurship becomes the engine or 'ultimate cause' of capitalist development, since 'the mechanisms of economic change in capitalist society pivot on entrepreneurial activity', Schumpeter (1947, pp. 222, 223). This is how Schumpeter (1961, pp. 82–3) summarises his position:

> hence, our position may be characterized by three corresponding pairs of opposites. First, by the opposition of two real processes: the circular flow or the tendency towards equilibrium on the one hand, a change in the channels of economic routine or a spontaneous change in the eco-nomic data arising from within the system on the other. Secondly, by the opposition of two theoretical *apparatuses*: statics and dynamics. Thirdly, by the opposition of two types of conduct, which, following reality, we can picture as two types of individuals: mere managers and entrepreneurs.

Thus, Schumpeter's main focus of attention is the process of technological and institutional change that takes place through an innovative process internal to the system.

But this innovation process is far from smooth. It comes in clusters and produces a wave-like movement, 'which pervades economic life within the institutional framework of capitalism', Schumpeter (1935, pp. 134, 141). Schumpeter calls this wave-like phenomenon the 'business cycle', and he con-siders it as the main explanandum in the analysis of capitalism. 'The pre-sence or absence', he says, 'of a fluctuation *inherent* to the economic process in time is practically and scientifically the fundamental problem', pp. 135, 139. In the now famous phrase, Schumpeter (1987, p. 83) describes it as a process of 'creative destruction':

> the same process of industrial mutation ... that increasingly revolutionizes the economic structure *from within*, incessantly destroying the old one, incessantly creating the new one. This process of Creative Destruction is the essential fact about capitalism.

This wave-like phenomenon became the exclusive focus of attention in his *Business Cycles*, where he identifies three different cyclical patterns: Long

Waves or Kontratieff Cycles of 54 to 60 years' duration; Juglar Cycles of nine to ten years' longevity; and the shorter Kitchin Cycles of three years' duration. He identified three Long Cycles until his day. The first is between 1783 and 1842 associated with the Industrial Revolution. The second runs between 1842 and 1897, and he describes it as the age of steam and steel. This wave is also linked with railroadisation, which 'is the dominant feature both of economic change and of economic fluctuations at that time'. Last, the third Long Wave rose about 1897 and is associated with electricity, chemistry and motor cars.

What is of interest, for our purposes, is the way Schumpeter goes about carrying out his analysis of this most 'fundamental problem' of capitalism. This is all the more interesting since *Business Cycles* represents Schumpeter's most mature effort at applying his version of *Sozialökonomik* to the analysis of capitalism. The basic contours of his broad vision of (social) economics are once again made plain by the very subtitle of the book: 'A Theoretical, Historical and Statistical Analysis of the Capitalist Process'. To these, it will be recalled, he later added economic sociology. He describes his attempt: 'from our historic and everyday knowledge of economic behavior we shall construct a "model" of the economic process over time, see whether it is likely to work in wavelike way, and compare the result with observed fact', Schumpeter (1935, p. 136).

Hence, although the main aim remains theoretical in character (the construction of a model of economic change), observed fact and historical experience represent both the point of departure and the testing ground for his theoretical discourse. The role of history, in Schumpeter's theoretical schema, however, goes even further. Indeed, he considers the very aim of his theoretical exercise itself to be historical in nature. This is made compulsory by the dynamic and evolutionary character of his theory: he calls dynamics and history 'the two indispensables', Schumpeter (1949e, p. 327). And the historical dimension of his theoretical discourse remains its most essential ingredient in providing causal explanations, without which statistical series 'remain inconclusive', and the 'theoretical analysis empty'. At the same time, however, he makes clear that he has 'no wish to advocate the historical approach to the phenomenon of business cycles at the expense, still less to the exclusion, of theoretical or statistical work upon it', p. 322. It is the sum total of these approaches that provides a complete analysis of the phenomenon in question. The historical schema that he ultimately attains is not the conventional, descriptive type of history but, much like Marx's and Weber's, a theoretically informed, analytical type of history, or *histoire raisonée*. Reasoned history, then, becomes the 'ultimate goal' of his scientific endeavour, Schumpeter (1982, p. 220):

> Since what we are trying to understand is economic change in historic time, there is little exaggeration in saying that the ultimate goal is simply a reasoned (= conceptually clarified) history ... of the economic process

in all its aspects and bearings to which theory merely supplies some tools and schemata, and statistics merely part of the material. It is obvious that only detailed historic knowledge can definitely answer most of the questions of individual causation and mechanism and that without it the study of time series must remain inconclusive, and theoretical analysis empty.

Economic change thus becomes the meeting place of the historian and the theorist. 'Economic historians and economic theorists can make an interesting and socially valuable journey together, if they will. It would be an investigation into the sadly neglected area of economic change', Schumpeter (1947, p. 221). Economic development and social change thus offers the template for the erection of Schumpeter's version of *Sozialökonomik* by bringing together the economic, social, historical and dynamic elements of this process.

5 Concluding remarks

Both Weber and Schumpeter were products of their age. They were lucky and skilled enough to draw upon and be influenced by very rich traditions in political economy, from classical political economy and Karl Marx, through the historical tradition to marginalism. Traces (or more) of these influences are scattered throughout their writings. This does not mean, however, that Weber and Schumpeter were unduly eclectic, combining different elements from these traditions in an ad hoc fashion. On the contrary, they put forward their own research agenda in the ambitious form of *Sozialökonomik*. In retrospect, this ambition was bound to fail. After all, this was an era of separation, not cooperation between the social sciences. It saw the birth of sociology and economic history as separate disciplines, both of which were looking for vital ground, and grounds on which to establish themselves. Economics was becoming an increasingly deductive science, dealing with strictly economic phenomena, however defined. So, in a sense, both sociology and economic history emerged as residual sciences to fill the space vacated by the desocialisation and dehistoricisation of mainstream economics although, at the time, that space was extensive.

Weber, Schumpeter and their programme of *Sozialökonomik* suffered a similar fate within economic science to that of the Historical School. Both fell victim to their own insistence, contrary to Marx and the Historical School, on a separation of the social sciences, on the basis of which close cooperation between them should be re-erected in the form of social economics. Having failed to place social economics on the economist's research agenda, they are nowadays remembered mostly as founders of one of the other social disciplines or subdisciplines they helped to establish, with Weber to the fore in sociology but Schumpeter marginalised within economics. As a result, in addition to Weber's immense influence on the emergence and subsequent development of sociology as a separate discipline, see also the next chapter, if the concept of *Sozialökonomik* has left any successors these are mostly to be found (at least until recently) in the subdiscipline of economic sociology. Most textbooks of economic sociology consider Weber, Sombart and Schumpeter, together with other prominent writers such as Karl Marx, Emile Durkheim, Karl Polanyi and Talcott Parsons, as the founders and towering figures of this subdiscipline, Trigilia (2002), Swedberg (2003) and Smelser and Swedberg (1994). Max Weber's impact on its emergence and evolution is so great that one of the leading modern exponents of this tradition considers Weber's *Protestant Ethic* as a 'paradigm and a guide for how to proceed in economic sociology', Swedberg (2003, p. xi). It is indicative of the developments around economics, and of the fate of the concept of social economics, that it should be located within sociology, using mostly the 'frames of reference, variables and explanatory models' of this social science, Smelser and Swedberg (1994, p. 3), see also Fine and Milonakis (2009).

12 Positivism and the separation of economics from sociology

'Human society is the subject of many researches. Some of them constitute specialized disciplines: law, political economy, political history, the history of religions, and the like. Others have not been distinguished by special names. To the synthesis of them all, which aims at studying society in general, we may give the name *sociology*'.

Pareto (1935 [1916], p. 3)

'Ever since the eighteenth century both groups (that is economists and sociologists) have grown steadily apart until by now the modal economist and the modal sociologist know little and care less about what the other does, each preferring to use, respectively, a primitive sociology and a primitive economics of his own to accepting one another's professional results'.

Schumpeter (1994, pp. 26–7)

'Apart from pure Logic and Mathematics, scientific knowledge, explanation, and prognosis can only be based ultimately on empirical regularities'.

Hutchison (1960 [1938], p. 163)

1 Introduction

The twin subjects examined in this chapter are: first the emergence and further consolidation of sociology as a separate discipline, in the context of the contemporary developments in and around economics, and second the explicit introduction of positivism into economics in the 1930s by Terence Hutchison (1912–2007), itself a response to the excesses of marginalism as exemplified through Lionel Robbins' 1932 work, *An Essay on the Nature and Significance of Economic Science*.

Both the concepts of positivism and sociology were invented by the French nineteenth century philosopher Auguste Comte (1798–1857). Indeed, for him, the two are closely associated, since in his works the emergence of sociology is conceived as the result of the triumph of positivism in scientific thought, Giddens (1977). However, although the origins of modern sociology can be traced back to Comte's vision of a new science of society, or of man as a social creature, which would become the 'Queen of the Sciences',

Gordon (1991, pp. 286–95), it did not fully emerge as a separate discipline until the turn of the last century. Following the developments taking place around economic science, sociology played its part in filling out the gap left by the desocialisation of economic science. As a separate discipline, sociology was to concern itself with the 'social', defined negatively as the 'non-economic', or, more exactly, non-economics.

Based on the distinction between rational and non-rational action, between the economic and the social, between the market and the non-market, the two social sciences started their separate journeys. In such a climate, it was difficult for a social economics that promoted a multi-disciplinary approach to economic phenomena to flourish. On the other hand, and despite Weber's and Schumpeter's attempts at keeping a broad scope of economics alive, the impact of the rising neoclassicism, especially in its Austrian version, left its clear imprint. Schumpeter and Weber should be seen as necessarily failing to hold in check what was going on at their time – the remorseless fragmentation of social science into separate disciplines. The tensions involved could at most be temporarily and partially resolved by their individual contributions, and these could even have served to support as well as to reflect the directions being taken by economics in its dispensing with historical and social content.

With the failure of Weber's and Schumpeter's project to gain a secure hold, despite the extent of their own individual prestige, the search for a broad scope in economics came to an abrupt end in Europe. By the end of the Second World War, the separation of sociology from economics was complete, see opening quote by Schumpeter. The two figures that presided over the inauguration of sociology as a separate discipline and played the leading role in its birth were Emile Durkheim (1858–1917) and Max Weber. Another figure, even if of lesser importance as far as his positive contributions to sociology are concerned, is Vilfredo Pareto (1848–1923), who is the subject of Section 2. Pareto typified so much of what was going on – embodying in one person the total split between sociology and economics – while also playing an active part in promoting it. Pareto is also the third (although chronologically the first, the other two being Weber and Schumpeter, see Introduction to Chapter 11) of the dramatis personae in this book to have been dubbed a 'bourgeois Marx', albeit with protestations against the accuracy of such a label for Pareto from Schumpeter (1949c, pp. 110–11).

As charted already in detail in previous chapters, in the wake of the marginalist revolution, the capacity to develop economics as a separate discipline was considerably enhanced by the breach with classical political economy and the narrowing of the scope of inquiry to market relations. But even these freedoms could not release the discipline from irresolvable tensions. The thrust of marginalism itself was to base economic analysis on the optimising behaviour of individuals. As discussed in Section 3, this found its methodological expression in Lionel Robbins' (in)famous and deliberate redefinition of economics as the allocation of scarce resources between competing ends. But Robbins' attempt to characterise the discipline as it was, or was becoming, with a helpful push on his own part, exhibited considerable strains and encountered considerable opposition.

Two such reactions came from within economics. One was from Ralph Souter (1897–1946), briefly covered in Section 4, who engaged in the futile attempt to defend old Marshallian-type economics against the increasing encroachment of Robbins' excesses. The other came from a more philosophically informed positivist perspective. As argued in Section 5, Hutchison (1960) was the first to introduce positivism explicitly into economic science, although traces of positivist thought are scattered throughout the history of economic thought, as well as in the history of economic methodology, before Hutchison. As seen already in Chapter 6, following the *Methodenstreit*, both sides of the debate were in a conciliatory mood, accepting the necessity of both deduction and induction in economic theorising, even if reserving priority for their particular side of the argument. Following the work of Mises, see Chapter 13, and Robbins, both of whom tried to defend what Hutchison (1998) has dubbed 'ultra-deductivism', and Hutchison's response from what Machlup (1978) has called an 'ultra-empiricist' perspective, the *Methodenstreit* is very much alive again. This time round, however, the empiricist side is not represented by the inductivism of the Historical School, which had in any case long since been on the decline in economic science, with their scientific endeavours having been channelled into the newly founded discipline of economic history, see Chapter 8. Its place has been occupied by Hutchison's positivism – if not always consciously – and with his degree of philosophical sophistication.

Another sharp reaction to Robbins came from outside economics. Talcott Parsons (1902–1979), informed in economic theory but arguing from the confines of the newly emerging sociology, perceived Robbins as defining a *method* and *not a subject matter*. The economy could as well be studied by sociologists deploying other, non-individualistic methods, and dealing more fully and properly with the functioning of the economy as a system. Equally, within economics itself, Robbins' definition was at jarring odds with the unavoidable realities of the inter-war period, not least in light of the unprecedented levels of unemployment at his time of writing.

As argued in Section 6, Parsons was strongly placed to promote the process of separating sociology from economics – the one, in his hands, complementing the other in removing social and historical content. He sought both an alternative method to economics and to keep the disciplines separate. In this respect, he was the mirror-image of Marshall along the economics/sociology divide and, consequently, defined himself in this way in seeking to keep Marshallian economics out of sociology as well as the Robbinsonian. This had profound implications, at least temporarily, for the nature of sociology as a discipline. But, as the concluding remarks suggest, neither Parsonian sociology nor the discipline's more general separation from economics could be so, or remain absolutely so, for long. No sooner had economics fully established its technical apparatus as a science of choice than it sought to extend it beyond the boundaries of the market, to colonise the subject matter of the other social sciences. And, partly in response to this, the explicit renewal of economic sociology in the 1980s rekindled the tensions broached by Parsons in the 1930s, the major difference being the stand-off between the consolidated reductionism of economics as opposed to the wider range of approaches attached to sociology than those offered by Parsons, see Fine and Milonakis (2009). For the moment, it is important to acknowledge that the separation of the disciplines in the 1930s took precedence over attempts to keep connections between them alive, influencing the extent and the way in which the social and historical were to be positioned across the social sciences.

2 Twixt logical and non-logical: Pareto and the birth of sociology

Pareto differs from the other two founders of modern sociology, Durkheim and Weber, in that, unlike them, he is considered to have contributed separately to both economics and sociology as such, but with a content so divergent that he is justifiably considered to have driven the process of separating the two disciplines. He was instrumental in the birth of sociology as a separate discipline not least through his distinction between logical (rational) and non-logical (non-rational) action, which gave sociology a rationale for developing independently of economics. Pareto identified logical with economic action and non-logical with social action. Hence economics became the science of rational action, and sociology the discipline of non-rational action. As a result, sociology did not have a well-defined subject matter, but dealt instead with issues that were not studied by economists, such as religion, morality and law, Pareto (1935, p. 231), but also marriage, deviance, suicide etc., lying outside the market where crude self-interest is presumed to prevail.

From the point of view of this book, Pareto is interesting for a host of other reasons. First, he considered economic and social phenomena to be closely interconnected: 'when economic and social phenomena are considered together, as we are considering them here, the development is in the concrete direction', p. 1191. Following this, second, one of his aims was to integrate economic science into a wider framework of social sciences, Allais (1968, pp. 400, 401). 'Political economy', he says, cited in Salanti (1998, p. 355), 'is but a part – and a small part – of the more general science of sociology … To complete our knowledge we must also consult other branches of social sciences'. He even accused other contemporary economists of paying no attention to such interrelations, Pareto (1935, p. 1413).[1] Third is that his contributions to both economics and sociology took place in an era when the separation of economics from sociology was becoming more and more pronounced. Yet, fourth, and partly as a result of, but also greatly contributing to this process, his economics differed widely from his sociology, the two intermingling to a minimum degree, Hutchison (1953, p. 230). 'Pareto's economics and sociology refer to spheres of thought with very tenuous links joining them; there is no real bridge between them', Cirillo (1979, p. 32). Indeed his distinction between logical and non-logical action became a sort of official demarcation line between economics and sociology. Hence Pareto's name, as far as sociology is concerned, is mostly remembered as a token symbol for the latter's separation from economics, rather than for any lasting effect he had on its theoretical corpus. Sociology is concerned with those actions not covered by economics and other fields dealing with logical action, Pareto (1935, ch. 1), Schumpeter (1949c, p. 141) and Parsons (1968a, pp. 411, 415).

Pareto's academic profile was different from those of Weber and Schumpeter. Instead of an academic background in the humanities, Pareto, much like Jevons and Walras, took his academic training in engineering, mathematics and physical sciences. After working for 20 years as an engineer, he started his academic career in 1893, taking up Walras' chair in Laussane, after the latter's retirement, hence helping to establish the 'Laussane School'. This succession has more than symbolic value. Pareto's early contributions were mostly in what he called pure or mathematical economics. The reason for this, as he explains, is that 'mathematical economics aims chiefly at emphasizing the interdependence of economic phenomena. So far no other method has been found to attaining that end', Pareto (1935, p. 20).

Pareto, to begin with, was a Walrasian. His early work on economics (*Cours de Economie Politique*, 1896–7) amounts to an attempt at perfecting the Walrasian general equilibrium system mathematically. Pareto's name is associated, first, with the (statistical) law of distribution bearing his name (which he developed in his *Cours*). However, according to Schumpeter (1949c, p. 135), 'although Pareto the economist touched upon a large number of extremely concrete and practical problems ... his purely scientific contribution is in the realm of the most abstract economic logic'. His main contributions to pure theory were developed later in his *Manual of Political Economy* (1971 [1906]), and included the establishment of ordinal rather than cardinal utility as the basis for economic science, following the pioneering works of Fisher and Cassel, and in introducing indifference curves into the theory of the consumer, following Edgeworth and Fisher. Last, his name is also associated with the concept of what was later to be called Pareto optimality or efficiency, a positive (i.e. distribution-blind) rule for comparing different welfare situations, which gave a (positive) basis for the justification of free market exchange insofar as it is associated with none being made better off without others being made worse off. Overall, one may say that Pareto's contribution to 'pure' economics was more in helping to establish what was already there than to introduce new concepts or herald new directions. It is more 'an attempt to preach a sermon' than 'a technical achievement of the first order', Schumpeter (1949c, p. 142), see also Schumpeter

(1994, pp. 858–61), Hutchison (1953, ch. 14), Roll (1992, pp. 373–9) and Pressman (1999).

As time went by, Pareto became increasingly disillusioned with formalistic and mathematical economics based on the rational aspects of human action. 'At a certain point in my research in economics I found myself in a blind-alley', Pareto says, quoted in Salanti (1998, p. 356). He began to give more and more emphasis to other (social) factors influencing human behaviour, such as feelings and sentiments, which are socially useful and effective although non-logical from a strictly scientific point of view, Aron (1970, p. 17) and Cirillo (1979, p. 29). As Hutchison (1960, p. 166) observes, Pareto (together with Wieser, see Chapter 13, and Weber, Chapter 11), 'have treated their work on Economics as essentially a preliminary to wider sociological investigations'. Indeed, both in his *Cours* and in his *Manual*, Pareto had already made extensive methodological comments, which later on became the foundations of his sociological work, after he had abandoned the realm of economic theory to concentrate his efforts on constructing his system of political sociology in his *Mind and Society*, first published in 1916, Hutchison (1953, pp. 217–18). As Aron (1970, p. 110) puts it:

> Pareto's sociology has its origins in the reflections and disappointments of an engineer and an economist. The engineer, unless he is making a mistake, behaves in a logical manner. The economist, so long as he is under no illusions as to his own knowledge, is capable of understanding certain aspects of human behaviour. Outside of these two particular areas, according to Pareto, sociology is generally at the mercy of men who behave neither like engineers nor like speculators.

The distinction, then, between logical and non-logical action plays a pivotal role both in drawing the boundaries between economics and sociology and in Pareto's thought. So it is important to have a clear conception of what these notions involve in order to understand both. All social phenomena, according to Pareto (1935, pp. 9–10, 76), involve two aspects: the objective ('as it is in reality ... without reference to the person who produced it') and the subjective ('as it presents itself in the mind of this or that human being'). And all human action involves a goal and a means of attaining this goal. Logical action for Pareto is action based on reasoning both objectively and subjectively, p. 77:

> *Logical actions* [refer] to actions that logically conjoin means to ends not only from the standpoint of the subject performing them, but from the standpoint of other persons ... in other words, to actions that are logical both subjectively and objectively.

This is a very tight and narrow conception of rationality, all the more so since any action that does not correspond to it is, by default, non-rational. In other words, any form of action which is non-logical – either from the point of view of the actor, or objectively, or both – is considered non-rational. These forms of action include those based on courtesy and custom, and instinctive acts, pp. 78–9. The same applies to action which is logical from both viewpoints, but in each of which the goals or the means (or both) of achieving these goals do not coincide. It should be noted here that for Pareto (1971, p. 30) non-logical does not necessarily mean illogical:

> Let us know, moreover, that non-logical action does not mean illogical; a non-logical action may be one which a person could see, after observing the facts and the logic, is the best way to adapt the means to the end; but that adaptation has been obtained by a procedure other than that of logical reasoning.

All these forms of action form the core of the first volume of *Mind and Society,* where Pareto attempts a scientific (i.e. logical) analysis of non-logical action, Aron (1970, pp. 111–15). How is this possible?

For Pareto, in typical positivistic fashion, and guided by the methods of the physical sciences, the only royal road to true scientific knowledge in social sciences is through what he called the logical–experimental method, which is firmly anchored in reality, and involves 'observation, experience, and logical inferences from experience', Pareto (1935, p. 23) and Schumpeter (1949c, p. 136). Pareto (1935, p. 12) concludes 'We can know nothing *a priori*. Experience alone can enlighten us'. In this, he follows Comte's positivist philosophy, as opposed to the idealist philosophy of the German Historical School, Cirillo (1979, p. 29). This is how he summarises his experimental method, quoted in Salanti (1998, p. 355):

> First, political economy – like chemistry, or physics or astronomy – is conceived as a natural science. Therefore it must be studied in the light of the experimental method, and every effort must be taken to exclude the personal element. Second, the economist of today has no practical end in view ... His work is merely to investigate the laws of phenomena, to discover uniformities in their workings.

And, he goes on to stress the role of abstraction and of concepts, which, however, must be firmly anchored in reality, p. 356:

> It is not that a work loses its experimental character if it starts from an abstraction to reach a representation of facts, but, in order to keep such a character, the abstraction concerned must remain a simple hypothesis that becomes true only after verification of the correspondence between the obtained results and the concrete facts.

Substantively, Pareto's main preoccupation in his *Mind and Society* revolves, first, around the explanation of non-logical forms of action through the concepts of *residue* (Volume II) and *derivation* (Volume III), and, second, around his theory of the circulation of *élites*. Residues are associated with man's instincts which represent the real causes of (non-rational) human conduct, while the notion of derivation expresses all the concepts, theories, ideologies etc., devised in order to rationalise these actions in the eyes of the actors themselves. The former then has to do with human impulses, while the latter with the human mind, Pareto (1935, vols II–IV), Schumpeter (1949c, pp. 140–2) and Aron (1970, pp. 124–45).

In contradistinction to Pareto's logico-experimental approach to social phenomena, Weber follows his ideal typical path in defining sociology (and social sciences more generally) as purely theoretical sciences. To this, however, should be added the other pillar of Weber's conception of sociology: *understanding* or *interpretation of meaning*, see Chapter 11, Section 3. This is how he defines sociology at the very beginning of his *Economy and Society*, Weber (1978, p. 4):

> Sociology (in the sense in which this highly ambiguous word is used here) is a science concerning itself with the interpretative understanding of social action and thereby with causal explanation of its course and consequences.

And he goes on to clarify that 'action' refers to the subjective meaning the active individual attaches to his/her action, this becoming 'social action' once 'its subjective meaning takes account of the behavior of others and is thereby oriented in its course'.

And at another point he adds that 'we have taken for granted that sociology seeks to formulate type concepts and generalized uniformities of empirical process ... Theoretical differentiation ... is possible in sociology only in terms of ideal pure types', p. 20. So Weber treats sociology as a purely theoretical social science, which deals with 'ideal types' and is concerned with 'the interpretative understanding of social action', see also Therborn (1976, pp. 278–9). As we have seen, these represent the most fundamental aspects of Weber's conception of sociology.

Weber's concept of rationality is much like Pareto's, and, similarly, plays a pivotal role in the identification of the different social sciences. As is well known, Weber distinguishes four (ideal) types of social action: 'instrumentally rational', which refers to rational action directed towards the attainment of a certain goal; 'value-rational', referring to social action governed by the value system of the actor (this includes 'ethical, aesthetic, religious, or other form of behavior'); 'affectual action', referring mostly to emotional or instinctive reactions; and 'traditional action', governed by custom and tradition, Weber (1978, pp. 24–5). The first, instrumentally rational, form of action refers to a means–end nexus mediated through reason, which is very close to Pareto's logical action. All other forms of rationality are closer to Pareto's non-logical forms of action. For Weber, in modern capitalist societies, instrumentally rational behaviour is becoming increasingly predominant over all other forms of (non-rational) action.

The difference between Weber and Pareto is that although the latter approaches rationality (action), both from the point of view of the actor (subjectively) and from the point of view of the observer (objectively), Weber focuses exclusively on the meaning of rationality (action) for the human agent, Aron (1970, pp. 186–8). He considers instrumental rationality devoid of any social, emotional and other influences, to be the aspect of human conduct studied by economic theory. 'Pure economic theory', Weber (1949, pp. 43–4) says:

> utilizes ideal-type concepts exclusively. Economic theory makes certain assumptions which scarcely ever correspond with reality but which approximate it in various degrees: how would men act under these assumed conditions, if their actions were entirely rational? It assumes dominance of pure economic interests and precludes the operation of political or other non-economic considerations.

So *homo economicus* reigns supreme in Weber's economic world as yet another ideal-type, and becomes the *raison d'être* of economic theorising.

Much like Pareto, and despite his programme of *Sozialökonomik*, Weber can also be interpreted as perpetrating the original sin of dividing up the social sciences into separate disciplines, Fevre (2003, pp. 13–14). He accepted the case for marginalism as the basis for constituting economics as a separate discipline. It offered one ideal-type of behaviour, for which sociology would serve as a complementary social science handling other forms of (non)rationality, especially those removed from the pursuit of simple and individual economic interests. With his acceptance of economic rationality as having some independent scope, classical sociology itself was induced to take a wrong turn by abandoning certain domains of analysis to the economists. From that point on, at most, 'the classical critiques were intended to keep economic rationality in check by shedding new light on it from an other-worldly viewpoint', p. 9. Hence economics became the science of rational action and sociology the discipline of non-rational action, while economic history was identified with institutional, descriptive, narrative-type methods, see Chapter 8.

3 Lionel Robbins: squaring off the marginalist revolution

In methodological terms, economics took a step away from the old marginalism of Marshall with the appearance of Robbins' (1935) *An Essay on the Nature and Significance of Economic Science*, first published in 1932 in the midst of the Great Depression. Whilst (in)famous for defining economics as the allocation of scarce resources between competing ends in the midst of unprecedented levels of unemployment, it is significant that Robbins' deliberate shift of the definition of the science away from pre-occupation with 'the study of the causes of material welfare', p. 4, is an explicit concern with 'the inspection of Economic Science as it *actually exists*', p. 72, emphasis added. Thus Robbins believes that he is characterising economics as it has become. No doubt he is more than happy with this state of the science, and did his best to consolidate its character as such. This is all so much so that he rejects the idea that Marxism should be considered the *Economic* interpretation of history because economics is to be redefined other than as the causes of material welfare, p. 45.

With Robbins, however, the confusion between the scope of application of the laws of economics and their confinement to the market is reproduced in a more extreme form. On the one hand, the laws are, indeed, universal. Economic analysis need not be confined to an exchange economy, because 'behaviour outside the exchange economy is conditioned by the same limitation of means in relation to ends as behaviour within the economy, and is capable of being subsumed under the same fundamental categories', pp. 19–20. Accordingly, 'The Law of Diminishing Returns ... follows from the assumption that there is more than one class of scarce factors of production'. 'This is obvious. If it were not so, then all the corn in the world could be produced from one acre of land', p. 77. Further, pp. 78–9:

> The main postulate of the theory of value is the fact that individuals can arrange their preferences in an order, and in fact do so. The main postulate of the theory of production is the fact that there is more than one factor of production. The main postulate of the theory of dynamics is the fact that we are not certain regarding future scarcities. These are not postulates the existence of whose counterpart in reality admits of extensive dispute once their nature is fully realised ... they only have to be stated to be recognised as obvious ... the danger is that they may be thought to be so obvious that nothing significant can be derived ... Yet ... it is from the existence of the conditions that they assume that the general applicability of the broader propositions of economic science is derived.

Without regard to the nature of any specific good, 'The theory of value as we know it has developed in recent times by the progressive elaboration of deductions from very simple premises. But the great discovery, the Mengerian revolution, which initiated this period of progress, was the discovery of the premises themselves', pp. 105–6.

On the other hand, there are two respects in which Robbins does limit the scope of economics. In explicit opposition to the 'Materialist Interpretation of History', he suggests, 'It asserts quite definitely, not only that technical changes cause changes in scarcity relationships and social institutions generally – which would be a proposition in harmony with modern economic analysis – but also that all changes in social relations are due to technical changes – which is a *sociological* proposition quite outside the limited range of *economic* generalisation', p. 44, emphasis added. So social relations lie outside economics. Perhaps this is due, secondly, to his exclusion of the formation of preferences from the subject matter of economics. He reckons that 'the general absurdity of the belief that the world contemplated by the economist is peopled only by egoists or "pleasure machines" should be sufficiently clear ... We take them [individual relative valuations] as data. So far as we are concerned, our economic subjects can be pure egoists, pure altruists, pure ascetics, pure sensualists or – what is much more likely – mixed bundles of all these impulses', pp. 94–5. What was crucial for Robbins, however, was that economics should be based on the presumption that preferences, whatever they might be and however they might be formed, are ordered and define the ends pursued by available means, Maas (2005a) for a discussion through comparison with Weber.[2]

Despite his refusal to recognise that economics 'as it actually exists' was putatively peopling the world with pleasure machines in the form of utility maximisation, Robbins' contribution did promote this approach as economics became a universal logic of abstract choice (over the allocation of scarce resources to competing ends). By contrast, within nineteenth century utilitarianism and its corresponding political economy and economics, there was at least some recognition of the nature of different individuals, and the nature of the goods and activities that might give them satisfaction or pain. There was also a lingering attachment to the concerns and traditions of classical political economy. These are all effectively eliminated in the shift from utility itself towards utility functions, indifference curves and, ultimately, ordered preferences by anonymous individuals over equally anonymous goods, Ingrao and Israel (1990, p. 281).[3] As Maas (2005a) indicates, the passage of the meaning of rationality through Jevons to Robbins involved a prior reductionism – to a mechanical image of humans, and of the economic as mechanical. It also required the elimination of physiological and psychological aspects other than those defined by choice, Maas (1999, pp. 616–17):

> Jevons in a sense surpassed Babbage by conceiving of human reasoning itself as mechanical. It fostered Jevons's most important invention, designated by Jevons's direct pupil Edgeworth as the economic agent. For Edgeworth and then, shortly after, for Marshall, it was completely unproblematic to speak about this agent as a 'machine' ... This conception of the economic agent became dominant within economics. For some decades in the early twentieth century it lost its mechanistic connotations. 'Economic man' came to be identified with 'rational man'.

Indeed, whilst both Jevons and Edgeworth sought a biological foundation for utility theory, derived from human physiology, and as a consequence of pleasure and pain experienced by the human body, Robbins explicitly rejected 'pretensions of this sort', Maas (2005b). Or, as McCloskey (1996, p. 123) puts it all, 'Neoclassicals are obsessed with Choice, and see choice where others see subordination to necessity'.[4]

By the same token, the transition from Jevons to Robbins had witnessed an even more dramatic transformation in the understanding of production. This is transparent in the arrival of production and cost functions, with the theory of production scarcely distinguishable in form and content from the theory of consumption, Fine and Leopold (1993, ch. 4) and Potts (2000, p. 18). Thus, Lazonick (2003) suggests that Marshall held to two different methodologies as far as production is concerned, one of constrained optimisation but the other pre-occupied with innovation in response to such constraints.[5] In this light, 'Marshall was central to a critical transition in the economics discipline from the broad concern of the classical economists with its focus on economic development to the narrow focus of neoclassical economists on the optimal allocation of scarce resources among alternative existing uses', p. 40. But, 'Rather than making this *transition* from optimizing firm to innovative enterprise, however, the followers of Marshall, and subsequent generations of economists, accepted the theory of the optimizing firm as a sufficient mode of analysis of the role of the business enterprise within the economy', p. 41.

Such a perspective is strikingly brought out by Robbins' disparaging remarks over the treatment of production in Marshall's *Principles*, although he is otherwise extremely praising. Robbins suggests in his *Essay*, p. 5, emphasis added:[6]

> We have all felt … *a sense of shame at the incredible banalities* of much of the so-called theory of production – *the tedious discussions* of the various forms of peasant proprietorship, factory organization, industrial psychology, technical education, etc., which are apt to occur in even the best treatises on general theory … One has only to compare the masterly sweep of Book V of Marshall's *Principles*, which deals with problems which are strictly economic in our sense, with the *spineless platitudes* about manures and the 'fine natures among domestic servants' of much of Book IV to realise the *insidious effect* of a procedure which opens the door to the intrusion of amateur technology into discussions which should be purely economic.

In place of Marshall's concerns, Robbins chooses to discuss the position of Robinson Crusoe; more generally, despite Frank Knight's careful, wideranging and well-recognised distinction between risk and uncertainty, dynamics are reduced to the knowable (if not the fully known) conditions of future scarcity, with time understood as the means by which to attain a given 'longrun' equilibrium. As Hutchison (2000, p. 277) puts it, 'At no point', does Robbins 'show any adequate recognition of the full-knowledge postulate, or of … its essential role, or its often profound unrealism; this is the more strange because Knight's great work is several times appreciatively cited in Robbins *Essay*'.

All this is attached to an essentially Millian methodology. Robbins sees himself as following in the footsteps of Senior and Cairnes who, as seen in Chapters 2 and 3, were two of the more strident supporters of the Ricardian abstract, a priori method, Robbins (1935, p. 82). But there was also one substantial change involved in the move from Mill to Robbins (through Cairnes and J. N. Keynes). This, according to Wade Hands (2001, p. 37), consisted of:

> The movement from *characterizing the method of economics as it contrasts with the different methods of other sciences* in Mill, to specifying *rules for the proper conduct of any science, and thus economics*, in Robbins.

This was a shift, however, whose substance and implications were neither unnoticed nor uncontroversial.

4 Souter's reaction

The implicit and casual disregard of Knight's reservations over the direction in which economics was being interpreted and pushed did inspire more wide-ranging and explicit opposition as soon as Robbins staked out the state of, and prospects for, economics from his own viewpoint. For our purposes, the responses of Ralph Souter, Terence Hutchison and Talcott Parsons are worthy of brief consideration for the light they shed on different aspects of the past, present and future of economics at Robbins' time of writing. In this section, we concentrate on Souter's response, leaving Parsons for Section 6, after considering Hutchison's positivist reaction in Section 5.

Souter was committed to sustaining the old marginalism, as previously described, associated with Marshall, whom Parsons (1934, p. 522) describes as 'his master'. Souter (1933a, p. 378) himself refers to 'the genuine Classical Tradition that has so far reached its highest integration in the work of Marshall', indicating the extent to which the latter is seen as marrying both classical political economy and marginalism. Irrespective of the analytical wrinkles that the disciple adds of his own, his opposition to Robbins should be seen as symbolic defence of the more rounded marginalism and economics associated with Marshall. More specifically, in his lengthy review, both tart and dripping with sarcasm, he is concerned that 'Robbins' *credo* ... is symptomatic of a general trend – by no means confined to the strict votaries of this school, and discernible in a number of directions on both sides of the Atlantic – towards static formalism and an alleged increase in "logical precision"', Souter (1933a, pp. 377–8).

In addition, this has depended upon narrowing the scope of economics to exclude relevant considerations from other social sciences, p. 378: 'It is in this way that "economic science" miraculously juggles "psychology" (not to mention sociology, technology, etc.) over the wall and so obtains its "independence"'.

By the same token, Robbins is perceived to have devalued the notion of ends, the means to achieve them, and the 'amateur' understanding of technology, p. 380:

> Failure to embark on a more intensive 'realistic' examination of the complexities of modern industrial technology (with its systems within systems of 'ends') need, of course, not proved lethal – given a little imagination – had it not been conjoined with the pellet theory of 'ends'.

The snide reference to realism is brought out by making a contrast with the natural sciences that the economist purports to emulate. For, in case of ends, the economist simply takes them as determining and yet unknown. This is not the habit of the endlessly curious scientist, p. 383:

> What, as a matter of ... scientific and philosophical fact ... the economist '*qua* economist', simply does not know: he is in the exalted company of the pure mathematical physicist – '*something unknown is doing we don't know what*'. The main difference is that the static formalist not only does not know, he refuses to know: whereas the mathematical physicist gives every indication of being most anxious to find out.

Instead of investigating what needs to be investigated, the world and the history of economic thought is made to fit the increasingly formal and static theory rather than vice versa.

In light of the latter, Robbins' understanding of the Austrian School is always placed in inverted commas. This is because he is judged to have collapsed the complexity of multiple ends into a single problem of alternative uses of scarce resources as opposed to the influence, for example, of psychological pulls and technological imperatives, pp. 380–1. But most remarkable in Souter's commentary is to spell out precisely what will result from these developments, p. 390:

> If economists who lack philosophical training are still puzzled by the foregoing discussion, I suspect the root of their difficulty lies in the fact that they have allowed themselves to be hypnotized by the mathematical apparatus of demand and supply functions, and the spurious compulsion, resulting from a basic lack of understanding of its significance in terms of reality, which this apparatus exercises over many minds.

So economics will fail to understand its limitations, and not even understand corresponding criticism once established. Even more prescient is anticipation of the self-contained ambition and success of such an 'economic science', again the quotations marks are his own, pp. 396–7:

> Perhaps, therefore, we shall one day produce a whole crop of Economic Einsteins, each equipped with his own Magic Equation, which will

display instantaneously to the eye the distilled quintessence of the vast panorama of shifting shadowy functions of his own favorite Economic Space-Time Continuum.

For Souter, then, Robbins is embarking upon a journey towards a mechanical and vacuous version of economic theory. As we now know, it is a voyage to which the discipline would increasingly attach itself, if not all at once and entirely consciously, Backhouse and Medema (2007a and b).

5 Introducing positivism: From Hutchison to Friedman

If Souter's reaction to Robbins came from the perspective of the more rounded Marshallian economics, Hutchison's response, *The Significance and Basic Postulates of Economic Theory* (1960 [1938]), came from an epistemologically positivist perspective. As seen in previous chapters, there have been challenges to the deductive method in economics arising out of the inductivist and historicist traditions in economics throughout the nineteenth century, which have been associated with such names as Malthus and Richard Jones, and the members of the German and British Historical Schools. At the same time, traces of positivist thought are scattered throughout the history of economics and the history of economic methodology. We have already discussed the empiricist outlook of Mill's general methodological position, which was inspired by Comte's positivism, although for political economy he adhered to the abstract, a priori method, Chapter 3, Jevons plea for the deductive method to be supplemented by the need for verification through the empirical method, and the strong empirical content of Pareto's logico-experimental method, Section 3 above.[7] Nonetheless, it is only from the 1930s that positivism made its explicit entry into economic methodology – initially through the pioneering work of Terence Hutchison, to be followed by Friedman's instrumentalism and Samuelson's operationalism.

At the time Robbins wrote his *Essay*, positivism as a philosophical trend was on the ascendancy. Two different brands of positivist have been identified in the literature. One is in social theory and is associated with the work of nineteenth century philosophers and social scientists, especially Auguste Comte, who was the first to use the term 'positive philosophy', and Ernest Mach. The other is in epistemology and is closely attached to the 'logical positivism' of the Vienna Circle, which offered its most developed form.[8] In epistemology, logical positivism was followed by logical empiricism, associated with the philosophers Braithwaite, Hempel and Nagel. What positivists share in common is the conception of reality as consisting of what our senses perceive, the desire for the clearing of scientific thought from all forms of metaphysics, and the 'unity of science' dogma, or the belief that both physical and social sciences share common logical and methodological premises with a strict distinction between facts and values, Giddens (1977, pp. 29–31) and Wade Hands (1998, p. 376).

Logical positivism, in particular, refers to the philosophical doctrine that 'stressed the provisional and hypothetical nature of all scientific knowledge and the consequent need for empirical confirmation of all theories', Lachmann (1981, p. vi). The only true scientific knowledge was evidential and empirical, and the only true science was empirical science, whose propositions were true only under specific circumstances. The verifiability principle was its most identifiable characteristic and became the positivist demarcation criterion between science and non-science. This view of scientific knowledge is contrasted with the true but purely a priori knowledge associated with mathematics and logic, whose propositions are based on purely formal analysis and are universally valid. Logical empiricism, or what also came to be known as the 'Received View', as an epistemological trend, emerged as a reaction against the empiricist excesses of logical positivism. The main difference between logical empiricism and logical positivism is the former's adherence to the more deductive rather than inductive nature of scientific theories. This is reflected in the introduction of the hypothetico-deductive method as opposed to induction, and the acceptance of the search for explanation as one of the aims of scientific inquiry, Wade Hands (1998, pp. 374–7 and 2001, pp. 72–88), and Caldwell (1982, chs. 2 and 3).

The 1930s also witnessed the publication of Popper's *The Logic of Scientifc Discovery* (1959 [1934]), which introduced the falsification principle, and which was to have a long-lasting impact on twentieth century epistemology and philosophy of science. Popper's epistemology should be seen in the context of being both influenced by, and a reaction against, the rising (logical) positivism of the Vienna Circle. His basic idea is that, since verification is never possible, this should be substituted for by the falsification principle as the main demarcation criterion between scientific and non-scientific thought. In other words, whether a theory is scientific or not depends on whether it makes falsifiable propositions.

As already indicated, Hutchison's 1938 book, *The Significance and Basic Postulates of Economic Theory*, represents the first attempt to introduce positivism fully into economic methodology, and is to economics what Popper is to epistemology (if considerably less acknowledged as such in principle let alone practice). It too had a durable effect on twentieth century economic methodology. It should also be seen against the backdrop of the rising positivism, and as a reaction against the excesses of what he later on dubbed 'empirically minimalist ultra-deductivism', Hutchison (1998, p. 44). Specifically, for Hutchison, p. 75:

> By 'ultra deductivism', or the 'more extreme forms' of the deductive method, I mean those versions which emphasized (1) the minimizing of any empirical elements in the postulates; and (2) the 'self-evident', indubitable, or even a-priorist character of these postulates.

In this tradition, Hutchison, pp. 44, 48, includes the likes of Ricardo, Senior, James Mill, John Stuart Mill (to a lesser extent), Cairnes, Robbins and Mises.

Of this list he only qualifies J. S. Mill's method as being 'less extreme' and 'more empirical than others'. The explicit target of his book, however, according to his own later recollection, was 'the dogmatic and extreme *a priorism* of Professor Mises', Hutchison (1960, p. xxi).[9]

In this work, Hutchison (1941, p. 735) is self-consciously drawing on two great empiricist traditions: the positivist tradition in philosophy (and more specifically the work of Mach, Schlick and Carnap) and the tradition of the British empiricists. To these should be added the influence of Karl Popper, to whom he refers on many occasions, Blaug (1980, p. 94n). Among the British empiricists, Hutchison singles out Robert Malthus as one of his forerunners. According to him, the conclusions reached in his book 'are broadly similar to those reached in the first great controversy on these issues by Malthus', Hutchison (1960, p. 174). Indeed, he closes his book with a quote by Malthus to the effect that 'the principal cause of error ... among scientific writers on political economy, appears to me to be a precipitate attempt to simplify and generalise', see also Chapter 2. And he also approvingly quotes Pareto's advocacy of what he called the 'logico-experimental method' which, as seen already, has strong positivistic overtones, p. 13. The first great divide in economic thought between empiricism and deductivism, which began with the methodological clash between Ricardo and Malthus, is revisited. This time, however, one side of the debate is engaged from a positivist perspective!

Following the logical positivists of the Vienna Circle and Popper, Hutchison comes out strongly in favour of establishing a demarcation criterion distinguishing scientific from non-scientific propositions and theories. As he puts it in his 1960 Preface to *The Significance*, 'The first point made in this book and one that attracted much criticism, concerns what Professor Popper has called the Demarcation Problem, or Demarcation Criterion for distinguishing "between the statements, or systems of statements, of the empirical sciences, and all other statements"', p. vii. His aim is to exclude all 'expressions of ethical and political passion, poetic emotion or metaphysical speculation from being mixed with so-called "science"'. According to Hutchison, all propositions used in economic theory can be classified according to whether they are or are not 'conceivably falsifiable by empirical observation', p. 161. As he puts it, pp. 9–10, see also p. 163:[10]

> If the finished propositions of a science, as against the accessory purely logical and mathematical propositions used in many sciences, including Economics, are to have any empirical content, as the finished propositions of all sciences except of Logic and Mathematics obviously must have, then these propositions must *conceivably* be capable of empirical testing or *be reducible to such propositions* by logical or mathematical deduction. They need not, that is, actually be tested or even be *practically* capable of testing ... their truth or falsity, that is, must make some conceivable empirically noticeable difference.

All scientific propositions must have empirical content, therefore. Testability and falsifiability become the demarcation criteria for distinguishing between 'empirical statements and tautologies or definitions', or between 'empirical science and non-science', pp. x, xi. From these empiricist premises, Hutchison mounts a relentless attack on the 'propositions of pure theory' based on the 'hypothetical method', which are 'not conceivably falsifiable ... [and] therefore devoid of any empirical content', pp. 161, 33–40.

The 'hypothetical' or 'isolating' method, according to Hutchison, p. 166, cannot lead to 'realistic' and useful propositions, see also pp. 73–6:

> Within Economics the 'optimistic' procedure of beginning with highly simplified 'isolated' abstractions, in the hope of gradually making these more 'realistic' and applicable by removing the simplifying assumptions, is apt to come to a dead end, and ... if one wants to get beyond a certain level of abstraction one has to begin more or less from the beginning with extensive empirical investigation.

Empirical investigation, then, should be the starting as well as the finishing point of any scientific inquiry. He pinpoints several of what he considers to be problematic aspects of the 'hypothetical method' and 'pure theory'. *Ceteris paribus* clauses, according to Hutchison (pp. 162, 40–6, 53–7, 65–72), are 'frequently hopelessly ambiguous', while the propositions of pure theory 'have no prognostic value or "causal significance"', leading to 'circular' or 'tautological' arguments. He specifically attacks what he calls the 'Fundamental Assumption' of pure theory, which involves the 'fundamental maximum principle' with its Utilitarian origins, because its concomitant 'perfect expectation' hypothesis essentially 'assumes all economic problems out of existence'. Related to this is his disavowal of the 'psychological method' of Senior and Cairnes, based on introspection, which starts from certain assumptions about human nature, chiefly the hedonistic 'desire for wealth', which is taken for granted a priori, as logically preceding experience. Granted all this, Hutchison concludes that, given the presence of uncertainty, 'the method of deduction from some "Fundamental assumption" or "principle" of economic conduct is more or less useless', pp. 83–4, 94–104, 118, 131–43, 162, 163.

Hutchison's positivist programme was followed by other major positivist-inspired works on economic methodology such as Friedman's (1953) instrumentalist approach, and Samuelson's (1947) operationalism, Wade Hands (1998, p. 377). It also, however, gave rise to a considerable amount of debate and controversy. The first response came from Frank Knight (1940, pp. 5–6) who defended an outright deductive approach as the only road to economic and social knowledge, different from the testable propositions of natural sciences, but in no way less real or arbitrary. The reason for the difference, according to Knight (1941, p. 752), lies in the purposiveness of human behaviour, and the fact that 'human behaviour is affected by error' in a way that natural phenomena are not. As a result, the function of economic principles is 'to describe an ideal, not a reality'. In short, Knight's main preoccupation is to deny that the basic postulates about economic behaviour should be empirically testable rather than being true as commonsense knowledge, that is, by introspection. For him, economic propositions 'are subject to no test except that of agreement among the members of such a community of discourse', p. 753. This, however, does not make economics any less scientific. To the contrary, for Knight, cited in Machlup (1955, p. 5, note 7), arguing in the same spirit as Walras and Jevons, 'There is a science of economics, a true and even exact science, which reaches laws as universal as those of mathematics and mechanics'.

Assertions such as these have led Machlup (1955, pp. 5–6) to classify Knight together with Senior, Cairnes, J. S. Mill, Robbins and Mises as belonging to the 'extreme apriorist' camp. At the same time, however, he charges Hutchison of 'ultra-empiricism', because of his insistence that all scientific statements, including the basic assumptions of a theory, must be directly verifiable through empirical evidence, pp. 7–11. Following Hutchison's (1956) reply, where he defends his position by saying that he never proposed that the basic assumptions should be testable, Machlup (1956) persists in his charges and dubs him a 'reluctant ultra-empiricist'. In place of Hutchison's ultra-empiricism, Machlup proposes that economic theories should be only indirectly testable through their conclusions or predictions.

Machlup's position is close to Friedman's (1953) famous instrumentalist, 'as if' methodology. According to the latter, if a theory produces accurate predictions as tested against the evidence, then it is immaterial whether the assumptions are realistic or not. 'A theory cannot be tested by the "realism" of its "assumptions"', Friedman proclaims, p. 224. One should go ahead as if the assumptions were realistic. Not only that, but, stretching the argument to its extreme, 'the more significant the theory, the more unrealistic the assumptions', p. 218. What makes a theory scientific is not the empirical validity of its assumptions, but its capacity to produce accurate predictions, pp. 213, 214:

> The ultimate goal of a positive science is the development of a 'theory' or 'hypothesis' that yields valid and meaningful (i.e. not truistic) predictions about phenomena not yet observed ... Viewed as a body of substantive hypotheses, theory is to be judged by its predictive power for the class of phenomena which it is intended to 'explain.' Only factual evidence can show whether it is 'right' or 'wrong' or, better, tentatively 'accepted' as valid or 'rejected' ... The only relevant test of the *validity* of a hypothesis is comparison of its predictions with experience.

In this way, theories become predictive instruments rather than explanatory devices, hence the label instrumentalism.

Friedman, unlike Hutchison, was not inspired so much by the philosophical debates around logical positivism and logical empiricism prevalent at the time, but was mostly concerned to respond 'to certain contemporary debates regarding the theoretical and empirical practices of the economics profession', Wade Hands (2001, p. 53). In particular, he was reacting in part against some empirical studies by Hall and Hitch (1939) and Lester (1946), according to which marginalist analysis is perceived to fail to explain the practices of businesses and firms. These results were quite disquieting for orthodox economics at that time, and Friedman's 'as if' methodology offered a methodological way out of the problem. This is why Friedman's essay, the single most widely read piece in the history of economic methodology, which has variously been described as a 'marketing masterpiece' or 'the centrepiece of postwar economic methodology', 'has proven most popular with economists', despite its almost total disavowal by economic methodologists, Caldwell (1982, p. 173), Blaug (1980, p. 103) and Hausman (1992, pp. 162–3).[11]

It is the argument against explanation in science that Friedman's instrumentalism shares with Samuelson's operationalism. Samuelson's (1947, p. 3) 'operationalism' places emphasis on the elaboration of *'operationally meaningful* theorems' as the goal of science, and hence of economics. By the latter, he refers to theorems consisting of refutable propositions, and hence able to be tested against empirical evidence. 'By a *meaningful* theorem', he says, 'I mean simply a hypothesis about empirical data which could conceivably be refuted if only under ideal conditions', p. 4. It is obvious from the above that what Hutchison's positivism shares with Friedman's instrumentalism and Samuelson's operationalism is their common adherence to some form of empiricism, and their endorsement of some form of testability criterion, as the road to true science. In this light, they can all be considered as bringing into economic methodology some combination of positivist thinking with Popper's falsificationism.

Indeed, several commentators have suggested that Samuelson's operationalism, despite its label, is more akin to Popper's falsificationism or to Hutchison's method of deriving propositions which are 'conceivably falsifiable by empirical observation', than to the true operationalism associated with the physicist Percy Bridgman. Statements such as the one quoted above by Samuelson give ample support to such an argument. Be that as it may, Samuelson's methodological position was soon to change. In a comment on Friedman's instrumentalism, Samuelson (1963) attacks Friedman's position that the unrealism of assumptions is not relevant to the validity of theory, which he calls the 'F-twist'. At the same time his adherence to what he himself called 'operationalism' gives way to 'descriptivism', a crude form of empiricism where the task of science is reduced to description of empirical regularities, rather than explanation of the phenomena under investigation, Samuelson (1965, p. 1171), Blaug (1980, pp. 99–100, 111–14), Caldwell (1982, pp. 189–95), Wade Hands (2001, pp. 60–9) and Hausman (1992, ch. 9).

These positivist-inspired works have generally been met with wide acceptance, at the abstract methodological level, among practising economists – if not by economic methodologists. Whether this acceptance has been translated into practice, however, is another and highly disputed matter. In other words, do economists practice what they preach? In general terms, the answer must be in the negative. Hausman (1992, p. 152) talks about 'the striking methodological *schizophrenia* that is characteristic of contemporary economics, whereby methodological doctrine and practice regularly contradict one another'. Such schizophrenia is sometimes even manifest in the works of single individuals. Hausman (pp. 156–8), following Machlup (1964) and Mirowski (1989a), picks up Samuelson's work as a typical example of such schizophrenia as revealed, for example, by the contrast between his operationalist or descriptivist methodological outlook and the deductive premises of both his revealed preference theory and his work on international factor price equalisation, see also Caldwell (1982, p. 193), on Samuelson see also Chapter 14, Section 5. And similar considerations apply to Friedman's work, pp. 162–9, especially given his committed exposition of monetarist doctrines.

In short, in the wake of the direction given to the marginalist revolution through Robbins' *Essay*, and the methodological and substantive excesses associated with this work, together with the contributions of extreme deductivists such as Mises, subsequent stances on economic methodology by Hutchison, Friedman and Samuelson responded by introducing strong doses of empiricism into economic methodology, the positivist tradition. This is the first time that positivism is explicitly introduced into economic methodology, replacing historicist inductivism as the main methodological opponent of the deductivist camp. Despite its wide acceptance by practising economists at the methodological level, however, they failed to put these methodological principles into practice. Hence positivism increasingly became second nature to economists so that it was neither justified nor indeed put into practice.

6 Talcott Parsons and the consolidation of sociology

Souter's and Hutchison's reactions to Robbins are pertinent for reflecting disquiet with the latter's work from *within* the discipline of economics, from the old marginalist and the positivist perspective, respectively. Parsons' (1934) critique is complementary as a response *to* economics *from* sociology, from outside. However, before examining Parsons' reaction to Robbins from the confines of sociology, which was struggling to establish itself as a separate discipline, it is instructive to start by briefly examining Parsons' role in this process. This will be followed by his treatment of Marshall's economics, before coming to his reaction to Robbins's *Essay*.

Parsons is generally seen as being at the forefront, as the midwife, in the creation of modern sociology as a distinct discipline. His credentials for assuming this role were extensive: he had translated Weber and was responsible for the introduction of the classical sociological thought of Max Weber and Emile Durkheim to an Anglo-American audience. And he situated himself, in relation to the major economists of the day, who were themselves negotiating the emergence and positioning of economics. In addition, Parsons also engaged extensively with – and was even taught by – the institutionalists of his time, see Chapters 9 and 10, ultimately critically rejecting their attempts to establish a more rounded economics than that offered by marginalism, see Hodgson (2001) for an extensive account.

Parsons' aim was to construct a general theory of society. He thought that economic relations are embedded in society and, thus, that the economy is only a part of a more general social system. He identified three different traditions in social theory. One was the utilitarian school, which promoted a rationalistic and individualistic approach to social phenomena. Second was the positivistic tradition, which tackles human behaviour in a fashion similar to the scientific laws of physical sciences. Last was the idealist tradition which emphasised cultural values as the chief factor in explaining social phenomena. Economic theory in particular, as part of the first tradition, would never become a general theory of economic behaviour, because human behaviour is never purely economic or purely rational. Hence economic theory could not explain other forms of action, except as the result of ignorance and error. Parsons thought that Pareto made an important step in the direction of solving this problem through his distinction between logical and non-logical action, and his treatment of the latter as a form of behaviour that can be analysed scientifically (i.e. logically), see above. Overall, Parsons thought that all these traditions tackled specific aspects of social reality, without, however, being able to offer a comprehensive theory of society. Thus, in his first major book, *The Structure of Social Action* (first published in 1937), Parsons sought to rectify this state of affairs by reconciling all these traditions, and especially the thought of such diverse figures as Marshall, Durkheim, Pareto and Weber, in a general theory of society or what he called a 'voluntaristic theory of action'. Later on, in his other major work, *The Social System* (first published in 1951), he switched his attention more to the institutional structures of society as the determinants of human action, in what amounts to what he himself called structural functionalist analysis, Devereux (1963).

Seen in retrospect, the end result of Parsons' work was the promotion and the further consolidation of sociology as a separate discipline. The substance that he gave to sociology reflected five factors. First, from the wide variety of influences upon him, he sought to distil out those that would allow for sociology as a general social theory. Second, such a theory should have little contact with, or be tangential/orthogonal to, economics, and especially its peculiar form of methodological individualism. Third, the theory also needed to be as powerful as economics in its scope of application and appeal. Fourth, whilst the classics of sociology from which Parsons draws are to a large extent motivated by the wish to explain modern (bourgeois and industrial) society as distinct from what came before, he takes modern society as given or as the norm, almost as a natural analytical starting point. Fifth, whether consciously or not, but as a condition of its widespread acceptance in the post-war period, Parsons' sociology needed to celebrate the virtues of modern (US) society.

As observed by Hodgson (2001), in parallel with economics, the result was for Parsons to create an ahistorical sociology based on universal principles (or those of modern society parading as universal). It drew upon structures, systems, action, order, the macro and the social, and functionally, all generalised out of selective choice from the analytical fragments of his predecessors or the characteristics of contemporary US society. That such a sociology should be influential in the United States in the first decades after the Second World War is hardly surprising, just at it would be later rejected for more radical, as well as more socially and historically specific, approaches dealing in power and conflict, dysfunction and disorder, poverty and exclusion, as well as the more critical introspection attached to postmodernism and the acknowledgement of other worlds within and without the United States.

Parsons's role, both intellectually and professionally, in the establishment of sociology as a separate discipline could be seen as the mirror image of Marshall's role in economics. At the same time, in a sense, for Parsons, the institutionalists were simply Marshall's broader canvas in another form and with different analytical balance with marginalism. Thus, whatever his sympathies, antipathies and debts to the old institutionalism, that they were attached first and foremost to *economics*, both professionally and, to some extent, intellectually (individual–rational as a *part* of human behaviour), meant that it would attract his open hostility, Velthuis (1999). For Parsons fully accepted the marginalist principles and approach in defining economics if only within its own domain alone, but equally feared that any unification of such analysis with other disciplines, especially sociology, would have invasive and destructive implications for alternatives, as was to occur through economics imperialism, Fine and Milonakis (2009). In this respect, Marshall must have appeared far more dangerous than Robbins, because at least the latter accepted the domain of economics in terms of method and scope and, for Parsons, allowed for a clear boundary between economics and sociology.

Parsons' extensive assessments of Marshall's work should be seen in this light.[12] For our purposes, the specific perspective from which Parsons undertakes his review (as a theory of social action) is less important as such than the fact that it accepts and deploys the distinction between social theory and methodological individualism. As a result, from his broader approach, Parsons is able to identify the social (or non-rational) within Marshall, and to highlight the tension with his economics. His argument runs along the following lines.

First, Parsons (1968b, p. 174) accepts the possibility of an 'analytically separable' economics, derived 'as a descendant of the utilitarian aspect of positivistic thought'. It will be based essentially on 'supply and demand schema … inherent in a science of economics thought of in these terms'. In this respect, Parsons is not so different from Weber and Pareto.

Second, in principle, such an economics provides the option for economics to become a universal social science. Indeed, p. 454:

> This path leads to the conception of economics, from a theoretical point of view, as an encyclopedic sociology in which all elements bearing on concrete social life have a place, with the result that the separate identity of economic theory as a discipline is destroyed.

This, then, is to recognise the tension between economics as market supply and demand, versus economics as the principles underpinning supply and demand being applied universally.

Third, though, for Parsons in practice, this opens up two 'insidious' tendencies. One is the total neglect of non-economic factors unless 'they can be brought into relation with the supply and demand schema', p. 174. The other is to exaggerate those non-economic elements that can be related to supply and demand, p. 175. Parsons recognises that it is only Marshall's empiricism that prevents him from universally extending the principles of marginalism, and 'This conclusion has been obscured mainly by the role in economics of supply and demand', p. 173, that is concentrated focus upon the market in the first instance.

Fourth, Marshall's methodological inclination, despite his *Principles*, is to eschew formal axiomatics and abstract reasoning for a large dose of inductive reasoning. 'His conception of economics was thoroughly empirical – a "study of man in the everyday business of life"', p. 452. There is also an emphasis on Marshall's empiricism, his being in touch with everyday realities as opposed to long chains of deductive reason, p. 130. The idea of satisfying given wants without explanation of the origins of those wants is circular and useful within limits, pp. 130–1.

Fifth, Marshall consequently complements his economics based on utilitarianism with consideration of a higher set of wants and drives attached to entrepreneurial spirit, pp. 702–3.[13] For Parsons, this is entirely appropriate, as utility is necessarily related to an independently 'given system of ultimate ends ... [and] the concept of maximization of utility is completely meaningless by itself ... without bringing in logically distinct elements, such as the nature of wants', p. 608.

Sixth, Marshall's broader perspective remains inadequate, and is weaker than that of both Weber and Pareto, for viewing the relationship between the pursuit of utility and of higher goals as independent of one another (thereby allowing for a separable economics based on the satisfaction of utility). Pareto, for example, takes a more realistic, cyclical view of development because of the shifting balance of economic and non-economic elements in action – as opposed to Marshall's teleological triumph of free enterprise. Significantly, Weber has now been totally excised from economics, and Pareto only survives in token but prominent form in the definition of efficiency and the apparatus of indifference curves.

Seventh, Parsons concludes that economics is at most an 'intermediate' science, one that is incapable of offering a full explanation by itself – 'the focus of interest of economic theory is in the intermediate sector of the intrinsic means-end chain', p. 265. Indeed, economic rationality is a sort of ideal type, but unlike Souter, Robbins and Marshall, Weber does not 'obscure the enormous empirical importance of coercion in actual economic life [as in] the great majority of liberal economists'. In this context, Parsons is particularly harsh on Robbins, whose, p. 658:

> Professed aim is to construct an abstract science of economics. But by merely refusing to discuss them, it is not possible to evade the questions of the relations of the elements formulated in economic theory to the other elements of a system of action ... The result is a profound laissez-faire bias which appears conspicuously in Professor Robbins' other works.

In short, in terms of this account of Marshall through the prism of Parsons, it is possible to decipher how the latter negotiated the tensions between economics and the other social sciences by imposing methodological and substantive bounds on the realm of economic rationality.

Coming to Parsons' reaction to Robbins' *Essay*, whilst he accepts much of Souter's critique on methodological grounds, he finds it unsatisfactory for failing to descend to the level of the positioning of economics itself within the social sciences. For Parsons, Souter's methodological critique of Robbins opens the possibility of enriching economics with insights drawn from across the other social sciences. But this has the drawback of inappropriately infecting those social sciences with the methods of economics – a recipe for 'economic imperialism' as explicitly espoused by Souter, Parsons (1934, pp. 511–12):

> He does not consider the scope of economics in relation to the current discussion of the neighbouring sciences, but rather attempts to settle the question on the grounds of 'economic philosophy' alone. This failure ... leads him into an 'economic imperialism' (to borrow his own phrase), which results not only in enriching these neighbouring 'countries', which of course it does, but in putting some of them into a strait jacket of 'economic' categories which is ill-suited to their own conditions.

Thus, Parsons is primarily concerned with the different view of, and approach taken to, action in economics as opposed to other social sciences.

At one level, this is a matter of purposefulness, something which separates social from natural science, p. 520:

> Celestial bodies do not 'strive' to follow their orbits whether by the Newtonian or the Einsteinian formulae, they merely *do*. These considerations make 'economic law' something quite different from 'positive' law even in the abstract sense.

This means that ends cannot be taken as given, but should be subject to investigation even if there is a role for economics as study of means to given ends, p. 525:

> A sociology which does not explicitly study the role of ultimate ends in human life is a poor thing indeed. But so long as there is realization of the presence of that factor and of its main characteristics, economics can study certain intermediate phases of action in abstraction from it. It is highly important to realize the fundamental difference of this view from that which postulates as the subject matter of economic theory an abstract 'individualistic' society. It ... deals with one aspect of an 'organic' (if you will) social process.

But, if following Robbins' approach to economics as a means–end dualism, then focusing on individual optimisation narrows the scope of economics unduly even on its own terms. For 'on the social plane the question arises whether all possible means of acquisition from others, or through the services of others, are to be called "economic". This involves the status of such factors as use of threat of physical violence, some aspects of fraud, and other milder forms of the use of power. All can undoubtedly serve as modes of acquisition', pp. 526–7. The result in legitimately establishing economics as 'a science concerned with one aspect of all human action', p. 530, is to take these other factors out of economics and to render them the subject matter of another discipline, sociology.

Interestingly, in light of developments today around the new institutional economics, Parsons sees this all in terms of the presence or absence of economic *institutions*. And, further, p. 533:

> economic institutions are in the causal sense a specifically *non*-economic factor ... they form at least one fundamental element in accounting for the specific qualitative form of organization of any particular 'economy" ... But neither Robbins nor Souter, tho both vaguely note their existence, have any clear conception of the relation of institutions to economic activities, nor any systematic place for a theory of institutions in their scheme of the social sciences. In my opinion it is one of the central elements of sociology.

This is because, 'To a sociologist ... it is quite clear that institutions ... cannot be analyzed theoretically in terms of supply and demand curves but require an analysis of a totally different kind', p. 535. Without this, he continues, there 'is the tendency to attempt to extend "economic categories" to cover the whole of concrete life. This is the objectionable "economic imperialism" of which I spoke'. So Parsons follows in the footsteps of Weber and Schumpeter in clearly delineating the boundaries between social sciences, economics and (in particular) sociology, but, although he thinks that economics stands to gain by incorporating insights from other social sciences, he finds the reverse trend, which takes the form of economics imperialism, objectionable. But through both Souter and Parsons, it is apparent how economics was situated, and was situating itself, in relation to the other social sciences, much to the consternation of those who wanted a different substance of economics itself and its division of labour with other disciplines.

Thus, following Hodgson (2001) and others, whilst it would be appropriate in retrospect to highlight the roles of both Robbins and Parsons in carving out a separation between economics and sociology as disciplines, it is nonetheless important not to exaggerate the extent to which the division between the disciplines and between subject matter was rendered either immediately or absolutely. For Hodgson (2007a) refers to 'intellectual circles that changed the prevailing definition of economics from the Marshallian study of the "ordinary business of life" to the narrower Robbinsian "science of choice" and shifted the definition of sociology from the Comtean science of society to the Parsonian emphasis on the origin and integration of values'. He suggests a consensus over demarcation of boundaries between the two disciplines, with economics deploying rational choice to meet given ends, and sociology determining the social origins of those ends. This interpretation, though, is too extreme in level and pace of change for Robbins and Parsons did not so much define their respective disciplines as reflect their situation and promote particular dynamics for them, see also Backhouse and Medema (2007a and 2007b) for the slow, contested but remorseless acceptance of Robbins.

For economics, the process of excising the historical and the social accelerated on the basis of its separation from sociology (and history). But, for sociology, the template laid down by Parsons was both partial and temporary across the discipline as a whole. The reintroduction or retention of the historical and the social in sociology was, in a sense, even promoted by the extremes to which Parsons had been driven in his reaction against economics.[14]

Indeed, so widespread is criticism of Parsons for his structuralist functionalism that he has become the whipping boy for the many deficiencies of social theory. It has now become commonplace to accuse Parsons of having promoted the separation between study of the economy and study of society.[15] This is hardly fair, even if motivated by the presumed damage that his functionalism has done to the discipline of sociology. His criticisms of economics, especially as it was becoming at his time of writing, for its study of the economy could hardly have been harsher. And he can hardly be blamed for wishing sociology to attach itself to a different methodology if not, it should be emphasised, an entirely different subject matter. But the point here is less to assess, or reassess, Parsons fairly as sociologist – he seems more palatable to beleaguered heterodox economists than he does to thriving heterodox sociologists; rather it is to see him as representative of profound opposition to economics in addressing the social at all as opposed to the individual. For Parsons, differences in method, not subject matter, defined the differences between economics and sociology, thereby implicitly rendering economics imperialism stillborn at the moment of its embryonic stage. And, as will be apparent, Parsons' anxieties were not ill-founded.

7 Concluding remarks

The 1930s was a decade of intense activity in economic science. As discussed in this chapter, it witnessed the squaring off of the marginalist revolution, through Robbins' reaffirmation of economics as an abstract deductive exercise and his pushing economics away from its traditional definition as the science of wealth or the science of the economy, towards its definition as the science of choice. With this redefinition, the notion of what constitutes the economic also changed. The latter is no longer tied to the economy or the market, but refers to anything that involves scarcity and hence choice. Granted this, the road was opened for economics as a theory of choice to be applied to areas outside its traditional subject matter of the (market) economy. This possibility, first anticipated by Souter, was realised later on through the process of what he first called 'economic imperialism' (or 'economics imperialism' our preferred term), a process discussed in detail in Fine and Milonakis (2009).

The consolidation of marginalism through Robbins' work with its excesses, did not go unopposed but was met with some resistance both from within economics and from outside its confines. If with Robbins (and Mises), the 'ultra-deductivist" tradition in economic methodology of Senior, Cairnes and J. N. Keynes reaches a climax, with Hutchison, the 'ultra-empiricist' trend in economics in the tradition of Malthus, Jones and the Historical Schools is reintroduced, this time with a positivist twist. As argued in detail in this chapter, Hutchison's (1960) book represents what amounts to the first explicit, book-length introduction of positivism into economic methodology, an introduction which did not signify its immediate introduction to economic practice as such, although it did have a more long-lasting impact. Statistical data and methods were already making headway and econometrics was taking its first steps.

As a concomitant development to the squaring off of marginalism, the 1930s witnessed the further consolidation of sociology as a separate discipline based on the work of Talcott Parsons, following the lead of the three founders, Max Weber, Emile Durkheim and Vilfredo Pareto. Sociology's demarcation as a distinct area of study was accompanied by its irrevocable split from economics, on the basis of Pareto's (and Weber's) distinction between rational and non-rational action. This separation was complete by the Second World War. 'Few persons competent in sociological theory', write Parsons and Smelser (1956, pp. xviii), quoted in Smelser and Swedberg (1994, p. 17), 'have any working knowledge of economics, and conversely ... few economists have much knowledge in sociology'. 'Indeed', they say, 'we feel that there has been, if anything, a retrogression rather than an advance in the intervening half century', i.e. since Max Weber's time, p. xvii. For Swedberg (1990, p. 13):

> In concrete terms this often meant that the economists tried to analyse economic problems while abstracting from social forces, and that the sociologists tried to analyse social problems while abstracting from economic forces.

The last, and perhaps the most important, innovation that took place in the 1930s was the emergence of moderm macroeconomics, through Keynes' *General Theory* (1973 [1936]), which was to become part of the newly emerging orthodoxy, despite its widely divergent methodological and substantive outlook to that of the triumphant marginalism and neoclassical economics. We come back to discuss Keynes' theory in Chapter 14, together with general equilibrium theory. Before this, however, we first turn our attention to the evolution of the Austrian School of thought.

13 From Menger to Hayek
The (re)making of the Austrian School

'And it is probably no exaggeration to say that every important advance in economic theory during the last hundred years was a further step in the consistent application of subjectivism'.

Hayek (1952, p. 281)

1 Introduction

Menger, as seen in Chapter 6, has left behind many legacies, one of the most important is his role as the founder of the Austrian School in economics. His *Principles* is considered to be its founding document. Indeed, as shown below, most of the important ideas of the Austrian School in all its versions, can be traced back, in one way or another, to having presence in Menger's work. To summarise, the basic elements of his approach include the stress on the necessity of theory, the clarification of the 'analytic-composite' or abstract/ deductive method in economics, the principle of 'atomism' or methodological individualism, and his subjective theory of value based on the principle of marginal utility. His theory also included strong doses of institutional development, of the primacy of process where time is important, and of knowledge, uncertainty, ignorance and error, Streissler (1973). In this way, he departed from other marginalists in important ways, Section 2. These elements of his method disappeared in the wake of the triumph of marginalism and of Marshallian neoclassical economics, only to resurface in the 1930s, mostly in the work of Hayek and, subsequently, neo-Austrianism, albeit with limited direct appeal to, and rediscovery of, Menger himself.

What is characteristic of the Austrian School is its specific trajectory. It started out as part of the marginalist revolution through Menger's work in the 1870s, and continued from the 1880s until the 1920s as a chief contributor to mainstream economic theorising. The main vehicle for the incorporation of the Austrians into the core body of neoclassical economic theory was the work of Menger's closest disciples and followers, Eugen von Böhm-Bawerk (1851–1914) and Friedrich von Wieser (1851–1926), examined in Section 3. Later on, however, in the 1930s and 1940s, mostly through the work of Ludwig von Mises (1881–1973) and Friedrich von Hayek (1899–1992), examined in

Section 4, it broke completely with marginalism while still remaining strongly subjectivist and individualistic. This time, however, it was in the context of subjectively held imperfect knowledge, uncertainty and ignorance.

What is disinctive about this school is that it is a typical example of one formed in opposition, Caldwell (2004, p. 126). To begin with, one of Menger's basic objectives was to reform and reconstruct (classical) political economy. In opposition to the German historicists, however, he did so using one classical tool, the abstract/deductive method. In the *Methodenstreit*, he adopted a methodological position in clear opposition to the historicists. During the 1880s and 1890s, Böhm-Bawerk used the subjective theory of value as a weapon in his attempt to demolish the Marxian labour theory of value. Coming to the 1930s and 1940s, the modern version of Austrian economics took shape in the writings of Hayek, who mostly wrote in response to the attempt by neoclassical economists such as Oskar Lange to provide a workable theoretical framework for a (market) socialist economy, in what came to be known as the socialist calculation debate.

Vaughn (1990) identifies five main phases in the evolution of the Austrian School. The first is the work of Menger himself, to be followed by its marginalist, neoclassical turn in the work of Böhm-Bawerk and Wieser. Then comes the revival of the Mengerian non-neoclassical themes in the work of Hayek and Mises in the 1930s and 1940s, followed by the 'quiet years' between 1950 and 1973. Recently, with the rise of neo-liberalism following the collapse of the post-war boom and the demise of Keynesianism, neo-Austrianism has benefited from something of a revival mostly in the work of Kirzner, Lachman, Rothbard and others. As observed in the closing section, however, the Austrian School's particular take on subjectivism, methodological individualism and deductivism – despite in general being more sophisticated than that of the mainstream – has exercised little leverage over it, not least because it is totally opposed to its substance. Rather, it has merely served to legitimise laissez-faire, but on grounds entirely at odds with those attached to the revival of (academic) monetarism, with which it is often and popularly conflated. The genuinely critical aspects of Austrian economics, concerning the impossibility of equilibrium and yet the positive role of the market in coordinating individual inventiveness and discovery, have been totally ignored or, at most, reduced to a more palatable calculus of imperfect but knowable information within the mainstream.

2 Carl Menger and the slippage from marginalism

As seen in Chapter 6, Menger is justifiably seen as one of the co-inventors of the concept (if not the word) of marginal utility. This has led many scholars to view marginalism as the 'keystone' of Menger's theoretical endeavour, Hutchison (1953, p. 141), a view that is no doubt reinforced by his association with Jevons and Walras as founders of marginalism. Later scholarship, however, has shown that, in contrast to Jevons and Walras, marginalism was certainly not the essence of Menger's inquiries, Streissler, (1973, p. 160). For one thing, this concept is introduced only half way through Menger's *Principles*, while, on the other hand and in this same work, Menger already incorporates, *'practically all the ideas which make the application of the marginal calculus difficult and hazy'*, p. 171. These include human perception, information, uncertainty, time and the possibility of error. 'Mengerian man', says Streissler, 'is constantly trying to *increase* his knowledge, creating *social institutions* to gather information ... Again and again Menger stresses the *time dimension* of goods and the amount of *uncertainty* this entails', p. 167. Or as Jaffé (1976, p. 521) puts it:

> Man, as Menger saw him, far from being a 'lightning calculator', is a bumbling, erring, ill-informed creature, plagued with uncertainty, hovering between alluring hopes and haunting fears, and congenitally incapable of making finely calibrated decisions in pursuit of satisfaction.

To this should be added Menger's aversion to the use of mathematics. 'We do not simply study quantitative relationships but also the NATURE of economic phenomena', he says in a letter to Walras, quoted in Hutchison (1973b, p. 17n). 'How can we attain to the knowledge of this latter (e.g. the nature of value, rent, profit, the division of labour, bimetallism, etc), by mathematical methods?' This is related to Menger's adherence to the 'analytic-composite method', through which he tries to uncover the underlying elementary causes of social phenomena, thus adhering to a type of generative causality, as opposed to Walras' logical causality, Jaffé (1976, p. 521). This aspect of Menger's work – the search for the essence of economic phenomena and of causal relations and exact laws – has led many commentators to describe his work as an application of Aristotelian essentialism, Chapter 6, Kauder (1965), Bostaph (1978) and Smith (1990). Caldwell (2004, p. 31) attributes Menger's failure to reach what he calls 'the standard results of marginal analysis', to his 'distrust of mathematics as a tool for understanding the social', which was to become 'a hallmark of much of the Austrian tradition', see also Hayek (1934, pp. 66–7).

Of particular interest is Menger's treatment of the origin and nature of social institutions. Its importance for him derives, first, from its strong connotations with the German historical writers, some of whom had made the issue of the evolution of institutions the core of their investigations. How are institutions to be dehistoricised relative to his opponents' approach *and* rehistoricised by his own? Second, and significantly, Menger is the only one among the marginalist writers (including his followers Böhm-Bawerk and Wieser) to have tackled this topic. This is not surprising, since such a qualitative issue, dealing with the *nature* of social phenomena, is not easily reconcilable with marginal analysis, as Menger himself had hinted, and as Wieser (1967 [1927], p. 165) fully admits, Section 3.[1] Indeed, this is yet another instance in Menger's work which, in Streissler's words quoted above, 'makes the application of the marginal calculus difficult and hazy'. This is probably the main reason why this anomaly, together with many others of a similar nature, have been lost in the wake of the marginalist revolution with its emphasis on quantitative relationships, rather than on the broader investigation of the nature of economic phenomena. And even when it did resurface, it did so under the rubric of such anti-marginalist schools as old institutionalism and the neo-Austrian School, associated with Mises and Hayek.[2]

According to Menger there are two ways of explaining the origins and existence of social institutions. First is the *pragmatic approach*, which examines the portion of social phenomena that is 'the result of agreement, of legislation, of the common will in general', Menger (1985 [1883], pp. 135, 145). For him, p. 145:

> There are a number of social phenomena which are the products of the agreement of members of society, or of positive legislation, results of the purposeful common activity of society thought of as a separate active subject ... Here the interpretation appropriate to the real state of affairs is the *pragmatic* one – the explanation of the nature and origin of social phenomena from the intentions, opinions, and available instrumentalities of human social unions or their rulers.

What is of more interest for Menger, however, is that portion of social institutions which are of *organic origin*, p. 158. Following Adam Ferguson, the Scottish philosopher of the Enlightenment, Menger uses this notion to refer to social institutions which are *not* the result of an '*intention aimed at this purpose*' but the '*unintended result of historical development*', p. 130. The crucial question for Menger is this, p. 146: '*how can it be that institutions which serve the common welfare and are extremely significant for its development come into being without a* common will *directed toward establishing them?*' Menger includes law, language, markets, communities and states among the institutions that were spontaneously created by historical development, p. 130.

By far his favourite example of such an institution is money. It first appears in his *Principles* and persistently reappears in his later works, for example Menger (1985 and 1892). Money, according to Menger (1985, p. 130), although an institution with immense implications for the welfare of society, is 'by no means the result of agreement directed at its establishment as a social institution'. Indeed, the task of science is exactly to understand how such an institution has come into being, 'by presenting the process by which, as economic culture advances, a definite item or a number of items leaves the sphere of the remaining goods and becomes money, without express agreement of people and without legislative acts', p. 153. He then goes on to describe the historical process through which money came into being, starting with the process of barter exchange and the difficulties and limits that this type of exchange faces (double coincidence of wants, etc.). Money, says Menger, comes into being as a result of people trying to do away with the obstacles to the exchange of goods presented by barter exchange, p. 154:[3]

> The economic interest of the economic individuals, therefore, with increased knowledge of their *individual* interests, without any agreement, without legislative compulsion, *even without any consideration of public interest*, leads them to turn their wares for more marketable ones, even if they do not need the latter for their immediate consumer needs ... Thus there appears before us under the powerful influence of custom the phenomenon to be observed everywhere with advancing economic culture that a certain number of goods are accepted in exchange by everybody.

There are two striking features of Menger's analysis of the emergence of money. One, which is neither new nor peculiar to him, but which is certainly at odds with his general methodological stance, is that he follows the historical method by tracing the origins of money from earlier times. As Hutchison (1973b, p. 32) says, he even 'complains that earlier economists had shown little interest in historical research so that the question he was concerned with was lost sight of until taken up by, among others, Roscher, Hildebrand, and Knies'. The second striking aspect of his analysis of the emergence of money is that he considers it to be 'the unintended result ... the unplanned outcome of specifically *individual* efforts of members of society', Menger (1985, p. 155). Menger, faithful to his 'atomism', and contrary to the then prevailing organicist interpretation, traces the origin and nature of these spontaneously created institutions, and of money in particular, in the unintended consequences of individual human action, what Hayek was later to call 'spontaneous order', see Section 4 below. This has affinities with Adam Smith's invisible hand explanation of the workings of the market economy.

So in Menger we find both the foundations of marginal analysis and, at the same time, all the necessary equipment to go beyond it. This apparent contradiction is seen by Streissler (1973, p. 164) as Menger's greatest strength. 'Menger', he says, 'was uniquely great because he surpassed marginalism at the same time that he created it'. Other authors have also stressed apparent inconsistencies in Menger's work. Kirzner (1978, pp. 36, 38), for example, points to the inconsistency between Menger's incorporation of problems of uncertainty and ignorance, and his otherwise neoclassical theory of price, see also Vaughn (1978). Lachmann (1978), on the other hand, has criticised Menger for what he calls his 'incomplete revolution of subjectivism'. By this he means that, although Menger focuses on value as a subjective judgement of economising men, at the same time he regards the ends towards which these judgements are directed, i.e. human needs, as objectively defined.

This ambivalence in Menger's founding document has spawned the development of two basic strands of the Austrian School, according to which of the two aspects of his work is stressed. In the hands of the second-generation

Austrians, Menger's immediate followers and disciples, Böhm-Bawerk and Wieser, the Austrian School witnessed a great marginalist impulse. Compared to them, Menger 'was the least marginalist of all the Austrians', Streissler (1973, p. 165). In the hands of the other two founders of the neo-Austrian School, Mises and Hayek, however, Austrianism moves away from marginalism towards a more subjectivist and a priori type of theorising, with the questions of human perception, knowledge, time and uncertainty taking the upper hand, rendering the concept of marginalism more or less redundant. Two distinguishing features of (neo-)Austrianism do, however, tend to prevail across each of Menger's progenies – methodological individualism and commitment to laissez-faire – something that each shares with monetarism, so that it is often rounded up as part and parcel of the same ideology if not economic theory.

3 The formation of the Austrian School: Böhm-Bawerk and Wieser

Before the 1880s, there certainly was not any identifiable Austrian School, and one was only really formed in the 1880s. Two important events took place during this decade to help in launching the school. One was the *Methodenstreit*; the other was the publication of Wieser's and Böhm-Bawerk's works of 1884 and 1886, respectively, see Howey (1973, pp. 26, 29) and Hutchison (1973a, p. 179).[4] Although the individual contributions of these two writers are not so profound, each helped immensely in both the further refinement of the marginalist principle and in its full incorporation into mainstream economic theory, and in the corresponding inauguration of the Austrian School. By 1890, it was already established, and both Böhm-Bawerk and Wieser were asked to write articles in the newly established *Annals of the American Academy of Political and Social Science* and the *Economic Journal* in order to introduce the school to English-speaking audiences, see Böhm-Bawerk (1890 and 1891) and Wieser (1891). In these articles both writers powerfully reasserted the need for theory. 'The province of the Austrian economists is *theory* in the strict sense of the work', says Böhm-Bawerk (1891, p. 361). Such theory should be built on the basis of the 'exact' or 'isolating' method, p. 363.

On the *Methodenstreit*, both Wieser (1891) and Böhm-Bawerk (1890, pp. 249, 250), as already seen, adopted a conciliatory stance, arguing for the 'equality of the two methods', although, naturally, leaning more towards the deductive method which 'is applied with rich results in almost all sciences, even in those which are pronouncedly empirical, like physics and astronomy'. On this basis, they powerfully reaffirmed that 'the value of commodities is derived wholly from their utility', Wieser (1891, p. 109), and that the principle of marginal utility is 'the cornerstone of the theory of value', Böhm-Bawerk (1891, p. 363).

Other than that, Böhm-Bawerk's main contribution is his theory of capital and interest, where he incorporates the dimension of time as the chief factor explaining the existence of interest. Because economic agents have preference for current over future consumption, and because production takes time, current production processes using capital must yield a portion of output to be paid in the form of interest to those who have invested in production processes in the past. For Schumpeter (1994, p. 846), Böhm-Bawerk's theory of capital and interest has a strong Ricardian root, because of the aggregative mode of reasoning. He also famously records Menger as having described this theory as 'one of the greatest errors ever committed', for much the same reason, p. 847n.

Wieser's work is of more interest from our point of view, for a number of reasons to be charted in what follows in this section. Wieser was a more idiosyncratic writer. His most important contribution to economic theory is his book *Social Economics* (1927 [1914]) which, however, according to Hayek (1968b, p. 49), cannot be regarded as representative of the Austrian School, 'but nonetheless constitutes a distinctly personal achievement'. This book has an interest, from the point of view of this book, not only because of its title – which points to an attempt by a marginalist at constructing social economics – but also because it is a product of its times with an interesting story behind it.

When Weber undertook to edit the *Grundriss der Sozialökonomik*, he asked Friedrich von Wieser, who was then one of the most famous economists of his age, to write one of the most important parts of the whole project, the book on economic theory – the result was *Social Economics*. That Weber should choose Wieser to write a book on economics theory is symbolic of the wide acceptance and influence of marginalism in the first decades of the twentieth century. That he chose to call his book *Social Economics* could be seen partly as a result of the influence of Weber's and Schumpeter's programme of *Sozialökonomik*, in which he was invited to participate. This book was widely appraised when it first appeared. According to Mitchell (1915, p. 225), it merits, 'in the literature of the Austrian school ... the place held by Mill's *Political Economy* in the literature of the classical school'. Equally, Schumpeter (1927, p. 300) considers it Wieser's 'last and ripest message on pure theory'.

Being himself a leading member of the Austrian tradition, Wieser's book bears all the birthmarks of its author's affiliation. However, it also tries to go beyond the strict boundaries of this tradition. Wieser considers himself a member of what he calls 'the psychological school', by which he means the theoretical tradition that 'takes its point of departure from within, from the mind of the economic man', Wieser (1967, p. 3). Unlike other marginalists, however, he considers the method of economic theory to be empirical; by this he does not mean inductivist. 'Economic theory', he says, 'need never strive to establish a law in a long series of inductions', p. 8. Neither is Wieser opposed to theorisation. What he simply means, reflecting a more positivistic and less deductivist attitude, in the spirit of Jevons as opposed to Walras and Menger, is that theory must be 'supported by observation and has but one aim, which is to describe actuality', p. 5. Simple description, however, is the work of the historian and the statistician. 'It is the historian's task to collect historical proofs and to assign their share of importance to the historical events', p. 5. The task of the economic theorist, more generally, is to present 'the typical phenomenon' by abstracting from 'all disturbing influences' and making simplifying assumptions through a process of 'isolation and idealization'. One such assumption is the creation of a 'model man', the abstract isolated individual. Starting 'from the most abstract isolating and idealizing assumptions', the theorist builds step by step a system of decreasing abstraction by rendering his assumptions 'more concrete and more multiform', p. 6.

In his *Social Economics*, Wieser follows closely, step by step, from abstract to concrete, the imperatives of his methodological principle. In Book I, he starts at the most abstract level, where the 'simple economy' is presented as consisting of a single person, p. 9. Hence the starting point and the unit of analysis is the 'model man', or abstract individual. At this level, the object of inquiry is the establishment of 'the most elementary laws of economic activity, especially those laws concerning value which provide the standard of economic comparison', p. 9. To do this, he deploys the concept of marginal utility, a term that he himself coined, and which, unlike with Menger, plays a pivotal role in his entire analysis, Mitchell (1915, p. 229). Starting at this most abstract of levels, in Books II–IV, he successively moves to lower levels of abstraction and closer to reality, by dropping step by step all the simplifying assumptions he made in Book I. Thus in Book II, the simplifying assumption of a single man economy gives way in order to examine what he calls the social economy, which, however, in typical neoclassical, reductionist fashion, he identifies with the exchange process. The object of inquiry now becomes the determination of prices. Private property and monopolies make their appearance, and exchange takes place in a context of power inequalities. In Book III, the assumption of a stateless economy is dropped, thus completing Wieser's vision of social economy through the introduction of the role of the state. 'Private households are [now] under the aegis of a central power, the state', Wieser (1967 [1927], p. 12). Last, in Book IV, he examines the theory of the world economy, where multiple states are allowed into the picture and the problems of their interrelations exposed.

For Wieser, economic theory should be firmly anchored in reality. This is why, although he appreciates the classical school as 'one of the most brilliant and practically significant efforts of the scientific mind', he was highly critical of it. For Wieser, first, the classical school was too abstract because it stopped at abstractions that were 'too remote from actuality' and, second, the classical economists failed to root their fundamental assumptions in adequate observation, p. 7. These critical points, however, apply with even greater force to his own theory, especially his 'model man', the abstract individual of orthodox economics which, by his own admission is a purely mental construct: 'thus', he says, 'the theorist assumes a model man, a man such as actually has never existed, nor can ever exist', p. 5. Wieser is also critical of the 'unreal fictions of the classical labor-theory' and its socialistic overtones, p. xx. Last, he considers the free-trade doctrine of the classical school as 'one of their disastrous errors', since they transfer the theorems derived in a national context to the international arena without taking into account the prevailing different socio-historical conditions, p. 12. These contradictions and drawbacks of the classical theory, according to Wieser, have been removed by the theory of marginal utility, p. xx.

Where Wieser departs from the marginalist paradigm, and concurs with Weber and Schumpeter, see Chapter 11, is in his admission of the role of the social and the historical element in economic theorising. 'The national economic process is a social one', he says, so that the individual, 'in his economic conduct ... is determined by social forces', pp. 152, 158. These social forces take the form of social institutions such as private property, law and morals, inequalities of power, submission and domination, and the 'feeling of fellowship' or 'social egoism', which mimics Adam Smith's principle of sympathy, pp. 149–66. As he puts it, p. 161:

> By reason of the social egoism a man is ready to fit into a social order which includes both submission and domination. The feeling of fellowship makes easier the submission of the masses to the historically maintained power or domination of the class of leaders – one submits more readily when others are seen also to submit.

The reason, however, why Wieser feels obliged to delve into these sociological issues is because 'sociology was still in the making', and therefore could not provide the required explanations, p. 152. The implication is that, once sociology is established and able to offer answers to these questions, then the economists could concentrate to the explanation of strictly economic phenomena on the basis of the rationalistic utilitarian 'model man'.

Wieser's adherence to psychological individualism and to his step-by-step, abstract to concrete, method does not mean that history is of no importance to economic theorising, pp. 4–5:

> The theorist ... will not have to dispense entirely with the consideration of the historical growth. There are numerous historical economic processes which, having filled decades and centuries, persist to this very day, while common experience discloses their interconnection. Instances of this kind are the evolution of the division of labor, the amassing of capital, the increase of the rent derived from land, additions to the store of money and the displacement of barter by the use of money. It is within the province of the theorist to deduce the law which regulates processes such as these, a law discoverable only in the general relationship of economic facts.

Hence the role of history is to supply raw material through the work of historians, which the economic theorist can then use in order to disclose the laws that regulate historical processes. There are several instances where Wieser himself makes use of the historical approach, especially in his account of the emergence of private property and other modern institutions, pp. 389–416. 'Law is of historical growth', he says, p. 398. And he adds, 'the historical growth of the private economic constitutions runs through thousands of years', p. 393.

Wieser's late admission of the role of social forces and history in his analysis is not unproblematic. On the contrary, it gives rise to some fundamental contradictions in his theory. The presence of social institutions, for example, strains and contradicts the 'model man' of his Book I. Wieser admits as much when he writes that, p. 165:

> in the presence of social institutions we must drop the rationalistic utilitarian assumption to which we might hold in the theory of the simple economy. The fundamental error of individualism appears in dealing with social institutions. It views individuals as though by nature they were entirely independent and carry through their activity entirely by their own will.

There is, in a sense, an anticipation of the bringing-back-in attached to economics imperialism, a later development in and around neoclassical economics, see Fine and Milonakis (2009). First make all the assumptions you need to establish economic rationality; then break them all, one by one, to incorporate the 'non-rational' and the social and historical.

In Wieser's hands, the Mengerian type of Austrian economics experiences two major points of emphasis. First, marginal utility is firmly asserted as the basis of the analysis of economic phenomena and, second, social institutions are no longer explained in terms of the unintended consequences of individual action. To the contrary, for Wieser, the existence of social institutions comes into direct conflict with the concept of economic man. These self-critical comments, however, were not enough for Wieser to abandon his adherence to the principle of psychological individualism, which remained one of his fundamental methodological pillars.

In short, Wieser's seems to be a more artificial and ad hoc way to construct a broader scope economics. Given its initial premises, his efforts were bound to lead to a cul-de-sac given the heavy weight of psychological individualism in his analysis and his adherence to the marginalist principle. He was neither marginalist economist pure and simple, nor social economist rounded and complex, but a bit of both.

4 Leaving marginalism behind: from Mises' praxeology ...

This brings us to the next phase in the evolution of the Austrian School in the 1930s and 1940s, which is associated with Mises and Hayek. Until the 1920s, the Austrians' journey was towards full incorporation within mainstream economics. According to Mises (2003 [1969], p. 19), 'About the time of Menger's demise (1921), one no longer distinguished between an Austrian school and other economics. The appellation "Austrian School" became the name given to an important chapter of the history of economic thought; it was no longer the name of a specific sect with doctrines different from those by other economists'. Such a state of affairs is considered by Hayek (1968b, p. 52) to be the best that any school of thought can hope for: 'A school has its greatest success when it ceases as such to exist because its leading ideals have become a part of the general dominant teaching'. If this is so, then Hayek's own trajectory is anything but a success as far as 'the general dominant thinking' in economics is concerned. Despite his many contributions, Hayek has failed by his own standards, since his views never really found their way into mainstream economics.

Hayek's major contributions are best assessed after an examination of the arguments put forward in Mises' methodological works. Mises has been described by Hayek (1992a, pp. 27, 29) as an 'isolated intransigent liberal', who combined a 'passionate interest in what we now call libertarian principles with a strong interest in those methodological and philosophical foundations of economics'. His main methodological works include *Epistemological Problems of Economics* (1981 [1933]), and his massive treatise *Human Action* (1949). The former is a compilation of methodological essays written in the 1920s, while the latter represents his major methodological work. Despite its idiosyncratic nature and the extreme form of its arguments, Mises' methodological work, especially *Human Action*, is interesting because it is the most exhaustive methodological account written after Menger's *Investigations* by a member of the Austrian School.

The academic climate in the 1920s was characterised by a reconciliatory mood as far as the *Methodenstreit* is concerned. Most writers considered it a thing of the past, and best forgotten, Lachmann (1981, p. vi). A general agreement seemed to have emerged that both theory and history are indispensable tools of any analytical endeavour, although, as seen already in Chapter 6, things were different in practice, with authors leaning heavily towards one or the other in their work, notwithstanding claims to the contrary in principle. Be that as it may, following the consolidation of the marginalist revolution, theoretical economics was becoming more and more the dominant force in Europe.[5]

At the same time, however, as seen in Chapter 12, positivism was also on the ascendancy in philosophical circles, and Vienna became the Mecca of logical positivism via what came to be known as the Vienna Circle. In such a climate, contrary to Weber and Schumpeter, Mises' objective was to keep the *Methodenstreit* alive, by defending Menger's Aristotelian position against the empiricist claims of the positivists. Judging from Hutchison's (1960) positivist reaction, whose main target, according to his own recollection, was Mises' 'dogmatic and extreme *priorism*', p. xxi, the latter's attempt, at least at a methodological level, was a success, see also Chapter 12, Section 5.

In his *Epistemological Problems,* Mises devoted his intellectual energies to exposing what he thought were the epistemological and methodological errors of the then prevailing philosophical and economic doctrines, such as 'logical positivism, historicism, institutionalism, Marxism and Fabianism or ... economic history, econometrics and statistics'.[6] In this way, Mises (1981a, pp. xiv–xv) cleared the ground 'for the systematic study of the phenomena of human action and especially also of those commonly called economic', to be provided in his *Human Action*.

He starts with a vehement attack on all those who confuse the methods of the natural and the social sciences, or the sciences of human action as he calls them. Indeed, the clear delineation of the methods used by each of these set of sciences is a prerequisite for any adequate explanation of social phenomena, p. xiii:

> The popular epistemological doctrines of our age do not admit that a fundamental difference prevails between the realm of events that the natural sciences investigate and the domain of human action that is the subject matter of economics and history. People nurture some confused ideas about a 'unified science' that would have to study the behavior of human beings according to the methods Newtonian physics resorts to in the study of mass and motion ... These doctrines misrepresent entirely every aspect of the science of human action.

And he goes on to list the differences between natural and social phenomena. Natural phenomena exhibit regularities that can be ascribed the status of a law, and which can be arrived at through laboratory experiments. On the basis of these experiments, theories can be built which can then be tested and be proved to be either correct or wrong. And he concludes in proper Aristotelian fashion: 'the natural sciences do not know anything about design and final causes', p. xiii. What Mises is describing here is the method espoused by positivism which, although suitable for the natural sciences, fails badly when it comes to the study of human action. The latter does not exhibit any 'discernible regularity', as it is governed by ideas and judgements. Human experience is very different from experimental experience, and as such cannot provide the template for the erection of a solid theoretical corpus, p. xiv:

> Experience of human action is history. Historical experience does not provide facts that could render in the construction of a theoretical science services that could be compared to those which laboratory experiments and observation render to physics.

Thus, for Mises, the differences between the natural and the human worlds mean different sources of evidence (laboratory and history, respectively) and different methodologies.

Mises calls for 'a universally valid science of human action', a science whose laws can claim validity irrespective of 'the place, time, race, nationality, or class of the actor', and whose method would totally break with positivism and the methods of natural sciences, pp. xviii, xxi–xxii. Any such laws are not empirical laws, and as such cannot be derived '*a posteriori* from historical experience', p. xxii. This is how Mises summarises his position for a 'universally valid science of human action'[7] that is based on the abstract, a priori method, pp. 12–13:

> The science of human action that strives for universally valid knowledge is the theoretical system whose hitherto best elaborated branch is economics. In all of its branches this science is a priori, not empirical. Like logic and mathematics, it is not derived from experience; it is prior to experiences. It is, as it were, the logic of action and deed.

Thus, from the prospective pretensions of economics as akin to a natural science, Mises is a peculiar creature. He rejects this out of hand, but accepts at least as strongly the merits of methodological individualism and deductive argument.

In this description of the method of social sciences other than history, Mises sides with the writers of the long deductivist tradition of classical thought, including Senior, Cairnes and Menger, as against the empiricist claims of the British and German Historical Schools, and American institutionalism, pp. xvii–xviii. Thus, in Mises' work, what Hutchison dubs 'ultra deductivism' takes its most extreme form. Further, for Mises, p. xxv:

> The Historical School in Europe and the Institutionalist school in America are the harbingers of the ruinous economic policy that has brought the world to its present condition and will undoubtedly destroy modern culture if it continuous to prevail.

Mises' opposition, then, to the latter schools lies not only in the methods used, but also in their policy recommendations, which he considers disastrous, threatening the very fabric of western culture itself.

In contrast to his totally dismissive attitude towards the historical and the intitutionalist schools, Mises' stance towards Max Weber is mixed. He praises him for clarifying 'the logical problems of historical sciences', mostly through the concept of the ideal type, pp. xviii–xix, but he also criticises him for his failure to distinguish clearly between economics and sociology (which are part of what in his *Human Action* he calls praxeology, see below), which are theoretical in nature, on the one hand, and historical investigation on the other, pp. xviii–xix: 'In Max Weber's view', he says, 'economics and sociology completely merge into history', also pp. 74–6. Contrary to Mises, Weber considers the difference between sociology and history to be one of degree rather than of a kind, p. 77, see also below.

Human Action represents an attempt to elaborate and build on all of these themes. Vaughn (1990, p. 395) has described this massive work as a:

treatise in the grand style: comprehensive, philosophical, non-mathematical, deductive, explicitly critical of Marxist and interventionist ideology and hence completely out of step with the times. Further it was contemptuous of the currently fashionable positivist methodology and held instead that empirical data (or 'history' as Mises referred to it) had to be organized according to a priori theory.

In *Human Action*, Mises treats economics as part of a wider and universal science, for which he now introduces the term *praxeology*, which he defines as 'the general theory of human action', p. 3. Since economic problems are first and foremost problems of choice, it follows that economics, in dealing with this specific form of human action, is part of praxeology. For Mises, all human action is purposeful, p. 11:

> Human action is purposeful behaviour. Or we may say: Action is will put into operation and transformed into agency, is aiming at ends and goals, is the ego's meaningful response to stimuli and to the conditions of its environment, is a person's conscious adjustment to the state of the universe that determines his life.

This is reminiscent of Weber's notion of *understanding* (*Verstehen*), see Chapter 11, in the sense that both refer to meaningful social action as the subject matter of social theory. Where the two writers differ, however, is that although Weber's *understanding* refers to individual's own meaning of his/her actions, Mises gives more emphasis to the *conceptualisation* (a sort of rational reconstruction) of the meaning of action. As Mises (1981, p. 133, 134) puts it, 'conception seeks to grasp the meaning of action through discursive reasoning. Understanding seeks the meaning of action in empathic intuition of a whole ... "Conception" of rational behaviour does not set goals for itself as ambitious as those that "understanding" pursues', see also Crespo (1997, pp. 44–5).

Mises is also a rationalist and a utilitarian. 'Science belongs completely to the domain of rationality', he declares. Contra Pareto and Weber, 'there can be no more a science of the irrational than there can be irrational science. The irrational lies outside the domain of human reasoning and science', p. 135. All human action is rational by definition, its ultimate aim being the satisfaction of desires, p. 19. After a thorough discussion of Weber's four types of human action (instrumentally rational, value-rational, traditional and affectual), see Chapter 12, Section 2, he reaches the conclusion that all these types of action are rational deep down, and that Weber's (and hence also Pareto's) distinction between rational and non-rational behaviour cannot be sustained, p. 85:

> The distinction Max Weber draws within the sphere of meaningful action when he seeks to contrast rational and nonrational action cannot

be maintained. Everything that we can regard as human action, because it goes beyond the merely reactive behaviour of the organs of the human body, is rational: it chooses between given possibilities in order to attain the most ardently desired goal.

In other words, for Mises, human (or meaningful) action becomes synonymous with rational action simply because it is mediated through the human mind (it always involves a choice in a means–ends nexus).

Granted all this, and consistent with the long Austrian tradition, Mises' work is strongly subjectivist based on an equally strong methodological individualism. In fact, Mises (1996, p. 42) has given one of the classic definitions of methodological individualism as the principle according to which 'all actions are performed by individuals', and 'a social collective has no existence and reality outside the individual members' actions'. Here the whole becomes a mere aggregation of its individual parts and has no existence outside of them.

Mises identifies two main branches of science of human action, praxeology and history. He differentiates between them in the strongest possible terms. History is totally empirical: 'History is the collection and systematic arrangement of all the data of experience concerning human action. It deals with concrete content of human action', p. 30. Praxeology, on the other hand, is an abstract, a priori science, which is totally devoid of any reference to empirical reality, on a par with logic and mathematics, p. 32. This is what differentiates it from the natural sciences and from positivism more generally. A priori problems, according to Mises, p. 34, refer 'to the essential and necessary character to the logical structure of the human mind. The fundamental logical relations are not subject to proof or disproof'.

Mises' method is perhaps the most anti-positivist and anti-empiricist approach to social science ever stated. For him, the science of human action is a purely deductive science, on a par with logic and mathematics, devoid of any empirical content. In his work, a priorism takes on its extreme form, as does utilitarian rationalism: praxeology becomes simply the science of *rational* individual action.

5 ... To Hayek's spontaneous orders

Mises, together with Hayek, and despite their many differences, offered the most formidable ultra-liberal duet of the twentieth century. Even so, as has already been hinted, their intellectual efforts have met with anything but success as far as influence within economics in their own time is concerned, despite a moderate recent revival of interest in their work. Hayek, who was a student of Wieser (as was Mises) and a close friend of Popper's, had Mises as his mentor. Politically, he was as committed a liberal as Mises, but less extreme and dogmatic in some respects when it came to his scientific endeavours. Being also extremely prolific, his thought kept on developing, at least in some respects, thus making him a moving target for any investigator. At the same time, his work spans more than half a century and almost the entire spectrum of social sciences, including economics, psychology, politics, philosophy, methodology and the history of ideas, Caldwell (2004, p. 4). For Hayek (1962, p. 267), talking in good classical manner and running contrary to the then (and even more so now) prevailing trend, 'he who is only an economist cannot be a good economist. There is hardly a single problem which can be adequately answered on the basis of a single special discipline'.

All this makes Hayek's work 'a daunting challenge for interpreters', Caldwell (2004, p. 4), and has indeed resulted in different interpretations of his intellectual trajectory. Some have stressed the elements of continuity in his work, what they consider to be the constant elements of his research programme, Birner (1994 and 1999). Others have emphasised the elements of change, either seeing his intellectual journey as a 'continuous transformation', Lawson (1994), or simply a transformation away from the study of narrow economic problems to more philosophical ones, Caldwell (1988), or as involving a complete U-turn, '*a fundamental shift*' away from Mises' extreme a priori method and the equilibrium concept, towards a more Popperian type of methodology and a subjective conception of knowledge, Hutchison (1981, p. 215), see also Caldwell (2004, pp. 409–22). For the second group of writers, the turning point in the evolution of Hayek's thought was what is perhaps his most famous article, 'Economics and Knoweledge', published in 1937. Indeed, this article contains most of the elements that dominated Hayek's thought since then, such as methodological individualism, subjectivism and his subjectivist conception of knowledge, in short most of the elements that we have come to associate with the Austrian School of thought. In what follows, we concentrate on Hayek's methodological writings in his post-1937 era, with one exception, his methodological comments in his *Monetary Theory and the Trade Cycle*, first published in 1933, to which we come back after an examination of his most important methodological work.

Hayek (1942–4), in his 'Scientism and the Study of Society', much like Mises, makes a clear distinction between the methods of the natural and social sciences. He sharply criticises what he calls the 'scientistic method' or scientism, by which he means the attempt to apply the methods of the natural sciences to social sciences. He identifies objectivism and collectivism as the two basic characteristics of scientism. Together with historism, they form the basic targets of Hayek's attack in his methodological essay. In this, he defines the object and method of social sciences as dealing not with 'the relations between things', p. 27:

> but with the relations between men and things or the relations between men and men. They are concerned with man's actions and their aim is to explain the unintended or undesigned results of the actions of many men.

Hayek's emphasis on 'man's conscious or reflected action', pp. 27–8, brings him close to Mises' praxeological description of the social sciences. At the same time, his treatment of social phenomena as the unintended result of human action – what he later called 'spontaneous order', see below – has strong Mengerian connotations and is very close to the latter's organic interpretation of social institutions, Section 2 above. Hayek's emphasis is on conscious human action and human perception – 'what men think and mean to do', p. 35 – but *not* on the explanation of human activity that is the subject of psychology, p. 40. For the social sciences, the types of conscious action, what Hayek variously calls opinions or beliefs or ideas or concepts, are taken simply as data or facts, pp. 28, 30, 36, 40: 'So far as human actions are concerned the things *are* what people acting think they are', p. 28, and 'the facts of social sciences are merely the opinions, views held by the people whose action we study', p. 30. It is this distinctly subjectivist character of the social sciences, as opposed to the objective nature of the natural sciences, that forms the differentia specifica of the former, pp. 29–30. So, unlike Mises, Hayek does not identify the a priori and abstract character of the social sciences as its basic feature that sets it apart from natural sciences. His emphasis on subjectivism is one of the most important attributes of Hayek's work, see opening quote.

The objectivism of the scientistic approach, according to Hayek, is closely related to methodological collectivism, p. 44. The latter has the tendency to treat 'wholes' such as 'society' or the 'economy' 'as definitely given objects about which we can discover laws by observing their behaviour as wholes', p. 44, what Hayek calls 'naïve realism', p. 45. He distinguishes between 'those ideas which are constitutive of the phenomena we want to explain and the ideas ... formed about these phenomena and which are not the cause of, but theories about, social structures', p. 36. For Hayek, collective entities such as 'society', the 'economic system' or 'capitalism' are no more than 'provisional theories and popular abstractions', and as such cannot be treated as facts, as is mistakenly thought by the 'scientistic method', pp. 37–8.

Last is Hayek's critique of 'historicism'. The two basic attributes of the latter are, first, that it tries to make theoretical generalisations out of historical research and the empirical study of society, and, second, that it lays emphasis on the 'unique character of all historical phenomena' (historical specificity), pp. 53–4. For Hayek, much like Mises, the validity of theory is universal and not historically specific, p. 64. He also considers theory as prior to historical knowledge, p. 60: 'the place of theory in historical knowledge is thus in forming or constituting the wholes to which history refers; it is prior to these wholes which are not visible except by following up the system of relations which connects the parts'. This, according to Hayek, makes theory and history logically distinct but complementary activities, but it does not make history theoretical or theory historical, pp. 61–2. Indeed, Hayek refers to the attempts to build a theoretical or philosophical history associated with the laws of historical development and the succession of stages as 'the darling vice' of the nineteenth century, associated with Hegel, Comte, Marx (particularly), Sombart and Spengler, pp. 62–3.[8]

Going back to Mises, the extreme form of his a priorism has given rise to considerable controversy. One of the chief critiques was delivered by Hayek himself. He accuses Mises of overreaction to the scientific positivism of his time, by moving to an extreme a priori position, Hayek (1968b, pp. 55–6):

> While it was true that the pure logic of choice by which the Austrian theory interpreted individual action was indeed purely deductive, as soon as the explanation moved to interpersonal activities of the market, the crucial processes were those by which information was transmitted among individuals, and as such were purely empirical.

And Hayek goes on to add that 'Mises never explicitly rejected this criticism but no longer was prepared to reconstruct his by then fully developed system'. Going back to his earlier study, *Monetary Theory*, Hayek (1966 [1933], ch. 1) argues that empirical work cannot provide insights into causal relationships and, as such, it cannot be used as the starting point of any theoretical investigation, p. 27. Much like Mises, his emphasis is on theory as against empiricism. Theory he says, referring particularly to trade cycle theory, 'must be deduced with unexceptionable logic from the notions of the theoretical system', and 'it must explain by a purely deductive method', p. 32. Statistical examination, however, can be used to supplement theory in order to make possible forecasts for the future, which is the ultimate aim of any theory, pp. 35–6. Although he considers statistical work of limited value as a means of verifying theories, p. 32, he admits the possibility that empirical studies can be used for the falsification of existing theories: 'such a theory', he says, 'could only be false either through an inadequacy in its logic or because the phenomena which it explains do not correspond with observed facts', p. 33. This is followed in the next page by the following statement:

> It is therefore only in the negative sense that it is possible to verify theories by statistics. Either statistics can demonstrate that there are phenomena which the theory does not sufficiently explain, or it is unable to discover such phenomena. It cannot be expected to confirm the theory in a positive sense.

In the last two statements, it seems that Hayek comes close to Popper's falsificationism, albeit in a very undeveloped and rudimentary form.[9] If this reading is correct, what makes these statements remarkable is that they were first made in 1929, the date of issue of the German edition of Hayek's book, five years before the first appearance of Popper's *The Logic of Scientific Discovery*, in German in 1934, which is considered the first official, complete, book-length statement of falsificationism.

Contrary to both Mises' overall methodological position, and Hayek's view expressed in his 'Scientism' essay, according to which natural and social sciences should be distinguished in the clearest possible manner, Popper

(1986, p. 130) proposed the 'doctrine of the unity of method' for both types of sciences.[10] This means that 'all theoretical and generalizing sciences make use of the same method, whether they are natural sciences or social sciences'. This, for Popper, much like the positivists, is supplied by the hypothetico-deductive method, which contributes 'in offering deductive causal explanations, and in testing them', as opposed to pure deduction or pure induction. Where Popper's position differs from the positivists is in his principle of falsification, according to which the aim of empirical testing of theories should be their falsification rather than their verification, as with positivism, which in any case is impossible since no number of confirmations can lead to verification. The hypothetico-deductive method, then, becomes the common method of both natural and social sciences, and falsifiability the demarcation line between scientific and non-scienific theories, in both types of sciences.

Although remaining a self-proclaimed anti-positivist, Hayek's adoption of Popperianism became explicit in his later methodological writings, Hayek (1955 and 1964) and Hutchison (1981, ch. 7). In them, Hayek (1955, pp. 4–5) accepts both the hypothetico-deductive system as the common method of both natural and social science, and the falsifiability principle as the main demarcation line between science and non-science. There is, however, one important hurdle on the way. This has to do with the complexity of some social phenomena, which makes falsifiability difficult to obtain, Hayek (1964, p. 29), and see also Hayek (1955, pp. 3–5):

> While it is certainly desirable to make our theories as falsifiable as possible, we must also push forward into fields where, as we advance, the degree of falsifiability necessarily decreases. This is the price we have to pay for an advance into the field of complex phenomena.

Indeed, it has been argued that the simple versus complex phenomena dichotomy, which is common to all forms of science and in accordance with the Popperian 'unity of method' doctrine, gradually replaced the natural versus social science division in Hayek's thought, as the new demarcation line between sciences, Hutchison (1981, p. 217) and Caldwell (2004, p. 311).

Closely related to his subjectivism, much like Mises and the other Austrians, is Hayek's commitment to methodological individualism. His 'basic contention' in his essay 'Individualism: True and False', is that 'there is no other way toward an understanding of social phenomena but through our understanding of individual actions directed toward other people and guided by their expected behaviour', Hayek (1945a, p. 6). His individualism, however, departs from Mises' in important ways. He accuses the latter of making undue concessions to rationalist utilitarianism, Hayek (1968b, p. 55).[11] In his 'Individualism', Hayek discerns two different strands of individualism: true and false individualism. He identifies false individualism with 'Cartesian rationalism' or 'rationalist individualism' of Rousseau and the physiocrats, and, one should add, Mises, although Hayek does not refer to him explicitly.

By true individualism, he refers to the (anti-rationalist) individualism of Locke, Mandeville, Hume, Tucker, Ferguson and Adam Smith, p. 4. The basic characteristics of Hayek's true individualism are, first, that it starts 'from men whose nature and character is determined by their existence in society', p. 6. Statements such as this have led at least one commentator to describe Hayek's individualism, following Agassi (1975), as 'institutional individualism', Caldwell (2004, p. 286). Second is its 'antirationalist approach, which regards man not as a highly rational and intelligent but as a very irrational and fallible being, whose individual errors are corrected only in the course of a social process, and which aims at making the best of a very imperfect material', Hayek (1945a, pp. 8–9). This echoes Menger's 'bumbling, erring, ill-informed creature', 'plagued with uncertainty', according to Jaffé's (1976, p. 521) lucid description, see above, and has led at least one commentator to describe Hayek's individualism as 'subjectivist individualism', where agents with imperfect and subjectively held knowledge act under conditions of uncertainty and ignorance, Zouboulakis (2002, p. 30).[12] Both of these characteristics/descriptions run contrary to the 'psychological individualism' adopted by the neoclassical school, which postulates 'the existence of isolated or self-contained individuals', Hayek (1945a, p. 6), and which treats the individual as a perfectly informed creature in a world of certainty.

Related to this anti-rationalist element is the treatment of institutions as the (unintended) results of human action rather than as the result of human (rational) design, Hayek (1945a, p. 8 and 1967b). Much like his distinction between 'true' and 'false' individualism, this is contrasted in the strongest possible terms with Cartesian rationalistic explanations of social phenomena – what he also calls 'naïve rationalism' or 'rationalistic constructivism' – which 'traces all discoverable order to deliberate design', and according to which, 'all the useful human institutions were and ought to be creation of conscious reason', Hayek (1945a, p. 8 and 1965, p. 85).[13] In treating institutions as arising spontaneously as a result of the actions of individuals, Hayek again follows a long string of writers, from the British moral philosophers of the eighteenth century to Carl Menger.[14] It is as a reaction against Cartesian rationalism that these thinkers 'built up a theory which made the undesigned results of individual action its central object, and in particular provided a comprehensive theory of the spontaneous order of the market', Hayek (1965, p. 99). If Bernard Mandeville was 'the author to whom more than any other this "anti-rationalist" reaction is due', Adam Smith's invisible hand explanation of the functioning of the market system was a 'profound insight into the object of all social theory'. An insight, however, that had to wait a whole century before it was resuscitated by Carl Menger from the 'uncomprehending ridicule' that was poured on it, and be given the form in which it was handed down to later generations.

Hayek's distinction between spontaneous orders and designed institutions follows closely Menger's division between 'organic' and 'pragmatic' explanations of social institutions. Much like Menger's explanation of the emergence of money and other institutions, Hayek opts for the organic explanation of social phenomena, Hayek (1945a, pp. 6–7). Thus, 'by tracing the combined effects of individual actions, we discover that many of the institutions on which human achievements rest have arisen and are functioning without a designing and directing mind'. Indeed, if all social phenomena were consciously designed, 'there would be no room for the sciences of society', p. 40. The spontaneous order explanation of the emergence and functioning of institutions – which for Hayek is one and the same thing – is tantamount to an evolutionary explanation. Hayek (1967a, p. 77) calls them 'the twin ideas of evolution and spontaneous order'.[15]

Hayek (1967a, p. 66) makes a further distinction between 'the systems of the rules of conduct which govern the behaviour of the individual members of the group, on the one hand, and the order or pattern of actions which results from this for the group as a whole', on the other. Spontaneous order, then, which refers to the 'social pattern' or 'the structure of actions of all members of a group', emerges as the unintended result of the individual actions of the members of the group, which act in the context of certain pre-given rules, either genetically (innate) or culturally transmitted (learnt). One such spontaneous order is the market process itself, which Hayek (1976, pp. 108–9) also calls catallaxy: 'the order brought about by the mutual adjustment of many individual economies in the market'. 'A catallaxy', he says, 'is thus the kind of spontaneous order produced by the market through people acting within the rules of the law of property, tort and contract', Hayek (1976, p. 109), quoted in Fleetwood (1995, pp. 148, 149, also pp. 147–55).

Turning to Hayek's more substantive contributions, some of the most important were formed both during and after the so-called socialist calculation debate, and mostly as a consequence of it, especially in response to Lange's market socialist proposal, see Lange (1938).[16] Lange's article is a response to Mises (1935 [1920]), who argued that under socialism there is a calculation problem, because of the absence of private property and a market for capital goods to determine the prices of these goods. Lange responded by constructing a model of a market socialist economy along Walrasian general equilibrium lines, and showing that this could work as efficiently as capitalism, if not more so. This could be done through the substitution of public ownership of the means of production for private ownership, and by the elimination of capital markets, but allowing for real markets to operate for consumer goods and labour. In this model, the function of the determination of prices of capital goods is undertaken by the Central Planning Bureau, playing the role of the Walrasian auctioneer, and thus solving the calculation problem.

As Lange's proposal proceeded with impeccable logic from the theoretical premises of neoclassical economics, Hayek's response focused on questioning its basic building blocks: stationary equilibrium, competition as price-taking behaviour and the assumption of perfect knowledge. In three important articles written between 1937 and 1948, he puts forward some of the ideas that were to become the cornerstone of subsequent Austrian theorising, Hayek (1937, 1945b, 1948a). In these articles, Hayek revisits Mengerian themes long forgotten, although as Hayek (1968b, p. 55) says, at that time he was not aware of this precedent.

So what did Hayek's alternative involve? First is the concept of tacit knowledge which has a strong subjectivist element: 'the knowledge of the circumstances of which we must make use never exists in a concentrated or integrated form but solely as the dispersed bits of incomplete and frequently contradictory knowledge which all the separate individuals possess', Hayek (1945a, p. 77). This knowledge can only be acquired through a competitive process that, rather than reflecting passive price-taking and quantity-adjusting behaviour, is defined as a rivalrous process through which knowledge is dispersed to all market participants. Here competition is portrayed as a 'discovery procedure', the vehicle through which knowledge is dispersed to all market participants, Hayek (1968a). Related to this is Hayek's critique of the neoclassical concept of equilibrium. In his conception of the market system, the basic role of the price mechanism is no longer the equilibriating function, but the communication/coordination of knowledge function (Hayek, 1945b, p. 86). In Austrian theory, the concept of equilibrium is replaced by the concept of market process, which captures the uncertainty, time and change aspects of real market functioning that are left completely untouched in the Walrasian framework, Mises (1996, p. 354) and O'Driscoll and Rizzo (1985, p. 85).

This treatment by Hayek of the market system as a process in time gives it a potentially dynamic character and is one of the distinctive characteristics of the neo-Austrian economic analysis, if not its 'ultimate goal'. Such a dynamic analysis, according to Hayek (1941, p. 17):

> When it is used in contrast to equilibrium analysis in general, it refers to an explanation of the economic process as it proceeds in time, an explanation in terms of causation which must necessarily be treated as a chain of historical sequences ... This kind of causal explanation of the process in time is of course the ultimate goal of all economic analysis, and equilibrium analysis is significant only in so far as it is preparatory to its main task.

Thus, what is distinctive about Hayek's contribution is its strong subjectivist element coupled with a heavy emphasis on anti-rational methodological individualism, his subjectivist conception of knowledge that is discovered and diffused in the market process through rivalrous competition, and the organic explanation of the emergence of social institutions as spontaneous orders.

With Hayek, Austrianism had turned full circle, restoring Menger in large measure. It did so by rescuing him from appropriation by neoclassical economics as one of its founders by virtue of his marginalism alone. Instead, via methodological debate (and remarkably), it managed to reject neoclassical economics both for its limited subjectivism and for its correspondingly limited grasp of the consequences for economic and social change. But it retained an unshakable commitment to its own versions of both methodological individualism and the virtues of the spontaneous order associated with laissez-faire.

6 Concluding remarks

The way in which the ideas of the Austrian School have evolved, and its shifting relation to mainstream economics are most instructive. Starting with Menger, what survived of his writings for the next 50 years after their initial appearance, was what was palatable and could be assimilated within the neoclassical framework: deductivisn, methodological individualism, subjectivism and the concept of marginal utility. It is these aspects of his work that were taken up by his disciples Böhm-Bawerk and Wieser, who were responsible both for the formation of the Austrian School of thought, but also for its dissolution within neoclassical economics. These aspects are also found in most standard history of economic thought textbooks, as is so for the work of Böhm-Bawerk and Wieser. All this was done at the expense of all those other aspects of Menger's thought, such as the evolution of social institutions, the role of knowledge, human perception, uncertainty, etc., which were largely forgotten and only to resurface in Hayek's writings half a century later, however unconsciously by the latter's own confession. In truth, these aspects of Menger's thought were only fully rediscovered by scholarship since the 1970s. In the writings of Mises and Hayek, Austrianism moves away from marginalism towards a more subjectivist and a priori type of theorising (more so for Mises than for Hayek). The price to pay for this departure from marginalism was marginalisation.

Both Mises and Hayek wrote at a time when (logical) positivism was in the ascendancy, Keynesian macroeconomics was winning more and more supporters, and mainstream economics was rediscovering Walrasian general equilibrium, see Chapters 11 and 14, a very unfavourable environment for the two champions of free market ideology and extreme conservative politics. Accordingly, Mises 'became the archetypal "unscientific" economist, and, given that his political views were, in the Age of Keynes, even more unpopular, the adjective *reactionary* was also often appended', Caldwell (2004, pp. 125–6). Hayek was to suffer a similar experience. He took part in two central debates – one with Keynes on trade cycles,[17] and the other on the feasibility of socialism with Oskar Lange – and, at the time, he was considered to have lost both, Vaughn (1990, p. 389). Both Mises and Hayek were cast aside by the rising new orthodoxy of Keynesianism and Walrasian general equilibrium, only to be rediscovered in the 1970s following the demise of Keynesianism and the emergence of a more favourable political and ideological environment – and, to the extent of these only, a more favourable intellectual environment. Even then (and now) the doctrines of the new bastions of Austrian economics were to remain on the fringes of mainstream economic theory.

14 From Keynes to general equilibrium

Short- and long-run revolutions in economic theory

'The composition of this book has been for the author a long struggle of escape, and so must the reading of it be for most readers if the author's assault upon them is to be successful, – a struggle of escape from habitual modes of thought and expression ... The difficulty lies, not in the new ideas, but in escaping from the old ones, which ramify, for those brought up as most of us have been, into every corner of our minds'.

Keynes (1973 [1936], p. xxiii)

'We can only speculate on what Keynes would have made of the Keynesian policies carried out in his name. What we can see more clearly, with the benefit of hindsight and experience, is that at the theoretical level Keynesian economics created a schizophrenia in the way that economics was taught, with micro-economics, typically concentrating on issues relating to allocation, production and distribution (questions of efficiency and equity) and courses in macro-economics focusing on problems associated with the level and the long-term trend of aggregate output and employment, and the rate of inflation (questions of growth and stability). The Keynesian propositions of market failure and involuntary employment expounded within macroeconomics did not rest easily alongside the Walrasian theory of general competitive equilibrium ... Although Paul Samuelson and others attempted to reconcile these two strands of economics ... [they] integrated about as well as oil and water'.

Snowdon and Vane (2005, p. 21)[1]

1 Introduction

During the 1930s, Robbins' work – and especially his famous definition of economics as the allocation of scarce resources between competing ends – seemed to be rounding off the process that started with the marginalist revolution. As charted in Chapter 12, however, this highlighted a number of conundrums, the resolution of which were to create an internal division within economics between microeconomics and macroeconomics (and between orthodoxy and heterodoxy). Microeconomics incorporated the spirit of marginalism, but the working of the economic system as a whole, or macroeconomics, and the influence of non-economic factors was perceived to fall outside of its purview, so narrow was it in method and content. Nonetheless, through the prism of Keynesianism, the analytical content of such macro-economics was itself considerably reduced by focusing on the level of effective demand and its determinants. As discussed in Section 2, the division of economic theory into micro and macro may have provided a fix for the inadequacies of marginalism, but it did so only at the expense of the scope of other economic factors and an uncomfortable inconsistency between the two branches of the discipline, however deeply and frequently acknowledged as such.

How, rather than whether, Keynes would himself have made that reduction has been controversial since his death in 1946 across the macroeconomics that he inspired and the various interpretations of him and Keynesianism.[2] In Section 3, however, we adopt a different perspective to highlight the extent to which Keynes' pioneering contributions to macroeconomic theory were based on a methodology that was to be entirely discarded by the orthodoxy that he inspired, and by economic theory more generally. This concerns the role of mathematics, methodological individualism, equilibrium, econometrics and the understanding of uncertainty. Keynes held views on these that directly contradict neoclassical orthodoxy. The inescapable conclusion would appear to be that the discipline was on a methodological and technical rollercoaster that smashed through any alternatives, however legitimate by virtue of their analytical content or personal prestige. For the latter, none could be greater than that of Keynes in the immediate post-war period. And yet, even in his own name, economics took a direction that was entirely at odds with his own methodological inclinations. As Dow (2008) has suggested, there might have been a Keynesian revolution in establishing macroeconomics, but there was no methodological revolution to reflect Keynes' own positions in this respect. Indeed, Dow might even be considered to be wrong in denying a methodological revolution with the post-war development of Keynesianism, if looking at the issue in terms of the degree of departure from Keynes and his contemporaries as mainstream orthodoxy increasingly established itself.

If Keynes could not halt the forward march of neoclassical economics – and the evidence is that he saw it as benign relative to macro principles – then who could? General equilibrium as the culmination of microeconomics and IS/LM as the standard interpretation for macroeconomics have delivered a resounding answer, and one that has only got louder with the subsequent passage of time: NOBODY going by the name 'economist'. Only after the Second World War did general equilibrium theory gain general acceptance, as the microeconomics to complement macroeconomics, but with the two branches of the discipline continuing to lie uneasily side by side. As demonstrated in Section 4, it was impossible to found macroeconomics on sound microeconomic principles, as was explicitly recognised by the leading economist of the time, Paul Samuelson. But the way in which Keynesian macroeconomics was formulated was heavily influenced by his location in the United States and the intellectual and political climate that this created for the acceptability of his approach, as opposed to others of a more progressive and/or intellectually challenging character.

With the collapse of the post-war boom and Keynesianism, and the rise of monetarism, the designs of the marginalist revolution were completed, but at an enormous cost in terms of the genuine reservations and hopes expressed at its birth. For commitment to realism, an inductive content, rounded and heterogeneous as opposed to mono-motive representative individuals, and the importance of non-economic factors and modes of expression, have all been sacrificed in deference to an axiomatic formalism that, arguably, fails even on its own terms. It could not provide for the existence of a unique and stable equilibrium in the presence of money, let alone for unemployment, growth, cycles and structural change. In short, with its theory stripped down to its conceptual bones of *homo economicus*, mainstream economics had achieved its goal of becoming a science by its own (equally stripped-down) criteria. The historical, social and methodological, as well as much else besides, were the costs to be paid, those that had previously been presumed not to be worth affording by those who first tentatively promoted marginalism as a core element of economics as a separate discipline standing on its own two feet. In this light, the concluding remarks point to the extent to which the discipline is now driven first and foremost by its own technical apparatus, irrespective of other criteria that it itself, let alone others, might consider desirable.

2 No micro without macro: the rise of Keynesianism

The treatments of (consumer) demand, production, and time (and uncertainty) in the wake of the marginalist revolution are all representative of the reductionism that was incorporated into economics as a way both of establishing it as a separate discipline and of setting aside broader considerations rather than resolving their interaction with the newly defined and narrow economic. The oppositions and tensions within the literature of the time are worthy of a full account, as, according to Hutchison (2000, p. 266) from 1876, 'for the next three to four decades ... the details of microeconomic marginal analysis absorbed the main attention of leading neoclassical economists, especially in Britain'. Indeed, the length of time involved could be doubled with the specific terminological distinction between microeconomics and macroeconomics only first coined by Ragnar Frisch in the early 1930s, as reported in Schumpeter's *History of Economic Analysis*, see Hutchison (2000, p. 272).

This left macroeconomics in a peculiar relationship with microeconomics, with the latter scarcely able to pretend it could address the major issues of the time, from the UK return to gold in the 1920s to the unemployment of the 1930s. It was not simply that marginalism was patently inadequate as a theory of the individual – let alone of the influence of non-economic factors upon the economy – it was equally at a loss when it came to major issues within economics itself, such as the unavoidable presence and influence of money and the need for explanation of the persistence of business cycles. In this case, the tensions between micro and macro were necessarily resolved in an entirely different way than reductionism (other than to explain unemployment as due to too high a real wage, with money as neutral in all respects). A separate macroeconomics was developed alongside the evolving microeconomics, which concerned vital policy issues such as the level of government expenditure in response to recession, and, for 'the position taken by the original "macro thinkers" … their aggregative functions were not usually based on putative microeconomic assumptions, but plausible conjecture or hypotheses as the behavior of the system as a whole', Smithin (2004, p. 57).

Interestingly in this context, in his autobiography, in the wake of the rise of Keynesianism, Robbins (1971, p. 154) recants on his opposition to Keynes in a policy committee in the 1930s, confessing to 'the greatest mistake of my professional career'. His opposition concerned 'the desirability of increased public expenditure during the slump', p. 152. To himself, it seems impossible in retrospect that he could have adopted such a position, for he asks 'How had I got myself into this state of mind', to which the answer is that 'the trouble was intellectual. I had become the slave of theoretical constructions which, if not intrinsically invalid as regards logical consistency, were inappropriate to the total situation which had then developed and which therefore misled my judgement', p. 153. Indeed, 'The theory was inadequate to the facts'. The inappropriate theory was simply one of adjustment from overinvestment in fixed capital, needful of correction but totally oblivious to the 'freezing deflation of those days', p. 154. Significantly, this subsequent correction of his blinded aberration of mind follows immediately upon the proud account of *An Essay on the Nature and Significance of Economic Science*, for which no apology is offered. This is so even though the connection between it and the theoretical commitment to balanced adjustment in supply (and demand) are more or less immediate.

No wonder, then, that the economics profession felt the need for a macroeconomics that was distinct from the microeconomics then flowing from the marginalist revolution, even if the microeconomics could become a badge of professionalisation and object of analysis in its own right. In respect of macroeconomics, uncontroversially, the commanding figure was J. M. Keynes and *The General Theory*. But it is worth emphasising in the first instance the extent to which macroeconomics and Keynesianism as it became after the Second World War was somewhat different in the inter-war period. For Keynes himself is well known to have been deeply attached to the Marshallian, or the *old* marginalist tradition, Leijonhufvud (2006). Much like Marshall, and unlike Walras, he was not trying to build a comprehensive theory, but rather one that is purpose-built (an 'economic organon') to solve particular problems, a characteristic of what Hoover (2006, pp. 80–2) calls a 'diagnostic science'.[3] He was a realist who was not afraid of deploying pure theory for appropriate purposes. He even accused Marshall of being otherwise, Keynes (1938a, p. 300): 'Marshall often confused his models, for devising which he had great genius, by wanting to be realistic and by being unnecessarily ashamed of lean and abstract outlines', see also Fontana (2006, p. 170). Much like Marshall, though, he remained sceptical of mathematical models. 'The object of our analysis', he says, Keynes (1973, p. 297):[4]

> is, not to provide a machine, or a method of blind manipulation, which will furnish an infallible answer, but to provide ourselves with an organised and orderly method of thinking out particular problems ... It is a great fault of symbolic pseudo-mathematical methods of formalising a system of economic analysis ... that they expressly assume strict independence between the factors involved and lose all their cogency and authority if this hypothesis is disallowed.

Mathematics and equilibrium were of limited applicability, not least because of death in the long run, see next section. At the same time, his theory of expectations concerned systemic uncertainty as opposed to calculable risk. Indeed, in responding to critics shortly after the publication of the *General Theory*, Keynes considered the introduction of radical uncertainty as the most important theoretical innovation separating his theoretical system from classical theory, cited in Backhouse (2006b, p. 25): 'I accuse the classical theory of being itself one of those pretty, polite techniques which tries to deal with the present by abstracting from the fact that we know very little about the future'. Lastly, for Keynes, macroeconomic relations, such as the consumption function and the multiplier, were not grounded in the optimising behaviour of individuals.

Not surprisingly, Keynes proves a rich vein of quotes for the impoverished thinking of the economist. But, as is apparent in microcosm from his dispute with Robbins over unemployment and government expenditure as a remedy, he could have been in little doubt over the task that faced him in persuading his fellow economists – and policymakers – of how to divorce micro from macroeconomics. To a large extent, it is academic whether Keynes himself believed in the burgeoning influence of the new microeconomics. As far as he was concerned, it was classical in its attachment to Say's Law of markets and the impossibility of a general glut of commodities and unemployment other than due to too high real wages. And if the classical theory was applicable in the special conditions of full employment, it was certainly totally inapplicable in the conditions of involuntary unemployment of the 1930s, Keynes (1973, p. 16, see also p. 3):

> The classical theorists resemble Euclidean geometers in a non-Euclidean world who, discovering that in experience straight lines apparently parallel often meet, rebuke the lines for not keeping straight – as the only remedy for the unfortunate collisions which are occurring.

According to Deane (1978, pp. 182–3), 'there are three respects in which the *General Theory* broke away from the classical mould and generated a new economics' to the extent that it did. 'The first was in the questions it asked, the second was in the conclusions and the third was in the route to these conclusions'. The central question was 'what were the determinants of the supply and demand for aggregate output', which emphasised deficiency in aggregate, macroeconomic, effective demand as the key factor. 'The iconoclastic conclusion of his analysis was that there was no invisible hand translating private self-interest into social benefit'. And 'the method was to set up an aggregative model of the economy as a whole'. As Keynes (1973, p. xxxii) puts it:

> I have called my theory a *general* theory. I mean by this that I am chiefly concerned with the behaviour of the economic system as a whole ... And I argue that important mistakes have been made through extending to the system as a whole conclusions which have been correctly arrived at in respect of a part of it taken in isolation.

This latter characteristic gave Keynes' approach a holistic and organicist outlook, both at odds with the individualistic overtones of neoclassical economics and more in line with some writers in the classical (in our sense of the word) tradition, and with the Historical Schools and American institutionalism.

In retrospect, the most obvious consequence of the Keynesian revolution was to create, or consolidate, a division within economics between micro and macro, with the former taking its lead from formalist marginalism and the latter from Keynes. This all became standardised in teaching and research at every level, especially with the corresponding formalisation of Keynesianism through Hicks' IS/LM model, and the Keynesian cross, popularised in the United States by Paul Samuelson, see below. Whilst there are alternative interpretations of Keynes, such as the reappraisal (quantity-constrained, fixed price, rationing or micro-foundations approach) at one extreme, and post-Keynesianism at the other, these only achieved limited and/or later prominence.

For our purposes, though, there are two more striking consequences of the Keynesian revolution, which have profound effects on how economics developed as a discipline out of the original division between micro and macro in the 1930s. First, the emergence of macroeconomics provided an extraordinarily powerful fix for the glaring deficiencies of microeconomics' capacity to address the major issues of the day – the business cycle, the financial system and massive levels of unemployment. All this is quite apart from the changing institutional and international environment of both rivalries between great powers and the rise of extensive state economic intervention across industry, health, education and welfare. Without macroeconomics, the evolving microeconomics could only have appeared even more unrealistic, not least in Robbins' definition and concerns for the discipline. With macroeconomics to answer the big questions of the day, microeconomics could claim legitimacy for its evolving formalisation of that, as yet unspecified, scope of application – but at least to include partial equilibrium, confined to supply and demand, where purely economic motives prevail.

Second, though, this division of labour between microeconomics and macroeconomics involved a considerable devaluation of macroeconomics itself in deference to some degree of attachment to microeconomics. With emphasis on effective demand (and the corresponding importance of money markets that is otherwise absent from microeconomics), there is an equally effective exclusion of other considerations, whether directly economic or not. Anything to do with major causal factors simply no longer figures. To list a few, these are the distribution between capital and labour, the structure or restructuring of industry (with the paramount importance of shift from old to new industries in the inter-war period and the rise of the modern corporation), with the sources and consequences of technical change, the dynamics of economic and social change, the role of the state and other institutions such as trade unions and modern finance, other than as manipulator of macroeconomic aggregates or the overall price level. In the post-war period, such matters tended to be put aside or increasingly downgraded – and even dropped altogether – as belonging to the descriptive or applied branch of the discipline as a whole (what those did who could not do theory or econometrics).

In short, the rise of Keynesianism was one way of resolving the tensions within Marshall between micro and macro, as well as other tensions concerning the formalism and lack of realism and historicism of the marginalist project. It allowed the latter to flourish, and, not surprisingly, it did so on both sides of the Atlantic. In the UK, it became extraordinarily well represented by Hicks, who provided both for micro-foundations prior to the Second World War and for IS/LM Keynesianism in its aftermath. In the US, though, such developments were comparable but far less pure – no doubt reflecting the absence of Keynes, the lesser Marshallian tradition, the influx of more rounded, European intellectuals, the greater commitment to economic history as an element of economics and the greater weight of an institutionalist tradition. The latter is important, for, as Yonay (1998, pp. 75–6) implicitly suggests, the tensions within Marshall were not resolved by Keynes(ianism) in the inter-war period, as institutionalism, especially in the United States, even strengthened, see Chapters 9 and 10.

One reason why old marginalism needed to be more wide-ranging than its core principles was in order to address the economic and social issues of the day. Pearson (2004) suggests that the old marginalism of Marshall placed an emphasis on altruism and other human motives because they were socially engaged, making 'heroic commitments to political movements, governmental institutions, professional organizations, social reform associations and the personal lives of their students', p. 39. It was even hoped that the evolution of the human spirit away from self-interest would undermine the need and rationale for state intervention. By contrast, the marginalists' core principles themselves could claim to be above such policy and normative considerations, and to display universal truths. Interestingly, whilst the corresponding claim to analytical neutrality within economic theory based itself on the universal truths of its abstract propositions, exactly the same sort of normative and political neutrality was being sought within the emerging discipline of economic history, by focusing on the discovery and ordered presentation of the facts with limited theoretical content, to be addressed in a contribution in preparation on economic history. Both economics and economic history sought to distance themselves from possible charges of bias and from the traditions of keen attachment to the controversies of the day and also, to a large extent, popular consciousness and engagement. With marginalism, though, there was a difference, in that its proponents tended to support laissez-faire, although, given the theory of market imperfections, this was not a logical requirement.

In this respect, the breach between old marginalism and its progeny as neoclassical economics is further highlighted. The inter-war period marked not only the rise of Keynesianism to deal with 'macro' policy, but also the issues associated with great power rivalries and the increasing economic role of the state in protecting and restructuring industries and promoting education, health and welfare. Only following the collapse of the post-war boom, the formulation of general equilibrium theory, the decline of Keynesianism and rise of monetarism, could the marginalist principles as such occupy the high ground as far as policy is concerned. With a wonderful irony and historical reversal, its professed neutrality and universal propositions sought to take command of policy by positing the superiority of the market (supply-side economics) and a minimalist role for the state. The latter's powers were, in any case, liable to be limited – if not undermined – by the constraints imposed by pursuit of self-interest through the market.

3 Keynes and the philosophical foundations of economics

Many of the observations of the previous section are illustrated, reinforced and enriched by considering the development of Keynes' thought in the 1930s. But our focus in this respect is not so much on the evolution of his economic ideas as on the corresponding evolution of the methodology underpinning them. For, first and foremost, Keynes sustained an abiding interest in philosophy at this time, and his outlook went through considerable change as he strove to base his economics on broader foundations. And he was also in a position to benefit from the circle of Cambridge philosophers with whom he had frequent contact and discussion. What we find is that, as he was drafting the *General Theory*, Keynes was experiencing an evolution in his own methodological understanding. It would take him further away from that of Robbins and that which underpinned microeconomics. The paradox is that the most important apparent influence on post-war economics, for his creation of Keynesianism, should have been so opposed to the direction in which the discipline's methodology and content were about to be taken.

Initially, the influences on Keynes were probably derived from his father and Marshall, see Chapter 7, and Russell and Moore, from all of whom he wished to extract the maximum by way of deductive, mathematical reasoning, but to which he wished to add something more. In this respect, it is significant that he wrote what is perceived to be a classic contribution to the theory of probability as the basis for understanding uncertainty. Russell had commented favourably on his *Treatise of Probability* and had been a major influence upon it. As Coates (1996, p. 10) observes:[5]

> Cambridge philosophy during the twenties and thirties was the scene of some very intense and fruitful discussions between Moore, Russell, and Wittgenstein, as well as the economist–philosophers Piero Sraffa and Ramsey. It has not been appreciated that Keynes was also an integral member of this group, and kept his finger on the pulse of new ideas.

Relatively rarely, Coates concentrates on Keynes' later philosophical development in order to bring out a substantial change in his thinking.[6] For, p. 76:

> To sum up, while Keynes had early in his career paid homage to both Russell and Moore, it is apparent that he had serious reservations about Russell's form of analysis, and was more naturally allied with Moore's common sense philosophy.

For our purposes, it is crucial that Keynes moved away from the approach of Russell – as did Wittgenstein, to whom Keynes increasingly and closely aligned himself.[7] Thus, continuing from above:

> This showed itself in Keynes' fundamental reservations about (1) the assumption that reductive symbolic analyses are more precise, or less prone to ambiguity, than everyday language; (2) the possibility of specifying sense data without interpretation; and (3) the possibility of reducing complex entities to the level of simples.

One reason for this is that Russell is perceived to be wedded to an atomistic and deductive methodology, rather than a tradition of commonsense reasoning.[8] Coates reports Keynes as commenting that, pp. 65–6:

> But beyond the fact that the conclusions to which [Russell] seeks to lead up are those of common sense ... he is not concerned with analysing the methods of valid reasoning which we actually employ. He concludes with familiar results, but he reaches them from premises, which have never occurred to us before, and by an argument so elaborate that our

minds have difficulty in following it ... [It] gives rise to questions about the relation in which ordinary reasoning stands to this ordered system.

And further, in critique of Edgeworth's atomism, Keynes comments, p. 75:

The atomic hypothesis which has worked so splendidly in physics breaks down in psychics. We are faced at every turn with the problems of organic unity, of discreteness, of discontinuity – the whole is not equal to the sum of the parts, comparisons of quantity fail us, small changes produce large effects, the assumptions of a uniform and homogeneous continuum are not satisfied.

The growing antipathy to Russell lay not in suggesting that he believed science could be reduced to a formal logical system, but rather that such a goal should even be approached as closely as possible. Thus, whilst Russell recognised pervasive vagueness in meaning, language appropriates what meaning it can by 'approaching the ideal language of logical atomism', p. 8. By contrast, Keynes (under the sway of Russell's former ally, Wittgenstein) positively embraces the vagueness of concepts as a means of incorporating the inexactitudes and uncertainties of (economic) life itself. Coates refers to 'The drift away from the canonical notation of analytic philosophy and logical atomism towards an analysis of vague concepts', p. xii.[9] Thus, 'During the transition to the *General Theory* Keynes increasingly used the term "vagueness" when writing about economic concepts', p. 81. This does not refer to imprecision in measurement of an exact quantity, but to an inability to reduce definitions to an exact and unchanging meaning, in part because concepts can be subject to a number of interlocking meanings, p. 85.[10] More specifically, in quoting Keynes, 'Much economic theorising to-day suffers, I think, because it attempts to apply high precise and mathematical methods to material which is itself much too vague to support such treatment', p. 83. The result is that precision in definition can have the negative effect of leaving concepts empty of meaning, as in excessive and inappropriate formalism as opposed to Marshall's suggestion that meaning should be inferred from the richness of context, p. 87. Indeed, for Keynes, 'those writers who try to be *strictly* formal generally have no substance', cited from a lecture, p. 88. Thus, Keynes is seen as reluctantly prefacing the *General Theory* with 'philosophical comments because of "the appalling state of scholasticism into which the minds of so many economists have got"', pp. 88–9. Indeed, by explicitly drawing the parallel with 'a similar critical assessment of analytic philosophy, he referred to Russell's method as "extravagantly scholastic". He thus reiterated the warning [from an earlier draft of the Preface to the *General Theory*] that "in writing economics one is not writing either a mathematical proof or a legal document"', p. 89.

As such, Keynes argued 'against Robbins, [in that] economics is essentially a moral science, and not a natural science. That is to say, it employs introspection and judgements of value ... it deals with motives, expectations, psychological uncertainties', Coates (1996, p. 102). But, it should be noted, as for Davis (1991, p. 94), Keynes' moral science is not ethics but one that 'must make significant use of introspection and judgements of value to be able to model individuals' behaviour', testing those ascribed by examining one's own inner thoughts, motives and intentions. But, whilst couched in these individualistic terms, and as already hinted, Keynes took the view that pinpointing these inner speculations or whatever, required a prior attention to their social determinants, so complex and shifting could they be in (collective) content and meaning. Thus, for Coates, Keynes' famous confession in the *Preface* to the *General Theory* of 'a long struggle to escape ... from habitual modes of thought and expression', is to be interpreted in broad philosophical terms rather than upon the narrow terrain of adherence to Say's Law and the breach with 'classical' economics in this respect, p. 63.[11] Runde (1997, p. 240) thereby draws the conclusion that Keynes's methodology in the *General Theory* suggests 'economic action and its consequences also have a material aspect in their dependence on social structures that are independent of any individual's conception of them'. And, for Carabelli (1991, p. 119), this involves Keynes view of the economy as a unity of interdependencies, for:

> Keynes's methodology of criticism of the classical theory was provided by the concept of organic interdependence – a concept which was at the base of his own positive approach to economics (his notion of 'macro' came from here!).

Thus, the priority of macro over micro, and the fallacy of constructing the latter out of the former, is a consequence of informal philosophical arguments. The philosophical underpinnings of Keynes' economics, then, increasingly rejected the shift towards mathematical formalism that accelerated in the aftermath of the Second World War. For Keynes, like Marshall, models are instruments of thought and, as such, most important to acquire, but not at the expense of seeking to turn economics into a pseudo-natural science through econometric estimation, thereby fixing numerical values of what are vague categories, Coates (1997, pp. 111–12).[12] As critical realists have emphasised, this is to close the model, render it deterministic, and preclude its continuing to serve as an instrument of thought.[13] As Keynes (1938b, p. 301) puts it, arguing against Tinbergen's use of econometric methods in the study of business cycles:

> In chemistry and physics and other natural sciences the object of experiment is to fill in the actual values of the various quantities and factors appearing in an equation or a formula ... In economics, that is not the case, and to concert a model into a quantity formula is to destroy its usefulness as an instrument of thought.

Rather, the attachment to vagueness allowed Keynes to appeal to common sense, the deployment of concepts in common use, and to engage both in persuasion and policy making.

This is not the place to interrogate this commonsense view, and the consistency and veracity of Keynes' methodology, only to observe its compromises in principle and practice. Keynes does use abstract concepts that are not in common use, and his rejection of methodological individualism is muted in deference to the sensibilities of fellow economists. In retrospect, Keynes may have accommodated too much, although the chances are that his philosophical foundations and their consequences would have been overwhelmed, come what may. For with the consolidated division between micro and macro, and their respective attachment to general equilibrium and IS/LM Keynesianism (and macro-econometrics), Keynes' philosophical concerns simply vanished without trace within the discipline of economics, despite his overwhelming (if partial) influence on macroeconomic theory. It is crucial to recognise just how much his intended macroeconomics differed from the microeconomics under development at the same time, not only in substance but also in method.

4 General equilibrium or trooping the techniques

It is not simply that Keynes' methodological concerns were considered, debated and rejected in the post-war period. Economists, beyond a small Cambridge circle, were not even aware of them, and they have only been brought to light as part of the history of economic thought and as a contribution to the methodology of economics, long after these slipped off the mainstream economist's radar. And, as already indicated, the period after the Second World War was very different in the realm of economic theory. Whilst institutionalism had been stronger in the USA, the ideological climate had shifted substantially. Leys (1996, p. 6) reminds us, with references, that 'The degree to which critical social science was systematically rooted out in the USA from 1948 onwards is apt to be forgotten'. Accordingly, its inter-war institutionalism was increasingly marginalised. By contrast, neoclassical orthodoxy could flourish. Samuelson finished off much of what was left over from Hicks as far as micro-foundations are concerned. For Cooter (1982, p. 1260), with pride and claim of self-image far in excess of achievement, 'In the process of absorbing Newton's mathematics, which began in the 1880s and was completed by the time Samuelson published the *Foundations of Economics* in 1947, economics gained technical superiority over other social sciences'. In addition, Hicks' IS/LM model stripped the understanding of the macroeconomy of all inductive content. And the extension of the micro-foundations to the functioning of the economy as a whole, the ultimate in (ultra-)deductivism, found an ideal home in the thrusting of general equilibrium theory to the forefront of research. The publication of Hicks' (1939) *Value and Capital* played an important role in the revival of interest in general equilibrium theory, which attained its pinnacle with the work of Arrow and Debreu (1954) and Debreu (1959), although it continued to provide a thriving programme of research until at least the appearance of Arrow and Hahn (1971).

Essentially, building upon the maximising behaviour of individuals, as preference-satisfying consumers or as profit-maximising entrepreneurs, general equilibrium theory sought to establish the existence of equilibrium prices and quantities across all markets simultaneously, and to investigate the relationship between such equilibrium and Pareto-efficiency. The result was the proof of the existence of a general equilibrium (but not of its uniqueness or stability), supplemented by the two fundamental theorems of welfare economics: the first stating that every competitive equilibrium is Pareto optimal, in the sense that no change from this equilibrium can make any one better off without making anybody else worse off; and the second that any Pareto optimal outcome can be achieved given an appropriate (re)distribution of initial endowments. Whilst ultimately achieving its goal in a limited sense, the success in doing so might be considered to be hollow, especially in light of the original motivations of marginalism. First, competition is reduced to the idea of all agents being price-takers. Second, conditions of production and the nature of products are taken as given. Third, preferences are also taken as given. Fourth, there is no uncertainty. Fifth, the economy is reduced to market interactions, with no non-market interaction between agents or with the economy (apart from the automatic transformation of inputs into outputs as representative of production – and similarly for preference satisfaction through consumption and, disutility of, work). Sixth, there is no money. Seventh, it is institutionally empty and institutionally neutral, Kaufman (2007, p. 10) and Chapter 6, Section 2. Last, for existence, uniqueness, efficiency and/or stability of equilibrium, highly stringent technical assumptions needed to be made concerning lack of increasing returns, the equivalent of diminishing marginal utility, no externalities and extreme limitations on the nature of substitution both in consumption and production.

By the same token, general equilibrium theory had become entirely reliant upon the deductive method, totally divorced from reality, and dependent upon deductive assumptions, or axioms, around production and consumption that bore little relation to common experience or the scholarship of the other social sciences. In Blaug's (1998a, p. 11) words, 'by the time we get to Arrow and Debreu, general equilibrium theory has ceased to make any descriptive claim about actual economic systems and has become a purely formal apparatus about a virtual economy'.[14] Similarly, for Ingrao and Israel (1990, pp. 273–4), especially with Debreu, the theory takes on a life of its own, independent of real world application (although such concerns are more compelling to Arrow if predominantly, it should be added in his other work). Debreu (1986, p. 1265) could not put the predominance of the deductive method and its relationship to reality more clearly:[15]

> An axiomatized theory first selects its primitive concepts and represents each one of them by a mathematical object ... Next assumptions on the objects representing the primitive concepts are specified, and consequences are mathematically derived from them. The economic interpretation of the theorems so obtained is the last step of the analysis. According to the schema, an axiomatized theory has a mathematical form that is completely separated from its economic content. If one removes the economic interpretation of the primitive concepts, of the assumptions ... its bare mathematical structure must still stand.

And the requirement of deductive logic is raised to the highest pedestal for 'A deductive structure that tolerates a contradiction does so under the penalty of being useless, since any statement can be derived flawlessly and immediately from that contradiction', Debreu (1991, pp. 2–3). This is itself an interestingly flawed argument, since just because logical contradictions make any statement possible, this does not mean that other valid conclusions cannot be drawn.[16] More significantly, Debreu's interpretative neutrality with respect to use of mathematical methods is not as innocent as appears at first sight. In response to Alan Krueger's (2003, p. 190) question on whether 'we don't need a separate field of macroeconomics', Edmond Malinvaud responds 'That was a vision Gerard Debreu was arguing with me in our interchanges ... at the Cowles Commission'. So, whilst there is no logical connection as such between methodological individualism, general equilibrium and mathematical methods, this was the direction pushed for by orthodoxy from an early stage, ultimately giving rise to the extreme form adopted by new classical economics, see below.

The point, then, was (at least in principle) for orthodoxy to elevate mathematisation as the form taken by a deductive system of economics, from which economic interpretation can be taken as a next and separate step. Yet, as Nadal (2004a, p. 47) confirms, 'In attempting to rely on the purity of mathematical discourse, economic theory has frequently sacrificed content for the sake of using mathematical tools'. But in immediately suggesting that Koopmans 'was one of the first to point this out' in 1957, there is an interesting oversight towards the antipathy to such mathematisation of economics from Say, Menger, Marshall, Keynes and others onwards.[17] What is illustrated is the extent to which those who developed general equilibrium were indeed conscious of the extent to which their use of formalism and increasingly unsatisfactory assumptions in order to attain the goal of general equilibrium was undermining the significance of their efforts. Solving the problem of equilibrium became the be-all and end-all; the substantive content and significance of the solution paled into the background. Earlier, Walras' general equilibrium had fallen into neglect, at least in part because its formalism was considered inappropriate for understanding the economy as a whole. With the resurrection of general equilibrium, formalism became an object in itself with realism at most secondary and a matter of interpretation, see concluding chapter.

This can be seen in a number of ways. First is in terms of the spirited and, it might be added, relatively rare defence of general equilibrium given by Hahn (1973) who nonetheless articulates what its proponents would most likely argue. This is that general equilibrium is not intended to be realistic, but rather a standard against which the real world can be judged. Of course, this is a considerable departure from the motivation of old marginalism for which other considerations were supposed to be integrated with core economic theory rather than to take it as a point of departure – this itself a compromise over inductive/deductive and historical/analytical contents. Methodologically, it simply smacks of opportunism, not least because of Hahn's now infamous suggestion that young economists should avoid methodology altogether and simply get on with the mathematical models, Lawson (1997, p. 12) (although this might have been sound career advice in view of the standards of the academic profession). For why should we judge the real world by its departure from an entirely imaginary construct? Or, by analogy, should we study the anatomy of the horse by first laying out the unicorn as a means for comparison?

Second, to a large extent, these reservations have been recognised by Hahn himself, albeit in the context of his extreme aversion to monetarism. For the latter effectively seeks to rely upon general equilibrium to underpin its faith in markets and a simple relationship between monetary factors and the level of economic activity. As general equilibrium fails to provide a satisfactory place for the role of money – why would its use persist in equilibrium for example? – then Hahn would be right to point to the fallacy in drawing upon it as a rationale for monetarism since it is a moneyless economy and cannot serve as a standard for the real world. But the same sort of argument applies more generally in light of all of the deviations of general equilibrium from realism – whether it be the absence of uncertainty or endogenous preferences and technology. This is to play fast and loose with the idea of realism, but the substantive point is to recognise the extremely limited extent to which general equilibrium gets to grips with economic processes, by virtue of purporting to set a standard against which they can be judged by way of deviation. Rather, so much of economic activity and causal factors are precluded by general equilibrium, for which the use and role of money is merely the most blatant example. For those who cared to see, this exclusion was honoured rather than addressed by complementing microeconomics with Keynesian macroeconomics.

Third, the relationship between general equilibrium theory and the history of economic thought is particularly troubled. It is not simply that conceptually and substantively it progresses little (other than in technique) beyond what had already been achieved by Walras almost a century before. It also suffers a collective amnesia over the old marginalists' reservations over his contribution. As Bridel (2002, p. 270) aptly concludes:

> Despite weak and early attempts at 'realism' including disequilibrium trading, Walras' *tâtonnement* mechanism is nothing more than (or not

even) an idealized representation of a virtual market process conducted as it is in terms of *numéraire* – and not money. Despite Walras' repeated claims that the mathematical solution of equilibrium is the selfsame problem that is solved in practice by a perfectly competitive market, his timeless and moneyless *tâtonnement* is nothing but a mathematical technique of iteration with scant relation to its intuitive content – and certainly void of any proper technology of exchange or institutional set-up in which money plays a role in the transaction process. After years of groping, and four different editions, Walras eventually fell victim to his relentless search for an internal coherence to his general equilibrium model that is only congruent with a purely static approach from which any claim of describing the price formation *process* is excluded. In short, for the sake of saving the internal coherence of his mathematical model, Walras progressively severed the relationship between scientific abstraction and empirical evidence throughout the various editions of the *Eléments*. And money was an obvious victim of this procedure.

Further, Bridel agrees that the 1930s marks the watershed between a rejection of such formalism at the expense of interpretative content. After it, 'like modern axiomatic general equilibrium theorist, Walras could write with confidence that, "pure economics does not expect any confirmation from reality". Half a century later, such a conclusion was obviously not going to be very palatable to crypto-Marshallians like Hicks ... and Patinkin trying to build a synthesis between Keynes and the "Classics"', p. 271. Accordingly, the period between Walras and Arrow/Debreu was not one of honing mathematisation and axiomatics although these have been central to the creation and development of general equilibrium, Ingrao and Israel (1990, p. x). For the delays are not simply a matter of 'mere "blunders" arising from technical "incapacity" [but] not infrequently reflect conceptual choices', p. 4. As illustrated above through the tensions identifiable in Marshall around micro/ macro, method, distribution, the economic and the non-economic, etc., antipathy towards general equilibrium, or embracing what became its goals, was deeply entrenched within the old marginalism in and of itself and through the continuing influence of classical political economy.[18]

Instead of revisiting the doubts over Walras, the push for acceptability of general equilibrium theory has looked back further in the past, drawing upon the idea, and continuing to do so, that it involves a formalisation of Adam Smith's invisible hand, Ingrao and Israel (1990, p. ix) for example, and Hutchison (2000, p. 313), who references Hahn, Tobin and Stiglitz for this view.[19] Hutchison could not be more dismissive of what is perceived to be a reinvention of the history of economic thought, p. 314–15:[20]

As regards what Smith wrote, and his methodology, it amounts to a profound misunderstanding and misrepresentation to claim that his 'vision' (Hahn) or 'conjecture' (Tobin and Stiglitz) was, accurately translated ...

either into 'something sufficiently precise to enable us to argue about it' (Hahn); or into 'a rigorous theorem' (Stiglitz); or was 'rigorously proved by Arrow and Debreu' (Tobin). Smith's 'conjecture' was, in fact, not so much 'translated' as *transformed*, both in content and cognitive nature. In fact, if the first rendition of the 'fundamental theorems of welfare economics' is 'the modern rendition' of Adam Smith's invisible hand conjecture, then this is a grossly distorting 'rendition'. For what GE analysis has done to Smith's conjecture is to eviscerate it of real-world content, and transform it into a piece of 'rigorous', empirically vacuous, hyper-abstract analysis, based on a range of fantastic, science-fictional assumptions.

As Loasby (1976, p. 47) concludes, cited by Hutchison (2000, p. 318), 'Hahn's assertion that general equilibrium theorists have made "precise an economic tradition which is two hundred years old" demonstrates that he has very little idea what that tradition is"'.

No wonder that Hutchison (1994, p. 290) tartly refers to 'the Mathematical Abstractionist version of the history of economic thought, which claims to be "translating" the insufficiently rigorous visions of the great writers of the past into "something sufficiently precise to allow us" (for the first time in the 1980s) to argue about them'. He is primarily concerned, relative to general equilibrium theory, with the much more complex and contingent arguments that Adam Smith made in favour of laissez-faire as well as the case he also made in favour of state intervention, his antagonism to the idea of perfect foresight, and a methodology far removed from the ultra-deductivism of modern mainstream economics. To some extent, though, this is to miss a major part of the picture. For Adam Smith ultimately favoured the opening up of markets in order to promote their extent, the division of labour, productivity and the wealth of nations, Chapter 4, an approach that simply does not sit inside general equilibrium theory either methodologically or substantively.

Fourth, though, there remains the enduring gap (or inconsistency) between microeconomic analysis and macroeconomics, or consideration of the economy as a whole even on the reduced basis that became standard with Keynesianism. Patinkin (1956) had demonstrated that the classical dichotomy between real and monetary analysis is invalid. In other words, either general equilibrium is a world without money – hardly realistic or one that could command policy or popular appeal – or it does include money and this must have an impact, at least in the short run, at every level. Further, whilst macroeconomic analysis insists upon the presence of money, general equilibrium offers no microeconomic rationale for it to be held other than that it might offer some utility in itself by lying in individual pockets. As Patinkin put it himself in the revised edition to his classic contribution, cited in Bridel (2002, p. 277):

> Most discussions of monetary theory ... simply assume (as I too do in this book) that money exists and serves as a unique medium of exchange in the economy.

Whilst some remedies have been sought to rectify this unjustified assumption, Hahn (2002, p. 262) could not be more disparaging about them, for they 'bring the use of mathematics in economics into disrepute'. Further:

> The algebra adds absolutely nothing to the argument or the theory and only shows that if efficient exchange requires an agent to accept a good which he does not directly desire and if trust is at a premium then money is needed. In other words, if there is not a 'coincidence of wants' money will be a good idea.

Instead, apart from highlighting that money is not neutral even in the long run if equilibrium is not unique, Hahn argues for a more sophisticated account of the interaction between transaction costs, information and trust.

However, this is a considerable step back from Patinkin's own understanding. For, as powerfully argued by Mehrling (2002) and Dimand (2002), he remained steeped in the earlier tradition of simply accepting that there remained an irresolvable inconsistency between micro and macro, especially as far as general equilibrium and value theory – as opposed to the theory of money and business cycles – are concerned. Attempts to reconcile the two, through money in the utility function or whatever, could only succeed by devaluing both the theory of money itself and the scope of macroeconomics (to short-run deviations around given trends or long-run equilibrium to the exclusion of business cycles). Nothing could better illustrate, at least analytically, the debased understanding of macroeconomics that was evolving, as well as its role in fixing the deficiencies of microeconomics as far as the functioning of the economy as a whole is concerned.

5 Paul Samuelson: synthesis versus revolution?

These conclusions are confirmed, and with wider significance, by considering 'The Coming of Keynesianism to America', a volume edited by Colander and Landreth, published in 1996.[21] J. K. Galbraith (1975, p. 141) takes for granted, possibly as late as was feasible in light of the imminent monetarist counter-revolution, that 'Keynesian policies are the new orthodoxy'.[22] He judges that Samuelson 'almost from the outset was the acknowledged leader of the younger Keynesian community', p. 136. With the comfortable hindsight of the victor, he also treats the ideological context of the construction of Keynesianism in the immediate post-war period as something of a joke, with those promoting it 'identifying Keynesianism with socialism, Fabian socialism, Marxism, Communism, Fascism and also literary incest, meaning that one Keynesian always reviewed the works of another Keynesian', p. 139. By contrast, those of 'conservative mood ... who objected to Keynes were also invariably handicapped by the fact that they hadn't (and couldn't) read the book. It was like attacking the original Kama Sutra for obscenity without being able to read Sanskrit. Still, where

social change is involved, there are men who can surmount any handicap',
pp. 138–9.

Such lingering sarcasm over the cursory knowledge and scholarship of
anti-Keynesians no doubt reflects the relatively mild and short-term dis-
comfort that Galbraith himself experienced as a result of the fall-out for
Keynesians from anti-communism.[23] His appointment to Harvard was held
up for a year in the late 1940s as a result of concerted opposition from
Harvard graduates, members of the inappropriately named Veritas Foundation,
with books such as *God and Man at Yale* in 1951, through to *Keynes at
Harvard* in 1960, published in the campaign against Keynesianism and
Keynesians, Colander and Landreth (1996, pp. 12–13). The latter cite the
President of Harvard at the beginning of this period to the effect that
'Keynes' name had taken on a symbolic value ... To a certain type of busi-
nessman, it was a proverbial red rag. In the eyes of many economically illit-
erate but deeply patriotic (and well-to-do) citizens, to accuse a professor of
being a Keynesian was almost equivalent to branding him a subversive agent',
p. 12. As Backhouse (2006a, p. 16) puts it, 'Prominent Keynesians, from
Galbraith to Samuelson were vilified and labelled Marxists or communists'.[24]

In short, Keynesianism in the immediate post-war period was a hot political and ideological potato, sharpening and representing major differences
between Republicans and Democrats, and differing responses both to the
experience of interwar depression and the way in which to preclude such in
the future. With the post-war boom and the passage through the extremes of
McCarthyite anti-communism, such differences were tempered as Keynesianism
became the orthodoxy. But, even if its ultimate triumph was inevitable – and
as long as the economy was doing well and this could be imputed to macroeconomic management – the forms and direction taken by Keynesianism
were not fixed at the outset.[25]

In this light, Colander and Landreth usefully point to the Keynesian
revolution as comprising theoretical, political and textbook elements. But it
is inappropriate to see these as separate from one another. Whilst Samuelson
became the leading figure in promoting Keynesianism in the United States,
he was not in the lead initially, especially as far as a textbook is concerned.
That he should be considered to have dominated Keynesianism in the
United States at the outset is understandable. His text *Economics* first
appeared in 1948, and is now in its eighteenth edition, with William
Nordhaus as co-author from 1985. It has spawned many imitators, apart
from its own adoption across the US and elsewhere as a textbook. It is sufficiently important as a text in the history of economic thought to have been
reissued in 1998 in its original edition. Significantly, Samuelson had published what was essentially the results from his own PhD thesis one year
earlier than his textbook. His *Foundations of Economic Analysis* is a classic
of a different type. It is based on the application of the principles of ther-
modynamics to economic problems, particularly those of individual optimisation and the corresponding equilibrium of economic systems.

It is easy to recognise that the two books are entirely different, especially as far as motivation and level are concerned. Through these two texts, Samuelson had 'a profound impact on the shape and structure of postwar economics', by setting the scene for the teaching of economics both at the undergraduate and postgraduate level, Wade Hands (2001, p. 60). But each contributed to the revolution in economic theory in its own way, across both theory and text. For, in the revolution in economic thought around Keynesianism, the distinction between theory and textbook (and politics) is not so sharp until the new ideas become orthodoxy. In the first decade after the Second World War, economics as a discipline was undergoing multiple shifts in content and technique. Significantly, in the forefront of Keynesian texts in the United States before Samuelson, was the now unknown Lorie Tarshis, someone who had had the advantage of studying at Cambridge in the 1930s. His text was published in 1947, and rapidly became adopted throughout the United States. As he puts it, Colander and Landreth (1996, p. 68):

> In the first two or three months in which the book came out I would get letters ... saying Brown had adopted it, maybe Middlebury adopted it, Yale had adopted it – one place after another had adopted it. Every time I got a letter like this that indicated ten more adoptions or twenty more adoptions, I thought, 'Boy, that bank account will be picking up'.

But then came the reaction: 'It was a nasty performance, an organized campaign in which they sent newsletters to all the trustees of all the universities that had adopted the book'. Orders started being cancelled, as universities became concerned about, even suffering threats of, loss of endowments. 'Sales, instead of staying at that beautiful peak, went down just like that ... But it really died in 1948 or 1949. And then Paul Samuelson's book came out a year later, in 1948'.

But why should Samuelson have been able to rescue, save, appropriate and/or promote the Keynesian revolution, and, in doing so, was it made into something different than it would otherwise have been? Tarshis himself is tart to the point of sarcasm about Samuelson's Keynesianism: 'Paul Samuelson was not in the Keynesian [discussion] group. He was busy working on his own thing. That he became a Keynesian was laughable', Colander and Landreth (1996, p. 64). In doing his own thing, Samuelson is extraordinarily revealing. For him, becoming a Keynesian was a matter of overcoming or, more exactly, unsuccessfully reconciling it with his prior predilection for micro-foundations. He confesses 'What I resisted in Keynes the most was the notion that there could be equilibrium unemployment', p. 159. Indeed, 'I was like a tuna: the Keynesian system had to land me, and I was fighting every inch of the line. I was worried about micro foundations', p. 161. He places considerable emphasis on his own personal experience of unemployment, finding himself unable to get a summer job as a student at any wage to relieve family poverty, p. 161. So Samuelson wanted to be a Keynesian, but could not marry it with microeconomic principles. How did he resolve this conundrum? The plain answer is that he did not, and simply accepted this. For, as he puts it, 'I was content to assume that there was enough rigidity in relative prices and wages to make the Keynesian alternative to Walras operative', the presumption being the presence of some 'substructure of administered prices and imperfect competition', p. 160. And, in retrospect, he judges that 'It's a modern desire to have impeccable micro foundations for macro ... I decided that life was more fruitful not worrying about it ... Moreover, the search today for micro foundations for macro does not have a rich set of results ... It's because I get a better positivistic macroeconomics to do some worrying about the micro foundations that I do the worrying, and not because I have a tidy conscience that everybody's micro foundations must be tidy', p. 162.

Samuelson's retrospective account has a modern ring about it in its mode of expression, with its reference to micro-foundations for macroeconomics. But his attitude is embedded in his and the discipline's past, with an ill-concealed contempt for such micro-foundations, in and of themselves, as a logical exercise in mathematical consistency (for which read new classical economics). For Samuelson's generation, Keynesianism was macro, and it floated systemically free from micro, although the latter might offer ideas on how to go about the former. Thus, Samuelson offers a remarkably frank confession, that his Keynesian macro had not been landed in the sense of being founded on sound micro foundations, and he had ceased to care about this. But it is a little bit too convenient that the presumed microfoundations are those of a little bit of rigidity in prices, derived from 'imperfect competition', and incorporated into an equilibrium, possibly at less than full employment for the economy as a whole. For the reference to imperfect competition, and the use to which it is put, scarcely begins to get to grips with the systemic consequences of the monopolisation of modern capitalism and its implications for its dynamic, let alone its level of economic activity. To some extent, this helps us to explain why Tarshis should have given way to Samuelson, even though both were Keynesians, and without relying upon relatively less important factors such as Samuelson's powers of exposition and his use of mathematics as a neutral and more acceptable form of exposition.

Interestingly, though, both Samuelson, p. 160, and Tarshis, p. 69, seem mystified over why one should have replaced the other. But it is worth ranging over Tarshis' (1947) text to understand why, bearing in mind that the slightest deviation from market fundamentalism is liable to attract outrage from his opponents. His treatment of Keynes comes at the end of his book, after a full cover of microeconomics and other topics. He bends over backwards to disassociate himself from political attachments. Thus, p. 347:

> A word must be said, before we begin our analysis, about the political implications of the Keynesian theory ... The truth is simple. The Keynesian

theory no more supports the New Deal stand or the Republican stand than do the newest data on atomic fission ... It is possible, as we shall see later, to frame either the Republican or the Democratic economic dogma in terms of the theory. After all, both good Republicans and good Democrats can analyze the causes of mental illness or of faulty timing in an automobile engine. And so the following chapters are neither an attack upon, nor a defense of, the beliefs of individual political parties. Rather, they are intended to show how a good many modern economists analyze this primary economic problem.

Now if you are anti-Keynesian and see it as the thin end of the wedge of communism, you are not going to take kindly to such claims of irrefutability across all political positions, and you might find it more palatable and (equally important) more difficult to contest if Keynesian economics were presented in neutral terms without political claims at all. And, the problem referred to as primary follows immediately in the next paragraph, 'The importance of avoiding unemployment cannot be overstressed'. And it can be avoided: 'The upshot of the analysis ... is that unemployment can be cured', p. 528. This is also taken, some might think provocatively, as meaning that capitalism does not have to be overthrown: 'Our knowledge of how capitalism works shows us that we can prevent that suffering [from unemployment]. And we have certainly found no reason to conclude that we have to scrap the system to do it', p. 529.

Tarshis has already indicated some sympathy for working people as far as employment is concerned. For him, wages should be raised as far as possible, inasfar as is consistent with full employment, not least because this is the most important way of improving the gains of all and, in veiled terms, of guarding against social unrest: 'Labor's primary interest is to maintain full employment; but that is not at all in conflict with the interests of other groups, for the employer, the farmer, and the investor all gain when we have peak prosperity. If we can keep the national income at its maximum, it will not be necessary for labor to live "across the tracks". Our economy can produce enough to provide a decent livelihood for all if we do away with depression', p. 657.

But such a community of interests, harmonised by Keynesianism, does not extend to monopolisation. For 'As long as so great a degree of monopoly exists, it is probable that output will be below capacity, distribution of the output will be unequal, and the pattern of production will remain unbalanced ... Thus, growing monopoly is likely to be harmful to the rest of the economy which is left behind in the race to secure monopoly status, and it may even injure the groups that achieve it, since their prosperity depends in part upon the prosperity of the economy as a whole. Nonetheless, it is difficult to control monopoly, as the most casual glance at the world about us will show', pp. 679–80. Whilst this does place monopoly capital in the dock, with labour potentially as unemployment victim, Tarshis closes his book in more neutral terms, with Keynesianism as the cure-all as opposed to detailed intervention, p. 687:

> While it may be legitimate for each group to improve its lot at the expense of competing groups, the struggle to do so becomes anti-social when it causes a reduction in the total output of the economy. The damage done by such a struggle can be most successfully prevented, not by legislative restraint, but by society's adopting measures to keep the total output as high as possible, its composition as nearly ideal as possible, and the distribution as fair as possible. When that is done, the economic problem will be solved.

Tarshis does combine an ethos of scientific neutrality and the preservation of capitalism with tinges of pro-labour sympathy and anti-monopoly antipathy. Place this in the context of Keynesianism for conservatives as representing a conscious – possibly deliberately veiled – or unconscious strategy for more deep-rooted change, and it is hardly surprising that he should attract a vitriolic campaign against his text being universally adopted across American universities.

It follows that the political climate may not have prevented the rise of Keynesianism in the United States, but it seems to have had some influence over both its theoretical direction and its textbook content, most obviously as dictated by Samuelson. As Backhouse (2006a, p. 16) puts it, surely too cautiously, 'doubts about its closeness to communism did not prevent Keynesianism from becoming widely accepted in academia, though that may have contributed to its being expressed in more careful, technical language than might otherwise have been the case'. But it is not simply a matter of *whether* Keynesianism but also of *what* Keynesianism. For there are sufficient differences in substance between Samuelson's treatment and that of Tarshis, whose style and content of analysis is unrecognisable by comparison with macroeconomic texts today. And it is not simply a matter of the differences as they were, but also as they might have become. Tarshis, for example, is not so far short of the approach being offered by Kalecki, the major difference being the latter's denial of the possibility of eliminating unemployment under capitalism for want of its capacity to discipline workers when jobs can be left without fear of being unable to gain another. But the emphasis on monopoly as a key characteristic of the Keynesian system – as output-restricting and distributionally disadvantageous to real wages and effective demand – was inspired by Kalecki but has only survived in the heterodoxy of post-Keynesianism.

That is but for one exception of possibly more than symbolic significance. The treatment of monopoly as a source of systemic stagnation was soon to become the major element in the leading Marxist approach to US capitalism, and most closely associated with Paul Sweezy, the country's leading Marxist over the last 50 years of the twentieth century.[26] For him, monopolies were capable of generating a surplus that they were incapable of realising through sale on the market. However, Sweezy had been an orthodox Harvard economist in the early 1930s, before converting via Keynesianism to Marxism during that decade. And he was a close associate of Lorie Tarshis. They first met in the early 1930s in London (at the well-known restaurant, Bertorelli's,[27] Sweezy being a student at the London School of Economics). As Tarshis puts it, 'he was so Hayekian, even Hayek was too far to the left for Paul Sweezy in those days', Colander and Landreth (1996, p. 58). They met again at Harvard in 1936: 'By then he'd already gone all the way over to Keynes and a little bit more'. For those, looking for reds under the beds, Tarshis innocently confesses 'I saw an awful lot of Paul from then till 1939 or 1940', p. 59. For those looking to associate Keynesianism with something worse, potentially or otherwise, Tarshis' text and his association with Paul Sweezy would appear to have been more than damning.

In a sense, this explains the Keynesianism that did not bark within the orthodoxy in relating monopoly, for example, to macroeconomic functioning. As indicated, microeconomic foundations (such as they were) existed uncomfortably side-by-side with macroeconomics. But rather than addressing the corresponding inconsistencies, as accepted by Patinkin and Samuelson for example, Keynesianism survived alongside general equilibrium until the collapse of the post-war boom at the end of the 1960s. The rise of monetarism, especially within the academic arena, had the effect of excising even the diminished scope of analysis of the macroeconomy. It began with Friedman's invention of a Chicago tradition, heavily criticised by Patinkin as an intellectual bastard, which had sought both to minimise the significance of Keynesianism and which purported to have anticipated it, Backhouse (2002a). With the subsequently even more extreme new classical economics as the new form of monetarism, the schism between micro and macro (and the concerns that the schism encompassed) is abolished by the simple expedient of relying exclusively on general equilibrium. This is irrespective of its deficiencies from the perspectives of the history of economic thought that inspired it.

Indeed, as one of its leading exponents, Robert Lucas is fanatically committed to general equilibrium, irrespective of its own problems that are simply ignored (stability, existence and uniqueness of equilibrium and no rationale for money). Methodological individualism takes on the extreme form of a representative individual with the perfect, if stochastic, foresight implied by rational expectations, and aggregate consistency across markets is paramount. Consequently, Lucas (1981, p. 278) strongly praises Patinkin's book, considering it to be 'perhaps the most refined and influential version of what I mean by the term "neo-classical synthesis"', cited in Bridel and de Vroey (2002, p. 156). But this is only because he wishes to set aside all of the tensions that Patinkin continues to recognise in the construction of a macroeconomics on micro-foundations. Indeed, Lucas writes to Patinkin of the latter's 'use of the term "mechanical" as a pejorative applied to theories, and our discussion of this in class. This helped to push me to the extreme view ... that well-formulated theories *are* machines, and therefore *necessarily* mechanical', cited in Backhouse (2002a, p. 189).

There can be no doubt, then, that mathematical methods have come to dictate economic theory, at the expense of realism, and that this is both reflected in and consolidated by the project of defining and refining general equilibrium. As McCloskey (1990a, p. 231) comments in retrospect:

> Since 1947, when Paul Samuelson published his Ph.D. dissertation, we in economics have been on a wild goose chase to find theorems provable by mathematical means that will miraculously give us a purchase on the world without having to venture out into it. Such a project had to be tried, I suppose, in view of human optimism, but unhappily the chase has not captured a single goose. Maybe a stray feather or two, but no complete animal.

One of McCloskey's enduring concerns had been the lack of realism of economics in terms of its correspondence to empirical evidence and significance in a sense other than statistical (what he dubs 'oomph').

But McCloskey, even if critically and like other critics, accepts what is a generally unquestioned image that economics has of itself. It is mathematically rigorous, for which it is prepared to sacrifice realism. But this is false – as is indicated by the extent to which mathematical rigour, or its consequences, are sacrificed when necessary for what is a higher claim on mainstream economic theory. As Giocoli (2005) reiterates, the deductive system of general equilibrium or otherwise is more concerned to hold to a particular system of thought than with attachment to empirical analysis, and formal content is examined in a way that removes it from substantive content (empirical or otherwise). As a result, there is no interest in experimental evidence on preferences for example, even from those who seek to combine the results of (a limited) psychology with economics. Giocoli asks:

> Why did this happen? In other words, why do most economists – even those of a more experimentalist penchant – go on refusing to *fully* account for the evidence offered by psychology? Why are they so little interested in describing the actual processes – not merely the outcomes – through which agents make their choices?

His answer is in terms of the wish for 'maximum generality', 'conceptual integrity' and 'image of economics as a scientific discipline'.

From there, however, it is but a short step to recognise that (important though it is) mathematics or its consequences are themselves dispensable should they prove unfavourable to the system of thought (especially the techniques) that are associated with the mainstream. After all, the mathematics shows that general equilibrium is not liable to exist, to be unique and stable, or to display efficiency properties. But general equilibrium is a core organising concept, and the techniques associated with its construction from supply and demand and optimisation are sacrosanct, and take priority over mathematics. This is so in that if the mathematics and the techniques contradict one another in some sense, then it is the techniques that prevail. For example, we almost always assume that the second order conditions for optimisation hold – not for reasons of mathematical rigour, let alone realism, but because these are required for the application of the techniques. As Moscati (2005) argues, the evolution of consumer demand theory within economics has, 'little empirical relevance and [is] regularly in contrast with commonsense evidence, observational data or experimental tests'. What drives the theory is not mathematical rigour, first and foremost, but an unwavering commitment to a system of concepts, the technical apparatus of utility and production functions that were to be derived from Marshall's organon but without any of his qualifications over their application.

6 Concluding remarks

All this sets the context for the excesses to which mainstream neoclassical economics has been driven in the most recent period, which is the subject of Fine and Milonakis (2009). Suffice it to observe here the extent to which that mainstream has departed from the concerns of those who inspired the marginalist revolution. Mathematics, deduction, the optimising individual in a knowable if stochastic world with money figuring at most in a token way, and the centrality of general equilibrium have all come to the fore. Lost have been the more rounded individual, the broader macroeconomic, social and institutional environment and causal factors, and endemic uncertainty and the corresponding dynamic change. The putative inductive content embedded in the axiomatic approach has long become subservient to standardised assumptions that are taken as much as articles of faith and universally true as they are left unexamined. In all of its dimensions, the historical and the social had become expunged from the world of economics, other than as data sets against which to test such speculative theory.

But, in all of this, there is one more paradox to be raised and resolved. For it is not simply with the rise of general equilibrium, and the eventual eclipse of a face-saving Keynesian macroeconomics, that microeconomics came to set aside all the troublesome anxieties that plagued the old marginalism. Even on its own terms, such microeconomics has been riddled with the deepest of problems and inconsistencies, observed by critics and proponents alike before either passing on or being studiously ignored. These comprise the conditions for the existence, uniqueness, stability and efficiency of general equilibrium itself, its dependence upon special assumptions around timelessness, moneylessness, a fictional Walrasian auctioneer, convexity of preferences and technology, and fixed preferences, technology and endowments of resources.[28] The real world – let alone the policy relevance – of such assumptions beggars belief, not least in light of the theory of the second best for which correcting some deviations from the perfectly competitive economy is no guarantee of improvement unless all deviations are corrected.

The paradox, then, is that a theory and approach that has come to pride itself against alternatives and other disciplines on the basis of its scientific rigour – by which is meant drawing out the implications of mathematical deduction – should be so careless over its own results. Nor is this confined to the issues so far covered. Consider, for example, the Cambridge capital controversy, or capital critique, that raged between MIT, USA, and Cambridge, England. The details need not concern us,[29] but, in part, the debate revolves around the legitimacy of the particular technique of deploying an aggregate production function that remains extraordinarily common across neoclassical orthodoxy. The consequences, however, range over a considerable proportion of the theoretical and empirical work undertaken within the mainstream – from distribution theory to the empirical measurement of economic performance. The outcome of the controversy was an unambiguous victory against the neoclassicals. So much so that one of the vanquished, Paul Samuelson (1966, p. 582) concluded the orthodoxy's capitulation in the following terms:

> If all this causes headaches for those nostalgic for the old time parables of neoclassical writing, we must remind ourselves that scholars are not born to live an easy existence. We must respect, and appraise, the facts of life.

These wise words have, subsequently, continued to be more observed in the breach, with the mainstream proceeding as if the Cambridge critique was never fought (and lost), the triumph of the neoclassical system of thought over its own mathematical logic when the two conflict, Giocoli (2005) and Moscati (2005).

And, of course, the old time parables of neoclassical writing are nostalgically retained, if only on a *selective* basis. None of the reservations of the old marginalism has been recalled. Rather, their fate, as well as that of rigour, has been commonly determined by a reductionism to a core set of techniques and axioms that have taken priority over all other considerations. In short, methodologically, neoclassical economics has sinned so enormously against its own origins within the old marginalism that a little more sinning against its own ethos is insignificant by comparison. Having imploded upon its own impenetrable and intolerant rationale and subject matter to the exclusion of all others, however, the ground had been prepared to venture back onto those pastures previously abandoned, as can be seen in our account of economics imperialism, Fine and Milonakis (2009).

15 Beyond the formalist revolution[1]

'Smith, Marx, Mill, Marshall. Keynes, Schumpeter, and Viner, to name but a few, were nourished by historical study and nourished in turn. Gazing down from Valhalla it would seem bizarre that their heirs would study economics with the history left out ... Yet this is what happened. It began in the 1940's, in some respects earlier, as young American economists bemused by revolution in the substance and method of economics neglected the reading of history in favour of macroeconomics, mathematics and statistics'.

McCloskey (1976, p. 434)

'Those who can, do science: those who can't prattle about its methodology'.[2]

Samuelson (1983, p. 7), cited in Holcombe (2008, online)

'My impression is that the best and brightest of the profession proceed as if economics is the physics of society. There is a single universally valid model of the world. It only needs to be applied. You could drop a modern economist from a time machine ... at any time, in any place, along with his or her personal computer; he or she could set up in business without even bothering to ask what time and which place'.

Solow (1986, pp. 25–6)

1 Introduction

In many ways, our account of the shifting methodological, social and historical content of economic theory appropriately ends in the immediate post-war period with the work of the first Nobel Laureate, Paul Samuelson, and other technically-oriented economists, and Laureates, such as Arrow and Debreu. Their formal contributions have set the pattern for, if not always the exact content of, the discipline up until the present day. As a Keynesian, Samuelson could hardly have welcomed the monetarist counterrevolution of the 1970s pioneered by fellow Laureate Milton Friedman. Nor has he found acceptable monetarism's purest progeny, with (fellow Chicago Laureate) Robert Lucas, to the fore. For, as we have seen, Samuelson rejected the idea of reducing macroeconomics to (optimising individual) microeconomics.[3] The new classical economics (NCE), on the other hand, has based itself entirely on the hyper-rational optimising behaviour of individuals, extending their pursuit of self-interest to the formulation and use of (narrowly conceived) expectations in the context of perfectly working markets – these themselves only disturbed from their harmony by unanticipated random shocks – and thereby rendering government policy totally ineffective other than in distorting outcomes at the microeconomic level.

Still, Samuelson (2003, p. 14), is obviously content to observe of yet another Nobel Laureate as 'a Joe Stiglitz, who exudes theorems hourly from every pore'.[4] Yet, with Stiglitz and the new information-theoretic economics in which he has played a leading role, we find that economics, including Keynesianism, is based on sound (optimising individuals) foundations and its principles are extended to cover most, if not all, areas of social theory. Gary Becker (another Chicago Laureate) may have inspired economics imperialism through treating the non-economic as if it were reducible to as if market activity. But the scope of economics imperialism is both considerably expanded and rendered more palatable across the social sciences in the form associated with the information-theoretic approach, treating the non-market as if a response to market imperfections.

These propositions concerning the development of economics and economics imperialism over the last 50 years or more are fully covered in Fine and Milonakis (2009). The purpose of this chapter is to close our account of how the social and historical was excised from economic theory by reflecting forward upon its consequences in providing the basis for mainstream economics as it is today. But we also reflect back upon the process of establishing the orthodoxy in the inter-war period in the wake of the marginalist revolution, i.e. the process of moving from 'interwar pluralism' to 'postwar neoclassicism', Morgan and Rutherford (1998). For that *process* was far richer than its *outcome* for it involved a recognition of the weaknesses and limitations of reducing the economic, let alone the social and historical, to marginalist principles, and of relying upon an increasing predominance of unquestioned technique over conceptual content and salience to issue under study.

Paradoxically, it seems precisely because it is so reduced in social, historical and methodological content, and wedded to technique, and (in these senses) unchanging, that mainstream economics is potentially subject to rapid change in substantive content at least within the (admittedly narrow) limits permitted by its core principles. So, whilst the continuing evolution of mainstream economics is neither arbitrary nor entirely stalled, its subordination to its technical apparatus, its deductivism and its statistical methods of enquiry, render it fluid for being without constraints imposed by wider or deeper concerns. In the following section, we reflect on how this situation has come about and what its prospects are, before concluding with an appeal for 'a *general* theory' that surely goes far beyond what Keynes had in mind in terms of its social and historical content as well as its method and interdisciplinarity.

2 From implosion of principle to explosion of application

Developments within economics between 1945 and 1955 have been described as a 'formalist revolution', Blaug (1999, 2001 and 2003) for example. Blaug highlights what is an uncontroversial process of change in which mathematical and statistical techniques have assumed much greater – and ultimately overwhelming – significance within the discipline of economics. The point here is not to question whether, in technique, the decade pinpointed by Blaug marked a revolution either in initiating change or the extent of change, thereby creating a fundamental break between before and after. Rather, the intention is to set the formalist revolution in the wider contexts both of the history of economic thought and of the relationship between economics and the other social sciences. In this sense, we are less concerned with the rise of formal techniques as an instrument of economic inquiry than with shift in substantive content and scope of application of economic theory.

In addressing this, however, we accept that the decade of the formalist revolution represents a watershed in the evolution of economic theory and in the relationship between it and the other social sciences – as significant over the long term, if not necessarily so acute and dramatic, as the process of formalisation itself. During this decade, the core technical apparatus associated with what is now neoclassical orthodoxy reached its analytical pinnacle, and became the standard for what was to follow. But the earlier process by which it was established involved a *narrowing* in scope of application, both within economics itself and through detachment from the other social sciences. By contrast, once established, the core apparatus has become the foundation on which both to appropriate the discipline internally to an almost exhaustive extent (otherwise discarding what does not fit) and to colonise the subject matter of other disciplines, economics imperialism.

In short, Blaug's notion of a formalist revolution raises a number of issues. If correct, it implies that there were both pre-revolutionary and post-revolutionary periods, as well as what is necessarily a relatively short period of revolutionary action itself. What is the nature and significance of this periodisation over and above what is presumably a passage from the informal, aformal, or is it non-formal, to the formal, and what were the mechanisms that brought this about?

The first of these questions – the nature of the revolution, if such it is – is open to a number of differing interpretations each of which is subject to contestation. Initially, there is the issue of what is meant by formalism itself, as covered in part amongst other things by the collection in the *Economic Journal* edited by Dow (1998). Rigorous and scientific argument is not restricted to, nor guaranteed by, mathematical expression or models based on deductivism, as there are requirements of conceptual consistency with empirical evidence and of the relationship between different parts of the analysis (a most obvious example being the need to invent a fictional

Walrasian auctioneer). Mainstream economists tend to view formalism in extremely narrow terms, if reflecting upon matters of methodology at all, see below. Essentially, protestations to the contrary in terms of attachment to realism through empirical evidence and the need to translate formal into informal discourse, Krugman (1998) for example within the collection, formalism has been seen as equivalent to science and rigour and, more important, whatever economists do in practice. All seem to accept that there is a role for formalism, however it be defined, but that, in and of itself, it is both insufficient and not liable to be exercised in practice in pure form other than in the deductive world of Debreu's interpretation of general equilibrium theory, see previous chapter.

In short, the formalist revolution involved a shift both in economics and how it interpreted formalism itself. Inevitably, for example, of significance is the changing status of mathematics in scientific inquiry in general – across social as opposed to natural science – and in application to economics in particular. Whilst mainstream economists have an image of themselves as rigorous and scientific in view of their use of mathematics, methodological debate within – or, more exactly, around – economics has pinpointed certain limitations that are imposed by the increasing reliance upon mathematical methods. These include undue attachment to deductivism, determinism and conceptual impoverishment, see Chick and Dow (2001) for an overview.

To these can be added two further considerations. First, the use of mathematics within economics is extremely limited. A colleague of ours has deplored the way in which economics has become the plaything of third-rate mathematicians.[5] This is certainly true in the sense of the breadth of mathematics that is used in economics, deriving primarily from calculus and statistical methods. Whilst the breadth and depth of the mathematics used by economists has undoubtedly ratcheted up across all levels of the subject, it almost certainly has not kept pace with developments within mathematics itself. It is extremely easy for a mathematician,[6] or someone from the natural sciences trained in the necessary techniques, to become an economist, but the transition in the opposite direction is, we suspect, almost unknown.

In addition, complementary to the limited use and knowledge of mathematics, economics has displayed little or no interest in the inner limitations of mathematics itself, as opposed to the greater (if now marginalised) attention paid to the limitations in applying it to economics. As argued elsewhere, problems in the philosophical foundations of mathematics – those associated with Russell's paradox – mean that there are corresponding problems in the application of mathematics to social science and so to economics, Fine (2007d).[7] Specifically, if we build up our theory from the aggregated behaviour of individuals or individual interactions, this imposes certain limitations upon the *social* properties that can be derived. In particular, for example, concepts such as liquidity, institutions, the state and identity cannot be satisfactorily accommodated within a mathematical approach, not as such, but in one that relies upon methodological individualism as does, of course, the core of mainstream economics, and increasingly so in its deployment of mathematics in practice. Not surprisingly, the leap from aggregation over individuals to the social is one of faith, and unsatisfactory in both conceptual and mathematical logic.[8]

It follows that, in the wake of the formalist revolution, if not before, the use of mathematics by economics has been for instrumental and deductive purposes and, as such, has been highly selective and careless in its use of mathematics. This has been most strongly highlighted, and criticised, by the critical realist school of economics, most closely associated with Tony Lawson. But it is also implicitly accepted by Backhouse (2007), for example, in part in opposition to critical realism on the grounds of the primary role that mathematics plays in providing models as instruments for problem solving rather than satisfying methodological niceties. One informal commentator on the implications of Russell's paradox for economics suggested that neither bridges nor economic theory fall down because of the philosophical foundations of mathematics. But the latter does shed light both on the nature and limitations of classical mechanics and neoclassical economics, irrespective of the motives, and success, of engineers and economists. At a more superficial level, the idea that the formalisation of economics has removed it from an attachment to real world problems has been strenuously denied by both Solow (2005) and Dasgupta (2002) in light of the extent to which theory has been heavily and increasingly attached to empirical work, Mäki (2002) for a broader assessment. There is a questionable assumption here of essentially equating realism (and problem-solving) with econometrics or more general interrogation of the data/facts. This is more evidence of the carelessness with which mathematical models *and* statistical methods are deployed, not least for example in the Barro-type regressions associated with new growth theory.[9] Indeed, there appears to be a reductionism of the issue of formalism within the mainstream as to whether mathematical modelling is attached to econometrics or not, with the presumption that, if so, the formalism is acceptable. The substantive content of the economic theory involved is simply overlooked.[10]

There is, then, a tension in much of the methodological literature around economics, in which formalism offers an excellent but not a unique illustration.[11] There are those (the heterodox, usually) who are more methodologically rounded and sophisticated and, generally critical of the mainstream to at least some degree, who tend to accept (and reasonably so) the virtues of formalism as a part of economic methodology and more generally. By contrast, those few from the mainstream who debate methodology at all remain much less well-informed over what is involved, and so readily accept the need for something more than formalism, most usually appealing to the extent to which the mainstream draws upon the empirical and engages in applied work. They see criticism as ill-informed and/or illegitimate, but, even more important, as a licence simply to get on with it.

As argued elsewhere, then, in light of the critical realism school, the nature of, and opposition to, mainstream economics and its mathematical methods cannot be taken much further without critically engaging with the substance of its economic theory, Fine (2004a, 2006a and 2007e). There are surely diminishing returns to debating both the nature of formalism within economics and what should be its more appropriate role. This is not least because mainstream economists themselves show little interest in (or self-awareness of) the nature of their own methodology and its weaknesses, or even that their claimed parallel with the methods of the natural sciences has long been superseded in principle and, to a large extent, in practice.[12] Thus, significantly, in his defence of orthodoxy, Dasgupta (2002, p. 57) opens by confessing that 'Most economists ... have little time for the philosophy of economics as an intellectual discipline. They have even less patience with economic methodology. They prefer instead to *do* economics ... There is much to be said for this habit ... I know of no contemporary practicing economist whose investigations have been aided by the writings of professional methodologists'. Further, neglect of history of economic thought is justified by reference to the methods of the natural sciences: 'You can emerge from your graduate studies in economics without having read any of the classics, or indeed, without having anything other than a vague notion of what the great thinkers of the past had written', for 'She reads Ricardo no more than the contemporary physicist reads James Clerk Maxwell', p. 61.

Given, though, that the formalisation of economics involved the heavy adoption of mathematical techniques, and that this also involved questionable change in both the form and content of economic theory, how (and why) was this brought about? The previous chapters have charted the intellectual process in the passage from classical political economy through the marginalist revolution to the Keynesianism and general equilibrium of the formalist revolution, and the corresponding division between macro and micro. To describe the creation of the technical apparatus that underpinned these developments (including its creation of a space for macroeconomics), we would emphasise a sort of methodological, theoretical and conceptual *implosion*, with the derivation of technical results from optimisation by individuals to aggregation over them to the economy as a whole taking absolute precedence over all other considerations.

And the corresponding outcome has been that the technical apparatus has taken precedence over all else – including conceptual content, realism, method, empirical evidence and alternative approaches. This is even so of mathematical rigour in the sense that, should such rigour come into conflict with the technical apparatus, then it is the latter that prevails. The evidence for this is compelling in the ubiquity of the technical apparatus across neoclassical economics, as well as the latter's disregard or contempt for anything that does not incorporate it. More specifically, we can see the imperative of the technical apparatus in the observation only in the breach of the results – even within neoclassical economics itself – that offer profound challenges to its continuing use. This begins with an acknowledgement of the failure to guarantee existence, uniqueness and stability of general equilibrium. Assume such problems away. The same applies to the profoundly destructive implications for use of production functions that arise out of the Cambridge critique. Yet neoclassical economics continues as if such lessons need not be learnt.[13] Much the same applies to the absence of money in anything other than a formal sense within economic models; the theory of the second best, the need to attach the technical apparatus to convexity and other assumptions, and the absence of factor reversals in trade theory, of externalities in many models, and of a mode of setting prices other than through a fictional auctioneer. The point is not that neoclassical economics never confronts these issues. On the contrary, the fact that it does so reveals how important they are in principle for its modelling and why they must be overlooked as a matter of formal convenience for the technical apparatus to be able to solve problems within a framework of its own making, Kirman (1989 and 1992) in context of representative individuals and optimisation.[14]

Indeed, the setting aside of the reservations that arise within the technical apparatus out of its own application are indicative of a much more profound difference across the watershed in economics signalled by the formalist revolution. Whilst marginalist principles were imploding upon the formalities required for derivation of the neoclassical technical apparatus, those involved in pushing forward and accepting it were often at pains to acknowledge both qualifications and reservations, both in content and scope of application.

Thus, for example, the theory, and consequences, of the optimising individual has its most profound if not earliest origins in the *Principles of Economics* of Alfred Marshall. There can be no doubt that he sought to establish an 'organon' of optimising individual behaviour. But he saw this as only part of economic and human behaviour and far from a basis on which to understand the functioning of the economic system as a whole. Indeed, forging a link between marginalism and macroeconomics proved to be a project that he failed to realise, not through his own inadequacies but because a solution would only lie along the unacceptable lines to be adopted following the formalist revolution. Significantly, though, Marshall's provision of an acceptable organon of marginalist principles to the economists of his own time depended upon rendering it palatable through stated limitations and reservations, not least in relation to historical and methodological concessions. By contrast, once the technical apparatus was in place, its expanding scope of application within economics, and across the subject matter of other social sciences, is increasingly taken for granted without apparent awareness of the reservations and limitations set aside in establishing it. For the latter, it is only necessary to observe the unconsidered confidence with which Robert Lucas (1987), for example, considers the functioning of the economy as a whole in terms of representative individuals alongside assertions to the effect that there is no such thing as macroeconomics distinct from microeconomics.

It follows that the changes in economic theory have in part been propelled by those who make them, inadvertently or not, by offering clear statements of reservations and limitations only for these to become secondary and, ultimately, discarded in the progress of the discipline. As a corollary, this also suggests that such changes can be rapid, within a generation or less, and become consolidated as a new conventional wisdom with little regard for what has gone before. A further corollary is that the explicit identification of such reservations by those pushing economic theory forward has decreased with the passage of time. In short, prior to the formalist revolution, hostile rejection of the reductionism attached to marginalist principles was relatively rare but it was complemented by its acceptance as a direction of research that corresponded at most to one *part* of an economic analysis. It was also clearly motivated by the idea that the rise of capitalism had historically and socially rendered such sort of behaviour more pervasive, especially within the market sphere, and worthy as such of exclusive attention. This is all apparent in case of Marshall but it is also true of Weber and Schumpeter in their search for 'social economics', of the Austrian School in their complementary appeal to uncertainty and inventiveness, and in Keynes and others in providing complementary material in macroeconomics, business cycle analysis, economic history and other areas of applied economics. This is not to deny presence of outright opposition to the newly emerging homo economicus from time to time. But the more general response was one of acceptance of the legitimacy of economic rationality as long as it be complemented by what was increasingly perceived as otherwise irrational although it is more correctly seen as social or non-rational to the extent that economic rationality is associated with the single-minded pursuit of self-interest through utility maximisation.

In addition, whilst the technical apparatus was confined only to a part of economics as a discipline, it was nonetheless increasingly detached and isolated from the other social sciences. This means that other forms of what would now be dubbed heterodox economics remained strong, American institutionalism, for example, at the time that the foundations for the formalist revolution were being laid, and the old or classic development economics could emerge untainted by the formalist revolution and its antecedents at the same time as the formalist revolution itself. And economic material and analyses found themselves located in other disciplines, not least with the emergence of economic history and the economic elements covered by sociology, see Chapters 8 and 12 for economic history and sociology, respectively.

In short, the process of creating the technical apparatus that provided the foundation for, and culminated in, the formalist revolution of the 1950s, did reflect something of an implosion in relation to the discipline of economics itself as well as in relationship to other disciplines. Apart from the reductionism required to establish the technical apparatus, it was also acknowledged only to have a limited scope of application and, equally, a limited scope of methodology. Consequently, the collection edited by Morgan and Rutherford (eds) (1998) can be seen as supporting the notion of a watershed in economic theory across the more narrowly conceived formalist revolution because the latter incorporated or induced a number of different additional elements. Before the event, considerable pluralism and plurality[15] prevailed across the discipline with open debates amongst different positions within what is now unduly homogenised in the vernacular as the old institutional economics, see Chapters 9 and 10. The commitment to an ethical economics with policy implications and inductive content was far more common and perceived to be part and parcel of a scientific method and to be engaged in the appropriate proportions according to subject matter. By contrast, after the event, the formalist revolution increasingly marked an attachment to, and a belief in the possibility of, a value-free and objective economic science based on deductive principles. Initially, at least, this prevailed at the microeconomic level, not surprisingly given how these principles were derived. But their stature was also enhanced by their perceived contribution to detailed planning during the war economy. Subsequently, claims of objectivity, neutrality and irrefutable scientific rigour allowed for negotiation of a degree of government intervention in the context of Cold War McCarthyism. Whilst Keynesian macroeconomics prospered, it was in diluted form relative to Keynes' own theoretical intentions and inclinations, but by virtue of its popular appeal, the relative weakness of the microeconomic principles in suggesting something else, the experience of inter-war depression, and despite the greater affront to McCarthyism for which it was presented as a communist front, Chapter 14.

The passage, then, to the formalist revolution is in complete contrast to the situation afterwards, with the implosion onto core principles followed by an *explosion* of scope of application of those principles. This explosion is grounded in what we term the historical logic of economics imperialism. Whilst the marginalist revolution began the process establishing the technical apparatus of the emerging neoclassical economics, it did so only by accepting its own limitations both analytically and in scope of application as the preconditions necessary to derive its formal results. If not absolutely, rational, optimising homo economicus was traditionally confined to the market and supply and demand of traded goods, and to microeconomic questions. This seems to have been taken for granted to a large extent, if not universally so, well after the formalist revolution, see Fine and Milonakis (2009). Such a compromise in practice and by tradition, however, over the intra- and inter-disciplinary boundaries around marginalist principles, was at odds with the universal nature, or unlimited scope of application of the technical apparatus itself. Utility and production functions are generalised, asocial and ahistorical, instruments without necessarily being confined to optimisation in response to the constraints imposed by prices and incomes.

As a result, once the formalist revolution had established itself through its corresponding technical apparatus, it was inevitable that the attempt should be made to recapture the ground conceded in scope of analysis. Over the post-war period there has been a dual process of colonising subject matter both within economics as a discipline and between itself and other disciplines.

The process of internal recolonisation is surely uncontroversial in the sense of being familiar to those who either are old enough to have lived through it to a greater or lesser extent and/or who have cared to look back upon it. Nonetheless, it is worth offering a few observations upon the process and on its substance and timing.

First, there can be little doubt that the formalist revolution promoted the recolonisation but, equally, it did not determine either its content or its timing. Thus, not least with the standard and universal IS/LM reduction of Keynes to the neoclassical synthesis, the focus on macroeconomic aggregates that make up aggregate supply and demand were undoubtedly formalised but not, in general, by appeal to optimising individuals attached to utility and production functions. Notably absent from IS/LM Keynesianism is Keynes' emphasis on uncertainty and his antipathy both to mathematical modelling and, especially, econometrics. Initially, though, Keynes' rejection of methodological individualism was both unknown and so, to a large extent, unwittingly accepted. Nonetheless, reductionism to individualism, with this label deployed by Coddington (1976), had to wait upon the reappraisal of Keynes, significantly offered as a radical rupture with the neoclassical synthesis. This enjoyed a brief but glittering career, Backhouse and Boianovsky (2005), until the stagflation of the 1970s and emergence of the monetarist counter-revolution, ultimately, the new classical economics, had dealt it a devastating blow (not least through perfect market clearing in place of fixed prices).

But this is not the full story. The first major application of the micro technical apparatus to the macroeconomy long preceded NCE, with the emergence of the old growth theory in the mid-1950s, and the presumption that an economy can be represented by a single production function (something carried over mindlessly into new growth theory). In addition, what is striking about the internal recolonisation is its limited progress relative to *micro-* not just macroeconomics. Of course, this is not true of its technical apparatus so much as the application of that apparatus to what were perceived to be applied topics – not least industrial economics, for example, and other fields presumed to incorporate a particularly heavy empirical or policy content. Applied economics, at both micro and macro levels, did not necessarily thrive without mathematical modelling, and econometrics, but nor did it fully, even partially on many occasions, embrace either methodological individualism or its corresponding neoclassical technical apparatus.

Comparison with today is marked, signifying some obstacle(s) to internal recolonisation in the past. It has been natural to offer explanation in terms of lower levels of technical capacity in the past, the most explicit case being that of the old or classic development economics as suggested by Krugman (1992). But we doubt whether the old classical development economists were incapable of matching Krugman in technique as opposed to not wishing to do so. Hence, the content, form and timing of the formalisation of economics following the formalist revolution is heavily influenced by a continuing, if eroding, commitment to its limited applicability within economics itself, especially in light of systemic and/or applied considerations (as opposed to undue reliance upon axiomatic deductive theory).

There are three compelling pieces of evidence, or symbolic illustrations, to support this view, although interpretation of them will remain controversial over their significance for the history of economic thought. One is the various contributions made by Coase (1937 and 1960) both on the existence of the firm and the settling of externalities through property rights in case of zero transaction costs. As is now apparent, these insights are now addressed within the technical apparatus of the mainstream but they did not become so fully incorporated until decades after the event, especially as far as the firm is concerned (and the firm was soon followed by institutions in general). Whilst much of the new institutional economics does remain free of mathematical formalism, especially as developed by Williamson, Coasean economics was only taken up by the mainstream itself when its subject matter was considered to be sufficiently suitable for reductionism to the optimising individual. Significantly, Coase himself was scathing about such 'blackboard economics', a term he coined, and preferred more inductive methods.

Coase offers a particularly sharp illustration of delayed formalisation of economics through its technical apparatus and beyond. A second is provided by rational expectations. For Muth's (1961) original contribution had to wait upon a decade or more for adoption within the new classical economics. Far from uncertainty being reducible to costly risk, macroeconomists in the Keynesian tradition must surely have retained some lingering understanding of, and commitment to, uncertainty as understood by Knight (and Keynes, Hayek and others). It is also a moot point whether general equilibrium theory, replete with a full set of timeless (or chronologically indefinite) contingent markets would have served to have promoted or impeded the attraction of risk in place of uncertainty within a systemic understanding of macroeconomics. But with new classical economics, expectations had been detached from uncertainty and attached to information in a way that is totally servile to reductionism to optimising behaviour.

A third example of delayed formalisation is the use of game theory, so important in recent times for the formalisation of so much microeconomics on the basis of its technical apparatus. Game theory was ready for adoption within economics at an early stage, certainly coincident with the formalist revolution itself. As revealed by Amadae (2003), it was heavily promoted by the RAND Corporation after the Second World War and, although familiar to economists situated there and at the Cowles Commission, made little inroad into economics. Whilst Amadae does see this promotion of game theory as an important element in the rise of rational choice theory within economics, and beyond, it did not have that effect immediately. It would, for example, have placed stable given preferences into question as the link between utility, optimising behaviour and choice would have been broken by interdependent strategic behaviour. By contrast, game theory has now become entirely acceptable but only by generally setting aside the conundrums associated with the definition and meaning of rationality that it implies.

As already indicated, just as the formalist revolution marked a watershed in the derivation and application of the neoclassical technical apparatus *within* economics, so it also signals a watershed in the relationship *between* economics and the other social sciences. With the increasing acceptance of the technical apparatus as a core component of the discipline, the historical logic of economics imperialism dictated that it should be applied more widely than within economics alone. This is now done with much less attention to the reservations and qualifications that were expressed in deriving the technical apparatus for the even more limited application to economic behaviour alone. Thus, paradoxically, there were much greater concerns expressed in making the assumptions to allow for the derivation and use of utility and production functions for the narrow application to supply and demand than there were in extending their application across the social sciences.

One example of this is provided by economic history and the rise of cliometrics, Fine and Milonakis (2003), Milonakis and Fine (2007), and a future volume on economic history in preparation for a fuller discussion. North (1963, p. 128), one of its pioneers, serves notice at an early stage of major change in the academic wind, 'A revolution is taking place in economic history in the United States'. It involves the application of economic theory to economic history. North suggests taking any leading article and seeing whether it is susceptible to formal modelling even if needing to rely upon the most favourable (unrealistic?) assumptions. More generally, a manifesto is provided for the fledgling field, North (1965, p. 91):

> In summary … we need to sweep out the door a good deal of the old economic history, to improve the quality of the new … and it is incumbent upon economists to cast a skeptical eye upon the research produced by their economic history colleagues to see that it lives up to standards which they would expect in other areas of economics.

Economic theory without history, then, is to provide the standard by which to judge (economic) history itself.

This excursion into economic history is a significant but far from isolated example of what we term the first phase of economics imperialism, with public choice theory being an equally prominent and early example. The leading proponent of such economics imperialism has been Gary Becker. Significantly, Demsetz (1997, p. 1) describes him as having 'earned Commander-in-chief ranking in the EEF (Economics Expeditionary Forces)'. But it would be a mistake to overlook that many economists by training, tradition and inclination remained wedded to more restrictive notions of the compass of economics, Swedberg (ed) (1990) offers examples. Their concerns did arise by way of (subsequently overlooked) reservations even whilst pushing forward the boundaries of economics imperialism. Akerlof (1990, p. 73), for example, even lampoons Becker in terms of his having learnt how to spell banana but not knowing when to stop.

In this light, it is paradoxical that it is with Akerlof's own contributions to economics that the floodgates are opened for a deluge of economics imperialism in a new phase, both in tempering reservations from within the discipline and in rendering its incursions more palatable to the colonised. In a nutshell, the information-theoretic approach to economics that he pioneered has yielded the following despite continuing to be based on the optimising behaviour of individuals in circumstances of imperfect markets:

1   Market failures explain economic structures.
2   Response to these explains non-market structures.
3   Hence history, institutions, culture, customs, norms, etc, matter and can be endogenised.

As a result, a new phase of economics imperialism has been prompted, literally promoting a whole range of 'new' fields or rejuvenating the old – new growth theory, new institutional economics, new economic geography, new labour economics, new development economics etc. Some of these build upon the old, others are new ventures. But what they all share in common is continuing commitment to the core technical apparatus. It can all be summarised by the two equations, if stretching the use of mi to two meanings to forge a parallel with Einstein:[16]

$$e = mi^2 \quad \text{and} \quad ss = e \quad \text{so that} \quad ss = mi^2$$

where e is economics, ss is social science and mi is both methodological individualism and market imperfections.

This has the effect of dividing the social sciences in relation to neoclassical economics, as previously, into three broad areas around the rational/non-rational divide. Pure models depend upon optimising agents only; mixed models somewhat inconsistently combine rational with non-rational motives, behaviour, culture, or whatever; and the rest that seeks to escape the rational/non-rational dualism as the basis for social theory. The boundaries of these first two categories have been symbiotically pushed out to a significant degree by the new phase of economics imperialism, as indicated by the range of new or newer fields, thereby appropriating both economic heterodoxy and the subject matter of other disciplines.

But these incursions do not necessarily prosper at the expense of the third category although there is presumably some crowding out involved as well as developments in parallel. The impact of economics imperialism across the social sciences is diverse, varying from discipline to discipline and from topic to topic, according to the continuing traditions and dynamics of scholarship. Economics imperialism is liable to be more influential to the extent that rational choice (a host factor) is already present and attention to the meaning of concepts (a hostile factor) is absent. But the latter is no guarantee of protection as economic imperialism can proceed by stripping out inter- pretative content of categories like culture in deference to its own meaningless technical apparatus. A striking example of this is provided by the economics of identity pioneered by Akerlof in which it appears as an otherwise unspecified variable in a utility function![17]

3 Concluding remarks

This is to paint a dismal picture within the dismal science and in its relations with other social sciences. But prospects are not exclusively bleak since the prospects for political economy within the other social sciences are currently brighter than for two or more decades, despite the challenges posed by eco- nomics imperialism. What political economy will be adopted and how is also remarkably open. This implies that the current generation of political econ- omists have a major responsibility in sustaining their critique of orthodoxy in and of itself and in constructively offering alternatives especially in rela- tion to interdisciplinarity – rather than retreating into a strategy for tenuous survival on or outside the margins of orthodoxy. By the same token, there is responsibility amongst non-economists to take political economy seriously rather than to dismiss all economic analysis as inevitably reductionist simply because it is dominated by an orthodoxy which is irretrievably so. Indeed, this book has sought to highlight the rich mixture of options open to those seeking to wed political economy to an apposite methodological, social and historical content.

Notes

1 Introduction

1 We have not always used first editions of works when citing them but, if of importance, we indicate first date of publication in square brackets usually only on the first occasion on which a citation appears in the book. We also indicate first date of publication in list of references although note that many of Marx's major works were not published in his lifetime. For some works, as indicated, we list the original date of publication in the text and references but accompanied by the later source used for page citation.

2 Gavin Wright, reporting on a symposium among economists and economic historians which took place at the meetings of the American Economic Association in 1984.

2 Smith, Ricardo and the first rupture in economic thought

1 See opening to Chapter 6 for these differences.

2 'By classical political economy I mean all the economists who, since the time of W. Petty, have investigated the real internal framework … of bourgeois relations of production, as opposed to the vulgar economists who only flounder around within the apparent framework of those relations … and seek there plausible explanations of the crudest phenomena for the domestic purposes of the bourgeoisie', Marx (1976 [1867], pp. 174–5n). Indeed, he pinpointed the year 1830 as the closing year of classical political economy and the beginning of 'vulgar economy'. In the former he included Smith and Ricardo while, in the latter, writers such as McCulloch, Senior, Bastiat and followers of Say, Dobb (1940, pp. 133–4).

3 '"The classical economists" was a name invented by Marx to cover Ricardo and James Mill and their *predecessors*, that is to say for the founders of the theory which culminated in Ricardian economics. I have become accustomed, perhaps perpetrating a solecism, to include in the "classical school" the *followers* of Ricardo, those, that is to say, who adopted and perfected the theory of the Ricardian economics, including (for example) J. S. Mill, Marshall, Edgworth and Prof. Pigou', Keynes (1973 [1936], p. 3n). Note though that Keynes' rough and ready identification of classical political economy with acceptance of Say's Law served his own polemical and analytical purposes of rejecting it in his *General Theory* through construction of his own stylised great divide in the history of economic thought.

4 See entries on various economists in Pressman (1999).

5 For Tabb (1999, pp. 18–19), classical political economy is first and foremost a *social* science whereas, with the change from political economy to economics,

economic science purports to become a social *science*. This corresponds to what he calls the A mode and the B mode of doing economics. The A mode 'is bolstered by a theorem-driven mathematical fundamentalism', while B mode economics 'is historical, institutional, and comparative'. This division, according to Tabb, reflects two ways of doing science in general. Chemistry and physics belong to the A mode, 'in which replicable experimental knowledge forms the core', while geology and paleontology to the B mode, 'in which history and detailed distinctions are central', p. 17. This, of course, begs the question of what exactly is meant by *science* and by *social science,* and whether each lives up to its own standards however valid and appropriate. Interestingly, Arrow (1986), a leading exponent of neoclassical general equilibrium theory, has also drawn the analogy between economics and geology. He does so by asking 'Is economics a subject like physics, true for all time, or are its laws historically conditioned?'. If the latter, then for Arrow, geology certainly is a better analogy for economics since it is 'in good measure a study of the specific. Geology is an historical study and a fascinating one', pp. 14–16. From Jevons' metaphor of 'statical mechanics' (see Chapter 6) to Veblen's and the institutionalists' analogy between economic investigation and evolutionary biology (see Chapters 9 and 10), such parallels have a long history in economics, with rough and ready correspondence between divisions between the sciences and between inductive and deductive methods across the social sciences. Such metaphors are useful as heuristic devices but they can also obscure the issues involved. In Tabb's analogies, for example, the divisions in the natural sciences to which he refers seem to be those between the experimental and the descriptive as opposed to the deductive and inductive methods in economics. In this respect, Lloyd (1986, p. 10) strikes the right note when, in referring to social history, he proclaims that:

> Some natural sciences such as cosmology, geology, and evolutionary biology are just as historical as social history and just as scientific as physics. It is not physics that should be our model, or geology, but the *idea* of science as a quest about causality – a quest that proceeds through the complex process of reasoning, theory, observation, and constant criticism.

6 Note here that historical investigation is a necessary companion of induction only in the social sciences.

7 And Dow continues: 'It is, however, only in mathematics that it is possible to establish incontestable axioms, because mathematics alone is a definitional system which can be pursued totally independently of observations of reality. The axiomatic method is aesthetically appealing because it allows a complete logical system to be constructed. Within this mode of thought, mathematics is thus regarded as the apex of scientific purity'.

8 For a more detailed account in these terms, see Fine (1982, ch. 2) and also Chapter 4.

9 See also Redman (1997, p. 207).

10 Of course, this comment at this time, and the (focus on the) wish to strike a balance between induction and deduction, as opposed to other methodological considerations, is characteristic of the passage through the marginalist revolution as the balance shifts in economics towards the deductive, see especially Chapters 6 and 7.

11 This distinction between 'orthodox' and 'theoretical or conjectural' history originates with another member of the Scottish historical school, Dugald Stewart, see Skinner (1975).

12 'These principles [of rent, profit and wages]', he writes in a letter to Trower, 'are so linked and connected with everything belonging to the science of political

economy that I consider the just view of them as of the first importance. It is on this subject, where my opinions differ from the great authority of Adam Smith, Malthus, etc. that I should wish to concentrate all the talent I possess, not only for the purpose of establishing what I think correct principles but of drawing important *deductions* from them', Ricardo (1952a, pp. 315–16), emphasis added.

13 H.S. Foxwell (1909), the British historical economist, in the Preface to Andreades' *History of the Bank of England*, designates Ricardo as the leader of the ahistorical school in economics, hinting at Marshall. Perhaps it was the Physiocrats who attempted the first deductive model in the history of economic thought, in the form of Quesnay's *Tableau Économique*.

14 Of course, this no doubt reflects the total rejection of the principal *theoretical* contribution of Ricardo, his absolute commitment to the labour theory of value.

15 One of the first to develop the distinction between economic science and ethics, long before J.N. Keynes, was Richard Whately in his book *Introductory Lectures in Political Economy*, first published in 1831, Karagiannis (1995, pp. 88–9).

3 Mill's conciliation, Marx's transgression

1 See also Chapter 12.

2 In view of this, it is ironic that, according to Blaug (1980, pp. 73–7), when Mill comes to apply these methodological principles in practice in his *Principles,* most of the predictions of the Ricardian system – rising price of corn, rising rents, a constant level of real wages and a falling rate of profit – as well as some of its premises – the growth of population at a rate at least as fast as the growth of foodstuffs – had already been empirically refuted.

3 According to Zouboulakis (1997, pp. 13, 11–12), Mill was 'aware of the fact that economic laws have a limited range of application, essentially because their premises are culturally bound'.

4 See also the articles by Kincaid (2005a and b), Callinicos (2005), Murray (2005), Bidet (2005), Hunt (2005), Albritton (2005) and the riposte by Arthur (2005), in the symposium organised around Arthur's book in *Historical Materialism*.

5 The discussion of the role of history in Marx's work draws on Milonakis (1990, ch. 3).

6 See also Fine (1979 and 1980b) in debate with Morishima and Catephores (1975 and 1976) and Catephores (1980), and Milonakis (1995).

7 The following draws on Milonakis (1990, ch. 8).

8 In the *The German Ideology*, Marx and Engels (1972 [1847], pp. 18–21) have substituted the Asiatic with the 'tribal' mode of production.

4 Political economy as history: Smith, Ricardo, Marx

1 See Fine (2002b and 2004b) for an overview of Kuhn and its application to economics, especially for its implications for the present phase of economics imperialism as scientific revolution.

2 See Skinner's (1970) introduction to Smith's *Wealth of Nations* for a penetrating overview of Smith's system of thought as a whole.

3 For a fuller account in general and on raw materials in particular, see Fine (1982, Chapter 5) where this treatment of what for Marx is constant capital is shown to give rise to further insights *and* problems.

4 See also Hahn (1973, p. 12), 'It now seems to me clear that there are logical difficulties in accounting for the existence of agents called firms at all unless we allow there to be increasing returns of some sort'.

5 The merits of this position and the debate over the transition is taken up in our future book on economic history. Note, however, with the exception of the so-

called historical transformation problem, how little value theory enters into these debates. See Engels (1981), Meek (1973b), Morishima and Catephores (1975 and1976), Fine (1979 and 1980b), Catephores (1980) and Milonakis (1995).

6 More exactly, Ricardo's value in agriculture is determined by the worst application of capital in use, which may be extra capital on a better land already in use. The details of the so-called intensive margin need not detain us.

7 For overviews of value theory and its implications from various points of view, see Aglietta (1979), Dobb (1940), Elson (ed) (1979), Fine (ed) (1986), Fine and Harris (1979), Fine *et al.* (2004), Fine and Saad-Filho (2004), Foley (1986), Lebowitz (1992), Lee (1993), Meek (1956), Rosdolsky (1977), Rubin (1972), Saad-Filho (2002), Steedman (1977), Steedman *et al.* (1981), Sweezy (1968) and Weeks (1981).

8 This aspect of the commodity is taken up at length in Fine (2002c, Chapter 3) in the context of consumption.

9 For an account of Marx's rent theory along these lines, see Fine (1979 and 1980a), and for the evolution and demise of rent theory more generally, Fine (1983).

10 On cliometrics as the neoclassical's revenge on the separated discipline of economic history, see our book currently in preparation on economic history.

11 For presentation and critique of which, see Fine (2001) and subsequent work on social capital. Note that within the social economics offered by the 'economic approach', we are now even offered the idea of 'habit capital', Becker and Murphy (2001, p. 17).

5 Not by theory alone: German historismus

1 The first part of the title of this chapter is borrowed from the title of Balabkins' (1988) book.

2 As argued in Chapter 7, Section 2, marginalism was not really consolidated until the end of the nineteenth century after the publication of Marshall's *Principles* in 1890, after having gathered some momentum in the 1980s, the decade when the *Methodenstreit* took place, through the work of Wieser, Böhm-Bawerk and Wicksteed.

3 By 'early' marginalists, we mean especially Walras, Jevons and Menger and those most closely associated with them. They used marginalist principles but in very different economic visions from one another. By 'old' marginalists, we mean Marshall and his followers who prescribed to a core set of marginalist principles but also considered that they could not exhaust economic analysis. See Chapters 6 and 7.

4 See Pearson (1999, p. 556) for francophone, Italian and US branches of the school, although 'all these counterparts to the German literature shared its brief moment of prestige in the late nineteenth century, and all were similarly swept into relative obscurity by the formalization and professionalization of the discipline early in the twentieth century'.

5 There has, however, been a limited revival of interest in the writings of the Historical School recently. See references in following note and Caldwell (2004, pp. 339–40).

6 On the Historical School, see for example, Schumpeter (1994, pp. 807–24), Roll (1992, pp. 276–83), Screpanti and Zamagni (1993, pp. 91–3, 161–2, and 170–3), Tribe (1995, ch. 4), Koslowski (ed) (1995), Lindenfeld (1997, ch. 5), Pearson (1999), Grimmer-Solem and Romani (1999), Hodgson (2001, chs. 4, 5, 6, 7 and 9), and Shionoya (ed) (2001). On Schmoller, see Balabkins (1987 and 1988), Shionoya (1995), Giouras (1992) and Psychopedis (1992). On Knies, see Kobayashi (2001).

7 But see later discussion of Roscher as unrepresentative of the school he founded.

8 Note that 'historicism' is here used as equivalent to the German *Historismus* rather than the older version 'historism' which was used by Schumpeter, see also

Betz (1988, p. 411n). Lenger (1997, p. 147) thinks that the term 'historism' is preferable, on the grounds that 'historicism' is closely associated with Popper's use and critique of it. Historicism in the former sense or 'historism' or the 'historical method' as Schumpeter variously called it, refers to the programme of the Historical School which, as will be seen shortly, consists in 'the results of, and in generalizations from, historical monographs' as a way of constructing scientific economics, Schumpeter (1994, pp. 807–8). Historicism in Popper's (1986, p. 45) sense, on the other hand, refers to 'the study of the operative forces and, above all, of the laws of social development [which] could be described as historical theory, or as theoretical history, since the only universally valid social laws have been identified as historical laws. They must be laws of process, of change, of development'. In other words, Popper uses the concept in broadly similar terms to the notion of 'philosophical history' or what Schumpeter has called *histoire raisonée*, see Chapters 3 and 11. As will be seen below, the attempt to provide a stages approach to economic development is also part of the programme of many members of the Historical School, but not its defining feature. It is no accident that Popper in his critique of historicism does not refer to the Historical School at all, but rather to Karl Marx's theory of history, p. 51, and see Chapter 3 above, and to Comte's and Mill's 'laws of succession', p. 116. For Comte's version of historicism see Moore (1999, pp. 58–9).

9 The so-called 'social question' refers to the problems created by the rapid changes taking place in capitalist societies of the nineteenth century associated with rapid urbanisation and industrialisation. These problems include the housing problem, the phenomenon of mass poverty and the labour question, Giouras (1992, pp. 128–31).

10 See Esping-Andersen (1990) and Fine (2002c) for a critique.

11 On the importance of the ethical dimension in the writings of the German Historical School, and of Schmoller in particular, see Betz (1995) and Koslowski (2002).

12 Through authors that include Hermann, Hufeland, Schäffle, Knies and Rau.

13 This question of whether the historical movement really formed a school has bothered historians of economic thought and is still being hotly debated. See, for example, the recent exchange between Pearson (1999 and 2001) and Caldwell (2001). To answer this question one has to ask some other questions first. What distinguishes one school from another? Does this involve homogeneity of method, content, purpose, subject matter, external environment, contemporary and/or future recognition of such, etc.? If so for all of these, we are not liable to be able to identify a single school of thought in any object of study let alone economics so demanding are the criteria if all have to be satisfied. For each of these elements itself has multiple dimensions so that the demands of intellectual homogeneity are heavy, and hardly liable to be met across numbers of writers offering significant contributions over time. In part, what is and what is not designated as school, and who belongs or not, depends upon convention and convenience. We are open to accept the notion of an Historical School, or schools, but do so despite, in part because of, dissonance within, and blurred boundaries around, the school. More rewarding, though, is to identify and to emphasise such heterogeneity as well as homogeneity within the school and in its relations with other schools.

6 Marginalism and the *Methodenstreit*

1 On the distinction between 'early' and 'old' marginalism see Chapter 5, note 3.

2 In his careful study, Streissler (1990, pp. 38–40) argues that it is not true that Menger's book received unfavourable reviews, but he fails to cite Schmoller's review. He cites one important, mostly favourable review, however, and the report

of the Vienna faculty for Menger's appointment as associate professor in 1873, to the effect that his book 'had met with very favourable reception by the experts', p. 39.

3 An exception that proves the rule is the school of American institutionalism, see Chapters 9 and 10.

4 The word marginalism itself was coined by John Hobson in 1914, Howey (1973, p. 14).

5 The concept of marginal utility had already been developed in 1844 by Dupuit in France, in 1854 by Gossen in Germany and, even before them, by Lloyd and Longfield in 1834 and Senior. Despite this early invention, however, there are two strong reasons why its use by Jevons and Walras amounts to (re)invention. First, when the concept was first invoked, it failed to have any impact whatsoever. Second, Walras came into contact with Dupuit's work only in 1874, while Jevons 'discovered' Gossen in 1878, only after they themselves had independently deployed the concept anew. All these developments have led Blaug (1997, pp. 287–9) to wonder whether the invention of marginal utility has been a case of 'multiple discovery' in Merton's sense of the word without, however, coming to a clear conclusion. See also Blaug (1973, pp. 6–7 and 2001, p. 159) and Howey (1973, pp. 25–6).

6 Black (1973, pp. 98–9) also argues in similar vein:

> The term 'marginal revolution' is attractive, and useful if employed with due caution, but so interpreted, it relates to a process and not an event comparable say to the Paris Commune. That process was neither begun nor ended in 1871, though it was certainly significantly forwarded.

And for Blaug (1973, p. 11), 'to try to explain the origin of marginal utility revolution in the 1870's is doomed to failure: it was not a marginal *utility* revolution; it was not an abrupt change, but only a gradual transformation in which old ideas were definitely never rejected; and it did not happen in the 1870's'.

And, last, for Dobb (1940, p. 133), 'If we fix our attention ... on the shift towards subjective notions and towards the study of exchange-relations in abstraction from their social roots, we shall see that essential changes came earlier in the century, or at any rate the commencement of tendencies which later assumed a more finished shape'.

7 Jevons' attempt to establish economics as a natural science could well be related to his own experience and training in natural sciences and especially in chemistry and meteorology, Black (1973, pp. 103, 106). See also White (2004).

8 Both Jevons (1957, pp. xxviii–xliii) and Walras pay tribute to the mathematical economists who wrote before them but who were then forgotten, especially Dupuit, Cournot, Gossen and von Thünen. As Jevons (1957, p. xliii) writes in 1879: 'The unfortunate and discouraging aspect of the matter is the complete oblivion into which this part of the literature of Economics has fallen, oblivion so complete that each mathematico-economic writer has been obliged to begin almost *de novo*.'

9 It is worth emphasising here, a point to which we will return in Section 3 below, that Menger does not accept the use of mathematics in economics.

10 See also Searle (2005, p. 1):

> When Lionel Robbins ... tells us that 'Economics is a study of the disposal of scarce commodities', he takes for granted a huge invisible institutional ontology. Two dogs fighting over a bone or two schoolboys fighting over a ball are also engaged in the 'disposal of scarce commodities', but they are not central to the subject matter of economics.

11 The word marginal was actually first introduced in English by Wicksteed in 1888 in his *Alphabet of Economic Science*, and adopted by Marshall in his *Principles*. It

was Wieser, however, who first introduced it in German (*Grenz-nutz*) as a translation of Jevons' 'final degree of utility', Caldwell (2004, p. 21n). Before this, the terms actually used were 'final degree of utility', 'final utility', 'terminal utility' by Jevons, 'importance of the least important of satisfactions' by Menger and 'intensity of the last unit satisfied' or '*rareté*' by Walras, see Howey (1973, p. 30).

12 This change had already been announced and implemented by Jevons in the second edition of his *Principles in 1879*, although he thought it 'undesirable to alter the title page of the book', Jevons (1957, p. xv).

13 According to Vaughn (1978, p. 60), 'it is widely recognised that Carl Menger was one of the most influential and least read and understood economists of the nineteenth century'. And she goes on to add that 'outside of standard history-of-thought textbooks, virtually the only authorities to have provided extensive analysis of Menger's works in English were Friedrich Hayek, George Stigler, and Emile Kauder'.

14 Ikeda locates his discussion in the context of a common vulgar interpretation of Smith by both Menger and the Historical School.

15 As Böhm-Bawerk (1891, pp. 361–2) puts it, 'in the conviction of the inadequacy of the classical political economy, the Austrian economists and the adherents of the Historical School agree. But in regard to the final cause of the inadequacy, there is a fundamental difference of opinion which has led to a lively contention over methods'.

16 As we shall in Chapter 8, it was a different story with the British Historical School which became more empiricist rather than more theoretical as time went by.

17 According to Popper (1986, pp. 28–9), 'methodological nominalists hold that the task of science is only to describe how things behave', while methodological essentialism refers to 'a school of thinkers ... [which] was founded by Aristotle, who taught that scientific research must penetrate to the essence of things in order to explain them'. It is interesting to note here that although both J. S. Mill and Menger espoused the same abstract, a priori method for economics, their philosophical starting points differed widely ranging from Mill's empiricism to Menger's Aristotelian essentialism, Wade Hands (2001, p. 39).

18 Kirzner (1990, pp. 94–7) refers to all the evidence in favour of this interpretation.

19 See also Koot (1980, pp. 178–9 and 1987, pp. 2, 10) and Deane (1978, p. 94).

7 The Marshallian heritage

1 Citing White (1994).

2 This is from an essay, 'Economics at LSE in the 1930s: A Personal View', first published in 1982.

3 See Lawson (1997 and 2003) and Lewis (ed) (2004a) for example.

4 See discussion in Coase (1994, ch. 10), first published in 1972: 'The Appointment of Pigou as Marshall's Successor'. It is apparent that Marshall also blocked the creation of an extra chair to accommodate Foxwell, although this may also have been due to differences over trade policy, with Marshall in favour of promoting free trade in contrast to Foxwell. Coase (1994) takes this view sufficiently seriously to dispute it.

5 See also Souter (1933b, p. 97), who refers to Marshall as 'the most profound and massive mind that has thus far devoted itself to the problems of economic science'. But, like Keynes, if for different reasons (see footnote 10), he finds that the introduction of money, credit and trade had yet to be attained, the reason being Marshall's dedication to statics rather than evolutionary dynamics with which Marshall's economic 'organon' needed to be integrated. Souter (1933b, p. 4) does, however, quote Marshall to the effect that 'What I take to be a Static state is ... a position of rest due to the equivalence of opposing forces which tend to produce motion', very different from equilibrium as the long run of today's economics.

6 By the 'theory of mechanics', Marshall is most probably referring to engineering rather than the laws of mechanics in a Newtonian sense, which were universal principles. See Marshall (1959, p. 642).

7 For all of this, see Pigou (1953, ch. 1) for example.

8 Cited in Maloney (1976, p. 440).

9 Indeed, Collini *et al.* (1983, pp. 253–4) view Marshall as attaching himself to the English tradition, one totally opposed to 'unalloyed deductivism'. Ricardo is noted as an exception, and Marshall's suggestion cited that 'the faults and virtues of Ricardo's mind are traceable to his Semitic origins; no English economist has had a mind similar to his'!

10 For striking evidence of which, see Pigou's (1953, Chapter IV) partial defence of Marshall against Keynes on the grounds that his *Principles* are concerned with micro alone, and that 'his more realistic approach' in *Money, Credit and Commerce*, by contrast, is a more worthy target being guilty of 'falling into serious error' for overlooking 'the set-up proper for short-period analyses, [for which] the proportion of available labour (and capital) actually at work obviously cannot be treated as constant', p. 34.

11 Marshall's failure to move to macro does not indicate lack of intention nor effort but lack of success. For, as Coase (1994, p. 128) observes, in an essay first published in 1975 ('Marshall on Method'), Marshall was extremely sensitive to criticism, suffering ('the agonies of hell when he discovered that he had made a mistake') following the childhood experience of an overbearing father.

12 This in response to Cunningham's (1892b) claim that Marshall's principles involve a perversion of economic history. See next chapter.

13 Cited in Ackerman (2004b, p. 91) who also correspondingly observes the lack of development of the (mainstream) economics of consumption, p. 86. See also Fine and Leopold (1993) and Fine (2002c).

14 As Persky (2000, p. 100) puts it, 'The empiricism of American institutionalism, far from retreat, was just gaining steam in 1900. Such research efforts were largely unaffected by the neoclassical emergence'. Further, he draws the distinction between a narrow marginalism and a rounded neoclassicism, for which 'the defining characteristic of neoclassicism, as opposed to mechanistic marginalists, lay in neoclassicism's insistence on not deserting the classical attention to broad historical explanation', p. 105. Indeed, 'At bottom, the early American neoclassicists showed themselves to be open-minded to a wide range of analytical approaches and policy suggestions', p. 107.

15 His own book, Hutchison (1960)[1938], does not seem to count! But see also Chapters 2 and 3 for other major methodological treatises of the classical period.

16 See also his Appendix 4, an entry for the deductive method reproduced from the Palgrave's *Dictionary of Political Economy*.

17 See Chapter 14, and for animal spirits in Keynes, and its neglect by economists until after 1980 when it was taken up in the context of rational expectations and the boom in stock markets, see DiMaggio (2002).

18 Coase (1994, p. 152) also reports:

> J. N. Keynes adds in his diary (a very typical reference on his part to Marshall): 'Marshall is the most exasperating talker I know. He will agree with nothing you say & argues & dogmatises so as to drive one wild'.

19 See Chapter 8.

20 In this and other light, it is hard to agree with Coase that 'when interpreting Marshall, one has to realise that he commonly becomes somewhat evasive whenever there is a hint of disagreement or controversy, a trait I attribute to the strict discipline exercised by his father when he was a child. But whatever the reason,

Marshall often states his views in a way which tends to minimise differences in viewpoint', p. 168. It seems more accurate to suggest that once feeling impelled to offer his viewpoint, Marshall can be incapable of being anything other than blunt, brutal and single-minded.

8 British historical economics and the birth of economic history

1 'British' is here defined to include Ireland before 1921, Backhouse (2004, pp. 108, 110). The more commonly used term 'English historical school' is a misnomer, according to Hodgson (2001, p. 66n), since two of its members (Leslie and Ingram) were in fact Irish and one (Rogers) Scottish. Hodgson uses the term 'the historical school of the British Isles' instead. It is, however, a moot point to what extent and in what way such differing national origins were reflected in their contributions.

2 According to Maines' historical jurisprudence, law was the outcome of slow historical evolution as societal institutions developed from status to contract. This is contrasted with Bentham's approach according to which law is the result of human design. The difference between Maines and the German Historical School of jurisprudence, which influenced the German Historical School, is that whereas the latter stressed the unique character of historical trajectories, Maines was willing to arrive at generalisations based on the comparative method, Moore (1995, pp. 71–2).

3 See also discussion of a dog and his bone on p. 97.

4 The letter continues: 'On Monday I hope to call on you a few minutes before 4 at 4 Savile Row if fine. Should there be much rain I take it for granted you will not come. The Statist had a civil paragraph on my article in the Fortnightly, taking my criticism of the Marriages Movement & the decennial change alleged in the management of mercantile firms, in good part.
Yours ever sincerely
TECLeslie'
Also bound into the volume is a letter to Mr Jevons from Reilly (indistinguishable initials) of 21, Delahay Street, Westminster, SW, (this is Leslie's home address from Preface to the book), dated Friday, 27 January, 1882, to the effect that 'I deeply regret to say I have a telegram today stating Leslie's death this morning. Sincerely yours'.

5 See also Leslie (1877, p. 252), written in response to Bagehot's death, in part confirming earlier observations as well:

> Mr. Lowe affirmed that 'political economy belongs to no nation, is of no country, and no power can change it.' Mr. Bagehot, on the contrary, emphatically limited the application of the postulates of the à priori and deductive method to England at its present commercial stage. And within this limit he further circumscribed and qualified what he termed 'the fundamental principle of English political economy,' by assuming 'only that there is a tendency, a tendency limited and contracted, but still a tendency, to an equality of profits through commerce'.

6 See also p. 148.

7 The expression is reminiscent of Marx's (1976 [1867], p. 104) in his Preface to the French edition of Volume I of *Capital*, where, referring to his own work and the difficulty represented to the reader by the deployment of his new method, he states that 'There is no royal road to science, and only those who do not dread the fatiguing climb of its steep paths have a chance of gaining its luminous summits'. See also Cunningham (1892a, p. 16) where he draws the contrast with the supposedly immutable laws of the natural sciences.

8 See discussion in Collini et al (1983, pp. 324–5).
9 He continues to explain why he has not responded to criticisms of his work for 'in the aggregate they are not much less bulky than the unwieldy Volume to which they refer: I do not work fast; and if I attempted to reply as I should wish to do, my progress with writing my second Volume, which is now slow, would altogether cease'. Note that the second Volume was never completed, see Chapter 6.
10 What follows in this Section draws on Milonakis (2006).
11 Coleman himself borrows the 'reformist' label from Clarke (1978). What follows draws from Coleman's (1987) book.
12 See for example Clapham's (1930) *magnus opus, An Economic History of Modern Britain*, and Ashton's (1959) *Economic Fluctuations in England 1700–1800*.
13 This was part of a trilogy devoted to the social effects of the Industrial Revolution.

9 Thorstein Veblen: economics as a broad science

1 Among those so influenced were Henry Carter Adams, J.B. Clark, Richard Ely and Edwin Seligman.
2 This is close to Schumpeter's verdict on Schmoller, according to which the latter's work is a prototype of economic sociology, Shionoya (1995, p. 67). See also Chapter 11, Section 2.
3 On Pareto and the distinction between rational (or logical, his own term) and non-rational (non-logical), see Chapter 12.
4 Having defined institutions as habits of thought, Veblen (1909, p. 241) goes on to suggest that 'institutions are an outgrowth of habit', thus adding some looseness in the way he treats these concepts, Walker (1977, p. 218).
5 For a critique of the psychological aspects of Veblen's work, see Rutherford (1984).
6 On conspicuous consumption, see Mason (1981, 1984 and 1998), Fine and Leopold (1993) and Fine (1994 and 2002c).

10 Commons, Mitchell, Ayres and the *fin de siècle* of American institutionalism

1 Rutherford (1990) in his introduction to the reprinted edition cites the last sentence as favourable opinion of Knight on Commons but the previous sentences, and much before, suggests otherwise in combination with a heavy dose of irony, if not sarcasm, see concluding remarks.
2 For example, whilst Veblen puts forward the theory of intangible assets, so it is also recognised legally for Commons (1990b, p. 651), 'The Supreme Court of the United States, when cases arose, rested its decisions on this same new phenomenon of intangible property, not, however, on Veblen's exploitation, but on its own historic concept of reasonable value'. And, he sees the corresponding Banker Capitalism, and its agglomeration of savings, as being able 'to finance these huge aggregations of machinery, and armies of employees, made feasible by science, invention, and worldwide markets'. But he adds, 'this is the reason, too, why the transition is being made from individualistic economics of the eighteenth and nineteenth century to what is coming to be named the "institutional" economics of corporations, unions and political parties', Commons (1950, p. 68). Yet, this anticipated rise of institutional economics, as opposed to twentieth century individualistic economics, was already dead in its tracks by the time these words were posthumously published!

11 In the slipstream of marginalism: Weber, Schumpeter and *Sozialökonomik*

1 Weber studied jurisprudence, the history of law and economics, while Schumpeter's training included law and economics. At some point in their careers they both

practised law, while Schumpeter also managed the finances of a princess during his stay in Cairo. Although both exhibited an immense interest in political affairs, only Schumpeter had a short and unsuccessful active participation when in 1919 he became Finance Minister of Austria, while Weber remained a 'frustrated politician', Aron (1970, p. 17) and Perlman (1999, pp. 105–6). General overviews of Weber's and Schumpeter's life and work can be found, inter alia, in Swedberg (1999) and Swedberg (1991a and 1991b), respectively.

2 'In a rare combination [Weber] united enormous erudition, great theoretical power and subtlety of thought, and concern with some of the central political and cultural problems of his time. Weber is often regarded as a "bourgeois Marx". This is an apt characterisation, both with regard to his intellectual stature and to his class position, Weber was a very class-conscious bourgeois', Therborn (1976, p. 270). 'This essay', says Catephores (1994, p.3), 'aims at presenting Schumpeter as a "bourgeois Marxist". The term is paradoxical, intentionally so: it aims at drawing attention to a small group of powerful thinkers of our century, who adopted many aspects of Marx's analytical approach but firmly rejected one thing: his commitment to the working class. They reinterpreted Marx from a bourgeois point of view trying, by this roundabout but very effective means, to confront and confound his great revolutionary challenge'.

3 Heinrich Dietzel was a student of Adolph Wagner and an important academic, although a sort of outsider. He tried to build an economic theory which would incorporate political, ethical and other elements. In the *Methodenstreit*, however, he took sides with Menger, accepting his theoretical abstractions, while at the same time rejecting his individualism. The term 'social economics' is considered to have originated in the work of Jean-Baptiste Say in 1828, while in Germany the word *Sozialökonomik* made its appearance in the writings of various authors such as Roscher, Knies, Menger and Sombart before it was used in the title of books by Dietzel and Wagner in 1895 and 1907, respectively, Swedberg (1998, pp. 177–8).

4 *Grundriss* consisted of more than a dozen volumes and covered more than 50 economists belonging to different schools of thought, from the Historical School (such as Max Weber and Karl Bücher) to the Austrian branch of the marginal utility tradition (Wieser). Hence, both sides of the *Methodenstreit* were represented, translating Weber's conciliatory stance in the 'Battle over Method' into practice. The pieces that have made a more lasting impression, however, are Weber's own *Economy and Society* (by far the most important work of the *Grundriss*), Schumpeter's work on the history of economics (*Economic Doctrine and Method*) and Wieser's book on economic theory (*Social Economics*), Swedberg (1998, pp. 153–62, 189–203).

5 Although Weber did occasionally make use of statistics, it occupied a minor role in his writings.

6 Raymond Aron (1970, pp. 185–6) arranges Weber's books in four different categories: first are his studies in 'methodology, history and philosophy' in which may be included his *Methodology of the Social Sciences*; second are his 'strictly historical works' which include his work on the eastern provinces of Germany, his study of the agriculture of the ancient world and his *General Economic History*; third come his studies in the sociology of religion; and last is his *magnus opus*, the major treatise on general sociology, *Economy and Society*.

7 Note though that *Modern Capitalism* was a product of Sombart's earlier, more radical period. Later on he became more conservative his politics moving from socialism to nationalism and, ultimately, to fascism.

8 This paragraph draws on Mitchell's (1929) review of Sombart's *Hochkapitalismus* (*High Capitalism*).

9 However, the conclusion he draws in referring to Weber's *Protestant Ethic* that, 'the whole of Max Weber's facts and arguments fits perfectly into Marx's system', contains a strong element of exaggeration.

10 See also p. 72.
11 See Marx in *Capital*, Volume 1, Chapter 28, on the dull compulsion of wage-labour once capitalism is established.

12 Positivism and the separation of economics from sociology

1 This is how he puts it in sarcastic style, Pareto (1935, vol. 3, p. 1413): 'Until economic science is much further advanced, "economic principles" are less important to the economists than the reciprocal bearings of the results of economics and the results of other social sciences. Many economists are paying no attention to such interrelations, for mastery of them is a long and fatiguing task requiring an extensive knowledge of facts; whereas anyone with a little imagination, a pen, and a few reams of paper can relieve himself of a chat on "principles"'.
2 Ominously, even at a much later stage with explicit reference to Robbins, Coase (1978, p. 207) advises that 'Economists do not study all human choices, or, at any rate, they have not done so yet'.
3 See also Davis (2003).
4 Note that, in this contribution, despite commitment to rhetoric, McCloskey's account of 'The Economics of Choice: Neoclassical Supply and Demand' is marked by no effective place either for the meaning of those choices or that they might lead to major socio-economic change as opposed to an 'analysis here [that] has moved from the mundanities of individual choice to the grandeur of general equilibrium', p. 157. Or, as she put it herself more specifically in account of her own sex change, 'But economists, whether conservative or radical, think the answer to a "why" question is always "some material advantage"', McCloskey (1999, p. 198).
5 And currently being revisited in terms of new or endogenous growth theory, with externalities and spill-overs, etc, for a critical assessment of which, see Fine (2000, 2003b and 2006b).
6 This passage does not appear to have survived into Robbins' second edition but is cited by Yonay (1998, p. 193).
7 See also next chapter, Section 3, for Wieser's advocacy of the need for theory to be supplemented by observation.
8 The Vienna Circle included a number of philosophically-minded mathematicians and scientists who took part in a seminar organised by the physicist and philosopher Moritz Schlick between 1925–1936. It included, amongst others, Rudolf Carnap, Philip Frank, Hans Hahn, Karl Menger (Carl Menger's son who was a mathematician) and the Marxist Otto Neurath, Caldwell (1982, p. 11) and Wade Hands (2001, pp. 72–4).
9 On the economic methodology of Mises, see Chapter 13. Hutchison's 'ultra deductivist' camp, is very similar, and follows closely, Machlup's (1955, pp. 5–6) 'extreme apriorist' camp, see below.
10 Commenting on this passage almost two decades later Hutchison (1956, p. 477) writes that 'This passage now seems to me rather old-fashioned, and even slightly crude and ungrammatical in the way it is formulated', without, however, distancing himself from its meaning in any substantive way. Later, however, he did distance himself from the doctrine of methodological monism, according to which the social sciences 'could and would develop in the same manner as physics and the natural sciences', cited in Blaug (1980, p. 99), although still insisting on 'Popper's methodological prescriptions for economics', p. 98.
11 Hausman (1992, p. 163n) lists a large number of works in economic methodology which 'uniformly condemned' Friedman's methodology, as compared to only three or four sympathetic studies.
12 Here we draw from Parsons' (1968b) *magnus opus* first published in 1937. Significantly, though, the substance first appears in a sequence of articles in the

Quarterly Journal of Economics, Parsons (1931, 1932 and 1934), something similar being totally inconceivable today for a prominent, mainstream journal of economics. On a personal note, the initial submission of a version of Fine (2002a) was returned by the editors without being refereed on the grounds that they did not wish to hold debate in the area of economics imperialism despite having published the triumphant Lazear (2000) in the first place!

13 A factor reflecting, for Parsons, Marshall's commitment to liberalism.

14 The ultimate put-down is provided by Wright Mills (1959, p. 40) who observed of Parsons' text 'one could translate the 555 pages of *The Social System* into about 150 pages of straightforward English. The result would not be very impressive'.

15 Most recently, see Lewis (2004b, p. 168) which, one suspects, is simply replicating a view of Parsons that has become an unexamined conventional wisdom. See also Guillén *et al.* (2003, p.6):

> The first fallacy is that the social is a realm separate from economics ... this fallacy was perpetuated not only by economists but by Parsons within the field of sociology.

13 From Menger to Hayek: the (re)making of the Austrian School

1 As Wieser (1967 [1927], p. 165) expresses it, 'in the presence of social institutions we must drop the rationalistic utilitarian assumption to which we might hold in the theory of the simple economy. The fundamental error of individualism appears in dealing with social institutions. It views individuals as though they were entirely independent and carry their activity entirely by their own will'.

2 Schneider (1985, p. 4), the editor of the first translation of the *Investigations* in English, mentions Menger's treatment of the origin and character of social institutions as 'the element that afforded me the motivation to bring out the present edition of Menger's book'.

3 See Lapavitsas (2003, ch. 6 and 2005) for a discussion of theories of the emergence of money, and of Menger's in particular as not having been attained, let alone surpassed, by more recent mainstream attempts to explain it as a spontaneous consequence of increasingly efficient barter.

4 Wieser refers to his *Über den Ursprung und die Hauptgesetze des wirthschaftlichen Werthes*, and Böhm-Bawerk to his 'Grundzüge der Theorie des wirtschaftlichen Güterwerts' which appeared in the *Jahrbücher für Nationalökonomie und Statistik*, see Howey (1973, p. 29)

5 As Hayek (1992a, p. 21) puts it talking about the climate in Vienna University at the time:

> Perhaps the most remarkable circumstance is how much the interest ... at a time when so many practical issues presented themselves, centred upon the purest of pure economics. Here the effects of the marginalist revolution ... were clearly felt.

6 This is how he puts it in his *Human Action*, Mises (1996 [1949], p. 4):

> Many authors tried to deny the value and usefulness of economic theory. Historicism aimed at replacing it with economic history; positivism recommended the substitution of an illusory social science which should adopt the logical structure and pattern of Newtonian mechanics. Both these schools agreed in a radical rejection of all achievements of economic thought. It was impossible for the economists to keep silent in the face of all these attacks.

7 Mises' use of the phrase 'universally valid science of human action' is rather misleading since in this he does not include history, which, however, he considers as part of the 'science of human action'. As we shall see below, he clarifies all this in his other work on methodology, *Human Action*, through the distinction between praxeology and history.

8 See also Popper's (1986) critique of historicism, and Chapter 3, Section 3 above.

9 Curiously neither Hutchison (1981, p. 210–19) nor Caldwell (2004, pp. 156–62) make any reference to this passage in considering Hayek's position in his *Monetary Theory* as leaning almost wholly towards theory. In our interpretation, theoretical analysis also plays the chief role in this work, but with the allowance of a possible falsificationist role for empirical work. If our interpretation is correct, then this brings into question Hutchison's view that there was a U-turn in Hayek's methodology brought about through Popper's influence after 1937, which was insignificant before that date. It might be true that Popper's influence in the direct sense was not there since his *Logic* was published after Hayek's book, but this does not preclude the possibility that something along falsificationist lines in embryonic form was developed independently and earlier by Hayek.

10 For a full exposition of Popper's views on these matters see his *The Logic of Scientific Discovery* (1959). For a summary statement of his position, see his *Poverty of Historicism* (1986, pp. 130–43).

11 Elsewhere, in commenting on a passage from Mises' (1981b [1922]) *Socialism* where the latter author states that liberalism 'regards all social cooperation as an emanation of rationally recognised utility', p. 418, Hayek (1981, p. xxiii) states that 'the extreme rationalism of this passage, which as a child of his time he could not escape from, and which he perhaps never fully abandoned, now seems to me factually mistaken'.

12 Zouboulakis (2002, p. 30), however, lumps together all members of the (neo-) Austrian tradition (including Mises) as belonging to this version of methodological individualism (subjective individualism). In doing so, he fails to apprehend the important differences between Hayek and Mises on this point, with the latter's adherence to an extreme form of rationalism, totally unsuitable as a candidate for this form of subjective individualism.

13 'The difference between this view, which accounts for most of the order which we find in human affairs as the unforeseen result of individual actions, and the view which traces all discoverable order to deliberate design, is the first great contrast between true individualism of the British thinkers of the eighteenth century and the so-called "individualism" of the Cartesian school', Hayek (1945a, p. 8).

14 Indeed, the title of his article 'The Results of Human Action but of Human Design' borrows from Adam Ferguson's *An Essay on the History of Civil Society*, where he states that 'Nations stumble upon establishments, which are indeed the result of human action, but not the execution of any human design'. And Ferguson goes on, 'the forms of society are derived from the obscure and distant origin; they arise, long before the date of philosophy, from the instincts, not from speculations of man ... We ascribe to a previous design, what came to be known only by experience, what no human wisdom could foresee, and what, without the concurring humour and disposition of his age, no authority could enable an individual to execute', Ferguson (1767, pp. 187, 188) quoted in Hayek (1945a, p. 7).

15 This is how he puts the matter, Hayek (1967b, p. 101):

> The theory of evolution of traditions and habits which made the formation of spontaneous orders possible stands therefore in a close relation to the theory of evolution of the particular kinds of spontaneous orders which we call organisms, and has provided the essential concepts on which the latter was built.

16 This paragraph draws on Milonakis (2003). Vaughn (1980), Murrell (1983) and Lavoie (1985) offer comprehensive reviews of the calculation debate from an Austrian perspective; for more general critical reviews of the whole debate on market socialism, see Adaman and Devine (1996 and 1997) and Milonakis (2003), and references therein.

17 On Hayek's battle with Keynes, see Caldwell (1995).

14 From Keynes to general equilibrium: short- and long-run revolutions in economic theory

1 Note, for certain periods, their description of the scope of micro and macro is unduly generous, in relation to equity and growth, respectively.

2 See Snowdon and Vane (2005) for a useful overview.

3 'The distinction between Walrasian and Marshallian methodology is not a distinction between general and partial equilibrium ... Rather it is between theory that is comprehensive and one that is purpose-built', Hoover (2006, p. 81).

4 And Hoover continues as if he is writing about the present state of economics, p. 298, 'Too large a proportion of recent "mathematical" economics are merely concoctions, as imprecise as the initial assumptions they rest on, which allow the author to lose sight of the complexities and interdependencies of the real world in a maze of pretentious and unhelpful symbols'.

5 See also Gerrard (1992).

6 Coates (1996, p. 121) suggests:

> In the historical and biographical work on Cambridge philosophy there has been very little written specifically on Keynes's friendships with Ramsey and Wittgenstein, and more generally on the fruitful collaboration between the economists and the philosophers.

This might be thought to be an exaggeration, if only in light of literature emerging at the time. There is a healthy, if neglected, literature on Keynes and the philosophers. Thus, for Bateman and Davis (eds) (1991), 'Another *new* area of interest has been the philosophical dimensions of Keynes's *early* thinking and its relationship to his *later* work in economics', p. 1, emphasis added. For Coates, though, it is a matter of Keynes's shifting philosophy and the relationship between his later philosophy and his economics. Note that Bateman (1991) offers a review of three contributions that present differing interpretations of continuities in the evolution of Keynes thinking around philosophy and economics. And for Backhouse and Bateman (2006, p. 150), with considerable reference to the subsequent literature, so significant does philosophy (and art) remain for Keynes throughout his career that 'There is a strong case for considering Keynes, not as an economist scientist in the modern sense of the term, but as a philosopher-economist comparable with Hume, Smith, Mill and Sidgwick'.

7 In Coates' account, there is no entry for Russell in discussion of 'The Cambridge Philosophical Community', his Chapter 6, although each of Wittgenstein, Ramsey and Sraffa warrants a subsection. See also Skidelsky (1992).

8 See also Davis (1999) in review of Coates.

9 See also Coates (1997).

10 Here, there is a wonderful affinity with the uncertainty of Knight. Samuels (2007, p. 166) quotes Knight (2005 [1933], p. 35): 'There is *no established* economic usage for anything in economics'.

11 See also Gerrard (1997).

12 See also O'Donnell (1997).

13 Hence, Keynes' dispute with Tinbergen over applicability of econometrics to the study of business cycles, Coates (1996, p. 70).

14 See also Blaug (2001, p. 160):

> The history of general equilibrium theory from Walras to Arrow-Debreu has been a journey down a blind alley ... because the most rigorous solution to the existence problem by Arrow and Debreu turns general equilibrium into a mathematical puzzle applied to a virtual economy that can be imagined but could not possibly exist, while the extremely relevant 'stability problem' has never been solved either rigorously or sloppily.

15 However, even such mathematical methods carry implications for application to economic theory, see Chick and Dow (2001). In addition, choices within mathematics have the same effect, Weintraub (1998). See also Weintraub (2002) for emphasis on the shifting nature of mathematics, economics and the relationship between the two. He indicates that what mathematics is deployed by economics, and how it is interpreted, does not track developments within mathematics itself. This leads to the point, taken up below, that mathematical rigour and interpretation are not the first call upon economics, despite its frequent claims to the contrary and its distinguishing feature from other social sciences.

16 And, as Fine (2007d) shows, the logic underpinning the use of methodological individualism does itself undermine the capacity of economic theory to address the economy as a whole in light of Russell's set theory paradoxes.

17 For latter, see especially Coates (1996 and 1997) and previous section.

18 Interestingly, Petri (2006) explains the success of a flawed general equilibrium theory in terms of a particular balance between consistency, realism and lack of memory (of history of economic thought, especially for him, in emphasising the problem of defining capital in both short and long runs in a consistent way). But note that some such balance will always prevail, whatever the outcome, and the issue of why it should be general equilibrium that prevails (or not) remains open.

19 Note that Stiglitz (2004b, p. 4) persists in that 'The fundamental theorems of welfare economics provided the rigorous interpretation of Adam Smith's invisible hand, the conditions under which and the sense in which markets lead to efficient outcomes'. And, further, market imperfections seem only to have been discovered in the 1970s, Stiglitz (2004a, p. 2), 'Advances in economic theory in the 70s showed that market failures are pervasive, especially in developing economies rife with imperfections in information, limitations in competition and incomplete markets'. This paves the way for the new or newer development economics, see Fine and Milonakis (2009).

20 Blaug (2001, p. 153) dubs the tribute by Arrow and Hahn 'to Adam Smith for having dimly perceived 200 years ago that perfect competition secures Pareto optimal multi-market equilibrium' as 'a historical travesty'. See also Blaug (2006, p. 4) for further list of those representing Adam Smith's invisible hand as anticipation of general equilibrium theory or, more exactly, imposing general equilibrium theory on Adam Smith in retrospect. See also discussion in Chapter 8 of nineteenth century misinterpretations of Smith as offered by Leslie.

21 This is the title of Colander and Landreth (eds) (1996), with subtitle, *Conversations with the Founders of Keynesian Economics*. Galbraith (1975) has the title, 'How Keynes Came to America'.

22 Note that this piece by Galbraith was originally published in 1971. The later interview in Colander and Landreth (1996) is much more measured and serious in tone.

23 See also Colander and Landreth (1996, pp. 12 and 142).

24 See also Backhouse and Medema (2007a) and especially Lee (2009).

25 See Lee (2009) for a detailed account of the politics and ideology influencing the evolution of mainstream (American) economics in the post-war period.

26 *Monopoly Capital* by Baran and Sweezy (1966) is the classic text, but Sweezy's (1946) first major text of Marxist political economy had already appeared twenty years earlier. See Fine (2007b) for an account of Sweezy's puzzling conversion to Marxism, and reference to wider discussion. See also Fine and Murfin (1984) for a critical account of monopoly capital.

27 Subsequently famous as a meeting place, not least in its association with the satirical magazine, *Private Eye*.

28 For deficiencies of general equilibrium on its own terms, and implausibility of its assumptions, see Ackerman (2004a), Keen (2001) and Kirman (1989 and 1992) for example.

29 On the Cambridge controversy, see Harcourt (1972 and 1976), Fine (1980c, Chapters 5 and 6), Hodgson (1997), Cohen and Harcourt (2003) and *Eastern Economic Journal*, vol 31, no 3, 2005, and Han and Shefold (2006) for example.

15 Beyond the formalist revolution

1 This chapter draws in part upon Fine (2007c).

2 But, it might be added, where does this locate economists?

3 For the lack of realism and mathematical formalism of the new classical economics, and the opposition of neoclassical Keynesians, see Seidman (2005) who concludes that it is in the realm of academia that NCE has been most influential. Yet, as suggested by de Long (2000, p. 85), the new micro-foundations Keynesianism is more monetarist than its name would suggest: 'We may not all be Keynesians now, but the influence of monetarism on how we all think about macroeconomics today has been deep, pervasive, and subtle'.

4 Samuelson shared Gary, Indiana as birthplace with Stiglitz, whom he is rumoured to have declared, modestly but humorously, the best economist ever to have come from the small steel town.

5 See also Weintraub (1998) who points both to the selective use of mathematics by economists and to the shifting meaning of formalism and scientific rigour within mathematics itself.

6 For one of us as example if not exemplar, see entry for Fine in Arestis and Sawyer (eds) (2001).

7 Note that such limitations also apply to the application of mathematics to the natural sciences, as was inevitably highlighted by those investigating the philosophical foundations of mathematics in the first instance.

8 Fine (1980c) makes the same point in arguing that external causal content within neoclassical economics is a consequence of the social content that is taken as given for the purposes of individual optimisation. And Hodgson (2007b) has questioned whether a pure form of methodological individualism is to be found in practice, let alone that it is possible given the necessity of taking something social as given in the first instance.

9 Whilst Sala-i-Martin (1997) reduced the number of regressions he ran from four to two million, this was subsequently raised to 89 million, although 33 million of these proved sufficient for his purposes, Sala-i-Martin *et al.* (2004). This is despite the extraordinarily unrealistic assumptions that need to be made in order to justify such statistical profligacy, Rodríguez (2006) for example. For Hendry and Krolzig (2004), one regression should suffice.

10 For a striking example of this, see the recent survey of associate professors in the leading universities in the United States by Oswald and Ralsmark (2008). Interestingly, they find that 'the great majority of these young economists are doing empirical work', p. 1. As a result, they continue, 'Many people who criticise economists as obsessively mathematical have a view of economics that is out-of-date'. It is not clear why the doing of empirical work is an alternative to, or even

an excuse for, the mathematical, with no discussion of the theory that underpins each. In any case, they somewhat undermine their case for major change (other than more empirical work as such) by observing 'that the most-studied areas of economics are now macroeconomics, econometrics, and labour economics (though these days this encompasses topics only obliquely related to labour markets)', p. 1. What is also revealing in their survey of 112 economists is that of the 70 or so research areas they cover, none mentions globalisation, neo-liberalism, new world order, etc, although there are six votes for 'political economy' and one for 'economics of terrorism'.

11 Most prominent is the acceptance of some degree of methodological individualism only to find it increasingly universalised!

12 See Mosini (2007, p. 5) for the very different relationship between theory and evidence in natural sciences as opposed to economics, with close 'reality checks' for the former throughout in contrast to the latter.

13 See Hodgson (1997) and, more recently, symposium in *Eastern Economic Journal*, vol 31, no 3, 2005, Han and Schefold (2006), and Fine (2006b) in context of new growth theory.

14 See also Hartley (1996), though, for the intellectual origins of the representative agent in Marshall.

15 The difference resides in pluralism involving debate between a plurality of positions rather than the latter co-existing in parallel. See collection edited by Mearman (2008), although pre-occupation with this issue might also be thought to involve self-indulgent diminishing returns in the debate with current orthodoxy given the latter's failure to recognise other positions let alone to debate them.

16 The first and last might be dubbed, respectively, the special theory of economics and the general theory of social science.

17 See Akerlof and Kranton (2000) for first contribution and Davis (2007) and Fine (2007a) for their further contributions and complementary critiques.

References

Ackerman, F. (2004a) 'Still Dead after All These Years: Interpreting the Failure of General Equilibrium Theory', in Ackerman and Nadal (eds) (2004).

—— (2004b) 'Consumed in Theory: Alternative Perspectives on the Economics of Consumption', in Ackerman and Nadal (eds) (2004).

Ackerman, F. and A. Nadal (eds) (2004) *The Flawed Foundations of General Equilibrium: Critical Essays on Economic Theory*, London: Routledge.

Adaman, F. and P. Devine (1996) 'The Economic Calculation Debate: Lessons for Socialists', *Cambridge Journal of Economics*, vol 20, no 5, pp. 523–37.

—— (1997) 'On the Economic Theory of Socialism', *New Left Review*, vol 221, pp. 54–80.

Agassi, J. (1975) 'Institutional Individualism', *British Journal of Sociology*, vol 26, no 2, pp. 144–55.

Aglietta, M. (1979) *A Theory of Capitalist Regulation, the US Experience*, London: New Left Books.

Akerlof, G. (1990) 'George A. Akerlof', in Swedberg (ed) (1990).

Akerlof, G. and R. Kranton (2002) 'Identity and Schooling: Some Lessons for the Economics of Education', *Journal of Economic Literature*, vol XL, no 4, pp. 1167–1201.

Albritton, R. (2005) 'How Dialectics Runs Aground: The Antinomies of Arthur's Dialectic of Capital', *Historical Materialism*, vol 13, no 2, pp. 167–88.

Allais, M. (1968) 'Pareto, Vilfredo: Contributions to Economics', in Silis (ed) (1968).

Amadae, S. (2003) *Rationalizing Capitalist Democracy: The Cold War Origins of Rational Choice Liberalism*, Chicago: Chicago University Press.

Amatori, F. and G. Jones (eds) (2003) *Business History around the World*, Cambridge: Cambridge University Press.

Amsden, A. (1989) *Asia's Next Giant: South Korea and Late Industrialization*, New York: Oxford University Press.

Andreades, A. (1935) [1909] *History of the Bank of England: 1640 to 1903*, translated by C. Meredith with a Preface by H. S. Foxwell, 3rd ed., London: P.S. King & Son.

Arestis, P. and V. Chick (eds) (1992) *Recent Developments in Post-Keynesian Economics*, Aldershot: Edward Elgar.

Arestis, P., G. Palma, and M. Sawyer (eds) (1997) *Capital Controversy, Post-Keynesian Economics and the History of Economics: Essays in Honour of Geoff Harcourt, Volume I*, London: Routledge.

Arestis, P. and M. Sawyer (eds) (2001) *A Biographical Dictionary of Dissenting Economists*, second edition, Aldershot: Edward Elgar.

—— (2004) *The Rise of the Market*, Camberley: Edward Elgar.

Arnott, R., B. Greenwald, R. Kanbur and B. Nalebuff (eds) (2003) *Economics for an Imperfect World: Essays in Honor of Joseph E. Stiglitz*, Cambridge: MIT Press.

Aron, R. (1970) *Main Currents of Sociological Thought 2: Pareto, Weber, Durkheim*, Harmondsworth: Penguin Books.

Arrow, K. (1986) 'History: A View From Economics', in Parker (ed) (1986).

—— (2000) 'Increasing Returns: Historiographic Issues and Path Dependence', *European Journal of History of Economic Thought*, vol 7, no 2, pp. 171–80.

Arrow, K. and G. Debreu (1954) 'Existence of an Equilibrium for a Competitive Economy', *Econometrica*, vol 22, no 3, pp. 265–90.

Arrow, K. and F. Hahn (1971) *General Competitive Analysis*, San Francisco: Holden Day.

Arthur, C. (2002) *New Dialectic and Marx's 'Capital'*, Leiden: Brill.

—— (2005) 'Reply to Critics', *Historical Materialism*, vol 13, no 2, pp. 189–222.

Ashley, W. (1893) 'The Study of Economic History', Inaugural Lecture delivered at Harvard University on the 4th January 1893, reprinted in, and cited from, Harte (ed) (1971).

—— (1894) 'Roscher's Programme of 1843', *Quarterly Journal of Economics*, vol 9, no 1, pp. 99–105.

—— (1927) 'The Place of Economic History in University Studies', *Economic History Review*, vol 1, no 1, pp. 1–11.

Ashton, T. (1959) *Economic Fluctuations in England 1700–1800*, Oxford: Clarendon Press.

Ayres, C. (1951) 'The Co-ordinates of Institutionalism', *American Economic Review*, vol 41, no2, pp. 47–55.

—— (1962) [1944] *The Theory of Economic Progress*, New York: Schoken Bokks.

Backhouse, R. (2002a) 'Don Patinkin: Interpreter of the Keynesian Revolution', *European Journal of the History of Economic Thought*, vol 9, no 2, pp. 186–204.

—— (2002b) *The Penguin History of Economics*, London: Penguin Books.

—— (2004) 'History of Economics, Economics and Economic History in Britain, 1824–2000', *European Journal of the History of Economic Thought*, vol 11, no 1, pp. 107–27.

—— (2006a) 'Economics since the Second World War', Paper to the History of Postwar Social Science Seminar Series, London School of Economics, March.

—— (2006b) 'The Keynesian Revolution', in Backhouse and Bateman (eds) (2006).

—— (2007) 'Equilibrium and Problem Solving in Economics', in Mosini (ed) (2007).

Backhouse, R. and B. Bateman (2006) 'John Maynard Keynes: Artist, Philosopher, Economist', *Atlantic Economic Journal*, vol 34, no 2, pp. 149–59.

Backhouse, R. and B. Bateman (eds) (2006) *The Cambridge Companion to Keynes*, Cambridge: Cambridge University Press.

Backhouse, R. and M. Boianovsky (2005) 'Disequilibrium Macroeconomics: An Episode in the Transformation of Modern Macroeconomics', available at http://www.anpec.org.br/encontro2005/artigos/A05A012.pdf

Backhouse, R. and J. Creedy (eds) (1999) *From Classical Economics to the Theory of the Firm, Essays in Honour of D. P. O'Brien*, Cheltenham: Edward Elgar.

Backhouse, R. and S. Medema (2007a) 'Defining Economics: Robbins' *Essay* in Theory and Practice', mimeo.

—— (2007b) 'Robbins' *Essay* and the Axiomatization of Economics', mimeo.

Balabkins, N. (1987) 'Line by Line: Schmoller's *Grundriss*: Its Meaning in the 1980s', *International Journal of Social Economics*, vol 14, no 1, pp. 22–31.

—— (1988) *Not by Theory Alone: The Economics of Gustav von Schmoller and its Legacy in America*, Berlin: Duncker & Humblot.

Baran, P. and P. Sweezy (1966) *Monopoly Capital: An Essay on the American Economic and Social Order*, New York: Monthly Review Press.

Bateman, B. (1991) 'Das Maynard Keynes Problem', *Cambridge Journal of Economics*, vol 15, no 1, pp. 101–11.

Bateman, B. and J. Davis (1991) 'Introduction', in Bateman and Davis (ed) (1991).

Bateman, B. and J. Davis (eds) (1991) *Keynes and Philosophy: Essays on the Origins of Keynes's Thought*, Aldershot: Edward Elgar.

Becker, G. and K. Murphy (2001) *Social Economics: Market Behavior in a Social Environment*, Cambridge: Harvard University Press.

Bentham, J. (1970) [1789] *An Introduction to the Principles of Morals and Legislation*, edited by J. H. Burns and H. L. A. Hart, in *The Collected Works of Jeremy Bentham*, with general editor J. H. Burns, London: Athlone Press.

Betz, H. (1988) 'How Does the German Historical School Fit?', *History of Political Economy*, vol 20, no 3, pp. 409–30.

—— (1993) 'From Schmoller to Sombart', *History of Economic Ideas*, vol 1, no 3, pp. 331–56.

—— (1995) 'The Role of Ethics as Part of the Historical Methods of Schmoller and the Older Historical School', in Koslowski (ed) (1995).

Biddle, J. and W. Samuels (1997) 'The Historicism of John R. Commons's *Legal Foundations of Capitalism*', in Koslowski (ed) (1997).

Bidet, J. (2005) 'The Dialectician's Interpretation of *Capital*', *Historical Materialism*, vol 13, no 2, pp.121–46.

Birner, J. (1994), 'Introduction: Hayek's Grand Research Programme', in Birner and Zijp (eds) (1994).

—— (1999) 'The Surprising Place of Cognitive Psychology in the work of F. A. Hayek', *History of Economic Ideas*, vol 7, nos 1–2, pp. 43–84.

Birner, J. and R. van Zijp (eds) (1994) *Hayek, Coordination, and Evolution: His Legacy in Philosophy, Politics, and History of Ideas*, London: Routledge.

Black, C. (1973) 'W. S. Jevons and the Foundation of Modern Economics', in Black *et al.* (eds) (1973).

Black, C., A. Coats and D. Goodwin (eds) (1973) *The Marginal Revolution in Economics*, Durham: Duke University Press.

Black, M. (ed) (1963) *The Social Theories of Talcott Parsons*, New Jersey: Prentice Hall.

Blackwell, R., J. Chatha and E. Nell (eds) (1993) *Economics as Worldly Philosophy: Essays in Political and Historical Economics in Honour of Robert L. Heilbroner*, London: Macmillan.

Blaug, M. (1958) *Ricardian Economics: A Historical Study*, New Haven: Yale University Press, reprinted by Westport: Greenwood Press, 1973.

—— (1973) 'Was There a Marginal Revolution?', in Black *et al.* (eds) (1973).

—— (1980) *The Methodology of Economics: Or How Economists Explain*, Cambridge: Cambridge University Press.

—— (1997) [1962] *Economic Theory in Retrospect*, Cambridge: Cambridge University Press, fifth edition.

—— (1999) 'The Formalist Revolution or What Happened to Orthodox Economics after World War II', in Backhouse and Creedy (eds) (1999).

—— (2001) 'No History of Ideas, Please, We're Economists', *Journal of Economic Perspectives*, vol 15, no 1, pp. 145–64.

—— (2003) 'The Formalist Revolution of the 1950s', *Journal of the History of Economic Thought*, vol 25, no 2, pp. 145–56.

—— (2006) 'The Fundamental Theorems of Modern Welfare Economics, Historically Contemplated', Erasmus Institute for Philosophy and Economics, Working Papers, February.

Böhm-Bawerk, E. von (1890) 'The Historical vs. the Deductive Method in Political Economy', *Annals of the American Academy of Political and Social Science*, vol 1, no 2, pp. 244–71.

—— (1891) 'The Austrian Economists', *Annals of the American Academy of Political and Social Science*, vol 1, no 3, pp. 361–84.

—— (1899) 'The Historical vs the Deductive Method in Political Economy', *Annals of the American Academy of Political and Social Science*, vol 1, no 2, pp. 244–71.

Bostaph, S. (1978) 'The Methodological Debate Between Carl Menger and the German Historicists', *Atlantic Economic Journal*, vol 6, no 3, pp. 3–16.

Bottomore, T. (1992) *Between Marginalism and Marxism: The Economic Sociology of J. A. Schumpeter*, New York: St. Martin's Press.

Boudon, R. (1997) 'The Present Relevance of Max Weber's *Wertrationalität* (Value Rationality)', in Koslowski (ed.) (1997).

Bowman, S. (1998) 'Introduction', in Veblen (1998).

Brette, O. (2003) 'Thornstein Veblen's Theory of Institutional Change: Beyond Technological Determinism', *European Journal of the History of Economic Thought*, vol 10, no 3, pp. 455–77.

Bridel, P. (2002) 'Patinkin, Walras and the "Money-in-the-Utility-Function" Tradition', *European Journal of the History of Economic Thought*, vol 9, no 2, pp. 268–92.

Bridel, P. and M. De Vroey (2002) 'Introduction', *European Journal of the History of Economic Thought*, vol 9, no 2, pp. 155–60.

Brodbeck, M. (ed) (1968) *Readings in the Philosophy of the Social Sciences*, London: Collier-Macmillan.

Burge, M. (ed) (1964) *The Critical Approach to Science and Philosophy: Essays in Honour of K. R. Popper*, New York: The Free Press.

Burns, A. and W. Mitchell (1946) *Measuring Business Cycles*, New York: National Bureau of Economic Research.

Cairnes, J.. (2001) [1857] *The Character and Logical Method of Political Economy*, 2nd edition 1888, Kitchener: Batoche Books.

Caldwell, B. (1982) *Beyond Positivism: Economic Methodology in the Twentieth Century*, London: George Allen and Unwin.

—— (1988) 'Hayek's Transformation', *History of Political Economy*, vol. 20, no 4, pp. 513–41.

—— (1995) 'Introduction', in Hayek (1995).

—— (2001) 'There Really *Was* a German Historical School of Economics: A Comment on Heath Pearson', *History of Political Economy*, vol 33, no 3, pp. 650–4.

—— (2004) *Hayek's Challenge: An Intellectual Biography of F. A. Hayek*, Chicago: University of Chicago Press.

Caldwell, B. (ed) (1990) *Carl Menger and His Legacy in Economics*, Annual Supplement to vol 22 of *History of Political Economy*, Durham: Duke University Press.

Callinicos, A. (2005) 'Against the New Dialectic', *Historical Materialism*, vol 13, no 2, pp. 41–60.

Callinicos, A. (ed) (1989) *Marxist Theory*, Oxford: Oxford University Press.

Carabelli, A. (1991) 'The Methodology of the Critique of Classical Theory: Keynes on Organic Interdependence', in Bateman and Davis (eds) (1991).

Catephores, G. (1980) 'The Historical Transformation Problem – A Reply', *Economy and Society*, vol 9, no 3, pp. 332–6, reprinted in Fine (ed) (1986).

—— (1994) 'The Imperious Austrian: Schumpeter as a Bourgeois Marxist', *New Left Review*, 205, pp. 3–30.

Chamberlain, N. (1963) 'The Institutional Economics of John R. Commons', in Dorfman *et al.* (1963).

Chandler, A. (1977) *The Visible Hand: The Managerial Revolution in American Business*, Cambridge: Harvard University Press.

Chang, H-J (2002) *Kicking Away the Ladder: Development Strategy in Historical Perspective*, London: Anthem Press.

Chick, V. and S. Dow (2001) 'Formalism, Logic and Reality: A Keynesian Analysis', *Cambridge Journal of Economics*, vol 25, no 6, pp. 705–21.

Cirillo, R. (1979) *The Economics of Vilfredo Pareto*, with a Preface by F. Oulès, London: Frank Cass.

Clapham, J. (1922a) 'Of Empty Economic Boxes', *Economic Journal*, vol 22, no 3, pp. 305–14.

—— (1922b) 'The Economic Boxes: A Rejoinder', *Economic Journal*, vol 32, no 128, pp. 560–3.

—— (1930) *An Economic History of Modern Britain*, Volume I, Cambridge: Cambridge University Press.

Clark, J. (1891) 'Distribution as Determined by a Law of Rent', *Quarterly Journal of Economics*, vol 5, no 3, pp. 289–318.

Clarke, P. (1978) *Liberals and Social Democrats*, Cambridge: Cambridge University Press.

Coase, R. (1937) 'On the Nature of the Firm', *Economica*, 4, Nov., pp. 386–405.

—— (1960) 'The Problem of Social Cost', *Journal of Law and Economics*, vol 3, no 1, pp. 1–44.

—— (1978) 'Economics and Contiguous Disciplines', *Journal of Legal Studies*, vol 7, no 2, pp. 201–11.

—— (1994) *Essays on Economics and Economists*, Chicago: Chicago University Press.

Coates, J. (1996) *The Claims of Common Sense: Moore, Wittgenstein, Keynes and the Social Sciences*, Cambridge: Cambridge University Press.

—— (1997) 'Keynes, Vague Concepts and Fuzzy Logic', in Harcourt and Riach (eds) (1997).

Coats, A. (1954) 'The Historist Reaction in English Political Economy 1870–90', *Economics*, vol 21, no 82, pp. 143–53.

—— (1969) 'Is There a "Structure of Scientific Revolutions" in Economics?', *Kyklos*, vol 22, no 2, pp. 289–96.

—— (1973a) 'The Economic and Social Context of the Marginal Revolution of the 1870s', in Black *et al.* (eds) (1973).

—— (1973b) 'Retrospect and Prospect', in Black *et al.* (eds) (1973).

Coddington, A. (1976) 'Keynesian Economics: The Search for First Principles', *Journal of Economic Literature*, vol 14, no 4, pp. 1258–73.

Cohen, A. and G. Harcourt (2003) 'Whatever Happened to the Cambridge Capital Theory Controversies?', *Journal of Economic Perspectives*, vol 17, no 1, pp. 199–214.

Cohen, G. (1978) *Karl Marx's Theory of History: A Defence*, Princeton: Princeton University Press.

Colander, D. and H. Landreth (eds) (1996) *The Coming of Keynesianism to America: Conversations with the Founders of Keynesian Economics*, Cheltenham: Edward Elgar.

Coleman, D. (1987) *History and the Economic Past*, Oxford: Clarendon Press.

Collini, S., D. Winch and J. Burrow (1983) *The Noble Science of Politics: A Study in Nineteenth-Century Intellectual History*, Cambridge: Cambridge University Press.

Colona, M. and H. Hageman (eds) (1994) *The Economics of Hayek, Volume I: Money and Business Cycles*, Aldershot: Edward Elgar.

Commons, J. (1924) *Legal Foundations of Capitalism*, New York: MacMillan.

—— (1931) 'Institutional Economics', *American Economic Review*, vol 21, no 4, pp. 648–57, reproduced with original page numbers in Samuels (eds) (1988a).

—— (1950) *The Economics of Collective Action*, New York: MacMillan.

—— (1990a and b) [1934] *Institutional Economics: Its Place in Political Economy*, Volumes 1 and 2, London: Transaction Publishers, first published as one volume.

Commons J. and S. Perlman (1929) 'Der Moderne Kapitalismus', *The American Economic Review*, vol 19, no 1, pp. 78–80.

Cooter, R. (1982) 'Law and the Imperialism of Economics: An Introduction to the Economic Analysis of Law and a Review of the Major Books', *UCLA Law Review*, vol 29, no 5/6, pp. 1260–9.

Court, W. (1970) *Scarcity and Choice in History*, London: Edward Arnold.

Crespo, R. (1997) 'Max Weber and Ludwig von Mises, and the Methodology of the Social Sciences', in Koslowski (ed.) (1997).

Cuningham, W. (1882) *The Growth of English Trade and Commerce*, Cambridge: Cambridge University Press.

—— (1892a) 'The Relativity of Economic Doctrine', *Economic Journal*, vol 2, no 5, pp. 1–16.

—— (1892b) 'The Perversion of Economic History', *Economic Journal*, vol 2, no 7, pp. 491–506.

Dasgupta, P. (2002) 'Modern Economics and Its Critics', in Mäki (ed) (2002).

Daunton, M. and F. Trentmann (eds) (2004) *Worlds of Political Economy: Knowledge and Power in the Nineteenth and Twentieth Centuries*, Basingstoke: Palgrave MacMillan.

Davis, J. (1991) 'Keynes' View of Economics as a Moral Science', in Bateman and Davis (eds) (1991).

—— (1997) 'New Economics and Its History: A Pickeringian View', in Davis (ed) (1997).

—— (1999) 'Common Sense: A Middle Way between Formalism and Post-Structuralism?', *Cambridge Journal of Economics*, vol 23, no 4, pp. 503–15.

—— (2003) *The Theory of the Individual in Economics: Identity and Value*, London: Routledge.

—— (2007) 'Akerlof and Kranton on Identity in Economics: Inverting the Analysis', *Cambridge Journal of Economics*, forthcoming.

Davis, J. (ed) (1997) *New Economics and Its History, History of Political Economy*, vol 29, Supplement, Durham, NC: Duke University Press.

Davis, J., D. Wade Hands and U. Mäki (1998) *The Handbook of Economic Methodology*, Cheltenham: Edward Elgar.

De Long, J. (2000) 'The Triumph of Monetarism', *Journal of Economic Perspectives*, vol 14, no 1, pp. 83–94.

De Vroey, M. (1975) 'The Transition from Classical to Neoclassical Economics: A Scientific Revolution', *Journal of Economic Issues*, vol IX, no 3, pp. 415–39.

Deane, P. (1978) *The Evolution of Economic Ideas*, Cambridge: Cambridge University Press.

—— (1983) 'The Scope and Method of Economic Science', *Economic Journal*, vol 93, no 369, pp. 1–12.

Debreu, G. (1959) *Theory of Value: An Axiomatic Analysis of General Equilibrium*, New Haven: Yale University Press.

—— (1986) 'Theoretic Models: Mathematical Form and Economic Content', *Econometrica*, vol 54, no 6, pp. 1259–70.

—— (1991) 'The Mathematization of Economic Theory', *American Economic Review*, vol 81, no 1, pp. 1–7.

Demsetz, H. (1997) 'The Primacy of Economics: An Explanation of the Comparative Success of Economics in the Social Sciences', Western Economic Association International 1996 Presidential Address, *Economic Inquiry*, vol XXXV, no 1, pp. 1–11.

Devereux, E. (1963) 'Parsons Sociological Theory', in Black (ed) (1963).

DiMaggio, P. (2002) 'Endogenizing "Animal Spirits": Toward a Sociology of Collective Response to Uncertainty and Risk', in Guillén *et al.* (eds) (2002).

Dimand, R. (2002) 'Patinkin on Irving Fisher's Monetary Economics', *European Journal of the History of Economic Thought*, vol 9, no 2, pp. 308–26.

Dobb, M. (1940) *Political Economy and Capitalism*, London: Routledge and Kegan Paul.

—— (1973) *Theories of Value and Distribution since Adam Smith: Ideology and Economic Theory*, Cambridge: Cambridge University Press.

Dorfman, J. (1955) 'The Role of the German Historical School in American Economic Thought', *American Economic Review*, vol 45, no 2, pp. 17–28.

Dorfman, J., C. Ayres, N. Chamberlain, S. Kuznets and R. Gordon (1963) *Institutional Economics: Veblen, Commons and Mitchell Reconsidered*, Berkeley: University of California Press.

Dow, S. (1996) *The Methodology of Macroeconomic Thought: A Conceptual Analysis of Schools of Thought in Economics*, Cheltenham: Edward Elgar.

—— (1998) 'Formalism in Economics', *Economic Journal*, vol 108, no 451, pp. 1826–8.

—— (2008) 'Was There a (Methodological) Keynesian Revolution?', Keynes conference in Copenhagen in April, http://www.ruc.dk/isg/nyheder/30082173/sheila_dow2/

Dowd, D. (2002) 'Thornstein Veblen: The Evolution of Capitalism from Economic and Political to Social Dominance', in Dowd (ed) (2002).

Dowd, D. (ed) (2002) *Understanding Capitalism: Critical Analysis from Karl Marx to Amartya Sen*, London: Pluto Press.

Dugger, W. and H Sherman (2000) *Reclaiming Evolution: A Dialogue Between Marxism and Institutionalism on Social Change*, London: Routledge.

Eatwell, J., M. Milgate and R. Newman (eds) (1987) *The New Palgrave: Marxian Economics*, London: Macmillan.

Ekelund, R. and R. Hébert (2002) 'Retrospectives: The Origins of Neoclassical Microeconomics', *Journal of Economic Perspectives*, vol 16, no 3, pp. 197–215.

Elson, D. (ed) (1979) *Value: The Representation of Labour in Capitalism*, London: CSE Books.

Elster, J. (1982) 'Marxism, Functionalism and Game Theory: The Case for Methodological Individualism', *Theory and Society*, vol 11, no 4, pp. 453–82, reprinted in Callinicos (ed) (1989).

Engels, F. (1968) [1883] *Socialism: Utopian and Scientific*, reprinted in Marx and Engels (1968).

—— (1970) [1859] 'Karl Marx, "A Contribution to the Critique of Political Economy: Part I"', in Marx (1970).

—— (1972) [1878] *Anti-Dühring*, reprinted in Marx, Engels and Lenin (1972).

—— (1981) [1894] 'Supplement and Addendum to Volume III of Capital', in Marx (1981), pp. 1027–47.

Esping-Andersen, G. (1990) *The Three Worlds of Welfare Capitalism*, Princeton: Princeton University Press.

Ferguson, A. (1767) *An Essay on the History of Civil Society*, reprinted in 1995 with a new introduction by Louis Schneider, London: Transaction Publishers.

Fetter, F. (1901) 'The Passing of the Old Rent Concept', *Quarterly Journal of Economics*, vol 15, no 3, pp. 371–89.

Fevre, R. (2003) *The New Sociology of Economic Behaviour*, London: Sage.

Fine, B. (1979) 'On Marx's Theory of Agricultural Rent', *Economy and Society*, vol 8, no 3, pp. 241–78, reprinted in Fine (ed) (1986).

—— (1980a) 'On Marx's Theory of Agricultural Rent: A Rejoinder', *Economy and Society*, vol 9, no 3, pp. 327–31, reprinted in Fine (ed) (1986).

—— (1980b) 'On the Historical Transformation Problem', *Economy and Society*, vol 9, no 3, pp. 337–39, reprinted in Fine (ed) (1986).

—— (1980c) *Economic Theory and Ideology*, London: Edward Arnold.

—— (1982) *Theories of the Capitalist Economy*, London: Edward Arnold.

—— (1983) 'The Historical Theory of Rent and Price Reconsidered', *Australian Economic Papers*, vol 22, no 40, pp. 132–43.

—— (1994) 'Consumption in Contemporary Capitalism: Beyond Marx and Veblen – A Comment', *Review of Social Economy*, vol LII, no 3, pp. 391–6.

—— (1998) *Labour Market Theory: A Constructive Reassessment*, London: Routledge.

—— (2000) 'Endogenous Growth Theory: A Critical Assessment', *Cambridge Journal of Economics*, vol 24, no 2, pp. 245–65.

—— (2001) *Social Capital versus Social Theory: Political Economy and Social Science at the Turn of the Millennium*, London: Routledge.

—— (2002a) '"Economic Imperialism": A View from the Periphery', *Review of Radical Political Economics*, vol 34, no 2, pp. 187–201.

—— (2002b) 'Economics Imperialism and the New Development Economics as Kuhnian Paradigm Shift', *World Development*, vol 30, no 12, pp. 2057–70.

—— (2002c) *The World of Consumption: The Material and Cultural Revisited*, London: Routledge,

—— (2003a) 'Value Theory and the Study of Contemporary Capitalism: A Continuing Commitment', in Westra and Zuege (eds) (2003).

—— (2003b) 'New Growth Theory', in Chang (ed) (2003).

—— (2004a) 'Addressing the Critical and the Real in Critical Realism', in Lewis (ed) (2004a).

—— (2004b) 'Economics Imperialism as Kuhnian Revolution', in Arestis and Sawyer (eds) (2004).

—— (2006a) 'Debating Critical Realism in Economics', *Capital and Class*, no 89, pp. 121–9.

—— (2006b) 'New Growth Theory: More Problem than Solution', in Jomo and Fine (eds) (2006).

—— (2007a) 'The Economics of Identity and the Identity of Economics?', *Cambridge Journal of Economics*, forthcoming.

—— (2007b) 'Enigma in the Origins of Paul Sweezy's Political Economy', *Review of Political Economy*, forthcoming.

—— (2007c) 'The Historical Logic of Economics Imperialism and Meeting the Challenges of Contemporary Orthodoxy: Or Twelve Hypotheses on Economics, and What is to Be Done', paper presented at EAEPE Conference, 1–3 November 2007, Porto, Portugal.

—— (2007d) 'The General Impossibility of the New Institutional Economics: Or Does Bertrand Russell Deserve a Nobel Prize for Economics?', mimeo.

—— (2007e) 'Rethinking Critical Realism: Labour Markets or Capitalism?', *Capital and Class*, no 91, pp. 125–9.

Fine, B. (ed) (1986) *The Value Dimension: A Collection of Essays on Value Theory from Economy and Society*, with new Introduction, London: Routledge and Kegan Paul.

Fine, B. and A. Saad-Filho (2004) *Marx's Capital*, revised fourth edition, London: Pluto Press.

Fine, B. and L. Harris (1979) *Rereading Capital*, London: Macmillan.

Fine, B. and E. Leopold (1993) *The World of Consumption*, London: Routledge.

Fine, B., C. Lapavitsas and A. Saad-Filho (2004) 'Transforming the Transformation Problem: Why the "New Solution" Is a Wrong Turning', *Review of Radical Political Economics*, vol 36, no 1, pp. 3–19.

Fine, B., C. Lapavitsas and J. Pincus (eds) (2001) *Development Policy in the Twenty-First Century: Beyond the Post-Washington Consensus*, London: Routledge.

Fine, B. and D. Milonakis (2003) 'From Principle of Pricing to Pricing of Principle: Rationality and Irrationality in the Economic History of Douglass North', *Comparative Studies in Society and History*, vol 45, no 3, pp. 120–44.

—— (2009) *From Economics Imperialism to Freakonomics: The Shifting Boundaries Between Economics and Other Social Sciences*, London: Routledge.

Fine, B. and A. Murfin (1984) *Macroeconomics and Monopoly Capitalism*, Brighton: Wheatsheaf.

Fleetwood, S. (1995) *Hayek's Political Economy: The Socio-Economics of Order*, London: Routledge.

Foley, D. (1986) *Understanding Capital: Marx's Economic Theory*, Cambridge, Mass.: Harvard University Press.

Fontana, G. (2006) 'Mr Keynes and the "Classics" Again: A Methodological Enquiry', *Atlantic Economic Journal*, vol 34, no 2, pp.161–74.

Foxwell, H. (1909) 'Preface' to Andreades (1935).

Friedman, M. (1953) 'The Methodology of Positive Economics', in Friedman (1953), reprinted in, and cited from, Hausman (ed) (1984).

—— (1953) *Essays in Positive Economics*, Chicago: Chicago University Press.

Galbraith, K. (1975) 'How Keynes Came to America', in Keynes (ed) (1975).

Gerrard, B. (1992) 'Human Logic in Keynes's Thought: Escape from the Cartesian Vice', in Arestis and Chick (eds) (1992).

—— (1997) 'Method and Methodology in Keynes's *General Theory*', in Harcourt and Riach (eds) (1997).

Giddens, A. (1976) 'Introduction', in Weber (1976).

—— (1977) *Studies in Social and Political Theory*, London: Hutchison.

Giocoli, N. (2005) 'In the Sign of the Axiomatic Method: Mathematics as the Role Model for Neoclassical Economics', Blanqui Lecture, European Society for the

History of Economic Thought, EHSET, Ninth Annual Conference, Stirling, June 9–12.

Giouras, T. (1992) 'Gustav Schmoller: Historism and Criticism', *Axiologica*, no 4, pp. 96–131 (in Greek).

Gordon, D. (1965) 'The Role of the History of Economic Thought in the Understanding of Modern Economic Theory', *American Economic Review*, vol 55, no 2, pp. 119–27.

Gordon, S. (1991) *The History and Philosophy of Social Science*, London : Routledge.

Grimmer-Solem, E. and R. Romani (1999) 'In Search of Full Empirical Reality: Historical Political Economy, 1870–1900', *The European Journal of the History of Economic Thought*, vol 6, no 3, pp. 333–64.

Groenewegen, P. (1995) *A Soaring Eagle: Alfred Marshall 1842–1924*, Aldershot: Edward Elgar.

Guillén, M., R. Collins and P. England (eds) (2002) *The New Economic Sociology: Developments in an Emerging Field*, New York: Russell Sage Foundation.

Hahn, F. (1973) *On the Notion of Equilibrium in Economics*, Cambridge: Cambridge University Press.

—— (2002) 'The Dichotomy Once Again', *European Journal of the History of Economic Thought*, vol 9, no 2, pp. 260–7.

Hall, R. and C. Hitch (1939) 'Price Theory and Business Behavior', *Oxford Economic Papers*, vol 2, no 1, pp. 12–45.

Hamilton, D. (1953) 'Veblen and Commons: A Case of Theoretical Convergence', *Southern Social Science Quarterly*, vol 34, Sept, pp. 43–50, reproduced with original page numbers in Samuels (ed) (1988a).

Hamilton, W. (1919) 'The Institutional Approach to Economic Theory', *American Economic Review*, vol 9, no 1, pp. 309–18.

Hammond, J. and B. Hammond (1970) [1911] *The Village Labourer, 1760–1932: A Study in the Government of England Before the Reform Bill*, New York: Harper and Row.

Han, Z. and B. Schefold (2006) 'An Empirical Investigation of Paradoxes: Reswitching and Reverse Capital Deepening in Capital Theory', *Cambridge Journal of Economics*, vol 30, no 5, pp. 737–65.

Harcourt, G. (1972) *Some Cambridge Controversies in the Theory of Capital*, Cambridge: Cambridge University Press.

—— (1976) 'The Cambridge Controversies: Old Ways and New Horizons – Or Dead End', *Oxford Economic Papers*, vol 28, no 1, pp. 25–65.

Harcourt, G. and P. Riach (eds) (1997) *A 'Second Edition' of The General Theory*, Volume 2, London: Routledge.

Harte, N. (1971) 'Introduction: The Making of Economic History', in Harte (ed) (1971).

Harte, N. (ed) (1971) *The Study of Economic History: Collected Inaugural Lectures 1893–1970*, London: Frank Cass.

Hartley, J. (1996) 'Retrospectives: The Origins of the Representative Agent', *Journal of Economic Perspectives*, vol 10, no 2, pp. 169–77.

Harvey, D. (1996) *Justice, Nature and the Geography of Difference*, Oxford: Blackwell.

Hausman, D. (1992) *The Inexact and Separate Science of Economics*, Cambridge: Cambridge University Press.

Hausman, D. (ed.) (1984) *The Philosophy of Economics: An Anthology*, Cambridge: Cambridge University Press.

Hayek, F. von (1934) 'Carl Menger (1840–1921)', *Economica*, vol 1, no 4, pp. 393–420, reprinted with some additions in, and cited from, Hayek (1992b).

—— (1937) 'Economics and Knowledge', *Economica*, vol IV, no 13, pp. 33–54, reprinted in, and cited from, Hayek (1948b).

—— (1941) *The Pure Theory of Capital*, London: Routledge.

—— (1942–4) 'Scientism and the Study of Society', originally published in three parts in *Economica*, vol 9, no 35, pp. 167–96, 1942; vol 10, no 37, pp. 34–63, 1943; vol 11, no 41, pp. 27–39, reprinted in, and cited from, Hayek (1952).

—— (1945a) 'Individualism True or False', Lecture delivered at University College, Dublin, reprinted in, and cited from, Hayek (1948b).

—— (1945b) 'The Use of Knowledge in Society', *American Economic Review*, vol XXXV, no 4, pp. 519–30, reprinted in, and cited from, Hayek (1948b).

—— (1948a) 'The Meaning of Competition', in Hayek (1948b).

—— (1948b) *Individualism and Economic Order*, Chicago: University of Chicago Press.

—— (1952) *The Counter-Revolution of Science: Studies on the Abuse of Reason*, Glencoe, Illinois: The Free Press.

—— (1955) 'Degrees of Explanation', *British Journal for the Philisophy of Science*, vol 6, no 23, pp. 209–25, reprinted in, and cited from, Hayek (1967c)

—— (1962) 'The Economy, Science, and Politics', Inaugural lecture, University of Freiburg, reprinted in, and cited from, Hayek (1967c)

—— (1963) 'The Economics of the 1920s as Seen from Vienna', lecture delivered at the University of Chicago, reprinted in, and cited from, Hayek (1992b).

—— (1964) 'The Theory of Complex Phenomena', in Burge (ed) (1964), reprinted in, and cited from, Hayek (1967c).

—— (1965) 'Kinds of Rationalism', *The Economic Studies Quarterly*, vol. XV, no 2, pp. 1–12, reprinted in, and cited from, Hayek (1967c).

—— (1966) [1933] *Monetary Theory and the Trade Cycle*, New York: Kelley

—— (1967a) 'Notes on the Evolution of Systems of Rules of Conduct', reprinted in, and cited from, Hayek (1967c).

—— (1967b) 'The Results of Human Action but not of Human Design', reprinted in, and cited from, (1967c).

—— (1967c) *Studies in Philosophy, Politics and Economics*, London: Routledge and Kegan Paul.

—— (1968a) 'Competition as a Discovery Procedure', Lecture delivered to a meeting of the Philadelphia Society at Chicago, reprinted in, and cited from, Hayek (1978).

—— (1968b) 'The Austrian School of Economics', *International Encyclopedia of the Social Sciences*, vol 4, London: Macmillan, reprinted in, and cited from, Hayek (1992b).

—— (1973) 'The Place of Menger's *Grundsätze* in the History of Economic Thought', in Hicks and Weber (eds) (1973).

—— (1976) 'The Mirage of Social Justice', reprinted in, and cited from, Hayek (1982).

—— (1978) *New Studies in Philosophy, Politics, Economics, and the History of Ideas*, Chicago: University of Chicago Press

—— (1981) 'Foreword', in Mises (1981b)[1922].

—— (1982) *Law, Legislation and Liberty*, London: Routledge and Kegan Paul.

—— (1992a) 'The Economics of the 1920s as Seen from Vienna', in Hayek (1992b).

—— (1992b) *The Fortunes of Liberalism: Essays on Austrian Economics and the Ideal of Freedom, The Collected Works of F. A. Hayek*, Volume IV, edited by P. Klein, London: Routledge.

—— (1995) *Contra Keynes and Cambridge: Essays, Correspondence*, Volume 9 of *The Collected Works of F. A. Hayek*, edited by B. Caldwell, Chicago: University of Chicago Press.

Hayek, F. von (ed) (1935) *Collectivist Economic Planning: Critical Studies on the Possibility of Socialism*, London: George Routledge & Sons.

Hendry, D. and H. Krolzig (2004) 'We Ran One Regression', vol 66, no 5, pp. 799–810.

Hicks, J. (1939) *Value and Capital: An Inquiry into Some Fundamental Principles of Economic Theory*, Oxford: Clarendon Press.

—— (1975) 'The Scope and Status of Welfare Economics', Oxford *Economic* Papers, vol 27, no 3, pp. 307–26, reprinted in Hicks (1981).

—— (1976) '"Revolutions" in Economics', in Latsis (ed) (1976).

—— (1981) *Wealth and Welfare: Collected Essays in Economic Theory*, Volume I, Oxford: Basil Blackwell.

Hicks, J. and W. Weber (eds) (1973) *Carl Menger and the Austrian School of Economics*, Oxford: Clarendon Press.

Himmelweit, S. and S. Mohun (1978) 'The Anomalies of Capital', *Capital and Class*, no 6, pp. 67–105.

Hobson, J. (1891) 'The Law of the Three Rents', *Quarterly Journal of Economics*, vol 5, no 3, pp. 263–88.

Hodgson, G. (1994) 'Institutional Economic Thought in Europe', in Hodgson *et al.* (eds) (1994)

—— (1997) 'The Fate of the Cambridge Capital Controversy', in Arestis *et al.* (eds) (1997).

—— (2001) *How Economics Forgot History: The Problem of Historical Specificity in Social Science*, London: Routledge.

—— (2004) *The Evolution of Institutional Economics: Agency, Structure and Darwinism in American Institutionalism*, London and New York: Routledge.

—— (2005) 'Fragment: "The Present Position of Economics" by Alfred Marshall', *Journal of Institutional Economics*, vol 1, no 1, pp. 121–37.

—— (2007a) 'Marshall, Schumpeter and the Shifting Boundaries of Economics and Sociology', mimeo.

—— (2007b) 'Meanings of Methodological Individualism', *Journal of Economic Methodology*, vol 14, no 2, pp. 211–26.

Hodgson, G., W. Samuels and M. Tool (eds) (1994) *The Elgar Companion to Institutional and Evolutionary Economics*, Aldershot: Edward Elgar.

Holcombe, R. (2008) 'Pluralism versus Heterodoxy in Economics and the Social Sciences', *Journal of Philosophical Economics*, vol 1, no 2, http://www.jpe.ro/?id=revista&p=2

Holton, R. and B. Turner (1989) *Max Weber on Economy and Society*, London: Routledge.

Hoover, K. (2006) 'Doctor Keynes: Economic Theory in a Diagnostic Science', in Backhouse and Bateman (eds) (2006).

Howey, R. (1973) 'The Origins of Marginalism', in Black *et al.* (eds) (1973).

Hunt, I. (2005) 'The Economic Cell-Form', *Historical Materialism*, vol 13, no 2, pp. 147–66.

Hutchison, T. (1941) 'The Significance and Basic Postulates of Economic Theory: A Reply to Professor Knight', *Journal of Political Economy*, vol. 49, no 5, pp. 732–50.

—— (1953) *A Review of Economic Doctrines 1870–1929*, Oxford: Clarendon Press.

—— (1956) 'Professor Machlup on Verification in Economics', *Southern Economic Journal*, vol 22, no 4, pp. 476–83.

—— (1960) [1938] *The Significance and Basic Postulates of Economic Theory*, New York: Augustus M. Kelley.

—— (1973a) 'The "Marginal Revolution" and the Decline and Fall of English Classical Political Economy', in Black *et al.* (eds) (1973).

—— (1973b) 'Some Themes from *Investigations into Method*', in Hicks and Weber (eds) (1973).

—— (1978) *On Revolutions and Progress in Economic Knowledge*, Cambridge: Cambridge University Press.

—— (1981) *The Politics and Philosophy of Economics: Marxians, Keynesians and Austrians*, Oxford: Basil Blackwell.

—— (1994) *The Uses and Abuses of Economics: Contentious Essays on History and Method*, London: Routledge.

—— (1998) 'Ultra-Deductivism from Nassau Senior to Lionel Robbins and Daniel Hausman', *Journal of Economic Methodology*, vol. 5, no 1, pp. 43–91.

—— (2000) *On the Methodology of Economics and the Formalist Revolution*, Cheltenham: Edward Elgar.

Ikeda (2006) 'Popularisation of Smithian Economics in German-Speaking Areas: With Special Reference to Carl Menger', 19th Annual Conference of the History of Economic Thought Society of Australia, 4–7 July, Ballarat, Victoria, http://www.ballarat.edu.au/ard/business/hetsa06/ikeda.pdf

Ilyenkov, E. (1982) *The Dialectics of the Abstract and the Concrete in Marx's Capital*, Moscow: Progress Publishers.

Ingram, J. (1915) [1888] *A History of Political Economy*, New and Enlarged Edition with a Supplementary Chapter by William A. Scott and an Introduction by Richard T. Ely, Chapter VI: 'The Historical School', London: A. and C. Black, http://oll.libertyfund.org/index.php?option=com_staticxt&staticfile=show.php%3Ftitle=1678&Itemid=27.

Ingrao, B. and G. Israel (1990) *The Invisible Hand: Economic Equilibrium in the History of Science*, Cambridge: MIT Press.

Jaffé, W. (1973) 'Léon Walras's Role in the "Marginal Revolution" of the 1870s', in Black *et al.* (eds) (1973).

—— (1976) 'Menger, Jevons and Walras De-Homogenised', *Economic Inquiry*, vol 14, no 1, pp. 511–24.

Jevons, W. (1876) 'The Future of Political Economy', *Fortnightly Review*, 20, pp. 617–31.

—— (1957) [1871] *The Theory of Political Economy*, 5th edition, New York: Augustus M. Kelley, first edition also reprinted by Harmondsworth: Pelican, 1970.

Jha, M. (1973) *The Age of Marshall: Aspects of British Economic Thought, 1890–1915*, London: Frank Cass.

Jomo, K. and B. Fine (eds) (2006) *The New Development Economics: After the Washington Consensus*, Delhi: Tulika, and London: Zed Press.

Karagiannis A. (1995) *History of Economic Methodology*, Athens: Interbooks Publishers (in Greek).

Kauder, E. (1965) *A History of Marginal Utility Theory*, Princeton: Princeton University Press.

Kaufman, B. (2007) 'The Institutional Economics of John R. Commons: Complement and Substitute for Neoclassical Economic Theory', *Socio-Economic Review*, vol 5, no 1, pp. 3–45.

Keaney, M. (2002) 'Critical Institutionalism: From American Exceptionalism to International Relevance', in Dowd (ed) (2002).

Keen, S. (2001) *Debunking Neo-classical Economics: The Naked Emperor of the Social Sciences*: New York: Zed Books.

Keynes, J. M. (1925) 'Alfred Marshall, 1842–1924', in Pigou (ed) (1925), reprinted from *Economic Journal*, vol 34, no 135, pp. 311–72, 1924.

—— (1938a) 'Letter to Roy Harrod', 4 July, in *Collected Writings of John Maynard Keynes*, Volume XIV, *The General Theory and After: Part II: Defence and Development*, edited by D. Moggridge, London: Macmillan, 1973, reprinted in, and cited from, Hausman (ed) (1984).

—— (1938b) 'Letter to Roy Harrod', 16 July, in *Collected Writings of John Maynard Keynes*, Volume XIV, *The General Theory and After: Part II: Defence and Development*, edited by D. Moggridge, London: Macmillan, 1973, reprinted in, and cited from, Hausman (ed) (1984).

—— (1973) [1936] *The General Theory of Employment, Interest and Money*, London: Macmillan.

Keynes, J. N. (1999) [1890] *The Scope and Method of Political Economy*, 4th edition 1917, Kitchener: Batoche Books.

Keynes, M. (ed) (1975) *Essays on John Maynard Keynes*, Cambridge: Cambridge University Press.

Khalil, E. (1987) 'Kuhn, Lakatos, and the History of Economic Thought', *International Journal of Social Economics*, vol 14, no 3, pp. 118–31.

Kincaid, J. (2005a) 'Editorial Introduction', *Historical Materialism*, vol 13, no 2, pp. 27–40.

—— (2005b) 'A Critique of Value Form Marxism', *Historical Materialism*, vol 13, no 2, pp. 85–120.

Kirman, A. (1989) 'The Intrinsic Limits of Modern Economic Theory: The Emperor Has No Clothes', *Economic Journal*, vol 99, no 395, Supplement: Conference Papers, pp. 126–39.

—— (1992) 'Whom or What Does the Representative Individual Represent?', *Journal of Economic Perspectives*, vol 6, no 2, pp. 117–36.

Kirzner, I. (1978) 'The Entrepreneurial Role in Menger's System', *Atlantic Economic Journal*, vol 6, no 3, pp. 31–45.

—— (1990) 'Menger, Classical Liberalism and the Austrian School of Economics', in Caldwell (ed) (1990), pp. 93–106.

Knight, F. (1935) Review of Commons (1990a and b), *Columbia Law Review*, vol 35, no 4 pp. 803–5.

—— (1940) '"What is Truth" in Economics?', *Journal of Political Economy*, vol. 48, no 1, pp. 1–32, reprinted in Knight (1956).

—— (1956) *On the History and Method of Economics*, Chicago: Chicago University Press.

—— (1941) 'The Significance and Basic Postulates of Economic Theory: A Rejoinder', *Journal of Political Economy*, vol. 49, no 5, pp. 750–3.

—— (2005) [1933] 'Notes and Other Materials from Frank H. Knight's course, Economic Theory, Economics 301, University of Chicago, Fall 1933', *Research in the History of Economic Thought and Methodology*, vol 23-B, pp. 3–86.

Kobayashi, J. (2001) 'Karl Knies's Conception of Political Economy: The Logical Status of *Analogie* and *Sitte*', in Shionoya (ed) (2001).

Koopmans, T. (1947) 'Measurement Without Theory', *Review of Economic Statistics*, vol 29, no 3, pp. 161–72.

Koot, G. (1975) 'T.E. Cliffe Leslie, Irish Social Reform, and the Origins of the English Historical School of Economics', *History of Political Economy*, vol 7, no 3, pp. 312–36.

—— (1980) 'English Historical Economics and the Emergence of Economic History in England', *History of Political Economy*, vol 12, no 2, pp. 174–205.

—— (1987) *English Historical Economics, 1870–1926: The Rise of Economic History and Neomercantilism*, Cambridge: Cambridge University Press.

Koslowski, P. (1995) 'Economics as Ethical Economy in the Tradition of the Historical School: Introduction', in Koslowski (ed) (1995).

—— (2002) 'Economics as Ethical Economy and Cultural Economics in the Historical School', in Nau and Schefold (ed) (2002).

Koslowski, P. (ed) (1995) *The Theory of Ethical Economy in the Historical School*, Berlin: Springer-Verlag.

—— (1997) *Methodology of the Social Sciences, Ethics and Economics in the Newer Historical School*, Berlin: Springer.

Krueger, A. (2003) 'An Interview with Edmond Malinvaud', *Journal of Economic Perspectives*, vol 17, no 1, pp. 181–98.

Krugman, P. (1992) 'Toward a Counter-Counterrevolution in Development Theory', *World Bank Economic Review*, Supplement, (Proceedings of the Annual Bank Conference on Development Economics), pp. 15–39.

—— (1998) 'Two Cheers for Formalism', *Economic Journal*, vol 108, no 451, pp. 1829–36.

Kuznets, S. (1963) 'The Contribution of Wesley C. Mitchell', in Dorfman *et al.* (1963).

Lachman, L. (1978) 'Carl Menger and the Incomplete Revolution of Subjectivism', *Atlantic Economic Journal*, vol 6, no 3, pp. 57–9.

—— (1981) 'Foreword', in Mises (1981a).

Lange, O. (1938) *On the Economic Theory of Socialism*, edited by B. Lippincot, Minneapolis: University of Minnesota Press.

Lapavitsas, C. (2003) *Social Foundations of Markets, Money and Credit*, London: Routledge.

—— (2005) 'The Emergence of Money in Commodity Exchange, or Money as Monopolist of the Ability to Buy', *Review of Political Economy*, vol 17, no 4, pp. 549–69.

Latsis, S. (ed) (1976) *Method and Appraisal in Economics*, Cambridge: Cambridge University Press.

Lavoie, D. (1985) *Rivalry and Central Planning: The Socialist Calculation Debate Reconsidered*, Cambridge: Cambridge University Press.

Lawson, T. (1994), 'Realism and Hayek: A Case of Continuous Transformation', in Colona and Hageman (eds) (1994).

—— (1997) *Economics and Reality*, London: Routledge.

—— (2003) *Reorienting Economics*, London: Routledge.

Lazear, E. (2000) 'Economic Imperialism', *Quarterly Journal of Economics*, vol 115, no 1, pp. 99–146.

Lazonick, W. (2003) 'Understanding Innovative Enterprise: Toward the Integration of Economic Theory and Business History', in Amatori and Jones (eds) (2003).

Lebowitz, M. (1992) *Beyond Capital: Marx's Political Economy of the Working Class*. London: Macmillan.

Lee, C. (1993) 'Marx's Labour Theory of Value Revisited', *Cambridge Journal of Economics*, vol 17 no 4, Dec, pp. 463–78.

Lee, F. (2009) *Challenging the Mainstream: Essays on the History of Heterodox Economics in the Twentieth Century*, in preparation.

Leijonhufvud, A. (2006) 'Keynes as a Marshallian', in Backhouse and Bateman (eds) (2006)

Lenger, F. (1997) 'Ethics and Economics in the Work of Werner Sombart', in Koslowski (ed) (1997). http://socserv.mcmaster.ca/econ/ugcm/3113/leslie/leslie06.html, reprinted in Leslie (1879b cited here and 1888).

Leslie, T. (1870) 'The Political Economy of Adam Smith', reprinted in Leslie (1879b, cited here, and 1888).

—— (1873) 'Economic Science and Statistics', Section F of the British Association for the Advancement of Science, September, reprinted in Leslie (1879b, cited here, and 1888).

—— (1875) 'The History of German Political Economy', *Fortnightly Review*, July 1st, reprinted in Leslie (1879 and 1888), and cited from http://socserv.mcmaster.ca/econ/ugcm/3ll3/leslie/leslie04.html without page numbers.

—— (1876) 'On the Philosophical Method of Political Economy', *Hermathena*, iv, reprinted in Leslie (1879b, cited here, and 1888).

—— (1877) 'Mr. Bagehot', *The Academy*, March 31st, reprinted in Leslie (1879b, cited here, and 1888).

—— (1879a) 'Political Economy and Sociology', *Fortnightly Review*, January 1st, Leslie, T. (1879b) *Essays in Political and Moral Philosophy*, Dublin: Hodges, Foster, & Figgis.

—— (1879c) 'Jevons' "Theory of Political Economy"', *The Academy*, July 26th, reprinted in Leslie (1888).

—— (1880) 'Political Economy in the United States', reprinted in, and cited from, Leslie (1888).

—— (1888) *Essays in Political Economy*, Dublin: Hodges, Foster, Figgis, & Co.

Lester, R. (1946) 'Shortcomings of Marginal Analysis for Wage-Employment Problems', *American Economic Review*, vol 36, no 1, pp. 63–82.

Lewis, J. (1975) *Max Weber and Value-Free Sociology: A Marxist Critique*, London: Lawrence and Wishart.

Lewis, P. (ed) (2004a) *Transforming Economics: Perspectives on the Critical Realist Project*, London: Routledge.

—— (2004b) 'Economics as Social Theory and the New Economic Sociology', in Lewis (ed) (2004a).

Leys, C. (1996) *The Rise and Fall of Development Theory*, London : James Currey Ltd.

Lindenfeld, D. (1997) *The Practical Imagination: The German Sciences of State in the Nineteenth Century*, Chicago: University of Chicago Press.

Little, D. (ed) (1995) *On the Reliability of Economic Models*, Boston: Kluwer Academic Publishers.

Lloyd, C. (1986) *Explanation in Social History*, Oxford: Basil Blackwell.

Loasby, B. (1976) *Choice, Complexity and Ignorance*, Cambridge: Cambridge University Press.

Lucas, R. (1981) *Studies in Business-Cycle Theory*, Oxford: Basil Blackwell.

—— (1987) *Models of Business Cycles*, Oxford: Blackwell.

Maas, H. (1999) 'Mechanical Rationality: Jevons and the Making of Economic Man', *Studies in the History of the Philosophy of Science*, vol 30, no 4, pp. 587–619.

—— (2005a) 'How Rationality Came to Economics', Department of Economics, University of Amsterdam, paper presented to Conference of the European Society for the History of Economic Thought, Stirling.

—— (2005b) 'Basic Instincts: Psychophysics and the Physical Groundwork of Economics', Department of Economics, University of Amsterdam, paper presented to a workshop at Max Planck Institute for the History of Science.

Macdonald, R. (1966) 'Schumpeter and Max Weber: Central Visions and Social Theories', *Quarterly Journal of Economics*, vol 80, no 3, pp. 373–96.

Machlup, F. (1955) 'The Problem of Verification in Economics', *Southern Economic Journal*, vol 22, no 1, pp. 1–21.

—— (1956) 'Rejoinder to a Reluctant Ultra-Empiricist', *Southern Economic Journal*, vol 22, no 4, pp. 483–93.

—— (1964) 'Professor Samuelson on Theory and Realism', *American Economic Review*, vol 54, no 5, pp. 733–6.

—— (1978) *Methodology of Economics and other Social Sciences*, New York: Academic Press.

Mäki, U. (2002) 'Symposium on Explanations and Social Ontology 2: Explanatory Ecumenism and Economics Imperialism', *Economics and Philosophy*, vol 18, no 2, pp. 235–57.

Mäki, U. (ed) (2002) *Fact and Fiction in Economics: Models, Realism and Social Construction*, Cambridge: Cambridge University Press.

Maloney, J. (1976) 'Marshall, Cunningham, and the Emerging Economics Profession', *Economic History Review*, vo 29, no 3, pp. 440–51.

—— (1985) *Marshall, Orthodoxy and the Professionalisation of Economics*, Cambridge: Cambridge University Press.

Malthus, T. (1986) [1820] *Principles of Political Economy*, 2nd edition (1836), New York: Augustus M. Kelley.

Marangos, J. (2006) 'John Rogers Commons on Power', *International Journal of Political Economy*, vol 35, no 4, pp. 50–66.

Marshall, A. (1892) 'The Perversion of Economic History: A Reply', *Economic Journal*, vol 2, no 7, pp. 507–19.

—— (1925a) 'The Present Position of Economics', in Pigou (ed) (1925), inaugural lecture of 1885.

—— (1925b) 'The Old Generation of Economists and the New', in Pigou (ed) (1925), reprinted from *Quarterly Journal of Economics*, January, 1897.

—— (1959) [1890] *Principles of Economics: An Introductory Volume*, London: MacMillan, eighth edition.

—— (1996) *The Correspondence of Alfred Marshall, Economist*, three volumes, edited by J. Whitaker, Cambridge: Cambridge University Press.

Marx, K. (1964) *Pre-Capitalist Modes of Production*, with an Introduction by E. Hobsbawm, London: Lawrence and Wishart.

—— (1968) [1888] *Theses on Feuerbach*, reprinted in Marx and Engels (1968), originally written in 1845.

—— (1969a) *Theories of Surplus Value: Part I*, London: Lawrence and Wishart.

—— (1969b) *Theories of Surplus Value: Part II*, London: Lawrence and Wishart.

—— (1970) [1859] *A Contribution to the Critique of Political Economy*, with an Introduction by M. Dobb, Moscow: Progress Publishers, London: Lawrence and Wishart.

—— (1972) [1852] *The Eighteenth Brumaire of Louis Bonaparte*, in Marx *et al.* (1972).

—— (1973) [1953] *Grundrisse*, originally written in 1857–8, London: Penguin Books.

—— (1976) [1867] *Capital: Volume I*, translated by Ben Fowkes with an introduction by Ernest Mandel, London: Penguin Books.

—— (1981) [1894] *Capital: Volume III*, translated by D. Fernbach with an introduction by Ernest Mandel, London: Penguin Books.

—— (1991) *Theories of Surplus Value: Part III*, reprinted in K. Marx and F. Engels (1991) *Collected Works*, vol 33, Moscow: Progress Publishers.

Marx, K. and Engels, F. (1848) 'Manifesto of the Communist Party', reprinted in, and cited from, Marx and Engels (1968).

—— (1968) *Selected Works*, London: Lawrence and Wishart.

—— (1972) [1847] *The German Ideology*, reprinted in Marx, Engels and Lenin (1972).

Marx, K., Engels, F. and V. Lenin (1972) *On Historical Materialism*, Moscow: Progress Publishers.

Mason, R. (1981) *Conspicuous Consumption: A Study of Exceptional Consumer Behaviour*, Farnborough: Gower.

—— (1984) 'Conspicuous Consumption: A Literature Review', *European Journal of Marketing*, vol. 18, no. 3, pp. 26–39.

—— (1998) *The Economics of Conspicuous Consumption: Theory and Thought since 1700*, Cheltenham: Edward Elgar.

McCloskey, D. (1976) 'Does the Past Have Useful Economics?', *Journal of Economic Literature*, vol 14, no 2, pp. 434–61.

—— (1990a) 'Their Blackboard, Right or Wrong: A Comment on Contested Exchange', *Politics and Society*, vol 18, pp. 223–32

—— (1996) 'The Economics of Choice: Neoclassical Supply and Demand', in Rawski *et al.* (1996).

—— (1999) *Crossing: A Memoir*, Chicago: Chicago University Press.

Mearman, A. (2008) 'Pluralism and Heterodoxy: Introduction to the Special Issue', *Journal of Philosophical Economics*, vol 1, no 2, http://www.jpe.ro/?id=revista&p=2

Meek, R. (1956) *Studies in the Labour Theory of Value*, New York: Monthly Review Press.

—— (1971) 'Smith, Turgot, and the "Four Stages" Theory', *History of Political Economy*, vol. 3, no 1, pp. 9–27.

—— (1973a) 'Marginalism and Marxism', in Black *et al.* (eds) (1973).

—— (1973b) *Studies in the Labour Theory of Value*, 2nd edition (1st edition 1956), London: Lawrence and Wishart.

—— (1976) 'Is There an "Historical Transformation Problem?" A Comment', *Economic Journal*, 86, June, pp. 342–47.

Mehrling, P. (2002) 'Don Patinkin and the Origins of Postwar Monetary Orthodoxy', *European Journal of the History of Economic Thought*, vol 9, no 2, pp. 161–85.

Menger, C. (1892) 'On the Origins of Money', *Economic Journal*, vol 2, no 6, pp. 239–55.

—— (1985) [1883] *Investigations into the Method of the Social Sciences with Special Reference to Economics*, New York: Lawrence H. White, original in German.

—— (2004) [1871] *Principles of Economics*, Translated by J. Dingwall and B. Hoselitz, with an Introduction by F. A. Hayek, Ludwig von Mises Institute, http://www.mises.org/etexts/menger/principles.asp

Michaelidis P. and J. Milios (2005) 'The Influence of the German Historical School on Schumpeter', paper presented at the 17th International Conference of the

European Association for Evolutionary Political economy, Bremen, Germany, November.

Michie, J., C. Oughton and F. Wilkinson (2002) 'Against the New Economic Imperialism: Some Reflections', *American Journal of Economics and Sociology*, vol 61, no 1, pp. 351–65.

Milford, K. (1990) 'Menger's Methodology', in Caldwell (ed) (1990).

Mill, J. (1836) 'On the Definition of Political Economy: and on the Method of Investigation Proper to It', reprinted in, and cited from, Mill (1968) [1844].

—— (1884) [1843] *A System of Logic, Ratiocinative and Inductive: Being a Connected View of the Principles of Evidence and the Methods of Scientific Investigation*, 8th edition, New York: Harper and Brothers.

—— (1962) [1863] 'Utilitarianism', reprinted in J. S. Mill (1962) *Utilitarianism, On Liberty, Essay on Bentham*, edited with an Introduction by M. Warnock, New York : Meridian Books.

—— (1968) [1844] *Essays in Some Unsettled Questions of Political Economy*, 2nd edition (1974), New York: Augustus M. Kelley.

—— (1974) [1859] *On Liberty*, edited with an Introduction by G. Himmelfarb, London: Penguin Books.

—— (1976) [1848] *Principles of Political Economy*, edited with an Introduction by Sir William Ashley, this edition first published in 1909, New York: Augustus M. Kelley.

—— (1994) [1848] 'Chapters on Socialism', in *Principles of Political Economy (and Chapters on Socialism)*, edited with an Introduction and Notes by J. Riley, Oxford: Oxford University Press.

Miller, W. (1971) 'Richard Jones: A Case Study in Methodology', *History of Political Economy*, vol 3, no 1, pp. 198–207.

Milonakis, D. (1990) *Historical Aspects of the Law of Value and the Transition to Capitalism*, unpublished Ph.D. thesis, University of London.

—— (1995) 'Commodity Production and Price Formation before Capitalism: A Value-Theoretic Approach', *Journal of Peasant Studies*, vol 22, no 2, pp. 327–55.

—— (2003) 'New Market Socialism: A Case for Rejuvenation or Inspired Alchemy?', *Cambridge Journal of Economics*, vol 27, no 1, pp. 97–121.

—— (2006) 'Pioneers of Economic History', in Jomo and Fine (eds) (2006).

Milonakis, D. and B. Fine (2007) 'Douglass North's Remaking of Economic History: A Critical Appraisal', *Review of Radical Political Economics*, vol 39, no 1, pp. 27–57.

—— (forthcoming) *Reinventing the Economic Past: Method and Theory in the Evolution of Economic History*, London: Routledge.

Mirowski, P. (1989a) 'How Not To Do Things with Metaphors: Paul Samuelson and the Science of Neoclassical Economics', *Studies in the History and Philosophy of Science*, vol. 20, no 2, pp. 175–91.

—— (1989b) *More Heat than Light*, Cambridge: Cambridge University Press.

—— (2000) 'Exploring the Fault Lines: Introduction to the Minisymposium on the History of Economic Anthropology', *History of Political Economy*, vol 32, no 4, pp. 919–32.

Mises, L. von (1935) [1920] 'Economic Calculation in the Socialist Commonwealth', in Hayek (ed.) (1935).

—— (1981a) [1933] *Epistemological Problems of Economics*, New York: New York University Press.

—— (1981b) [1922] *Socialism*, Indianapolis: Liberty Fund.

—— (1996) [1949] *Human Action: A Treatise in Economics*, 4th revised edition, San Francisco: Fox & Wilkes.

—— (2003) [1969] 'The Historical Setting of the Austrian School of Economics', New York: Arlington House, 1984; also Ludwig von Mises Institute, http://www.mises.org/etexts/histsetting.pdf, 2003.

Mitchell, W. (1910a) 'The Rationality of Economic Activity I', *Journal of Political Economy*, vol 18, no 2, pp. 97–113.

—— (1910b) 'The Rationality of Economic Activity II', *Journal of Political Economy*, vol 18, no 3, pp. 197–216.

—— (1913) *Business Cycles*, Berkeley: University of California Press.

—— (1915) 'Wieser's Theory of Social Economics', *Political Science Quarterly*, vol XXXII, no 1, pp. 95–118, reprinted in, and cited from, Mitchell (1937).

—— (1924) 'The Prospects of Economics', in Tugwell (ed) (1924), reprinted in, and cited from, Mitchell (1937).

—— (1925), 'Quantitative Analysis in Economic Theory', *American Economic Review*, vol XV, no 1, pp. 1–12, reprinted in, and cited from, Mitchell (1937).

—— (1927) *Business Cycles: The Problem and Its Setting*, New York: National Bureau of Economic Research.

—— (1929) 'Sombart's Hochkapitalismus', *Quarterly Journal of Economics*, vol XLIII, no 2, pp. 303–23, reprinted in, and cited from, Mitchell (1937).

—— (1937) *The Backward Art of Spending Money and Other Essays*, London: McGraw-Hill.

Moore, G. (1995) 'T. E. Cliffe Leslie and the English *Methodenstreit*', *Journal of the History of Economic Thought*, vol 17, no 1, pp. 57–77.

—— (1999) 'John Kells Ingram, the Comtean Movement and the English *Methodenstreit*', *History of Political Economy*, vol 31, no 1, pp. 69–90.

Morgan, M. and M. Rutherford (eds) (1998) *From Interwar Pluralism to Postwar Neoclassicism*, *History of Political Economy*, vol 30, Supplement, Durham, NC: Duke University Press.

Morishima, M. and G. Catephores (1975) 'Is There an "Historical Transformation Problem"?', *Economic Journal*, 85, June, pp. 309–28.

—— (1976) 'The "Historical Transformation Problem": A Reply', *Economic Journal*, vol 86, no 342, pp. 348–52.

Moscati, I. (2005) 'History of Consumer Demand Theory 1871–1971: A Neo-Kantian Rational Reconstruction', Università Bocconi, Milan, mimeo.

Mosini, V. (ed) (2007) *Equilibrium in Economics – Scope and Limits*, London: Routledge.

Moss, L. (1978) 'Carl Menger's Theory of Exchange', *Atlantic Economic Journal*, vol 6, no 3, pp. 17–30.

Murray, P. (2005) 'The New Giant's Staircase', *Historical Materialism*, vol 13, no 2, pp. 61–84.

Murrell, P. (1983) 'Did the Theory of Market Socialism Answer the Challenge of Ludwig von Mises? A Reinterpretation of the Socialist Calculation Controversy', *History of Political Economy*, vol 15, no 1, pp. 92–105.

Muth, J. (1961) 'Rational Expectations and the Theory of Price Movements', *Econometrica*, vol 29, no 3, pp. 315–35.

Nadal, A. (2004a) 'Behind the Building Blocks: Commodities and Individuals in General Equilibrium Theory', in Ackerman and Nadal (eds) (2004).

—— (2004b) 'Freedom and Submission: Individuals and the Invisible Hand', in Ackerman and Nadal (eds) (2004).

Nau, H. and B. Schefold (ed) (2002) *The Historicity of Economics*, Berlin: Springer.

North, D. (1963) 'Quantitative Research in American Economic History', *American Economic Review*, vol 53, no 1, pp. 128–9.

—— (1965) 'Economic History: Its Contribution to Economic Education, Research, and Policy', *American Economic Review*, vol 55, no 2, pp. 86–91.

O'Donnell, R. (1997) 'Keynes and Formalism', in Harcourt and Riach (eds) (1997).

O'Driscoll, G. and M. Rizzo (1985) *The Economics of Time and Ignorance*, Oxford: Basil Blackwell.

Oser, J. and W. Blanchfield (1975) *The Evolution of Economic Thought*, New York: Harcourt Brace Jovanovich.

Oswald, A. and H. Ralsmark (2008) 'Some Evidence on the Future of Economics', Warwick Economic Research Paper, no 841.

Pareto, V. (1935) [1916] *The Mind and Society: A Treatise on General Sociology*, edited by A. Livingston, translated by A. Bongiorno and A. Livingston, New York: Dover Publications, 4 Volumes.

—— (1971) [1927] *Manual of Political Economy*, edited by A. Schwier and A. Page, translated by A. Schwier, New York: Augustus M. Keley.

Parker, W. (ed.) (1986) *Economic History and the Modern Economist*, Oxford: Basil Blackwell.

Parsons, T. (1931) 'Wants and Activities in Marshall', *Quarterly Journal of Economics,* vol 46, no 1, pp. 101–40.

—— (1932) 'Economics and Sociology: Marshall in Relation to the Thought of His Time', *Quarterly Journal of Economics,* vol 46, no 2, pp. 316–47.

—— (1934) 'Some Reflections on "The Nature and Significance of Economics"', *Quarterly Journal of Economics,* vol 48, no 3, pp. 511–45.

—— (1951) *The Social System*, Glencoe, Illinois: The Free Press.

—— (1968a) 'Pareto, Vilfredo: Contributions to Sociology', in Silis (ed) (1968).

—— (1968b) *The Structure of Social Action: A Study in Social Theory with Special Reference to a Group of Recent European Writers*, Volumes I and II, New York: The Free Press, first edition of 1937.

Parsons, T. and N. Smelser (1956) *Economy and Society: A Study in the Integration of Economic and Social Theory*, Glencoe, IL: The Free Press.

Patinkin, D. (1956) *Money, Interest, and Prices: An Integration of Monetary and Value Theory*, Evanston, Illinois: Row, Peterson and Co.

Pearson, H. (1999) 'Was There Really a German Historical School of Economics?', *History of Political Economy*, vol 31, no 3, pp. 547–62.

—— (2001) 'Response to Bruce Caldwell', *History of Political Economy*, vol 33, no 3, pp. 655–61.

—— (2004) 'Economics and Altruism at the *Fin de Siècle*', in Daunton and Trentmann (eds) (2004).

Perlman, M. and C. McCann (1998) *The Pillars of Economic Understanding: Ideas and Traditions*, Ann Arbor: University of Michigan Press.

Persky, J. (2000) 'The Neoclassical Advent: American Economics at the Dawn of the 20th Century', *Journal of Economic Perspectives*, vol 14, no 1, pp. 95–108.

Petri, F. (2006) 'General Equilibrium Theory and Professor Blaug', Università degli Studi di Siena, Dipartimento di Economia Politica, Working Paper, no 486.

Pheby, J. (1988) *Methodology and Economics: A Critical Introduction*, London: Macmillan.

Pigou, A. (1953) *Alfred Marshall and Current Thought*, London: MacMillan.

Pigou, A. (ed) (1925) *Memorials of Alfred Marshall*, London: MacMillan.

Pilling, G. (1980) *Marx's 'Capital': Philosophy and Political Economy*, Routledge and Kegan Paul: London.

Popper, K. (1959) *The Logic of Scientific Discovery*, London: Hutchinson.

—— (1986) [1957] *The Poverty of Historicism*, London : Routledge.

Potts, J. (2000) *The New Evolutionary Microeconomics: Complexity, Competence and Adaptive Behaviour*, Cheltenham: Edward Elgar.

Pressman, S. (1999) *Fifty Major Economists*, London: Routledge.

Price, L. (1900) *A Short History of British Commerce and Industry*, London: Edward Arnold.

Psychopedis, K. (1992) 'Formalism, Historism and Value Judgement in the Foundation of Political Economy (G. Schmoller)', *Axiologika*, no 4, November, pp. 132–90 (in Greek).

Ramstad, Y. (1994) 'Veblen, Thornstein', in Hodgson *et al.* (eds) (1994).

Randall, J. (1965) 'John Stuart Mill and the Working-Out of Empiricism', *Journal of the History of Ideas*, vol. 26, no 1, pp. 59–88.

Rawski, T., S. Carter, J. Cohen and S. Cullenberg (1996) *Economics and the Historian*, Berkeley: University of California Press.

Redman, D. A. (1997) *The Rise of Political Economy as a Science*, Cambridge: MIT Press.

Ricardo, D. (1952a) *The Works and Correspondence of David Ricardo*, edited by P. Sraffa with collaboration of M. Dobb, Volume 6 (Letters 1810–1815), Cambridge: Cambridge University Press.

—— (1952b) *The Works and Correspondence of David Ricardo*, edited by P. Sraffa with collaboration of M. Dobb, Volume 6 (Letters 1819–1821), Cambridge: Cambridge University Press.

—— (1973) [1817] *The Principles of Political Economy and Taxation*, Introduction by Donald Winch, London, Melbourne and Toronto: Everyman's Library.

Riley, J. (1994) 'Introduction' to Mill, J. S. (1994) *Principles of Political Economy (and Chapters on Socialism)*, edited with an Introduction and Notes by J. Riley, Oxford: Oxford University Press.

Robbins, L. (1935) *An Essay on the Nature and Significance of Economic Science*, London: MacMillan, first edition of 1932.

—— (1971) *Autobiography of an Economist*, London: MacMillan.

Rogers, J. (1910) [1866] *A History of Agriculture and Prices in England*, Volume I, 5th edition, Oxford: Clarendon Press.

Rodríguez, F. (2006) 'Growth Empirics When the World Is Not Simple', http://www.un.org/esa/policy/backgroundpapers/rodriguez_2.pdf

Roll, E. (1992) [1937] *A History of Economic Thought*, 5th edition, London: Faber and Faber.

Roscher, W. (1882a) *Principles of Political Economy*, Volume I, translated from the thirteenth German edition of 1877, Chicago: Callaghan and Co.

—— (1882b) *Principles of Political Economy*, Volume II, translated from the thirteenth German edition of 1877, Chicago: Callaghan and Co.

Rosdolsky, R. (1977) *The Making of Marx's 'Capital'*, London: Pluto.

Roth, G. (1978) [1968] 'Introduction' in Weber (1978).

Rubin, I. (1972) *Essays on Marx's Theory of Value*, Detroit: Black and Red.

Runde, J. (1997) 'Keynesian Methodology', in Harcourt and Riach (eds) (1997).

Rutherford, M. (1983) 'John Commons's Institutional Economics', *Journal of Economic Issues*, vol 17, no 3, pp. 721–44, reproduced with original page numbers in Samuels (1988a).

—— (1984) 'Thornstein Veblen and the Process of Institutional Change', *History of Political Economy*, vol 16, no 3, pp. 331–48.

—— (1990) 'Introduction', in Commons (1990a and b).

—— (1994) *Institutions in Economics: The Old and the New Institutionalism*, Cambridge: Cambridge University Press.

—— (2001) 'Institutional Economics: Then and Now', *Journal of Economic Perspectives*, vol 15, no 3, pp. 173–94.

Saad-Filho, A. (2002) *The Value of Marx: Political Economy for Contemporary Capitalism*, London: Routledge.

Sala-i-Martin, X. (1997) 'I Just Ran Four Million Regressions', mimeo, Colombia University, revised to appear as, 'I Just Ran Two Million Regressions', *American Economic Review*, vol 87, no 2, 1997, pp. 178–83.

Sala-i-Martin, X., G. Doppelhofer and R. Miller (2004) 'Determinants of Long-Term Growth: A Bayesian Averaging of Classical Estimates (BACE) Approach', *American Economic Review*, vol 94, no 4, pp. 813–35.

Salanti, A. (1998) 'Pareto, Vilfredo', in Davis *et al.* (eds) (1998).

Samuels, W. (2007) 'Equilibrium Analysis: A Middlebrow View', in Mosini (ed) (2007).

Samuels, W. (ed) (1988a) *Institutional Economics: Volume I*, Aldershot: Edward Elgar.

Samuelson, P. (1947) *Foundations of Economic Analysis*, New York: Harvard University Press.

—— (1948) *Economics: An Introductory Analysis*, New York: McGraw-Hill, with W. Nordhaus (since 1985), eighteenth edition, 2005, first edition republished in 1998.

—— (1963) 'Problems of Methodology: Discussion', *American Economic Review*, vol 53, no 2, pp. 231–6

—— (1965) 'Professor Samuelson on Theory and Realism: Reply', *American Economic Review*, vol 55, no 5, pp. 1164–72.

—— (1966) 'A Summing Up', *Quarterly Journal of Economics*, vol 80, no 4, pp. 568–83.

—— (1983) 'My Life Philosophy', *The American Economist*, vol 27, no 2, pp. 5–12.

—— (2003) 'A Small Pearl for Doctor Stiglitz's Sixtieth Birthday: When Risk Averters Positively Relish "Excess Volatility"', in Arnott *et al.* (eds) (2003).

Sayer, D. (1979) *Marx's Method: Ideology, Science and Critique in 'Capital'*, Sussex: The Harvester Press, New Jersey: Humanities Press.

Schabas, M. (1995) 'Parmenides and the Cliometricians', in Little (ed) (1995).

Schefold, B. (1987) 'Schmoller, Gustav von (1939–1917)', in Eatwell *et al.* (eds) (1987).

Schmoller, G. (1893–4) 'The Idea of Justice in Political Economy', *Annals of the American Academy of Political and Social Science*, vol 4, translated by Ernest Halle and Carl Schutz, first published in German 1881, http://socserv.mcmaster.ca/econ/ugcm/3ll3/schmoller/index.html

—— (1897) 'The Mercantile System and Its Historical Significance', English edition, a chapter from *Studien uber die Wirthschaftliche Politik Friedrichs des Grossen*, published in German, 1884, http://socserv.mcmaster.ca/econ/ugcm/3ll3/schmoller/index.html

—— (2004) [1873] 'Review of Menger's *Principles*', translated by T. Caldwell, in Caldwell (2004), pp. 407–8.

Schneider, L. (1985) 'Introduction', in Menger (1985).

Schumpeter, J. (1927) 'Friedrich von Wieser', *Economic Journal*, vol XXXVII, no 146, pp. 328–30, reprinted in, and cited from, Schumpeter (1997).

—— (1931) 'Recent Developments of Political Economy', text based on a speech given in 1931 in Japan, reprinted in, and cited from, Schumpeter (1991).

—— (1935) 'The Analysis of Economic Change', *Review of Economic Statistics*, vol 17, pp. 2–10, reprinted in, and cited from, Schumpeter (1989).

—— (1937) 'Preface to the Japanese Edition of "The Theory of Economic Development"', reproduced in, and cited from, Schumpeter (1989).

—— (1947) 'The Creative Response in Economic History', *Journal of Economic History*, vol 7, no 2, pp. 149–59, reprinted in, and cited from, Schumpeter (1989).

—— (1949a) 'Science and Ideology', *American Economic Review*, vol 21, no 1, pp. 345–59, reprinted in, and cited from, Schumpeter (1989).

—— (1949b) 'The Communist Manifesto in Sociology and Economics', *Journal of Political Economy*, vol 57 no 3, pp. 199–212, reprinted in, and cited from, Schumpeter (1989).

—— (1949c) 'Vilfredo Pareto: 1848–1923', *Quarterly Journal of Economics*, vol LXIII, no 2, pp. 147–73, reprinted in, and cited from, Schumpeter (1997).

—— (1949d) 'Economic Theory and Entrepreneurial History', in *Change and the Entrepreneur*, prepared by the Research Center in Entrepreneurial History, Harvard University, Cambridge: Harvard University Press, pp. 63–84, reprinted in, and cited from, Schumpeter (1989).

—— (1949e) 'The Historical Approach to the Analysis of Business Cycles', *Universities National Bureau Conference on Business Cycle Research*, November 25–7, reprinted in, and cited from, Schumpeter (1989).

—— (1950) 'Wesley Clair Mitchell: 1874–1948', *Quarterly Journal of Economics*, vol LXIV, no 1, pp. 139–55, reprinted in, and cited from, Schumpeter (1997).

—— (1961) *The Theory of Economic Development*, translated by R. Opie, New York: Oxford University Press.

—— (1967) [1912] *Economic Doctrine and Method: An Historical Sketch*, translated by R. Aris, New York: Galaxy Book.

—— (1982) [1939] *Business Cycles: A Theoretical, Historical, and Statistical Analysis of the Capitalist Process*, Volume I, Philadelphia: Porcupine Press.

—— (1987) [1943] *Capitalism, Socialism and Democracy*, with an Introduction by T. Bottomore, London: Unwin.

—— (1989) *Essays on Enterpreneurs, Innovations, Business Cycles, and the Evolution of Capitalism*, edited by R. Clemence, with a new Introduction by R, Swedberg, New Brunswick: Transaction Publishers.

—— (1991) *The Economics and Sociology of Capitalism*, edited with an Introduction by R. Swedberg, Princeton: Princeton University Press.

—— (1994) [1954] *History of Economic Analysis*, edited from manuscript by E. B. Schumpeter and with a new Introduction by M. Perlman, London: Routledge.

Screpanti, E. and S. Zamagni (1993) *An Outline of the History of Economic Thought*, translated by D. Field, Oxford: Clarendon Press.

Searle, J. (2005) 'What Is an Institution?', *Journal of Institutional Economics*, vol 1, no 1, pp. 1–22.

Seidman, L. (2005) 'The New Classical Counter-Revolution: A False Path for Macroeconomics', *Eastern Economic Journal*, vol 31, no 1, pp. 131–40.

Senior, N. (1965) [1836] *An Outline of the Science of Political Economy*, New York: Augustus M. Kelley.

Shionoya, G. (1995) 'A Methodological Appraisal of Schmoller's Research Program', in Koslowski (ed) (1995).

Shionoya, Y. (1991) 'Schumpeter on Schmoller and Weber: A Methodology of Economic Sociology', *History of Political Economy*, vol 23, no 2, pp. 193–219.

—— (2001a) 'Rational Reconstruction of the German Historical School: An Overview', in Shionoya (ed) (2001).

—— (2001b) 'Schumpeter on the Relationship between Economics and Sociology from the Perspective of Doctrinal History', in Shionoya (ed) (2001).

Shionoya, Y. (ed) (2001) *The German Historical School: The Historical and Ethical Approach to Economics*, London: Routledge.

Silis, L. (ed) (1968) *International Encyclopedia of the Social Sciences*, New York: Free Press, 18 Volumes.

Skidelsky, R. (1992) *John Maynard Keynes: The Economist as Saviour, 1920–1937*, London: MacMillan.

Skinner, A. (1970) 'Introduction to *Wealth of Nations*', Harmondsworth: Pelican.

—— (1974) 'Adam Smith, Science and the Role of the Imagination', in Todd (ed) (1974).

—— (1975) 'Adam Smith: An Economic Interpretation of History', in Skinner and Wilson (eds) (1975).

Skinner, A. and T. Wilson (eds) (1975) *Essays on Adam Smith*, Oxford: Clarendon Press.

Small, A. (1924) *Origins of Sociology*, Chicago: University of Chicago Press.

Smelser, L. and R. Swedberg (1994) 'The Sociological Perspective on the Economy', in Smelser and Swedberg (eds) (1994).

Smelser, N. and R. Swedberg (2005) 'Introducing Economic Sociology', in Smelser and Swedberg (eds) (2005).

Smelser, N. and R. Swedberg (eds) (1994) *The Handbook of Economic Sociology*, Princeton: Princeton University Press.

—— (2005) *The Handbook of Economic Sociology*, second edition, Princeton: Princeton University Press.

Smith, A. (1976) [1759] *The Theory of Moral Sentiments*, Oxford: Clarendon Press.

—— (1981) [1776] *An Inquiry into the Nature and the Causes of the Wealth of Nations*, Volume I, a reproduction of the edition published by Oxford University Press in 1976 with general editors R. H. Cambpell and A. S. Skinner and textual editor W. B Todd, Indianapolis: Liberty Fund.

Smith, B. (1990) 'Aristotle, Menger, Mises: An Essay in the Metaphysics of Economics', in Caldwell (ed) (1990).

Smithin, J. (2004) 'Macroeconomic Theory, (Critical) Realism and Capitalism', in Lewis (ed) (2004a).

Snowdon, B. and H. Vane (2005) *Modern Macroeconomics: Its Origins, Development and Current State*, Cheltenham: Edward Elgar.

Solow, R. (2005) 'How Did Economics Get That Way and What Way Did It Get?' Daedalus, vol 134, no 4, pp. 87–100.

Solow, R. (1986) 'Economics: Is Something Missing?' in Parker (ed.) (1986).

Sombart, W. (1929) 'Economic Theory and Economic History', *Economic History Review*, vol II, no 1, pp. 1–19.

Souter, R. (1933a) '"The Nature and Significance of Economic Science" in Recent Discussion', *Quarterly Journal of Economics*, vol 47, no 3, pp. 377–413.

—— (1933b) *Prolegomena to Relativity Economics: An Elementary Study in the Mechanics and Organics of an Expanding Economic Universe*, New York: Columbia University Press.

Sowell, T. (1994) *Classical Economics Reconsidered*, with a new Introduction by the author, Princeton: Princeton University Press.

Spadaro, L. (2004) 'Editor's Note', in Menger (2004).

Spiethoff, A. (1952) 'The "Historical" Character of Economic Theories', *Journal of Economic History*, vol 12, no 2, pp. 131–9.

Stedman Jones, G. (1987) 'Dialectical Reasoning', in Eatwell *et al.* (eds) (1987).

Steedman, I. (1977) *Marx after Sraffa*, New Left Books: London.

Steedman, I. *et al.* (1981) *The Value Controversy*, London: Verso.

Stigler, G. (1958) 'Ricardo and the 93% Labor Theory of Value', *American Economic Review*, vol 48, no 3, pp. 357–67.

—— (1973) 'The Adoption of the Marginal Utility Theory', in Black *et al.* (eds) (1973).

Stiglitz, J. (2004a) 'Introduction: From the Washington Consensus towards a New Global Governance', Barcelona, September, available at, http://www2.gsb.columbia.edu/ipd/Barcelona/Book_5.29.06/Ch.001_Barcelona_Intro_4.12.06.doc

—— (2004b) 'The Post Washington Consensus Consensus', Barcelona, September, available at, http://www2.gsb.columbia.edu/ipd/Barcelona/Book_5.29.06/Ch.004_Stiglitz_5.10.06.doc

Streissler, E (1973) 'To What Extent Was the Austrian School Marginalist?', in Black *et al.* (eds) (1973).

—— (1990) 'The Influence of German Economics on the Work of Menger and Marshall', in Caldwell (ed) (1990).

Sumiya, K. (2001) 'Max Weber and the Critical Succession of the German Historical School', in Shionoya (ed) (2001).

Sutton, J. (2000) *Marshall's Tendencies: What Can Economists Know?*, Cambridge: MIT Press.

Swedberg, R. (1990) 'Introduction', in Swedberg (ed) (1990).

—— (1991a) *Joseph A. Schumpeter: His Life and Work*, Cambridge: Polity Press.

—— (1991b) 'Introduction', in Schumpeter (1991).

—— (1998) *Max Weber and the Idea of Economic Sociology*, Princeton: Princeton University Press.

—— (1999) 'Introduction', in Weber (1999).

—— (2003) *Principles of Economic Sociology*, Princeton: Princeton University Press.

Swedberg, R. (ed) (1990) *Economics and Sociology, Redefining Their Boundaries: Conversations with Economists and Sociologists*, Princeton: Princeton University Press.

Sweezy, P. (1946) *The Theory of Capitalist Development: Principles of Marxian Political Theory*, London: D. Dobson.

—— (1968) *The Theory of Capitalist Development*, New York: Monthly Review Press.

Tabb, W. (1999) *Reconstructing Political Economy*, London: Routledge.

Tarshis, L. (1947) *The Elements of Economics: An Introduction to the Theory of Price and Employment*, Boston: Houghton Mifflin.

Tawney, R. (1932) 'The Study of Economic History', reprinted in, and cited from, Harte (ed) (1971).

Tawney, R. (1938) [1922] *Religion and the Rise of Capitalism*, London: Penguin Books.

Therborn, G. (1976) *Science, Class and Society: On the Formation of Sociology and Historical Materialism*, London: New Left Books.

Todd, W. (ed) (1974) *Hume and the Enlightenment*, Edinburgh: Edinburgh University Press.

Tribe, K. (1995) *Strategies of Economic Order: German Economic Discourse, 1750–1950*, Cambridge: Cambridge University Press.

Trigilia, C. (2002) *Economic Sociology: State, Market, and Society in Modern Capitalism*, Oxford: Blackwell.

Tugwell, R. (ed) (1924) *The Trend of Economics*, New York: F. S. Crofts

Urquhart, R. (1993) 'Adam Smith between Political Economy and Economics', in Blackwell *et al.* (eds) (1993).

Vaughn, K. (1978) 'The Reinterpretation of Carl Menger: Some Notes on Recent Scholarship', *Atlantic Economic Journal*, vol 6, no 3, pp. 60–4.

—— (1980) 'Economic Calculation Under Socialism: The Austrian Contribution', *Economic Inquiry*, no 18, pp. 535–54.

—— (1990) 'The Mengerian Roots of the Austrian Revival', in Caldwell (ed) (1990).

Veblen, T. (1958) [1904] *The Theory of Business Enterprise*, New York: The New American Library.

—— (1898a) 'Why is Economics Not an Evolutionary Science', *Quarterly Journal of Economics*, vol XII no 4, pp. 373–97, reprinted in, and cited from, Veblen (1990).

—— (1898b) 'The Beginnings of Ownership', *American Journal of Sociology*, vol 4, no 3, pp. 352–65, reprinted in, and cited from, Veblen (1998).

—— (1898c) 'The Instinct of Workmanship and the Irksomeness of Labor', *American Journal of Sociology*, vol IV, no 2, pp. 187–201, reprinted in, and cited from, Veblen (1998).

—— (1901) 'Gustav Schmoller's Economics', *Quarterly Journal of Economics*, vol 16, no 1, pp. 69–93, reprinted in, and cited from, Veblen (1990).

—— (1906a) 'The Socialist Economics of Karl Marx and his Followers I', *Quarterly Journal of Economics*, vol XX, no 4, pp. 575–95, reprinted in, and cited from, Veblen (1990).

—— (1906b) 'The Place of Science in Modern Civilisation', *The American Journal of Sociology*, vol XI, no 5, pp. 585–609, reprinted in, and cited from, Veblen (1990).

—— (1907) 'The Socialist Economics of Karl Marx and his Followers II', *Quarterly Journal of Economics*, vol XXI, no 2, pp. 299–322, reprinted in, and cited from, Veblen (1990).

—— (1908) 'Professor Clark's Economics', *Quarterly Journal of Economics*, vol XXII, no 2, pp. 147–95, reprinted in, and cited from, Veblen (1990).

—— (1909) 'The Limitations of Marginal Utility', *Journal of Political Economy*, vol XVII, no 9, pp. 620–36, reprinted in, and cited from, Veblen (1990)

—— (1958) [1904] *The Theory of Business Enterprise*, New York: Charles Scribner's Sons.

—— (1964a) [1923] *Absentee Ownership and Business Enterprise in Recent Times*, New York: Kelley.

—— (1964b) [1914] *The Instinct of Workmanship*, New York: Norton.

—— (1975) [1899] *The Theory of the Leisure Class*, New York: Kelley.

—— (1990) [1919] *The Place of Science in Modern Civilisation*, with a new Introduction by W. Samuels, New Brunswick: Transaction.

—— (1998) [1934] *Essays in Our Changing World*, edited by L. Ardzrooni, with a new Introduction by S. Bowman, New Brunswick: Transaction.

Velthuis, O. (1999) 'The Changing Relationship between Economic Sociology and Institutional Economics: From Talcott Parsons to Mark Granovetter', *American Journal of Economics and Sociology*, vol 58, no 4, pp. 629–49.

Viner, J. (1991) *Essays on the Intellectual History of Economics*, edited by Douglas A. Irwin, Princeton: Princeton University Press.

Wade Hands, D. (1998) 'Positivism', in Davis *et al.* (eds) (1998).

—— (2001) *Reflection Without Rules: Economic Methodology and Contemporary Science Theory*, Cambridge: Cambridge University Press.

Wagner, R. (1978) 'Final Remarks', *Atlantic Economic Journal*, vol 6, no 3, pp. 64–9.

Walker, D. (1977) 'Thornstein Veblen's Economic System', *Economic Inquiry*, vol 15, no 2, pp. 213–37, reproduced with original page numbers in Samuels (ed) (1988a).

—— (1979) 'The Institutionalist Economic Theories of Clarence Ayres', *Economic Inquiry*, vol 17, no 4, pp. 519–38.

—— (1987) 'Walras's Theories of Tatonnement', *Journal of Political Economy*, vol 95, no 4, pp. 758–74.

Walras, L. (1954) [1874] *Elements of Pure Economics*, translated by W. Jaffé from the Edition Définitive (1926), reprinted in 1977, London: Augustus M. Kelley.

Watkins, J. (1968) 'Methodological Individualism and the Social Sciences', in Brodbeck (ed) (1968).

Weber, M. (1927) 'The Evolution of the Capitalist Spirit', excerpt from M. Weber, *General Economic History*, reprinted in, and cited from, Weber (1999).

—— (1949) *The Methodology of the Social Sciences*, translated and edited by E. A. Shils and H. A. Finch, with a foreword by E. A. Shils, New York: The Free Press.

—— (1975) [1903–6] *Roscher and Knies: the Logical Problems of Historical Economics*, translated by Guy Oakes, New York: The Free Press.

—— (1976) [1904–5] *The Protestant Ethic and the Spirit of Capitalism*, translated by T. Parsons with an Introduction by A. Giddens, London: Allen and Unwin.

—— (1978) [1922] *Economy and Society: An Outline of Interpretative Sociology*, edited by G. Roth and C. Wittich, with an Introduction by G. Roth, second re-issue, Los Angeles: University of California Press, two volumes.

—— (1999) *Essays in Economic Sociology*, edited with an Introduction by R. Swedberg, Princeton: Princeton University Press.

Weeks, J. (1981) *Capital and Exploitation*, London: Edward Arnold.

Weintraub, R. (1998) 'Controversy: Axiomatisches Mißverständnis', *Economic Journal*, vol 108, no 451, pp. 1837–47.

—— (2002) *How Economics Became a Mathematical Science*, London: Duke University Press.

Westra, R. and A. Zuege (eds) (2003) *Value and the World Economy Today*, London: MacMillan.

Whately, R. (1832) [1831] *Introductory Lectures on Political Economy*, London: B. Fellowes, second enlarged edition.

Whewell, W. (1999) [1862] *Six Lectures on Political Economy*, Kitchener: Batoche Books.

White, M. (1994) 'Bridging the Natural and the Social: Science and Character in Jevons's Political Economy', *Economic Inquiry*, vol 32, no 3, pp. 429–44.

—— (2004) 'In the Lobby of the Energy Hotel: Jevons's Formulation of the Postclassical "Economic Problem"', *History of Political Economy*, vol 36, no 2, pp. 227–71.

Wieser, F. von (1891) 'The Austrian School and the Theory of Value', *Economic Journal*, vol 1, no 1, pp. 108–21.

—— (1967) [1927] *Social Economics*, New York: Kelley.

Winch, D. (1973) 'Marginalism and the Boundaries of Economic Science', in Black *et al.* (eds) (1973).

Wright Mills, C. (1959) *The Sociological Imagination*, New York: Holt.

Wright, G. (1986) 'History and the Future of Economics', in Parker (ed.) (1986).

Yonay, Y. (1998) *The Struggle over the Soul of Economics: Institutionalists and Neoclassical Economists in America between the Wars*, Princeton: Princeton University Press.

Zafirovski, M. (2001) 'From Market Catallactics to Universal Social Theory: Another Look at the Paradigm of Rational Choice', *Theory and Science*, http://theoryandscience.icaap.org/content/vol002.001/01zafirovski.html

Zeleny, J. (1980) *The Logic of Marx*, translated and edited by Terrell Carver, Oxford: Basil Blackwell.

Zingler, E. (1974) 'Veblen vs Commons: A Comparative Evaluation', *Kyklos*, vol 27, no 3, pp. 322–44, reproduced with original page numbers in Samuels (ed) (1988a).

Zouboulakis, M. (1997) 'Mill and Jevons: Two Concepts of Economic Rationality', *History of Economic Ideas*, vol V, no 2, pp. 7–25.

—— (2002) 'John Stuart Mill's Institutional Individualism', *History of Economic Ideas*, vol X, no 3, pp. 29–45.

Author index

Subject index

abstraction: abstract science, political economy as 31; abstract theorisation, Marx's favour for 36; German School and realism of abstraction 86; power of 37; 'rational' abstraction and material reality 37; role of 222–23
abstract/deductive method 1, 11, 18, 23, 78, 88, 120, 129, 144, 243, 245, 246; classical political economy 16, 20–22, 26, 32–33, 34–36, 54–58; dialectics and history, Marx's perspective 32–33, 34–36; marginalism and 91, 92, 94, 96, 99, 107, 113
accumulation, consequences of 66
acquisitive ethic 207
aggregate reasoning 14
American Economic Review 123
American institutionalism 302; applied economics 160; Ayres and 186–88; business cycles 157, 184–85; business enterprise 167–68, 173–74; capitalism and 167–68, 169–70, 178–79, 181, 187, 189; capitalist order, disintegration of 169–70; ceremonialism 187; collective action 176–77, 178, 180–81; Commons and 176–82; conflict of interest 176–77, 178; decline of 188–89; dynamic approach 161–62; elements of 189; empiricist drift 175–76, 182–86; emulation, principle of 166–67; evolution and history 159–62, 163–64, 171–74; globalisation, comparison of attitudes to 189; habits of thought, material circumstances and 164–70; Historical School and 158, 159, 162, 164, 171, 174, 176; historical specificity 160, 177, 183–84; historicism of Commons 179–80;

industrial organisation 167–68; instinct-habit psychology 164–65, 166–67; institutional individualism 180; interdisciplinarity 159, 160, 171–72, 183; leisure class, institution of 166; long-run development, issues of 158–59; marginal utility 179; marginalism and Commons 180; Marxism, Veblens critique of 162–64; materialism 162, 163, 168, 169, 190; method and history 170–74; methodological individualism 180; Mitchell and 182–86; national income, notion of 184; optimism of 189–90; pecuniary exploitation 166–67, 168, 169, 170, 172–74, 183; psychologism 171, 172; roots of 158; scarcity 176–77, 182, 186; self-interest 167, 171, 173; social concepts and institutions, role of 183–84; social individual, focus on 160–61, 164–65; social sciences, boundaries between 160; stages, theory of 158; technology and change 165–66, 169, 186–87; Veblen and marginalism 162–64; workmanship 164–65
analytical neutrality 275
Annals of the American Academy of Political and Social Science 250
applied economics 160
art and science of economics, distinction between 31–32
ascetic Protestantism 207–8
asocial reductionism 109
asocial subjectivity 29
atomism 98, 106, 245, 249, 277
Austrian School 229; analytic-composite method 102, 245, 247; distinctiveness 246; economics

dialectics, method of 36–37;
economic structure of material life
42–43; historical dialectics 38;
historical materialism 42; historical
specificity 38–39; historical
transformation problem 40–41;
history integral to Marx's method
39–40, 41–42, 43–44; holistic analysis
37; inquiry, method of 37;
labour-process 43; labour theory of
value 33, 34, 35, 36; logico-historical
presentation 40; material reality,
'rational' abstraction and 37;
materialist conception of history 42;
materialist-dialectical perspective 38,
39, 60; methodological eclecticism of
Smith, Marx's criticism of 34; 'new
dialectic,' distinction between
systematic and historical dialectics
38; philosophical history,
'historicism' and 44; political
economy as unified social science
38–39; presentation, method of 37;
presentation, modes of 39–40;
production mode as social entity
42–43; reasoned history 42; relations
of production 43; scientific
deficiencies in Ricardo 35–36; social
change, history and explanation of
process 44; socio-economic formation
43; systematic dialectics 38;
technological determinism 43;
theoretical corpus of Marx, pillars
of 33
Marxism 5, 76, 89, 115, 158, 188, 192,
225, 256, 285, 291; Veblen's critique
of 162–64
material reality, 'rational' abstraction
and 37
materialism: American institutionalism
162, 163, 168, 169, 190; materialist
conception of history 42; materialist-
dialectical perspective 38, 39, 60
mathematics, use of 298–99
mathematisation 122, 123
meaning, interpretation (and
understanding) of 200
mechanics 30, 121, 122, 124, 128, 234,
299; statical mechanics 109
mercantilism 13, 75–76
method 296, 298–99, 300–301, 307;
compartmentalisation 246–47;
eclecticism of Smith, Marx's criticism
of 34; economic methodology and

positivism 231–32; foundations of
German Historical School 78–82;
history and 170–74; hypothetical
method 233; hypothetico-deductive
method 193, 231, 263; individualism
in 14, 79–80; methodological
schizophrenia 236; political economy
as history 49; pure deduction 98;
rejection of individualism in 79–80;
schism over 15–16, 22–26; scope and
method of economic inquiry 11, 109;
see also methodological individualism
Methodenstreit ('Battle of Methods')
152–53, 156, 181, 218; Austrian
School formation and the 250; British
Methodenstreit 141–42, 150, 152, 154;
German Historical School and 72–73,
88, 90; issues behind the 112–14;
marginalism and the 91, 92, 93, 111,
116, 118; Marshall, marginalism and
the 119, 122, 125; Menger and the
101–8, 246; political economy as
history 46, 47, 58; reconciliatory
mood towards 255; *Sozialökonomik*
and the 192, 193, 198
methodological individualism 98,
109–10, 201, 267, 281, 304; American
institutionalism and 180; Austrian
School and 259, 260, 263–64
microeconomics *126*, 269–70, 270–71,
303; micro- and macro-, division
between 272–74, 278–79
Mill's theory: blending of classical and
anticlassical elements 27, 28–33;
abstract science, political economy as
31; ambiguities in Mill's view 30; art
and science of economics, distinction
between 31–32; assumed premises,
deduction from 31–32; cooperative
socialism 32; deduction/induction
dichotomy 30–31; duty 29; empiricist
epistemology, challenge of
reconciliation 30, 31; ethical
utilitarianism 28–29; historical
dimension, potential importance of
32; *homo economicus* 31; human
nature 29; individualism 29; inductive
inference 30–31; influences on Mill
30; labour theory of value 29; moral
science 28; objective theory of value
29; practical relevance 32; radical
empiricism 30; subjective theory of
value 29; subjectivist utilitarianism
28; value, theories of 29